STAND

**NAPIER POLYTECHNIC
of EDINBURGH**

THE QUEEN'S LIBRARY

Sighthill Court
Edinburgh EH11 4BN
Tel: 031–444 2266
Ext: 3426

This book is due for return on or before
the last date stamped below

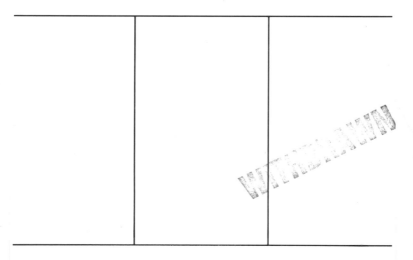

High Performance Leadership:

STRATEGIES FOR MAXIMUM CAREER PRODUCTIVITY

Philip R. Harris

SCOTT, FORESMAN AND COMPANY
Glenview, Illinois   London

Library of Congress Cataloging-in-Publication Data

Harris, Philip R. (Philip Robert),
    High performance leadership: strategies for maximum productivity
/ Philip R. Harris.
        p.   cm.
    Bibliography: p.
    Includes index.
    ISBN 0-673-38363-6
    1. Leadership.   2. Management.   I. Title.
HD57.7.H37 1989   88-23325
658.4'092—dc19   CIP

1 2 3 4 5 6 RRC 93 92 91 90 89 88

ISBN 0-673-38363-6

Scott, Foresman professional books are available for bulk sales at quantity
discounts. For information, please contact Marketing Manager, Professional
Books Group, Scott, Foresman and Company, 1900 East Lake Avenue,
Glenview, IL 60025.

DEDICATION

To two notable futurists and developers of human resources, my friends GORDON L. LIPPITT and HANK E. KOEHN, whose memories I honor with this volume—and with the author's gratitude.

To my colleagues at Leadership Resources, Inc. and the NTL Institute of Applied Behavioral Sciences, from whom I learned so much, as well as to the members of the United States Marine Corps and the thousands of global managers who were the subjects of this research into leadership development.

Foreword

There has always been a need for leadership in society, particularly in the business world. What is new is the increased emphasis on the need for high performance leaders. For some people high performance leadership means that leaders are more active, get more done, and generally function like hurricanes each time they arrive at the office or participate in a meeting. Such people are *heavy* performance leaders, not *high* performance leaders. The challenges of today call for leaders whose level of performance is not hectic, but *highly directed toward helping organizations reach goals and accomplish missions.*

There have been many books, in recent years, addressing the topic. Very few, however, have focused on the responsibility of high performance leaders in the area of human resources. This recognition is what makes this book distinctive and so important for those who seek to become or remain high performance leaders.

Given the constant accumulation of new knowledge and the rapidity of change, it is essential that high performance leaders become directly involved in continuous learning, as Harris points out in this book. It is essential for those leaders to provide learning (human resource development) for all those in their organizations, including themselves.

In recent years it has been surprising, but satisfying, to find an increasing recognition of the impact of culture on organizations. Those of us who have worked in the international arena and with multinational companies have come to understand the importance of recognizing cultural differences. Until recently, one only talked of culture when discussing other countries; for most people, the terms *international* and *cross-cultural* meant the same thing. The recognition has slowly emerged that culture exists within every group, organization and country, and is an important factor in understanding relationships, in communicating and providing leadership.

At one time in the United States, we groped towards a melting-pot society. That is, new people coming into the country were expected to slowly lose their "cultural baggage" and become "Americans." This was symbolized by a big pot, with a spigot at the bottom. Various kinds of people entered the pot at the top, but when the spigot was turned on at the bottom, what came out were people that all looked exactly the same. They were "Americans." As years passed and immigration slowed down, it was possible to take a look at ourselves and to recognize the reality—that we were not a melting-pot society, but a pluralistic society. Even more important is the realization that a pluralistic society can endure and become successful just because of the diversities that stimulate that society.

The same trend is now apparent in our organizations. At one time it was important for new employees to be indoctrinated (beyond merely receiving orientation) and to change to fit the company image. Of course, this attitude still exists today, but it is not nearly as pervasive as in the past. Organizations have recognized that diversity is not to be equated with disaster. Even an occasional organizational deviant can be helpful, and they are often among the most creative people in the organization. The pluralistic organization calls for a different kind of leadership than we have had in the past. It requires a leader prepared to accept cultural behavior that is constantly changing, and who may even be a catalyst in fostering the change.

The insights that Harris provides in this book are an important contribution to the literature in this area. In addition, he has provided interactive exercises and instrumentation that can take abstract theories and put them into the organizational perspective.

This is certainly not a volume to be read once and then placed on a leader's shelf or in the corporate library. It is a book to be read and then selectively reread, from time to time, as needed. The full value of the instruments may not be apparent at first reading, but subsequent reading will provide significant tools for the person who seeks to be a high performing leader. This is a text to be utilized as a continuing resource by managers and trainers!

Leonard Nadler
Professor of Adult Education
George Washington University
Washington, D.C.

Preface

All managers are not necessarily leaders. But if they are high performance managers, they exercise effective leadership. With the world of work in transition, such leadership requires managers to transform the work environment through people, beginning with their own self-development. The meaning and scope of that leadership will be explored in this book, but the rationale can be simply stated: *Increasing productivity, service, and profitability depends primarily upon improved human performance,* which can be stimulated by effective leadership in today's organizations.

Corporations, agencies, associations, and other organizations have limited material, technological, and capital resources. As Peter Drucker reminds us, the fourth factor, though — human resources — is virtually unlimited in its potential. The leadership challenge in organizations today is to learn how to capitalize on human assets to enhance a system's effectiveness. Managers confront this task during times of unprecedented change when the use of technology increases and its cost seemingly decreases, while the number of human workers decrease within individual organizations as their costs and quality go up.

To energize information and knowledge, workers, managers and administrators, therefore, have to exercise greater leadership skills with people. At a *Business Week* executive conference on "Gaining the Competitive Edge," Hank Koehn, when chairman of the Trimtab Consulting Group, forecast that we are moving away from a capital-intensive, physical-resource-based economy toward a human resource-based, knowledge-based-economy (*Business Week,* 1985). By the year

2000, Peter Strassman predicted at the same session, the American economy will have experienced a total growth in the work force to 157 million. This, though, will be largely among people who are classified as professionals, whereas growth in the managerial group will not be significant. The repositioning will result in a need for fewer managers, especially at the middle level, but for more managers who are truly leaders—instead of those who get kicked screaming into the twenty-first century by irate customers and frustrated personnel.

High Performance Leadership is written for managers who, responding to this leadership challenge, aim to be top performers themselves and to enable those associated with them to join them in this process. It is based on the premise that all supervisors, managers, and executives have a human resource development (HRD) responsibility. It takes cognizance of the organizational trend toward decentralization of HRD functions and of the fact that as the manager's role changes, such individuals will spend more time in their own and others' career development. Because the postindustrial work environment requires that leaders be learning facilitators, this book was composed to meet their needs.

Because the subject matter deals with the "human" aspects of work performance and learning, it may also appeal to any professional practitioner in the people business, from health service and criminal justice to real estate and sales. It is especially relevant to engineers, technicians, and computer experts whose education and training may not have emphasized people skills or for those in the expanding service occupations.

Within organizations today, many are assigned to a training function on a lateral transfer, often on a temporary basis. Too often they have no background in the behavioral sciences, group dynamics, or adult education, and are expected to pick up such knowledge on the job. For them, as well as for beginning HD specialists and meeting planners, this text may be of value.

High Performance Leadership is intended for those with leadership responsibilities for people. In the disappearing industrial work culture, such individuals were designated as "subordinates" or employees. In the emerging metaindustrial work situation, these human resources are perceived by managers as coworkers, colleagues, associates. The new paradigm of managerial thought envisions this work force as the capital investment of an enterprise. As futurist Hank Koehn reminded us, talent is more important than tenure. A worker's values and competencies are to be treasured. Thus, this book is written for those in management who wish to make the most of that more diverse, complex, multicultural work force, often better informed and educated than in previous generations.

There is now a readiness in the executive suite to grant that organizational leadership is necessary for attuning the corporate culture and management style to the demands of the "Information Society" and its people, whether consumers or knowledge workers.

In the Prologue of *High Performance Leadership,* the reader is asked to view his or her organization as an energy exchange system. With that model as our rationale, the opening chapter examines contemporary strategies for a high performance work environment, particularly relative to the role of leadership.

In a review of behavioral science literature for the Office of Naval Research (ONR), a team of eighteen highly qualified consultants led by the author concluded that the essence of managerial leadership and effectiveness with people could be summarized around five themes (Harris, 1973a). These aspects of the leadership process centered around (1) understanding human behavior and performance, (2) communications, (3) cultural influences, (4) organizational relations, and (5) change. Thus, these same factors are the focus of our next five chapters.

That same action research for ONR resulted in a *professional development system* for personnel that comprises the substance of our last two chapters. Since continuing education is critical for today's knowledge worker, Chapter 7 examines that issue of learning and Chapter 8 highlights the manager's leadership role regarding meetings.

Each of these eight chapters or learning modules is framed in terms of:

1. *Introduction* for the objectives or overview of that information segment or learning module.
2. *Input* that summarizes behavioral science management thinking on each subject for a manager's consideration.
3. *Interaction* that illustrates the possibilities for sharing the information and insights by the leader with his or her team through group process.
4. *Instrumentation* that can be used for human factor data-gathering and development relative to the chapter theme.

Finally, the Appendices offer the thinking manager further resources to advance leadership capability. There is a directory of organizations and publications useful in the HRD efforts of managers, as well as a reference section, which constitutes a bibliography of helpful readings. The total text is organized with a view to the leader sharing the learning obtained through its reading and discussion. The assumption is that every leader has human resource management and development responsibilities.

In previous books, I have defined *human resource management* as those personnel activities that range from recruitment and selection to health and safety, benefits and incentives, performance evaluation, and the like. In the new work culture, these activities are no longer left to personnel *specialists;* rather, line management plays an active role in such matters, especially in smaller, fast-growth companies. Akin to that effort is *human resource development,* a series of organized learning activities conducted within a specified time and designed to produce behavioral change, such as through education and training sessions (Nadler, 1984).

Again, the metaindustrial manager does not abdicate HRD responsibilities solely to a training staff, but undertakes direct involvement in developing the human potential of his or her team. Chapters 7 and 8 are designed to help the manager do that more professionally. As indicated above, these units point out how managers may engage in action learning and research and improve meetings as a means of advancing high performance.

To increase the yield on the organization's human capital, I offer in this book some specific ways a manager can exercise leadership in development of his or her people. I recommend that a formal leadership development program be inaugurated by the manager who aims to create a high performing work environment as described in the Chapter 1. As a beginning, I propose that leaders use the materials in Chapters 2 through 6 on the core topics of human performance, communication, culture, work relations, and change. In effect, each unit becomes a learning module to which we allocate as much time as feasible. Three to four hours per module is usual, and each action learning session can be scheduled once a week, once a month, or over one to three consecutive days. This mutual learning under the manager's leadership can occur in the course of regular staff meetings, or be formalized into some type of Professional or Management Development Institute.

The arrangements and details for this learning program can be handled by a professional trainer or consultant, but we urge that a task force be established to coordinate this learning systematically. Such a planning group could be composed of high performing members of the organization; later, they should be involved in the project. The last two chapters provide the information which these educational planners require. The payoff should be enhanced learning and improved performance by all who participate in both the planning and the intensive learning experience. Certainly, it should promote more shared leadership relative to the "human side of enterprise." Once this learning strategy has been made operational and internalized, it can be expanded to include other concerns in the management and marketing process or to take up topics related to technical training and computer literacy.

The introduction of such a planner personnel development program under the manager's leadership helps the one in that role to get to know his or her people better, and vice versa. It becomes another manifestation of participative management, which enables employees or members to realize more of their potential through high performance.

Philip R. Harris, Ph.D.
La Jolla, California

Acknowledgments

There are many persons who contributed to the database upon which this volume has been developed. Back in 1964, it emerged as "The Thomas Murray Leadership Training Program" with the assistance of two CEOs—Joseph Kearns of D. F. Young Inc., and Thomas Murray, Jr. of the Murray Manufacturing Corporation. The author increased his material while teaching group dynamics at Temple University in Philadelphia, in the late 1960s, so he is indebted to his graduate students. Simultaneously, his knowledge of the subject matter and experience were enriched as a consultant through his association with the NTL Institute of Applied Behavioral Sciences and Leadership Resources, Inc., both in the Washington metropolitan area. Of his many helpful colleagues then and now, one stands out in terms of this book—Leonard Nadler, professor of adult education and human resource development at George Washington University, whose foreword introduces this volume.

However, as indicated in the dedication, the primary contributors to this learning system were my clients. Among the chief ones were ONR's Organizational Effectiveness Research Programs office under Drs. Bert King and William Gaymon, as well as the USMC's human resource specialists under the leadership of Capt. David Penman. Among the team of behavioral scientists who assisted me on that professional development research project, I am especially mindful of the work of Drs. Dorothy L. Harris, Woodrow H. Sears, Jr., Maneck Wadia, Charles Newman, David Chigos, David Wigglesworth, and Lawrence Solomon. Of the two hundred client systems who permitted me to validate this material, two were outstanding in their advancement of the program—Dr. Walter

Schratz of the Westinghouse Learning Corporation, and the late June Inglima, regional director of training in Los Angeles for the U.S. Customs Service. To these and all the thousands of managers I have been privileged to learn with as a consultant in human and organization development, *thank you!*

Contents

Prologue: The Organization as an Energy Exchange

Have you ever thought of organizations as energy exchange systems? Behavioral scientists suggest this as a new way to look at the institutions with which we are affiliated. This dynamic view helps us to envision our corporation, agency, or association as a system for the exchange of natural and human energy, both physical and psychic. Our image of the organization not only affects our behavior and performance, but also that of our coworkers and clients. If we are to encourage high performance by people, perhaps we should begin by revising obsolete notions we have about the enterprises in which we are involved. In any event, this is the conceptual model we offer as the backdrop for the messages in this book.

A concept is like an intellectual hook around which we may string many ideas; it is a construct that can be formulated into numerous applications. "Concept" is similar to the Greek word *paradigm,* which refers to a framework of thought that helps us to organize human experience. Too often people think only in terms of words or sentences; leaders think in terms of concepts. That is why this book will share many concepts with readers, starting with the model of the organization as an energy exchange system (OEE). Our concern in this text is to foster top performance, so perhaps we should begin by examining how our organization channels or uses the energies of its human assets.

Each organization receives input from its environment and a pattern of internal activity transforms that energy into output, thus provoking new input of materials, information, and effort. Sound familiar? It is the cybernetic model of how our own human system—the body—operates, and is replicated in communication and computer exchanges. Jonas Salk maintains that humankind replicates biological models in the social systems we create, so it is understandable that the operation of our body may provide us with prototypes for organizational activities.

As managers adapt or abandon archaic organizational models from the industrial age, innovative leaders adopt more creative concepts such as OEE. In this way of thinking, our enterprise is seen as an open system engaged in constant transactions with its environment. This system includes many subsystems, called subsidiaries, branches, divisions, departments, or offices. All are continuously engaged in energy exchanges within the organization and outside with other systems. These energy transactions affect the behavior and performance of personnel in a corporation, an industry, a region, a country, and even internationally, because our company or agency is but a microsystem, part of one or more macrosystems. The definitive book on the subject, *Living Systems* (Miller, 1978), examines the concept in terms of cell, organ, organism, group, organization, society, and global systems.

Now this may sound like heady stuff straight from the world of biology and physics, but it has practical implications for executives and managers. Let's look at some of the applications for those who aspire to be leaders in high performance:

1. *Quality of the Work Environment.* There is much concern today about the quality of life and our environment. Therefore, we rightly organize to combat energy waste and pollution and preserve or conserve natural resources. Real leaders are equally concerned about the quality of work life and the organizational environment. They analyze their systems to counteract human energy waste and pollution, such as underused employees or workers whose energies are misdirected. Such leaders study how machines and technology can enhance human performance, for instance through the introduction of office automation or factory robotics. Leaders in the new work culture give priority to the conservation and development of human resources.

Physicists tell us that energy transactions take place in a field of force, such as a magnetic field, operating in space and time. Behavioral scientists such as the late Kurt Lewin conceive of the organization as also having a unique space at a point in time. It, too, is a field of driving and resisting forces that alter the status quo (the equilibrium between the forces that affect growth and development). For example, if a reader tries to introduce some of the insights obtained from this book into his or her office, one may anticipate that some people or forces will support this effort to improve performance, while others will oppose the concepts for a variety of reasons.

Inside every organization's space, a variety of energy exchanges or transactions take place among the personnel. The pattern of these interchanges represents the individual desires and aspirations, prejudices and biases, information and misinformation of the people who make up that human system. The same may be said for external systems that impact the organization, such as customers, suppliers, contractors, unions, and government agencies. Thus, a high performance manager is not only concerned about the performance of one's workers or management, but also about the clients, competitors, regulators, and all those outside the enterprise who impact employee productivity.

2. *The Management Process.* Every aspect of the management or leadership process can be reexamined in the context of the OEE paradigm. If we take the core concepts which make up the themes of this book, each can be redefined in terms of the energy exchange conceptual model. For example, in Chapter 1, we view leadership as guiding the generation of worker and group energy toward achieving personal and organizational goals through excellent performance. Such leadership involves control of the management and record-keeping of energy efforts by personnel. It also may include reward, which is the reinforcement or support of proper energy.

In Chapter 2, we consider human behavior and performance in terms of an individual effort toward personal and organizations goals. In Chapter 3, we look at communication as an exchange of energy between persons and groups. In Chapter 4, we regard culture as establishing the values and customs to which a particular group of people devotes its energies. In Chapter 5, we examine organizational relations as mechanism for maximizing cooperative energy. In this context, conflict between people or groups represents a disagreement on energy use. If it is not properly channeled, conflict energy may undermine performance. In Chapter 6, we analyze change as the altering of energy priorities, while planning becomes the setting of such priorities for energy use.

Every dimension of management, then, can be perceived in this framework of energy and its exchange. With reference to work performance, leaders seek effective use of human energy to improve morale and teamwork. As a result, productivity and service increase. Leaders also discover ways to minimize the waste of organizational energy. People can learn better ways to direct their energies, as shown in Chapter 7. Since so much time of managers and their colleagues are spent at meetings, Chapter 8 suggests means for making them more productive by properly using the energies of all involved.

Management expert Peter Drucker, as previously indicated, has wisely observed that capital is often scarce and physical resources are not inexhaustible. However, in the high-technology, fast-growth environment requiring top performance, leaders learn to capitalize on the organization's human resources. Play with the OEE concept, analyze it from different angles, then share it with coworkers. Devote a staff meeting to getting input from colleagues on how it could be applied to improve performance in one's own organizations. Our associates may have many valuable ideas for conserving employee energy, including their own. Given the opportunity to contribute, we may be surprised by their proposals for more creative employment of their own energies. For example, when this is done with a sales team, members may come up with imaginative approaches for focusing group energies in the achievement of targets and objectives.

Researchers estimate that the average person only realizes about 40 percent of his or her potential. The leader's goal should be to foster a creative environment that stretches people's capacities, energizing them to perform beyond their present level. The pages that follow provide some strategies for tapping into that 60 percent of unused ability or promise within all of us.

Leading in a High Performance Work Environment

INTRODUCTION

What is leadership? Leaders are more than excellent executives or managers: They make things happen to achieve organizational goals and influence planned change and organizational renewal. What *makes* a leader is the first question we address in this chapter—in the form of a briefing that offers only an overview. Next, we look at what contributes to a creative work environment, one that "turns people on" and stretches their capacities. What can leaders do with the organizational climate and culture, as well as their own management style, to stimulate high-performing workers? These are the two key questions to be addressed in the Input section of this learning module.

The Interactive segment of this chapter will review two strategies that foster peak performance among workers. One is a problem-solving session with top performers, and the other is a way to encourage intrapreneurialism in the organization. (Intrapreneurialism is a type of entrepreneurial policy and practice that innovative corporations or agencies promote. It fosters risk-taking, creativity, autonomy, and enterprise within existing institutions or systems. [Harris, 1985, pp. 88-98])

Finally, the Instrument provided for this chapter is the *High Performance Management Inventory* (HPMI), a self-analysis tool that can be used by a leader or by the managers and supervisors who report to that leader. The information and insight that the HPMI provides can really maximize performance.

INPUT

The Random House dictionary says that to *lead* is to go before, to show the way, to guide or influence, to take the initiative, and to demonstrate how something can be accomplished. The various meanings of the term include to precede, to persuade, to excel, and to be in the vanguard. Perhaps we should settle for the interpretation offered in the Prologue's conceptual model, namely, that leadership is the generation and direction of people's energies toward the achievement of personal and organizational goals. — def

Our concern here is, in general, creating a new work culture; more specifically, designing a high performance environment within an organization. The *new management* is that those who lead are attuned to the changing natures of societies and organizations, of the economy and market, of work and the worker, of leadership and management. To transform an industrial mindset and environment into a high performance, metaindustrial work culture calls for innovative managers who lead by example and by learning (Kuhn, 1987; O'Toole, 1987). The principal characteristic of the unique transformational leadership called for by the emerging postindustrial scene are summarized below (Harris, 1983, 1985).

CHARACTERISTICS OF THE NEW WORK CULTURE LEADERSHIP

LEADING IN

- Providing improved, more open communication and information to personnel, customers, and suppliers. This is accomplished both personally and electronically, such as through effective utilization of communication and computer technology. Because work is increasingly information-oriented, data need to be distributed and differentiated more rapidly, then shaped and pared into information that, when refined, becomes knowledge.
- Creating more autonomy and participation, so that workers have increasing control over their own work space and opportunities for involvement in the enterprise. This is achieved in a variety of ways that offer employees psychological or actual ownership in the business. The democratization in the workplace ranges from sharing in planning, problem-solving, and decision-making to team management and profit-sharing.

2

- Promoting an entrepreneurial spirit in innovative ventures, especially of a technological or service nature. This can be done through encouragement and funding of new start-up, fast-growth enterprises or by fostering intrapreneurial activities within existing organizations.
- Enhancing the quality of work life, so that it is more meaningful, fulfilling, and psychologically rewarding. This incorporates the above strategies but builds into human systems wellness programs, sabbatical leaves, incentives, and other entitlements that strengthen loyalty and morale, as well as peak performance.
- Generating innovative, high performing norms and standards that foster competence and excellence, a means to productivity and profitability. This is attained by cultivating work attitudes, agreements, and policies that develop a new work ethic of professionalism in which personnel strive to give of their best, to offer quality service at all cost.
- Utilizing more informal, synergistic organizational relations, so that cooperation and trust are reinforced among the workforce. This can be furthered by resisting hierarchical and status relations in preference to adaptive, temporary, cross-functional, or interdisciplinary collaborative activities and networking.
- Advancing technology transfer and venturing, as well as research and development. Because work is becoming more technically oriented, this trend involves more than the introduction of office automation and robotics. It means investing more in R&D by the private sector, more technical training and the use of technology for education of people, seeking more applications of new technologies to improve productivity and performance.

There are examples of these characteristics of tomorrow's organizational culture at work today, particularly among some of the high-tech, take-off companies. James Treybig, president and principal founder of Tandem Computers, Inc., has described such a work environment. Among the principal features of this Silicon Valley firm:

- *Fast-growth by high performers.* Only 10 years old, Tandem is already listed in the *Fortune 500;* in that time, it has grown from zero to half a billion dollars in sales, and from 4 to 5000 employees.
- *High productivity and creativity.* These traits come from competent people who continue to learn, especially about customer

satisfaction. *Datamation* magazine rates Tandem first in customer satisfaction because of outstanding, motivated, dedicated personnel.

- *Open-door policy toward workers, visitors, and customers.* Managers are responsive to their employees and treat them as equals. These attitudes are demonstrated in the weekly "Friday Popcorn," where employees from all levels meet and mix for two hours of unstructured communication.

- *Self-management and peer management emphasis.* Tandem employees are expected to take on responsibility and are held more accountable; as a result, they are involved in the computer business, they feel like a part of the corporation, and they enjoy working.

- *Information and technology.* Tandem prides itself on being a "paperless factory"; personnel not only build computers, they use them exclusively to conduct their business. The computer is every worker's tool—each has a terminal for setting personal quality standards and reviewing personal quality production; everyone controls quality, not members of a separate department. Electronic mail connects personnel from California to Switzerland, and Tandem encourages all employees to use the system to help one another, especially in global problem-solving. The company also has used its electronic network to produce a daily, real-time, internal newspaper that combines print, graphics, and media; employees from all over the world submit news. Other innovations include a journal that discusses corporate strategy, a TV network of 43 locations to promote organizational communications and trust as well as marketing, and a program of training through computer business simulations.

- *Participation—everyone is part of the management process.* Everyone shares supervisory responsibility through membership in various manufacturing committees concerned about everything from quality to asset management. Worker democracy extends to voting on corporate policy. As workers contribute to the success of the enterprise, they earn reward in the form of bonuses, stock, sabbaticals, or other forms of recognition. All concerned, including worker families, know where the company is going; the five-year corporate plan is shared, even with spouses of employees.

Organizational relations at Tandem are such that contributors have the ability to influence the decision process through systematic representation. (Chapter 5 will examine this subject in detail.)

When I first heard Tandem's chief executive give the speech that included the above information, I was amazed at how well their corporate culture paralleled my own research findings, as previously summarized. Here is a demonstration of management who actually *lead* in the creation of a high-performance work environment. Perhaps, then, it is fitting to end this section with a quotation from Jim Treybig that is not only the essence of his management philosophy, but the principal message of this book:

> The key to productivity in our business, and in fact in 90 percent of the jobs in our company, comes from its emphasis on people. We develop people concepts; we involve people in what we do. . . . The bottom line for business is that the major change facing companies in the United States today is the shifting roles of managers and individuals. Managers must integrate several functions—caring about people, working on strategy, expanding communication, generating creativity and innovation, raising productivity, improving quality, and strengthening the organization. (Smilor and Kuhn, 1986, pp. 5-7)

In essence, leaders are agents of planned change. These concepts will be more fully developed in Chapter 6.

Exhibit 1.1 illustrates this emerging role in terms of the management

Exhibit 1.1   The Leadership Continuum.

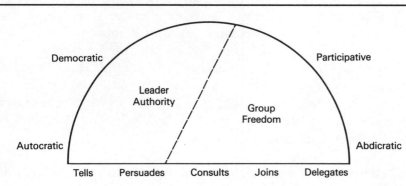

function. Leadership involves a delicate balance between the leader's authority or responsibility, in contrast with the work group's freedom. An autocratic leader reserves complete authority and allows subordinates or followers little freedom. A democratic leader equally shares authority with the group and seeks consensus. An "abdicratic" leader abdicates authority to the work unit; by total delegation, he or she permits the group to exercise complete control or freedom over decision-making and other managerial activities. Abdicrats totally delegate their authority and power to the group.

The leader response can range from telling and persuading to joining in group decisions to total delegation. The issue in this approach is how much authority the leader shares with members of a work unit or team (the dotted center line represents the division of authority and moves on a continuum). During an emergency or crisis, the line moves to the right and the leader makes rapid decisions to facilitate the safety of all or quickly resolve problems. On the other hand, with knowledgeable workers, such as those in an R & D laboratory, a project manager may let the line move considerably to the left, so that team members have more freedom of action. In this conceptual model, leadership is perceived as responding to the time, place, situation, and people involved.

CHANGING CONCEPTS OF LEADERSHIP

Formal research on the subject of leadership has been going on among social scientists for over 60 years. Four schools of thought have emerged. One tries to explain leadership in terms of general traits or characteristics practiced. The second looks at behavior, especially in terms of managerial or administrative style. The third theory explains leadership in terms of situational traits or effective response in *specific* circumstances with subordinates. The fourth, more recent theory, focuses also on situational behavior, but emphasizes learning a repertoire of responses to varied circumstances and people (Hunt, Hoskins, Schriesheim, and Stewart, 1984). Although the latter is a more dynamic approach to leadership, Behling and Rauch (1985) believe that a functional analysis of the leader's performance is helpful. The leader's function has been categorized in two ways:

1. *Task*. Getting a job done well. This includes setting the direction for subordinates and influencing peers; task-oriented functions may be formal activities, such as making work assignments, or informal

endeavors, such as when an unofficial leader of a group of workers determines the group's direction.

2. *Maintenance.* Supporting or influencing behavior. The leader affects group morale, performance, and results. Executives, for example, can influence a corporate or team culture so that it motivates and sustains top performance by the group members.

Hersey and Blanchard (1988) have developed a learning system for managers that is centered on situation leadership. These consultants describe a leadership style with varying emphases on task accomplishment and maintenance activities. This model envisions a manager developing leadership skills in understanding, diagnosing, and influencing human behavior at work. The purpose of this approach is to develop personnel so that they contribute to achieving organizational results and success.

These contemporary concepts of leadership are performance- and result-oriented, and the effort is usually measurable and can be evaluated in terms of outcomes. Anyone who has read the autobiography of Lee Iacocca or knows of his accomplishments at Chrysler Corporation has a demonstration of such leadership. In the process of turning that troubled auto manufacturing company into an economic success story, he observed:

> I learned more about people in three years at Chrysler than thirty-two years at Ford. I discovered that people accept a lot of pain if everybody's going through the chute together. I call this equality of sacrifice. (Iacocca with Novak, 1985, p. 201)

Interestingly, this corporate leader who has captured his nation's imagination admitted that most of his life has been spent "selling"—products, ideas, values. That is, he has been persuading people! It is a quality of leadership that Conger and Kanungo (1988) describe as *charismatic*—providing a strategic vision which motivates employees to achieve ambitious goals.

I agree with Bernard Bass, professor of organizational behavior at the State University of New York (SUNY) in Binghamton, that too much of current management theory focuses on transactional rather than transitional leadership; it is that latter kind of leadership that most institutions need today. This concept was first described by James McGregor Burns (1978). Bass (1985) rightly maintains that leadership research has been too long focused on the issues of autocracy and democracy or participation, and that a new paradigm of leadership is required, one that transforms individuals and systems. Bass concludes that quantum leaps in performance may result with a leader who has innovative or revolutionary ideas and offers a vision of future possibilities. Exhibit 1.2 contrasts the two styles of leadership.

A transactional leadership approach can work for managers, but is dependent upon giving positive or negative reinforcement. But contingent rewards do not necessarily lead to above average performance, and may fail or lead to unintended consequences because of employee contrariness. Transformational leadership is needed to supplement such a style. Primarily because this type of charismatic leadership with its individualized considerations and intellectual stimulation is appropriate for our times of transition into a different work culture.

Transformational managers can provoke extraordinary effort among workers. Leaders who have a personal approach to people and can instill in them a sense of larger mission create a high performance atmosphere, one in which the manager becomes a coach, cheerleader, facilitator, and consultant. Bass's research (1985) with senior executives and military officers confirmed that they had known such transformational leaders whose vision and expectations inspired them to work ridiculous hours,

Exhibit 1.2 Transactional and Transformational Leadership. (Source: Bass, B. M., "Leadership: Good, Better, Best," *Organizational Dynamics,* Winter 1985, Vol. 13, no. 2, pp. 26–40.)

Transactional:	Transformational:
* Recognize what actions subordinates must take to achieve outcomes; then clarify these role requirements for them, so as to instill confidence.	* Raises consciousness level about importance and value of designated outcomes and ways of reaching these, thus contributing to confidence building by members.
* Identify subordinates needs and wants so as these are satisfied, employees make the efforts to achieve the desired outcome.	* Raise the need level of members from survival and security to higher levels of recognition and self-actualization, thus heightening motivation for extra effort
* Leadership training and other positive re-inforcements to sustain performance, such as raises, promotions, or desirable assignments.	* Inspire individuals to transcendence over self-interests for sake of the team, organization, or larger cause leading to higher expectations and performance.

produce outstanding results, and express total commitment. Bass's informants described these high performance leaders as persons they wished to emulate.

These leaders

- Gave followers a sense of autonomy and fostered their self-development
- Treated followers in a friendly, informal, and equal way, like a benevolent parent who was always accessible
- Provided a model of integrity, fairness, and high standards while being capable of formality and firmness and of reprimanding or correcting as appropriate
- Encouraged subordinates with advice, help, support, recognition, and openness, while sharing knowledge and expertise
- Prompted reactions of trust, enthusiasm, admiration, respect, pride, and loyalty

Walt Ulmer, now president of the Center for Creative Leadership, demonstrated the validity of the above observations when, as the commanding general of the Army's Fort Hood, he implemented a leadership program based on such "power down" concepts.

Thus, transformational leaders are role models who offer followers individualized attention and consideration—the opportunities for inputs of information and inspiration. John Watson of IBM, John Welch of General Electric, and Akio Morita of Sony are corporate examples of transformational leadership. In an era of knowledge workers,* such leaders transmit intellectual stimulation by getting people to think and stretch their minds—to visualize the future and what might be done to arouse awareness. Such leaders cause their group to restructure their constructs or mind-sets for more timely and relevant responses. As Burns (1978) reminded us, these are moral leaders who reach down to express people's fundamental and enduring needs, mobilizing followers toward more meaningful and comprehensive values. He also warned that such leaders could be immoral when the need level elevated was not authentic or ethical.

Certainly, this kind of leader is in stark contrast to those exec-

---

*The postindustrial work environment is dominated by personnel engaged in the development, storage, or transmission of information that is used in the creation of knowledge.

utives who wish only to assemble or rearrange portfolios of assets, "number-crunchers" who forget that their companies are human systems to be developed. As Harvard's Robert Reich (1983) rightly noted, no manager transforms an economy, an industry, or a corporation by failing to innovate with new products and processes or by junking human capital and trust. If you aim for high performance, seek to become a transformational leader! Remember to think of the organization as a human system (as described in the Prologue) and concentrate on developing that energy. That is the perspective recently confirmed and restated in volumes of contributions by behavioral scientists (Tannenbaum, Margulies, et al, 1985; Tichy and DeVanna, 1986). For the latter researchers, the concept of transformational leadership implies leading in change, innovation, and entrepreneurship, especially by empowering personnel. Exhibit 1.3 presents the ideas of Professors Noel Tichy and Mary Anne DeVanna in a dramatic format—the three acts or stages of change managed by transitional leadership.

In *Leaders: The Strategies of Taking Charge,* Bennis and Nanus (1985) interviewed ninety leaders on the personal qualities that contribute to organizational effectiveness. This group listed persistence, self-knowledge, willingness to take risks and accept loss or failure, commitment, consistency, and ability to respond to challenge. Above all, those interviewed emphasized that learning is the high-energy fuel of leaders. They meant learning about what is going on inside and outside one's organization. This is especially critical as the United States changes into an information-based or "knowledge" society.

Futurists Bennis and Nanus counsel that this learning must be for more than maintenance, keeping an established system or way of life intact; instead it must be learning for innovation. This kind of learning requires "unlearning" obsolete information and attitudes, reinterpreting organizational history, experimenting with change, and analyzing trends and emerging issues. If an enterprise is a dynamic energy exchange system, then it is a learning organization, as AT&T discovered when reorganizing for deregulation. Bennis and Nanus suggest that the leader's role is to encourage learning about changes in both knowledge and people, in the environment, or in technology (Exhibit 1.4). That kind of learning is examined in Chapter 6, which discusses planned change. (This book has been organized so that managers may share learning from the input sections with others. The last two chapters offer ways for doing this through training and meetings.)

Exhibit 1.3 Transactional Leadership: A Three-Act Drama. (© 1986, American Society for Training and Development. Reprinted with permission. All rights reserved.)

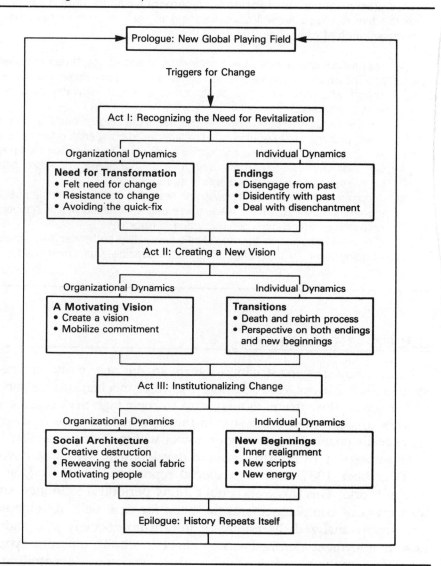

Exhibit 1.4 Leadership Qualities to Cultivate. (from "Presidents at CEOs" by Warren Bennis, *Los Angeles Times,* March 6, 1988, Part IV/p. 3.)

Warren Bennis, distinguished behavioral scientist and business professor at the University of Southern California, is working on a 1989 book, *Learning to Lead.* Based upon a decade of studying corporate leaders, here is a summary of the five qualities he will be discussing in that volume as essential for successful chief executive officers:

□ *Technical Competence*—the combination of knowledge, broad experience, and the ability to do whatever one does as well as possible; usually pragmatists who have risen through the ranks as smart, insatiably curious and tireless workers.

□ *People Skills*—the possession of self understanding of one's talents and flaws, plus the ability to eliminate the latter or to compensate for them; also the capacity to understand and work with others in terms of common needs;

□ *Conceptual Skills*—a viewpoint and a vision that permits one to capitalize on existing opportunities and anticipate future ones.

□ *Judgment*—the artful mix of brains and heart that translates into understanding and steadiness; with it, leaders see and understand what's happening, responding immediately, decisively and intelligently.

□ *Character*—the perfect balance of ambition, ability, and conscience; capable of doing the right thing and taking full responsibility for one's actions and those of his/her organization.

LEADERSHIP FOR RENEWAL

Many businesses are striving to adapt to the new work climate by strategic self-analysis, restructuring, and other mechanisms for survival and renewal. How many, though, turn to their high-performance employees to share their leadership in these processes? How many managers really channel the energy or power within their people?

The magazine of human resource development, *Training,* devoted its December 1987 issue to a special report on "The Changing Nature of Work." This Lakewood Publications' periodical examined America's crisis of competence and the need for new skills development. The report analyzed the emerging Information Society jobs and the new employment contracts that reflect a wholly different type of employee-employer relationship. With downsizing, decentralization, and deregulation, 13 million jobs have been eliminated in the United States during the past five years. It is only reasonable that personnel would be less committed to a company with dwindling job security and increasing part-time or contract work. The *Training* report cites a 1984 study of the Opinion Research Corporation that confirms the thesis of this book, namely, that today's employees must know the standards of job performance, the connection between achieving these standards and rewards to be received, and the provision of a system for effectively evaluating performance. Less concerned about job security, the modern knowledge and service worker wants the freedom to accomplish such goals.

THE HIGH PERFORMANCE WORK ENVIRONMENT

We have seen that leadership that establishes a creative organizational environment, can boost performance and productivity, as well as the quality of customer service and profitability. The next chapter will go into detail on improving individual behavior and performance. Now we wish to concentrate on some specific organizational strategies that have been successfully employed to encourage top performance in both public and private sectors.*

Two company models of corporate cultures that inspire outstanding performance are Intel Corporation and People Express (before its acquisition).

Intel Corporation is a high-tech firm in Northern California. Its president, Andrew Grove (1983) has authored a book, *High Output Management,* on how they produce. They adapt management style to personnel; structure decision-making to enlist employee support; work hard at forecasting and resolving potential problems; enhance meeting performance and productivity; systematize performance indicators and reviews; encourage high performance through raises, bonuses, and promotions; and improve employee career interviewing.

People Express was a "high-flying" company before its acquisition by another airline. This enterprise had taken advantage of deregulation in its industry and flourished for a short time. Yet, even though the company eventually fell on hard times, there is something to be learned from its founder, Donald Burr, and the innovative people he assembled.

---

*Waldentapes (201 High Ridge Road, Stamford, CT 06904) has an audio cassette album entitled "How to Manage for Peak Performance," a title that epitomizes the issue concerning us here.

13

They created a "performance culture" that was totally organized toward people and cutting costs. *All* employees were owners of stock and, as such, were designated "customer service managers." All were dedicated to life-style improvement and becoming better people by doing their work better. Such ideas and values deserve to live on.

So what really works for high performing organizations? A search of management literature reveals the following:

- Joint goal-setting by managers and workers; objectives and targets are always a bit beyond current levels, so that people stretch themselves and strive toward greater achievement.
- Installing and sustaining norms of competence and high performance in the system; accomplished with worker cooperation and consensus, these standards of excellence are incorporated into corporate culture (for instance, with a company slogan or logo, such as "We aim to be the best").
- Continual reinforcement of positive behavior and accomplishment, particularly with support services.
- Constructive feedback to redirect worker energies from ineffective to effective work habits and activities, so that people learn from failure.
- Capitalizing on human assets and potential by giving individuals and work groups more flexibility, responsibility, and autonomy— while maintaining accountability for top performance and results.
- Encouraging, by managerial example (including risk-taking and experimentation), a spirit of innovation and entrepreneurialism.
- Recruiting, selecting, promoting, and rewarding top performers, and highlighting them as role models to all employees.
- Fostering synergy among personnel, so that individual competition is replaced by teamwork and group achievement.
- Using training, education sessions, and self-learning methods to develop people's potential for success and metaperformance; these methods include personal growth input, self-image building, and achievement counseling.
- Eliminating underachievers who do not respond positively.
- Altering organizational structure so that it is more decentralized, mission-oriented, and responsive.
- Making work meaningful and fun by cultivating informality and fellowship in a context of production achievement and joyful accomplishment.

- Leading by staying close to personnel, suppliers, and customers, so that managers respond quickly to market and employee needs.
- Providing a mix of benefits, rewards, and incentives to encourage talented performance.

These are successful strategies for achieving maximum performance at work; imaginative leaders translate them into concrete programs in their company or agency, and then devise even better ones. For instance, relative to the last point above, Robert Cawley, a senior manager at Price Waterhouse, has proposed

1. Incentive awards based on achievement over last year's performance goals, or in comparison to peer accomplishment—balanced as to both both short- and long-term goal achievement
2. Compensation ranges for executive performance with appropriate minimum, midpoint, and maximum money amounts
3. Achievable, measurable (both quantifiably and qualitatively) targets and performance standards
4. Evaluation of performance based on defined goals and business strategies

Reinforcement of high performance can be accomplished by other rewards in addition to money and has to be designed to suit individual personality. For some, a leave from regular duties to pursue research, further education, or enriching travel can be more significant and prevent burnout. For others, psychological rewards are more desirable; these may come in various forms, including assignment to leadership position or membership in elite groups. People are "turned on" by different rewards, and it is the responsibility of management to discover which "button to push" and to treat everyone as an individual.

In *Vanguard Management,* futurist researcher James O'Toole (1987) surveyed 200 top-performing managers in successful companies to ascertain characteristics in their work environment that accounted for that success. Perhaps it would be well to end this section with a summary of those findings, to illustrate what is different about a vanguard corporate environment:

- A careful balance of and attention to the interests of the various stakeholders

- A dedication to high purpose—visionary, concerned with long-term performance, and forward-looking
- A commitment to continual learning, including the fullest development and utilization of human resources
- An orientation toward technology to improve both product and service
- A passion for free enterprise, and the dictates of the market
- Openness to new ideas

Notice how these various research reports confirm over and over certain values and behaviors in high-performing work environments.

INTERACTION

There are many opportunities to exercise leadership in the application of this chapter's insights by sharing the learning with colleagues. For example, some of the issues and strategies we have reviewed here could be placed on the agenda of staff meetings. Among the possibilities for group action about performance improvement through the work environment, here are two approaches known to succeed.

HIGH PERFORMANCE MANAGEMENT WORKSHOP (HPMW)

Bruce Qualset, of Professional Development Services, and I have been engaged in research with top-performing employees that pays off with results. The model developed has been successfully tested with Navy pilots, savings and loan personnel, public utilities supervisors, and moving company managers. The HPMW process goes like this:

1. *Preliminary data gathering.* The first step in this phase is identification of five critical management concerns, such as performance, productivity, or communications. Then executives define a top-performing employee by listing what is required for top performance and describing how such people are selected. Finally, participants nominate the high-achieving employees capable of effectively resolving the targeted issues.
2. *Designing and conducting a workshop.* Participants schedule and plan a 2-day session to deal with the problems they have identi-

fied. Twelve to fifteen high-achieving personnel participate in this session, with a facilitator. The entire session is videotaped in color. Groups are assigned to produce handouts and instruments to help in data-gathering and analysis. The focus of the problem-solving session is narrowed to two subjects: (1) How did these participants become top performers—what are their success stories? and (2) How will they solve the five critical problems presented by management?

3. *Analysis and Reporting.* The consultants present during the action learning session then play back and analyze the videotapes for feasible solutions and organizational insights. They later give top management an oral briefing on their findings and guidelines for tape review. The videotapes provide powerful feedback for management, either in summary or in full.

4. *Implications and Applications.* This organizational development strategy seeks employee input from outstanding personnel. It recognizes the high achievers within the enterprise and uses them as behavior models for ordinary workers. The videotapes can be edited and excerpted for use in training sessions. For example, high-performing overseas managers can be recorded and the tapes shown to newly assigned managers and technicians who are being prepared for overseas service.*

Top performers are today's innovators who help to establish tomorrow's organizational standards. They are vital to any organization, yet in two·such workshops with field and customer service supervisors at Michigan Consolidates Gas and Electric Company, I learned that many of the participants had never been told before that they were outstanding workers; selection for the workshop was the first recognition of this type. See Exhibit 1.5, the High Performance Management Inventory. By using one of the two strategies discussed here, managers give recognition and confirmation to personnel who excel at work.

THE OUTSTANDING PEOPLE SEMINAR (TOPS)

An annual conference of an organization's highest achievers and their spouses or loved ones can help maintain high morale and productivity

---

*For further information about this process, contact Harris International, 2702 Costebelle Dr., La Jolla, CA 92037)

and reward their extra effort and sacrifice for the past year. Slow business periods can be used for this purpose. Tandem Computers, Inc. does this through the program called TOPS; seven percent of their people, the outstanding performers for that year, are invited to a resort for a holiday with their personal companions. Groups of seventy include guest managers so that there is a mix of every level and function of the company. Because they all are outstanding workers, special relationships are formed that engender professional respect regardless of status or education and strengthen a family atmosphere. Executives are convinced that this group socializing builds mutual respect and creativity, as well as an effective and unstructured communication network that contributes to further business success. (For more information, contact Tandem Computer Corporation, Office of the President, 19333 Ballco Park, Cupertino, CA 95014.)

SPECIAL CHAPTER RESOURCE

At the end of this book, there is a Directory of Human Resource Organizations and Publications. The primary aid on the subject of this chapter is the Center for Creative Leadership listed on page 332 which offers worldwide programs for managers. The reader may wish to write for their annual catalogs of programs and products and request to be placed on the mailing list for their free newsletter based on the findings of the Center's leadership research. (See Appendix A for additional resources.)

INSTRUMENTATION

HIGH PERFORMANCE MANAGEMENT INVENTORY (HPMI)

Exhibit 1.5 The High Performance Management Inventory.

Directions: This instrument is useful for assessing your own management competencies for high performance, and provides indicators for continuing professional development. The inventory can also be used for more objective performance appraisal when a supervisor or colleague employs it to evaluate your managerial proficiency. The comparison of ratings obtained between its administration by yourself and by others can provide valuable

Exhibit 1.5   The High Performance Management Inventory, *cont'd.*

insights for further learning and growth as an effective global manager. Finally, HPMI can be used as an assessment instrument with those who report to you, or by project managers with team members.

HPMI not only helps to identify one's professional management strengths, but where to focus efforts for career development. The evaluation utilizes a nine point scale in which you rate yourself or another (or someone else rates you) from low to high proficiency. This is done by locating a place from left to right which best describes the current state of achievement, and then recording that number for the item under consideration:

0	1	2	3	4	5	6	7	8	9

NO COMPETENCY	BASIC COMPETENCY	INTERMEDIATE COMPETENCY	ADVANCED COMPETENCY

This analysis will be on 105 items which have been divided into twelve categories of management functions. These cover a range of activities and responsibilities in a leadership role as a manager. Kindly review the meaning of the classifications before beginning the rating process:

1. *Cultural Awareness*—Being conscious of and up-to-date on organizational culture, policies, priorities, and power issues (microculture) in relation to external issues, trends and development (macroculture—economic, political, social, technological conditions and trends).
2. *Communication*—Internal organizational communications and information exchanges, such as keeping subordinates informed, interpreting work unit activities and priorities, information interface with other units.
3. *Public Relations*—Work unit relations with its internal and external publics, or stakeholders in its professional activities; this involves representation of what the unit or team is doing to other managers or units within the organization, and to persons/groups outside in the community, industry, or government.
4. *Coordination*—Performing liaison functions and integrating work unit activities so as to create synergy with other organizational units, or with externals, such as suppliers, contractors, consultants, consumers, regulatory officials, etc.
5. *Planning*—Developing and deciding upon long-term objectives/goals, strategies, and priorities; planning for change or alternative courses of actions.
6. *Implementation*—Converting the above plans into short-term targets and activities by sequencing/scheduling and appropriate decision-making.
7. *Financial Management*—Inaugurating and monitoring financial controls, such as budgeting which includes preparing, justifying, and administering funds invested in unit activities.
8. *Materials Resource Management*—Assuring availability of adequate raw materials and/or supplies, equipment, and facilities to carry on the unit's activities; overseeing procurement/contracting functions of the unit.

Continued

Exhibit 1.5 The High Performance Management Inventory, *cont'd.*

9. *Human Resource Management*—Projecting number/type of staff requirements for the unit, and effectively using the human resource development (HRD) systems of the organization or community for recruitment, selection, promotion, training, performance appraisal and improvement.
10. *Supervision*—Providing continuous monitoring, guidance, and coaching of subordinates so that unit activities are accomplished, while recognizing and rewarding high performance, as well as correcting low productivity situations.
11. *Unit Monitoring and Scanning*—Keeping informed on overall status of unit culture and activities, identifying problem areas for corrective actions (e.g., rescheduling or relocating resources, using external consultants of resources); then being able to compare unit activity with performance or trends among comparable organizational units and industry or foreign competitors through environmental scanning and forecasting.
12. *General Performance Evaluation*—Action research to critically assess the degree to which the unit is achieving program/project goals and targets, as well as its overall effectiveness in work operations; also evaluation of miscellaneous practices of the manager which affect both personal and unit performance at home and abroad.

These are the twelve dimensions of management, which when performed very well, contribute to a high performing leader and work environment. Within the context of these defined categories, now proceed with the judgements. No one else is to see these results unless you decide to share them. Remember, if you are to advance your personal and professional development, or that of others, through this exercise, be discriminating and authentic in your ratings. Recall that you are assessing individual proficiency in a range of managerial activities and responsibilities relative to a work unit or team—that is, the part or level of the organization that you or the individual under consideration manage or supervise (a project team, an office, plant, branch, division, bureau, regional or national territory, subsidiary, etc.).

(If a colleague or supervisor is using this instrument to assess the performance of another person, follow the same procedure.)

Record the most appropriate rating from the nine point scale on the blank space to the left of each numbered item. Thank you for your cooperation. Please begin the assessment process.

Part I: Cultural Awareness

_____ 1. Involved in the transition to the new work culture for myself and my unit by planning change.

_____ 2. Keep up-to-date on the socio-economic developments that affect my work unit.

_____ 3. Keep up-to-date with technological changes and developments affecting area of expertise for myself and the work unit.

_____ 4. Keep aware of changes in corporate or organizational culture.

Exhibit 1.5   The High Performance Management Inventory, *cont'd.*

———— 5. Keep up-to-date on changing organizational objectives, roles, norms, activities, priorities, and politics.

———— 6. Develop a strong work unit or team culture that enhances high performance and excellence.

———— 7. Aware of and sensitive to the varied cultures, both macro and micro, in which the unit operates.

———— 8. Develop cultural empathy/sensitivity to difference in unit members/colleagues, customers/clients, contractors/suppliers.

———— 9. Have knowledge and language skills for the host culture in which the unit operates.

———— 10. Apply understanding of roles, expectations, or regulations relative to unit performance from the perspective of *officials* in this organization, its unions, its industry association, or the government.

Part II: Communication

———— 11. Explain/clarify changing organizational culture, policies, priorities and procedures to unit members.

———— 12. Extract and apply organizational communications pertinent to unit members (e.g., information and directives from higher management).

———— 13. Keep unit members informed of pertinent external issues, and developments that impact their work.

———— 14. Ensure that work unit activities reflect organizational goals, policies, and directives.

———— 15. Prepare required written and oral communications for unit with conciseness, accuracy, competence, and cultural sensitivity.

———— 16. Communicate respect for the recipient/listener by transmitting both verbally and non-verbally positive concern, interest, and encouragement, especially by trying to get into the receiver's world or life space.

———— 17. Communicate reciprocal concern and non-judgmental attitude by a dialogue which shares interaction responsibility, promotes circular communication, and avoids moralistic, value-laden, evaluative statements.

———— 18. Communicate flexibility and capacity to tolerate ambiguity by adjustments to the receiver's mind-set and needs, as well as being able to cope with cultural differences and uncertainties.

———— 19. Communicate changes in organizational policies, procedures, and programs to external clients, suppliers, and stakeholders.

Part III: Public Relations

———— 20. Identify work unit's diverse publics or stakeholders in its activities and performance.

Continued

Exhibit 1.5 The High Performance Management Inventory, *cont'd.*

_____ 21. Represent/promote work unit before groups and individuals within and without the organization.

_____ 22. Respond effectively to inquiries and requests for unit information and service.

_____ 23. Explain work unit programs and functions to nonexperts in terms they can understand and which are culturally appropriate.

_____ 24. Persuade other interested parties to "buy into" and support a desired course of unit action.

_____ 25. Use formal and informal resource networks effectively to achieve unit objectives and targets, or to obtain information.

_____ 26. Resolve conflict within unit or with other units by negotiation and compromise, so energies can be constructively channeled.

_____ 27. Develop positive unit *image* for performance excellence, resourcefulness, and cooperation.

_____ 28. Create unit reputation for innovation and adaptability to varied circumstances, results that are usually on time and within budget, and synergistic relationships.

_____ 29. Demonstrate unit respect for host country or area locals, culture, and work habits.

_____ 30. Maintain concern for environmental or ecological impact of unit activities.

Part IV: Coordination

_____ 31. Maintain helpful, supportive, productive relationships within the work unit.

_____ 32. Maintain influential relationships with higher level management whose attitudes and decisions affect unit.

_____ 33. Maintain productive work relationships with other units within the organization, obtaining cooperation from those not under direct control.

_____ 34. Maintain productive working relationships with other companies within the industry (or other agencies within government if in public sector).

_____ 35. Maintain effective community relations with other pertinent organizations and government bodies within the area.

_____ 36. Keep higher level management informed in a timely and relevant manner of unit developments and of significant information obtained from the above contacts.

Exhibit 1.5   The High Performance Management Inventory, *cont'd.*

Part V: Planning

——— 37. Utilize established dynamic planning techniques, environmental scanning, technological forecasting, or even future studies to develop unit goals with other members and higher levels of management.

——— 38. Establish a balance among competing objectives and targets to accomplish overall work unit goals.

——— 39. Assess technical feasibility for alternative courses of action.

——— 40. Assess financial feasibility for alternative courses of action.

——— 41. Assess sociopolitical feasibility for alternative courses of action.

——— 42. Anticipate obstacles to achieving work unit goals, identify means for overcoming them, and apply contingency plans when necessary.

——— 43. Plan specifically for changes, adjusting long-term work unit goals accordingly.

——— 44. Maintain a balance between needs/goals of specialized or unit interests, and larger organizational mission.

Part VI: Implementation

——— 45. Identify specific projects and actions necessary to accomplish work unit goals.

——— 46. Establish priorities among competing unit projects and activities.

——— 47. Set challenging, but realistic deadlines for completing work units projects.

——— 48. Sequence and schedule work activities to maximize efficient use of available resources.

——— 49. Consider long-term goals while devising short-term plans and schedules.

——— 50. Provide unit guidance on how to assess or measure goal accomplishments.

Part VII: Financial Management

——— 51. Prepare unit budget with members in context of organizational constraints and financial resources.

——— 52. Project long-term financial needs and resources of work unit.

——— 53. Explain and justify persuasively the unit budget requests both orally and in writing.

Continued

Exhibit 1.5 The High Performance Management Inventory, *cont'd.*

_____ 54. Apply financial systems reports and mechanisms in managing work unit costs and/or income.

_____ 55. Seek entrepreneurial opportunities to supplement unit budget or expand its income production.

_____ 56. Consider national or community financial situation relative to pricing and compensation recommendations, expenditures and contributions, as well as other manifestations of unit social responsibility.

_____ 57. Consider return on investment in unit activities, especially if in the private sector and stockholder dividends are involved or loans are to be repaid.

Part VIII: Materials Resource Management

_____ 58. Plan for the acquisition of needed equipment, facilities, supplies, or services to carry out unit mission.

_____ 59. Apply organizational contract and procurement rules and regulations in managing work unit.

_____ 60. Oversee or participate in procurement management of key unit material resources, including lease of purchase decision's on equipment and contractors.

_____ 61. Oversee or participate in managing and evaluating contractor or supplier activities for the unit.

_____ 62. Ensure that local and minority contractors or suppliers given equal opportunity for unit business.

_____ 63. Ensure that illegal, unethical or unjust financial practices are not practiced within or by the work unit.

Part IX: Human Resources Management

_____ 64. Plan for needed changes in size and composition of work unit staff and supplementary personnel.

_____ 65. Take an active role in recruiting, selecting, and retaining staff for the work unit.

_____ 66. Seek and maintain competence as performance criteria, regardless of sex, race, or other factors in worker's background.

_____ 67. Apply personnel policies and regulations, particularly regarding equal employment opportunity and affirmative action to prevent job discrimination.

_____ 68. Seek synergistic labor/management relations and high performing work culture which enhances people's potential.

_____ 69. Develop meaningful performance standards, and conduct helpful performance appraisals.

_____ 70. Capitalize on human assets by appropriate training and development programs, especially in new technologies.

Exhibit 1.5 The High Performance Management Inventory, *cont'd.*

_____ 71. Take corrective and constructive actions with work unit members whose behavior or performance is inappropriate.

_____ 72. Consult with unit members and higher management for meaningful reward and recognition program.

Part X: Supervision

_____ 73. Clarify roles and relationships, so all unit members understand work assignments and expectations.

_____ 74. Encourage participative and team management approach.

_____ 75. Delegate responsibility with commensurate authority and resources.

_____ 76. Provide positive re-inforcement for high performance through appropriate recognition and rewards.

_____ 77. Coach and counsel unit members on technical problems, productivity, career development, and appropriate changes in performance or behavior.

_____ 78. Maintain equal concern for task accomplishment and people maintenance within the unit.

Part XI: Unit Monitoring and Scanning

_____ 79. Establish systems for monitoring work progress, so as to ensure unit excellence.

_____ 80. Adjust to changes in workload, resources, priorities, or schedule in dynamic and timely manner.

_____ 81. Use cooperative relations, direct observation, or informal contacts with general management, users, customers and suppliers to ascertain needs and unit effectiveness—manage by walking or moving around and staying in touch with unit publics.

_____ 82. Anticipate trends, changes, needs and problems, readjusting and reallocating as appropriate.

_____ 83. Encourage innovation and entrepreneurial spirit within the work unit, and especially in relations to externals.

Part XII: General Performance Evaluation

A. Unit Assessment:

_____ 84. Evaluate unit effectiveness in a systematic and objective manner, emphasizing both quantity and quality.

_____ 85. Assess unit climate in terms of cooperative actions that enhance people performance and potential.

Continued

Exhibit 1.5 The High Performance Management Inventory, *cont'd.*

_____ 86. Identify specific ways for improving unit's procedures, processes, structures, and cost effectiveness.

_____ 87. Identify specific ways for improving the unit's culture, morale, relationships, and achievement level.

_____ 88. Develop strategies toward achieving unit long-term goals by continuing system refinements and improvements.

_____ 89. Utilize individual member performance appraisals and input as means for improving unit productivity and excellence.

B. Personal Assessment:

_____ 90. Evaluate personal effectiveness as a unit manager in a systematic, objective and periodic manner, so as to identify strengths, limitations, and plans for improvement.

_____ 91. Conduct unit meetings to achieve desired objectives by improved skills as a facilitator.

_____ 92. Present ideas clearly and persuasively in both oral and written communication by improved skills as a communicator.

_____ 93. Share helpful feedback with members by improved skills as a listener, observer and constructive critic.

_____ 94. Practice diplomacy, tact, and consideration of others by improved human relations skills.

_____ 95. Practice leadership in a results-oriented and proactive, rather than reactive, way by improved planned change and strategist skills.

_____ 96. Take responsibility, exercise initiative, and seize opportunity by improved entrepreneurial skills.

_____ 97. Manage information resources for wider input and applications by improved skills in communication technologies and informal networking.

_____ 98. Exercise power by influencing others to get things done through improved skills in negotiations, bargaining, and coalition building.

_____ 99. Apply imagination and creativity by improving problem-solving and decision-making skills.

_____ 100. Implement and sustain a wellness program which reduces stress and tension, while improving the quality of life and the management of time and leisure.

_____ 101. Manage for transition, ambiguity, uncertainty, and differences by improved transformational management skills.

_____ 102. Act to personalize knowledge and perceptions by improved cross-cultural management skills, so as to recognize the influence of one's own culture on your values, perceptions, attitudes, communications, and management practices.

_____ 103. Endeavor to function in the metaindustrial or technological work culture by improving technical skills and scientific comprehension.

Exhibit 1.5   The High Performance Management Inventory, *cont'd.*

_____ 104. Endeavor to function in global economy and marketplace by improving skills and understanding of international economics, global regional markets, international management and business protocol, foreign languages.

_____ 105. Practice synergy by improving skill development in cooperative and collaborative actions, cultural sensitivity and open-mindedness, team building and joint ventures.

_____ TOTAL SCORE

Scoring Procedure

1. Add up the ratings provided for the 105 items.
2. Determine an overall evaluation of high performance management proficiency by comparing the total score with these approximations—a score between 210–315 would indicate basic competency; between 420 and 630 would be intermediate comparing; and between 235 and 945 would be advanced competency.
3. Go back and analyze the implications of any scores rated below 4—such items are targets for immediate improvement. Those with ratings in the 5–6 range would be secondary targets for professional development if one aspired to become a high performing manager.
4. Observe the twelve parts and the ratings provided within each category. Any selection with a preponderance of scores in the 2–6 range would seem to be an area to focus upon for further career development.
5. If one's supervisor or a colleague were asked to provide a more objective performance appraisal of you on the 105 items, then compare the total score supplied by that observer in contrast to one obtained through self-evaluation. Furthermore note discrepancies in scores for individual items and categories. A conference with that observer on such matters may offer additional self-knowledge and career guidance.

The assessor simply adds up the total of the management proficiency ratings to ascertain whether the evaluation indicates basic, intermediate, or advanced competency. A rating on any item below 4 identifies areas for performance improvement. The same instrument can be used during performance evaluation sessions by an individual and the supervisor to whom he or she reports; discrepancies in ratings can serve as a basis for discussion on how to increase performance.

The *High Performance Management Inventory* may not be reproduced and is available in quantity from Management Research Systems/Talico Inc., 2320 S. Third St. #7, Jacksonville Beach, FL 32250. Other instruments by the author, which expand upon some of the items in HPMI, are available from the same source. For example, within the HARRIS SERIES, these titles are related: *Change Inventory for Leaders; Human Resources Inventory; Intercultural Relations Inventory; Inventory of Transformational Management Skills; Management Communications Inventory; Organizational Communication Analysis; Organizational Culture Survey; Organizational Roles & Relationships Inventory; Team Synergy Analysis Inventory;* and *Quality of Life Index.*

For further reading on the subject matter of HMPI and the new work culture, two other books by Dr. Philip R. Harris are recommended: *Management in Transition* (1985), Jossey-Bass Publishers, 350 Sansome Street, San Francisco, CA 94104; and *New Worlds, New Ways, New Management* (1983), Masterco Press, P.O. Box 7320, Ann Arbor, MI 48107.

2
Increasing Performance at Work

To improve performance and productivity in the workplace, the leader does more than shape a creative environment. Managers must endeavor to understand and motivate people, beginning with themselves. Thus, our first objective in this chapter will be to better comprehend human behavior, then to learn how to energize personnel, especially by one's managerial style.

The second purpose will be to examine individual performance and the factors that contribute to high achievement. The leader who is concerned about performance management should become in that regard a behavior model for other workers to emulate. Then executives or managers have a responsibility to hold those who report to them accountable, by developing mechanisms that objectively appraise the work effort and encourage top performance.

Individuals are also energy exchange systems in themselves; as leaders, we must energize ourselves and others in goal achievement. Motivation becomes the mobilizing of our energy forces, both physical and psychic, toward specific goals, objectives, and targets.

A metaindustrial leader does not seek workers who are submissive, passive, and dependent, but rather stimulates personnel who grow personally and professionally and who optimize their talents and resources.

29

INPUT

Leaders need greater comprehension human behavior and motivation—simply, what makes people "tick"? The way leaders answer this question influences how they structure an organization, their philosophy and practices of management, and their strategies to influence personnel and improve performance. For many decades, behavioral scientists have contended that the best way for leaders to maintain a competitive edge is to develop the organization's human assets. To take advantage of the human potential in a corporation or agency, management must deal with complex issues of human nature and achievement.

A REVIEW OF MANAGEMENT THEORY

Twenty five years ago, Douglas McGregor produced a seminal book on the human side of enterprise. In it, he described two kinds of managers. One has a view of human nature that is quite negative but prevalent in the industrial age. These *Theory X* types, as he labeled them, believe that the average person has an inherent dislike of work and avoids it and responsibility when possible, because most individuals have relatively little ambition. According to Theory X managers, workers prefer to be directed and must be controlled, coerced, and even threatened with punishment in order to make them perform effectively.

McGregor (1985) maintained that this type of management was replaced in the postindustrial period with a management style based upon very different assumptions about human nature, which he called *Theory Y*. Theory Y holds that the expenditure of energy in work is as natural as play or rest, and high performance depends on self-direction and self-control. From this perspective, commitment to organizational objectives is a function of rewards associated with their achievement; given the right organizational environment, the average worker learns to accept and seek responsibility. The leader's task is to create those conditions that unleash the human capacity for imagination, ingenuity, and innovation.

Other behavioral scientists have rejected what can be called *pull approach* to worker motivation, which depends on external controls used in an almost punitive way. Like Rensis Likert (1961), these theorists did not conceive behavior as dependent solely upon forces in the environment, responding only to demands and pressures, rewards and punishments, and deprivations and inducements. Their research in industry during the last half of the twentieth century has demonstrated the dynamic possibilities of human growth when workers are given meaningful work, are permitted to participate with management, and are challenged to achieve. Frederick Herzberg, for instance, proved to managers that it is not enough to take care of the needs of employees relative to pay, benefits, and working conditions; instead, the real motivators are to be found in achievement, growth, recognition, responsibility, and advancement. The manager's job, then, involves more than manipulating the work environment to induce and channel human energies. Workers themselves are changing in terms of their education and economic income, and they have a new set of needs and requirements for motivation.

MASLOW'S HIERARCHY OF NEEDS

One of the most helpful contributions toward understanding human motivation came from the humanistic psychologist, Abraham Maslow. He said that human needs vary according to immediacy and can be arranged in a *hierarchy,* or graded rank, according to the order in which they must be met. Exhibit 2.1 reproduces his conceptual model for us.

Exhibit 2.1   Maslow's Hierarchy of Needs.

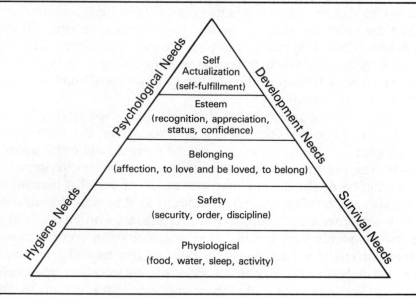

The foundation of Maslow's motivation theory is that we humans must satisfy certain needs before we can act or achieve. In other words, we first seek to satisfy our basic survival or physiological needs, such as food or sex. When these are sufficiently satisfied, we become concerned with another level of need related to safety and security, either physiological or psychological; such needs prompt such behaviors as locking homes, organizing neighborhood watch programs, building up bank accounts, and striving for the right job classification and tenure. Once these lower needs are provided for, according to this theory, we are freed for higher-level concerns, such as belonging and love, which find expression in yearning to be loved by someone, in membership in some group, and in general acceptance by others. Finally, near the top of the hierarchy are such "esteem" needs as self-respect, recognition, and prestige. Such ego needs can be prime movers toward self-determination, control over one's fate, and achievement. People operating at this need level work in order to have others acknowledge their capacities and power; if such needs are thwarted, such a person may feel weak, inferior, and even helpless. For some who distort the satisfaction of these needs, human drive may lead to excessive demands for power and control.

At the pinnacle of human needs in the Maslow model is the inner drive for self-fulfillment or actualization of one's potential. This drive propels some people to strive to become what they are capable of becoming, to seek excellence of achievement. At its best, it motivates the search for ultimate value, perfection, justice, truth, beauty, and other nonselfish ideals. It is manifest in high achievers, superior athletes and performers, accomplished artists and writers, and outstanding scholars and researchers. It leads to the highest expressions of human creativity and nobility of actions.

Maslow theorized that we all have all the varied needs, but that people may focus on one level or another. Thus, the homeless urban dweller of necessity concentrates on survival, while the suburban middle-class person may be centered on security needs, trying to preserve what he or she has attained. The theory allows that humans may move up and down on the need hierarchy as time and circumstances dictate. For instance, a young urban professional who loses his or her job may suddenly have a reordering of priorities. A second example is that citizens of a First World, affluent society have the luxuries of time and means to be concerned about the environment and ecology and to strive to prevent pollution or eradicate disease; many in Third World communities, on the other hand, must focus on fighting to stay alive and on counteracting the effects of drought, plague, starvation, and other disasters.

Dr. Maslow also maintained that there was a reverse side to his hierarchy; all the needs had associated complaints, which he labeled "gripes or grumbles." Humans perpetually seek fuller lives; their complaints also rise in a hierarchy that corresponds to their needs. Thus, as we have corrected some of the past abuses of the factory system, such as child labor, we become more concerned about higher issues of social justice, such as the employment of minorities or equal opportunities in management for women. If an employer takes care of personnel needs for cleanliness and safety in a plant, then the employer can expect workers' gripes or demands to move up the scale; perhaps they will demand child-care centers or sabbatical leaves.

Maslow actually applied his research to the work environment of a small California plant and wrote a book in 1965 on what he termed "eupsychian management." His point was that a more productive work situation would result when management created a corporate culture that emphasized satisfaction of the three higher levels of needs. In a sense, he anticipated what today is termed the *new management* or the *new work culture.* Leaders who hope to design a high performance corporation or agency would do well to analyze and apply these concepts.

HUMAN BEHAVIOR IN THE WORKPLACE

Psychiatrists, psychologists, sociologists, and other social scientists have propounded many theories for explaining why humans behave as they do. As a management psychologist, I have synthesized a viewpoint from that myriad research that has made sense to me in counseling or consulting with different people and systems. Below is a summary, which can be applied to problems of management—coping with coworkers and attempting to lead them toward higher performance.

Each of us lives within his or her own life space, which is as unique as a fingerprint. This space has both psychological and physical dimensions. Behavioral scientists call it our *perceptual field.* Each individual views reality from within this space or perspective and develops a way of reading meaning into it.

Think of life space, for a moment, in terms of concentric circles. At the core is the sense of self—how we view ourselves as persons, positively or negatively. From that core, moving outward in ever-larger circles, next comes our systems of needs, values, standards, expectations, and ideals. Together, these influence our perception of what happens outside of ourselves; it is the mind-set that ultimately affects our acts or inaction. Thus, we are each different, so that we may disagree as to what is real, true, beautiful, right, or wrong. Perception is relative, and explains why disagreements or arguments may occur, say, for instance, between ourselves and fellow workers. Knowing this makes a good case for being more tentative, less absolute, in our expression of opinions and viewpoints.

Being a part of a cultural group can further influence and reinforce an individual's perception and behavior (see Chapter 4). Suffice it now to recall that just as our life spaces or private worlds are unique, so is each of our need systems. As we seek to satisfy these needs, we are motivated or energized toward certain goals for ourselves. Exhibit 2.2 provides a visual presentation of the concept.

We motivate ourselves or get aroused when we direct and sustain effort to attain or to avoid something, so as to satiate a need (see Exhibit 2.2). When we are hungry, for example, we are motivated or aroused to seek food. Behavior is largely motivated, but there are several different forces within each person's life space that move us to act or avoid in a certain way.

Furthermore, behavior can be affected by habit, culture, or the activities of others. Although originally a course of behavior may have been a conscious choice, over a period of time people may act unconscious of the forces in the past or the culture that dictated their behavior. I was jolted at lunch one day when I was asked why I never used pepper; mulling over the question, I eventually remembered that my grandmother often told me as a child, "Pepper puts holes in your heart." Since I consciously recalled the reason for this foolish behavior, I regularly use pepper, especially as a healthier substitute for salt.

Exhibit 2.2 A Model of Human Behavior.

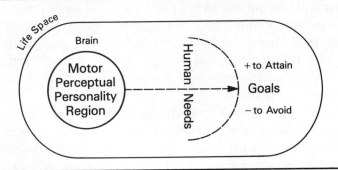

My point is that our behavior can be conditioned by others, by past experience and culture.

Behavior, then, can be modified toward what increases performance. This knowledge allows us to correct abuses in terms of smoking, alcohol, drugs, and other unhealthy or undesirable behavior. In addition, effective leaders learn to reinforce positive or desired behavior in employees, especially through some form of reward or recognition.

Exhibit 2.3 amplifies the behavior model we are proposing for consideration. In striving to meet our goals or objectives, we sometimes meet barriers, physical or psychological, that can frustrate the satisfaction of needs. We may cope with such realities by an adjustment that permits us to circumvent the obstacle or by engaging in conflict within ourselves or with others, such as blaming someone for the problem. This type of aggressive reaction to frustration—finding a "scapegoat"—can result in racism and other forms of bigoted behavior. Other responses to frustration range from withdrawal and apathy to rebellion and revolt.

To put this in a work context, consider this situation. A supervisor and her subordinate work out some career objectives for the latter during the course of performance appraisal. The plan calls for the employee to take courses that will lead to better job performance and

Exhibit 2.3   Motivations and Behavior Responses: Achievement or Adjustment.

Two motives act at once—choice as to which to satisfy, inability to express feeling causes frustration.

Conflict   Life Space

Adjustment = Satisfaction of motives and regulation of tension level

Adjustment

Need Satisfaction
Striving for Meaning/Purpose

Frustration   Fulfillment   Goals

Aggressive ◄ Reactions Defensive ◄

Note: When a need is consistently frustrated, the behavior reaction becomes a pattern; personality trait is formed.

Conflict/Hostility
Rebellion/Revolt
Displacement/Transfer
Withdrawal/Inactivity
Apathy/Indifference

Aggression can also produce frustration.

Cope with unsatisfied needs by denial.
Projection/Rationalization
Repression/Sublimation

advancement. Frustration may arise when the person discovers a barrier to attendance, for instance, by lack of time, money, or qualifications. The employee is in conflict. One positive adjustment would be to take the program independently, using audiotape or videocassette to teach himself. A negative adjustment would be to deny the need for the training, project the problem on the company, or even blame the supervisor for suggesting the idea in the first place. The healthy response to frustration is to channel one's energies in constructive, instead of destructive ways. Frustrated energy, for example, can be sublimated into service. Repressing that energy, for example, by dropping the course and blaming someone else, undermines one's position. Seeking alternative solutions to problems, on the other hand, contributes to personal growth, for we develop coping skills.

Mother Teresa of Calcutta, as an example, was once frustrated as a teacher of science to elite students in a private academy. Sensing the needs of the poor surrounding her in India, she sublimated her energies into a new form of service by founding an order or movement dedicated to the most needy humans. Her global achievements and leadership in serving the poor resulted in world acclaim and the Nobel Prize.

Deviant behavior occurs when the action differs from what is considered normal by a group. Deviant behavior can be creative, as in the case of those who advocate change of obsolete laws and regulations because the norms or standards are no longer appropriate, or it can be delinquent, as in the case of a worker who is frequently tardy or absent or who undermines order on the job. Creative deviants alter the status quo and promote renewal. Delinquent behavior may range from the abnormal to the illegal—it is always disruptive to the organization. Sometimes, with counseling or reeducation, a delinquent deviant will change behavior; if not, the employee may have to go.

Undesirable behavior may result in a worker being ignored, criticized, or unrewarded by the manager. Punishment is a less effective way of altering people's behavior over the long run. It may for the moment stop the negative actions but does not permanently change the delinquent. This is, in part, why our criminal justice system, based on punishment, is so inadequate.

Scientific research today recognizes that some individuals are genetically predisposed to criminality. James Q. Wilson, the author of *Crime and Human Nature,* reports studies that show that some criminals have low regards for the feelings or values of others and are prone to pursue immediate gratification of their own needs at the expense of others. Behavioral differences between the sexes have been linked to hormonal differences, which to some partially explains the ten'ency for males to be more predisposed toward criminal deviant behavior than are females. Dr. Wilson believes that the time is coming when we can provide more effective therapy early in life to those with such predispositions, who presently become menaces to society.

The best management strategy is to focus on healthy behavior so that the group will exclude those whose behavior is unacceptably disruptive. What are the criteria of healthy behavior that a leader seeks to encourage and develop in organizational members? Here are some characteristics of mentally healthy persons that leaders would do well to cultivate in themselves and seek in their work force:

- Healthy persons have a strong sense of self; they have resolved the fundamental questions "Who am I?," "Where am I going?," and "How do I get there?"; they are self-accepting and comfortable with themselves and not in perpetual conflict with themselves.
- Healthy persons have a unifying purpose or philosophy of life and realistic views of the world around them.
- Healthy persons have self-esteem balanced with a realistic assessment of their own abilities and skills.
- Healthy persons are able to experience warm and meaningful relationships.

High performers normally have healthy personalities. It has been observed that top performers are usually among the healthiest, happiest, and most enthusiastic people. Leaders, too, of course, should have such personalities.

THE CULTIVATION OF HIGH PERFORMANCE

Our second concern in this learning module is to identify the behaviors that contribute to high achievement and the ways to foster that kind of behavior on the job. For more than a decade, professor of organizational behavior Jean Lipman-Blumen and her colleagues at Stanford University have been studying human achievement, particularly how to measure such traits. She and Harold J. Leavitt have created the *L-BL Achieving Styles Model,* which classifies people in three achieving groups: direct, instrumental, and relational (Abrams, 1985):

1. The *direct class of achiever* has been subdivided into three further categories for greater comprehension:

- *Intrinsic-direct* achievers become totally absorbed in the task and get gratification from doing it well; such persons have an internalized standard of excellence and do not depend on external accolades or incentives.
- *Competitive-direct* achievers have to surpass all others or all others who are considered standards of reference.
- *Power-direct* achievers wish to take charge in nearly every situation regardless of motivations or intentions.

2. There are also three categories within the *instrumental* classification:

- *Personal-instrumental* achievers do not distinguish between means and ends, but use whatever will accomplish their purpose; for instance, the intellectual who uses knowledge to accomplish social goals, such as to prevent child abuse.
- *Social-instrumental* persons are likely to employ relationships, rather than abilities, to attain objectives; for instance, a lobbyist targets a relationship for what it can deliver.
- *Reliant-instrumental* achievers look to everyone or every relationship to help them advance; they depend upon others to carry out their goals for them. Such a type might become a teacher or counselor.

3. In the final, the *relationship,* class, there are also three subcategories:

- A *contributory* type identifies with another achiever, takes on that person's goals, and helps the other achieve those goals; the spouse of a corporate executive or government official might very well be a contributory achiever.
- *Collaborative* persons are team players who achieve, actively or passively, through the group relationship.
- *Vicarious* achievers accomplish through force of circumstances that bring people together, and enable one to achieve in place of another or the experience of the other (e.g., Jim Belushi's achievement of high status as an actor after the death of his talented brother, John).

Leaders may find this model helpful in the analysis of work achievement among diverse personnel and in varying their own managerial style to suit the personality of the employee or colleague. For example, an executive may be able to encourage contributory persons to adopt his or her own organizational goals as if they were their own. Lipman-Blumen suspects from her research with Leavitt that women are changing their styles of achieving to meet new demands upon them. Furthermore, for successful team building and management, she believes the group needs strong people of all nine types. A leader can also use this concept of achieving styles to resolve conflicts by helping personnel to modify or alter their style.

A 5-year study of top performers by Benjamin Bloom, an education professor at the University of Chicago, concluded that drive and determination, not great natural talent, led to the outstanding success of the high achievers interviewed (Harris, 1985, p. 208). The 120 leading artists, athletes, and scholars expressed an early interest in their fields and experienced continuing encouragement from parents and other adults. Bloom's findings show how moral support and training contribute to extraordinary performance levels. Leaders should bear this in mind when considering how work and organizational culture contribute to this process of achievement.

Various researchers on high performers have concluded that:

- Metaperformance is linked to a strong self-concept and self-esteem; average persons will improve their performance when they are helped positively to visualize themselves as achievers and winners.
- Creative, top performers seem to be more whole-brained—they use both right-brain capacity of perception and intuition along with left-brain logic.
- High performers are flexible, not rigid, and learn to get around bureaucratic obstacles and obsolete and ineffective policies, rules, or regulations, in order to get a job done well.
- High-achieving executives have been found to be as caring about their employees as about their profits, and to seek advice from subordinates.
- Peak performers demonstrate unusual qualities of creativity, risk-taking, and commitment to both their work and change.
- Managers who encourage employees to do their very best and to upgrade their performance are usually rated high by workers.
- Employees exhibit high internal motivation, work satisfaction, and performance when their work is meaningful and given larger purpose, when they feel responsible for its outcome, and when they have a continuing knowledge of the results of their work activities.
- Peak performance can be increased through human resource development methods.

CASE STUDIES ON SELF-ACTUALIZED LEADERS

A doctoral dissertation was recently completed in June 1987 at Northwestern University by Thomas P. Brennan on the subject of *Case Studies of Multilevel Development*. (It is available on microfilm from University Microfilms International, Ann Arbor, MI 48106).

Dr. Brennan's investigation builds upon the description of the characteristics of self-actualized people developed by the humanistic psychologist, Abraham Maslow, and the theories of emotional development set forth in the prior research of K. Dabrowski and M. M. Piechowski. Brennan conducted in-depth interviews with self-actualized persons and eventually composed four case studies.

Among the traits common to these high-performing individuals were:

- A strong desire to accomplish for the benefit of mankind; focus on problems outside oneself; a life mission
- A strong philosophy of life; guiding principles or transcendent values; a spiritual or religious orientation
- A concern for personal growth or change and self-acceptance
- A sense of responsibility; fairness; concern for ethics, justice, and the growth of others
- The ability to make decisions; autonomy; self-control
- An ability to establish exclusive relationships combined with a need for solitude in order to be productive; ability to use contemplation to cultivate inner harmony
- A high level of energy and physical well-being

This study not only provides insights about high performance by examining such self-actualized lives, but offers an efficient method for selecting and interviewing people who have achieved higher levels of self-development.

Dr. Brennan's research contributes to a consensus emerging from investigations into metaperformance. High achievers are generally people who are self-disciplined, in the sense of being oriented toward self-caring and self-development. Such individuals can not only set achievable goals for themselves, but delay gratification of pleasure in order to attain objectives. This discipline involves making tough choices as to what they will do and will avoid in order to reach the target or gain the prize. It is, however, a self-generated and self-maintained discipline; balanced and not rigid, a joy and an incentive toward positive change and accomplishment in one's life.

Dr. Brennan's summary of behavioral science research gives us something of a profile on high achievers. In a doctoral dissertation on the experience of top performers, Yates (1979) discovered that the 10 to 20 percent of the work force in this category were effective because of the vigorous manner in which they applied their skills and energies in the right tasks; because they gained knowledge from success and continually refined their experience and perpetuated their success. In today's information and service economy, such attitudes and skills are critical to a high-performance organization.

Too many companies or agencies permit their norms to degenerate to the lowest common denominator instead of using the top performers to help set standards so that everyone is stretched. Top performers often devise their own systems, which work better than those in place, and ordinary employees should be encouraged to emulate them. Today's high performer frequently sets tomorrow's norms, procedures, roles, and goals. Learning experiences, therefore, should be designed so that the high achiever's insights can be shared with coworkers.

For almost three decades the most outstanding research on human achievement and motivation has been done by David C. McClelland, Harvard University professor of psychology and founder of Boston's McBer and Company, a consulting firm specializing in job competency analysis based on the high performers. From his 1967 book, *The Achieving Society,* to his current works, McClelland (1984) has maintained that people can learn to achieve. Among his findings are that achievement-oriented personalities achieve success because of their need to experience success or avoid failure. From school to workplace, people can be taught or trained to achieve. McClelland suggests six steps for doing this:

1. Study your own achievements, strengths, and weaknesses, and examine the characteristics of achievers.
2. Get ideas on what goals to achieve, especially through brainstorming with others.
3. Set a realistic goal that is both challenging and achievable.
4. Develop a plan that outlines the tasks to be undertaken in order to accomplish this goal; include a needs and resource assessment, a self-inventory relative to the goal and the problems to be resolved,

and a look at the implications of the proposed actions upon yourself and others.

5. Carry out the plan and check on your progress regularly; according to your results, seek advice or help or even change the plan or the goal.

6. Evaluate your effort, including the reasons for success or failure, and list improvements to be made in accomplishing the next goal.

Behavioral scientists have long advocated goal-setting as the key to peak performance. Consultants such as Maria Arapakis (Software Resources, Inc., 6121 Rockridge Blvd., So, Oakland, Ca. 94618) have attempted to provide guidelines to translate such research into effective management practice. In a newsletter to clients, she proposes eight steps for improved performance:

1. Define your goals clearly in writing.
2. Identify the obstacles preventing the accomplishment of these.
3. Determine the principal barrier to achievement of the main goal.
4. Identify the choices for overcoming this obstacle and write down these potential solutions.
5. Make a schedule to meet deadlines for obtaining results in goal achievement.
6. Reward self for accomplishing mini deadlines, and share this sense of accomplishment with others.
7. Daily check-up on progress in attaining goals, and make necessary modifications to keep moving ahead.
8. Create mental images on final results, and be flexible on how you will achieve these goals.

HIGH PERFORMING ORGANIZATIONS

Finally, studies of contemporary successful corporations have more than demonstrated the impact of organizational culture on human performance (Harris, 1983, 1985.) Exhibit 2.4 offers a summary of these findings in terms of leadership style—what an executive or manager should emphasize and avoid in order to cultivate a high-performance work environment.

Leaders in high-performance management create a corporate culture that excites people and makes work fun. The work experience can be joyful because it encourages informality, fellowship, and teamwork, as

Exhibit 2.4 Characteristics of the High Performance Work Culture.

The High Performance Organization Emphasizes:	The High Performance Organization Avoids:
* Human resources as assets to be fully used and developed	* Underemploying, manipulating, and exploiting employees
* Personnel involvement in the management processes of goal-setting, problem-solving, and decision-making	* Autocratic, unilateral, and secretive approaches that exclude subordinates from power and authority
* Innovation, creativity, intuition, and orientation to the future by all	* Perpetuating the status quo, the tried and true, and advocating the safe "way we have always done it"
* Open, circular, authentic communications, networking, and information systems	* Downward communication, shielding top management from unpleasant news, telling them what they want to hear
* Alternative strategies and solutions and the search for unconventional answers or markets	* Simplistic solutions and clinging to only proven strategies and markets
* Calculated risk-taking, brain storming, the use of decision trees and simulations	* Insistence on orderly and traditional decision-making, limiting input and participation
* Energized management who serve as behavior models, who are informal, and are open to creative deviancy	* Managerial vacillation and inertia; overreliance on hierarchical policy-making; slavish adherence to all norms
* Tentative and temporary groupings and solutions that permit flexibility and fluidity of response	* Rigid scheduling, solid structures, chain of command, and precise procedures
* Reinforcing worker goals and achievements consistently, with constructive feedback	* Annual performance evaluation and the formal checklists in evaluating employees; focus on corrections and punishments
* Competence and high performance as behavior norms.	* The use of average performance standards according to contract
* Recognition and reward of productive behavior and merit	* Recognition and reward based on status and tenure
* Entrepreneurial spirit and personal commitment to projects	* Becoming corporate autocrats that control everything
* Capitalizing on personnel differences and unique talents, especially through teams	* Encouraging conformity; striving for organizational unity and a "corporate look"
* Wellness programs that continuously support a healthy life style; stress management; safety programs; and multiple insurance options	* Reliance on standardized health and accident insurance benefits; such inadequate care for personnel as the policy of annual physicals only

well as productive behavior. Steve Becker, president of Learningcom, Inc., learned from his research with high performers that they not only have superior intellects and are professionally or emotionally mature, but they are self-reliant and self-directing. This Framingham, Massachusetts consultant confirms that top performers need management that

- Offers new challenges and opportunities to relate to other professionals whom they respect
- Reinforces their enormous pride in the results they achieve by demonstrating respect for them
- Provides independence for them to do the tasks assigned without frustrating interference from supervisors
- Gives them more freedom by making occasional exceptions to rules and dress codes, being flexible about work hours and working at home, and supplying necessary equipment and support services
- Removes organizational obstacles to their performance on the job, allowing them to maintain intensity while maintaining a balanced control

I have learned many things about management from Dr. Dorothy Lipp Harris, particularly the way she achieved high performance in her administrative staff of almost a hundred people. As a dean at Pennsylvania State University, Dr. Harris always acted toward her colleagues as if they were one step beyond their actual performance. Because she cared for their needs and treated each of them as an accomplished, high-achieving professional, these people outdid themselves to attain that level of competence. As a result, the whole group became a very high-performing unit. (Exhibit 2.5 shows a further example of how managers can negatively influence the work environment toward low performance.)

INTERACTION

Managers who are leaders want to always be fully informed. Continued, shared learning with colleagues is one way to hone leadership skills. The following group dynamic process can be used in a staff meeting, in formal management development sessions, or in informal get-togethers, such as at the lunch hour. As a starter, the group can use this process to share learning with some of the topics in this book. In

Exhibit 2.5 Minicase on Work Environment: A dramatic account of a negative work culture.

To illustrate how managers can influence a work environment in a way that can undermine productivity, consider this recent news report:

Attorney Catherine Broderick worked for five years in a Washington regional office of the Securities and Exchange Commission. In a suit against the SEC, she described the work environment as a "brothel," a place where senior managers had affairs with their secretaries, gave them cash awards and promotions in return for promiscuous relationships, and encouraged an atmosphere of drinking, jogging, and little work—the accepted behavior for those who were part of their "team." Broderick testified that she was trapped in that office and could not get out; it took away her spirit, causing her to experience hopelessness and powerlessness. By not cooperating, she experienced severe harrassment, her outstanding work went unrecognized, and she was blackballed from transfer or promotion by the "good-old-boy network of the securities bar." After struggling against the situation for nine years, justice finally triumphed. . . . In June 1988, U.S. District Judge John H. Pratt II ruled in her favor after finding the SEC's regional office was a work environment permeated by sexual harassment and discrimination in which managers retaliated against complainers. Pratt ordered that Broderick be granted three promotions with retroactive pay plus interest, and all negative evaluations be removed from her file. The Judge also ordered an end to the sexually hostile environment, and initiated investigations and reforms within the agency. ("She Beat the SEC Team Over Sex Harassment," *Los Angeles Times,* June 17, 1988, Part V, pp. 1, 22–23.)

any HRD or training effort, variety of inputs, methods, and forms of participation are essential. This strategy has that advantage, plus it keeps stretching people's minds with fresh input and discussion.

INPUT BOMBARDMENT (IB)

The first step of this process is the formation of a small group, usually between six and twelve. This might be a natural work unit, a group of buddies interested in professional development, or a project team. The approach can also be used with a large audience divided into smaller groups. (In that case, each group should be given a different reading, for instance each covers a different article on the general subject of motivation.)

The group selects or is assigned a reading for review. This may be a book chapter, an article from a technical or professional journal, or a newspaper feature article. Each person has a copy of the reading. For example, the group could reproduce and distribute the two short essays on human behavior in the Input section on pages 30-37, or an article on high performance or productivity from a popular business magazine or a trade or technical journal. Choose content that is timely, interesting, stimulating, and relevant to the theme under discussion.

Third, each member of the group is assigned to cover a portion of the material. This can be done quickly by going around the circle and assigning paragraphs or sections to each person in order, until all the article is assigned. (A variation on this procedure, time permitting, is to give each person a separate chapter or article on the same theme to scan on behalf of the whole group.)

The fourth step to follow in the IB process is Read, React, and Report (R.R.&R.). Everyone reads his or her assignment individually, reacts to its message in terms of the group or the organization, and reports to all his or her findings. The reading is a rapid scanning, so that the essence of the writer's ideas are extracted. The report is an overview of the major points in the assigned reading and that individual's reaction to its implications here and now. That is, can the input be adopted, adapted, or applied within this group for personal and organizational improvement? After each member has provided input to the total group, the group together discusses the insights obtained from all the reports. At the end, group members should at their leisure study the complete reading in greater depth. (Another possibility is to give out the assigned reading before the IB session, so that people have an opportunity to study a larger portion of data in greater detail.)

Normally, this process can be accomplished in 40 to 60 minutes, or more as time permits. Let us assume that there is an hour and fifteen minutes available for IB during lunch, a staff meeting, or a training session, and that we have an ideal group of eight persons. One person—the manager, trainer, consultant, or someone elected by the group—assumes the role of facilitator. The facilitator is both time-keeper and discussion leader. The material in question is divided into eight parts, and each group member is allowed 3 minutes to privately read his or her assignment. Each then, in topical sequence, takes 3 minutes to react to what he or she has read. The process at this point will have taken up to 50 minutes. This leaves about 25 minutes for the general discussion, which might also include some action planning to apply this input back on the job.

Many variations can be made on this group dynamic technique. The facilitator can use a blackboard, overhead projector, or flip chart to outline the principal points of the material as it is reported by each person. If there is a large audience of say, sixty-four, provision can be made for eight group reports to the total assemblage; each group chooses a reporter to summarize that unit's findings.

I have used this method successfully hundreds of times with managers and professionals throughout the world, from small teams to audiences of 2000. Its values are

- A lot of information is covered in a relatively short time.
- The stimulation of new ideas can prompt one to read the material more critically.
- The opportunity to learn together and share in group communication furthers professional development.

Thinking managers will find input bombardment an ideal mechanism for exposing peers and work groups to research and developments that normally might not be discussed. Readers who wish to share the insights in this volume with their coworkers can use the Input sections in this book. The process can be used to cover the latest trends and concepts in your field or industry, marketing, manufacturing, and public and community relations.

Organizational leaders have employed this technique to cover

1. *Best selling management books.* Every manager does not have the time to read the many new books on the new management. IB is a chance to divide and conquer this database by having various groups or individuals in a group R.R.&R. on a specific title. Readers may wish to start with the reference books listed at the end of this text. Management book clubs and the Consultants Bookstore (Templeton Road, Fitswilliam, NH 03447) may help with selecting titles. You can request publishers of management books to put you on their mailing lists for new book announcements and catalogs. A representative sample of suggested titles and publishers will be found at the end of this book, along with recommended periodicals and journals.
2. *Contemporary periodicals.* These range from business magazines to international publications such as *The Economist;* to management journals such as those of the American Management Associations (e.g., *Organizational Dynamics*); and to the *Harvard Business Review* and *New Management* (all are cited in the Resource Section, Appendix A).

   You might ask a work team to look for articles relating to productivity. Arrange to have these articles reproduced for a monthly input bombardment session. For example, *Time,* featured in its Health & Fitness section (November 18, 1985, p. 98) an article on "Giving Goodies to the Good," which reported on the wellness life-style and its contribution to high performance. The item summarized corporate trends, such as company-sponsored programs and incentives to reward employees for taking positive steps to safeguard their health and increase their fitness. Finally, we urge readers to obtain the free publications catalog of the American Productivity Center (123 North Post Oak Lane, Houston, TX 77024).

3. The first two volumes of Tom Peters, for example, described many excellent companies, and his latest work, *Thriving on Corporate Chaos* (1987), is a handbook for a management revolution based on a company's ability to respond quickly and flexibly to ever-changing markets and technology. Peters' *The Leadership Alliance* (1988) examines the employee-employer partnership. Similarly, a new work by John Belcher, *Productivity Plus* (1987) shows how today's best-run companies are gaining the competitive edge. It gives the inside story on how Xerox, Tenneco, and Westinghouse met new challenges with innovative improvements. Selections from any or all these books are excellent material for IB.

MANAGING RESPONSIBILITY

When people clearly understand what is expected of them and are held accountable for fulfilling these expectations, performance improves and productivity increases. Clarifying roles and relationships among personnel is a continuing responsibility of leadership. In *Management in Transition* (Harris, 1985), I provided an instrument to facilitate this clarification among a manager and work unit. Now, consider an interaction process for the same purpose (Exhibit 2.6), contributed by Dr. Woodrow H. Sears, a management consultant in Los Angeles, California. The author of *Back in Working Order: How American Institutions Can Win the Productivity Battle* (1983), Sears designed this group exercise especially for use in team-building. "Expect/ inspect" is his way of summarizing the leader's charge to monitor and manage work performance. (Note: This interaction works best in groups that work together on a regular basis. If it is a large work unit, break it down into smaller teams of six to eight workers. The facilitator will require a flip chart with newsprint paper, large colored marking pens, and masking tape.)

Exhibit 2.6   The Critical Pay-Off Functions Exercise. (*Source:* Woodrow H. Sears, published in a column, "Tools for Training," by P. R. Harris in *Successful Meetings,* Sept. 1975, pp. 1, 29, 78.)

Critical Pay-off Functions.   Group members are asked to make a list of the things they do on their jobs. Then subgroups are formed to share the data, note common activities from each list, and draft a consensus report for their group. Manager or trainer then drafts a master list on a blackboard or newsprint sheets composed of the information supplied by the subgroup.

The various groups meet a second time to come to agreement on what they perceive as the "critical pay-off functions" on that master list, activities which must be performed if they are to succeed on the job. The facilitator underlines or stars each item that the groups report as critical.

Self-Assessment.   At this point a break should be taken for individual work, or the task can be given as a home assignment.

The participants are asked to review their personal lists and the comprehensive list compiled by the group, and decide upon 4 to 7 key elements of their jobs which they see as essential to the proper performance of their jobs. After this review and evaluation, they are asked to write down these functions in detail on a carbonized sheet of paper: One copy for them and one for the facilitator.

Now responsibility for job performance can be pinpointed in the written word of the individual doing the work. It would be ideal if that person's supervisor could review the list for feedback to the individual on whether his or her manager perceives such activities as critical functions.

To stimulate the trainee in the assessment process, questions might be raised, such as: Are you doing things you are not paid to do? Is your daily work schedule filled up with busy work or tasks with which you are most comfortable *because* you are unsure of the nature and scope of your job?

Synthesis.   During the next group session, the small groups meet again to share their assessments, and to develop a total group report on major categories of job functions which are critical in their work. This data is again visually displayed as the reports come in from the subgroups. They might include such topical headings as planning, communication, budgeting, etc. Then the trainees are given another management model to aid them in becoming more responsible in carrying out their job duties.

Need/Problem.   Group members are asked to identify either individually or in groups the needs they are seeking to satisfy by doing their jobs, or the problems they are trying to resolve through job performance. The data is then recorded on a blackboard or newsprint sheet under the major heading: Need/Problem; the same procedure is followed for the next four categories.

Objectives/Goals.   Based on the results of the above exercise, the participants are invited to set down one or more principal objectives/goals which

Continued

Exhibit 2.6   The Critical Pay-Off Functions Exercise, *cont'd.*

they should have for adequate performance of their jobs. They are encouraged to describe these aims with an action verb, to include a key outcome, to qualify and quantify, to set a time frame and budget dimension. Again the results are collected and visually recorded.

Resources Required.   To accomplish the above objectives/goals, what help or assistance is required? The individuals or groups are then requested to note the human/material/financial resources which are necessary for them to carry out their job purposes and perform the critical functions.

Action Steps.   To satisfy the needs or resolve the problems identified above, to achieve the objectives/goals set, what actions must be undertaken? The trainees are asked to develop a set of steps, phases or stages to be followed in accomplishing the critical job functions.

Evaluation.   To assess what has been done, particularly in terms of cost, the participants are asked to indicate some quantifiable standards or criteria or performance. How do they plan to measure the results of their efforts?

Finally, as a home assignment the trainees are asked to refine the above data in terms of their own job. Using the model provided, they are to write down on carbonized sheets their personal plan of action in terms of the categories or processes presented in the training session. One copy should eventually get to the participant's supervisor. How effectively the latter uses the information will influence the degree of payoff on the learning experience.

Sears often introduces the procedure with this astute observation:

> The continuing reality is that in most organizations, many employees are vague about the exact nature of their duties, the goals of the organization, and the specific objectives which must be reached to make possible goal achievement by the total organization. In short, most people who go to work still don't know what their jobs really are about, and how the functions they are supposed to perform relate to work done by others . . . Furthermore, most supervisors and managers cannot describe what it is they are supposed to do in specific terms that are tangible, achievable and measurable. Instead they talk in generalities about motivating people, seeing that the work gets done and even getting the work done through others.

INTERACTIVE JOB INSTRUCTION WORKSHOP

A leading adult educator, Dugan Laird, joined with author Ruth House to produce a unique group learning experience for managers to conduct with employees. They produced two related volumes, *Training Today's Employees* and *Interactive Classroom Instruction*. The latter is accompanied by a *Facilitator's Manual* with interactive training techniques for use in job instruction, so the manager can guide them to do what he or she intends them to accomplish. The whole learning package with workbook and audio cassette is available from Scott, Foresman and Company, 1800 East Lake Avenue, Glenview, Illinois 60025, USA.

INSTRUMENTATION

LEADERSHIP MOTIVATION INVENTORY (LMI)

This simple instrument may be used by a manager for personal assessment of his or her own need pattern or to ascertain the motivations of subordinates or a work team. It is based upon the research of Dr. Abraham Maslow described above in the Input section, pages 31-33. The thirty items are arranged in five categories that match his Hierarchy of Needs (Exhibit 2.1). Needs are grouped under these classifications: *P* (physiological or survival); *S* (safety or security); *B* (belonging or affiliation); *E* (esteem or ego); and *A* (actualization or self-fulfillment).

The respondent is asked initially to place an X next to five items on the list that most energize that person to perform or do better work. These first selections are considered to be the pattern of primary motives. The next task is to review the choices again, excluding those already picked, and to place a check next to one's secondary motives from among the remaining items.

Transfer this information to the pyramid diagram (Exhibit 2.7) so that one can see his or her major needs in the context of the Maslow paradigm. If the leader is working with a group using the same inventory, then a flip chart, blackboard, or overhead projector can be used to draw a large version of Exhibit 2.7. Each person then inserts his or her primary motives on that display at the proper level by marking Xs where they appear on one's individual inventory sheet (or the facilitator can simply take a hand count of those in the group who had a

Exhibit 2.7 Leadership Motivation Inventory Score Sheet.

LMI Score Sheet

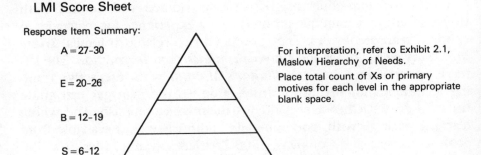

Response Item Summary:

A = 27–30

E = 20–26

B = 12–19

S = 6–12

P = 1–4

For interpretation, refer to Exhibit 2.1, Maslow Hierarchy of Needs.

Place total count of Xs or primary motives for each level in the appropriate blank space.

primary motive marked for each of the levels). In this way members can see the total group motivational picture and can be encouraged to discuss the implications in terms of performance and productivity.

The results included in Exhibit 2.8 (the LMI) are from a national study using a similar inquiry format by Dr. David S. Brown of George

Exhibit 2.8 Leadership Motivation Inventory (LMI). (*Source:* © Philip R. Harris/Harris International, 1984. Quantity copies of this instrument (#508) and the related *Organizational Roles and Relationship Inventory* (#513) and *Quality of Life Index* (#510) are available from Management Research Systems/Talico Inc., 2320 S. Third St., #7, Jacksonville Beach, FL 32250.)

Part A

A. Please place an X next to the five items below which you believe are *most important* in motivating you to do better work:

    1. Assurance of regular employment.   ———

(P) 2. Satisfactory physical working conditions.   ———

    3. Suitable rest periods and coffee breaks.   ———

    4. Adequate vacation arrangments and holidays.   ———

Exhibit 2.8 Leadership Motivation Inventory (LM), *cont'd.*

5. Good pay. _____

6. Having an efficient supervisor who tells me exactly what's expected. _____

7. Clear organizational objectives so that I know where I stand. _____

(S) 8. A good performance rating so I know where I stand. _____

9. Pensions and other fringe benefits (insurance, *et al.*). _____

10. A written job description which tells what's expected of me. _____

11. Maintenance of adequate living standards for my family. _____

12. Means for knowing what is going on in the organization (inclusion). _____

13. Being told by my boss that I am doing a good job. _____

14. Getting along with others on the job by being cooperative. _____

(B) 15. Participation in management activities (*e.g.*, attending staff meetings). _____

16. Receiving appreciation feedback when work is well performed. _____

17. Being kept informed on what's happening in the organization. _____

18. The support received from fellow workers in a work unit. _____

19. Means for promotion and advancement. _____

20. Feeling my job is important. _____

21. Respect of me as a person and/or as professional at my job. _____

(E) 22. Chance to turn out quality work. _____

23. Opportunity to gain status in the organization. _____

24. Means of achieving and proving myself. _____

25. Obtaining more freedom and independence on my job. _____

26. Opportunity to do challenging and meaningful work. _____

(A) 27. Opportunity to experience sense of accomplishment. _____

28. Others:_____

Continued

Exhibit 2.8 Leadership Motivation Inventory (LM), *cont'd.*

B. Place a check (√) now next to five other items which you consider to be of secondary importance in motivating you to do better work. Now go to Exhibit 2.7, and do the next task.

C. Please take accompanying Maslow pyramid and write down the *numbers of your primary* motivations (those marked X in A, above), and secondary motives (the checks) and insert the numbers in one of the categories.

D. You may wish to compare your own or your group's results with those of national survey that was similar to this assessment.

E. As a follow-up to the use of this instrument, you may wish to obtain extra copies of this instrument from Talico, Inc. and administer it to your work team or subordinates. Then compile a profile for the group when all the scores are entered into the pyramid.

Part B

JOB MOTIVATIONAL FACTORS

Summary of 1522 responses from both government and private business to the following request

"Please indicate the five items from the list below which you believe are important in motivating you to do your best work."

RANK ORDER	NUMBER OF RESPONSES	PERCENTAGE
1. Feeling my job is important	920	61
2. Opportunity to do interesting work	863	57
3. Opportunity for self development and improvement	757	50
4. Respect for me as a person	665	44
5. Chance for promotion	654	43
6. Good pay	651	43
7. Chance to turn out quality work	494	32
8. Knowing what is going on in the organization	423	28
9. Large amount of freedom on the job	356	24
10. Steady employment	315	21
11. Being told by my boss when I do a good job	294	20
12. Getting along well with others on job	251	16
13. Chance to do work not under direct or close supervision	225	15
14. Having an efficient supervisor	179	12

Exhibit 2.8 Leadership Motivation Inventory (LM), *cont'd.*

15. Agreement with agency objectives	162	12
16. Good physical working conditions	137	09
17. Getting a good performance rating so I know how I stand	94	06
18. Pensions and other security benefits	64	04
19. Miscellaneous	34	02
20. Attending staff meetings	16	01
21. Having a written description of duties of my job	16	01
22. Fair vacation arrangements	15	01
23. Knowing I will be disciplined if I do a bad job	9	006
24. Not having to work too hard	6	004
25. Adequate rest periods and coffee breaks	5	003
26. Having an employee council	3	002
27. Having a local house organ, employee paper, bulletin	3	002

NOTE: Compare your results, or that of your group's profile, with the above study.

NOTE: Maslow also maintains that one's gripes or grumbles vary with the need level. Man is ever seeking for the fuller life, so as his complaints are satisfied at the level of basic needs, he becomes more aware of other concerns, such as social injustice.

RESPONSE ITEMS SUMMARY:

A = 27 - 30
E = 20 - 26
B = 12 - 19
S = 5 - 12
P = 1 - 4

Washington University. An individual or group can compare responses with that sample of managers' motivations. This data-gathering and comparison raises peoples' awareness of their own needs and that of others associated with them. When a manager has some insight as to what motivates an employee or team, it may be possible to lead in meeting those needs better. How can one lead without knowledge of what "turns these people on" to achieve more?

HUMAN RESOURCES INVENTORY (HRI)

This instrument (Exhibit 2.9) was designed for personal and career development. Because life is a dynamic process, individuals should periodically assess their progress and growth. Recall in the Input section that psychologist David C. McClelland proposed six steps in achievement learning, the first of which is self-study, that is, systematic analysis of past achievements, strengths, and weaknesses. HRI enables a person to do this in terms of aptitudes, competencies, skills, and experiences. There are fifty opportunities for respondents to record their self-evaluation and accomplishments.

The inventory is divided into three components for analysis—life values, individual competencies, and human relationships. The first section of twenty-eight items uses a 10-point rating scale on such matters as self-awareness, leadership, affection, independence, and self-appreciation. Respondents mark a capital *P* to indicate present self-estimates, a small *p* to indicate past rating over a five-year period, and an *F* to reveal their aspirations for future growth. Provisions are made for reexamination of each rating. In the next competency section, respondents examine their professional and educational attainments in the context of intellectual, judgmental, social, physical, aesthetic, actualizing, and personal competencies. In the last part, respondents rate the quality of their human relationships as of *unsatisfactory, adequate,* or *very satisfactory*; a final review is offered as to objectives to seek and obstacles to be anticipated.

Developed by the author as part of an Office of Naval Research project, HRI is a one-hour exercise in personal review and reflection. It can also be used in a group setting. This exercise yields maximum benefits when results are shared with a trusted friend or family member who knows the person well or are discussed with a counselor or mentor. The HRI is intended to release some of the untapped human potential within every individual and organization. It advances personal and professional growth because it aids the respondent to improve self-insight and image. As a means for continuous life planning, HRI is a mechanism for pointing up those performance possibilities that need to be developed. An honest self-appraisal, checked out with others, can help the person to become a more effective worker, team member, and leader. As a follow-up to using this inventory, you may wish to utilize the *Quality of Life Index* (see page 52.). This is a wellness assessment divided into five sections of 30 items. The index permits self-appraisal in terms of (1) physical self-care; (2) psychological aspects; (3) philosophical or spiritual aspects; (4) social well-being; and (5) life style. The basic assumptions of this instrument are that staying well gives one greater control over life, increases performance, and is less costly than rehabilitation.*

Exhibit 2.9   Human Resources Inventory (HRI).

Life Values:

Below are several descriptions of major life purposes or primary motives. For each category read the description and place a capital *P* at the scale position that describes best your *present* estimate of self. Then, place a small *p* at the scale position that describes best your past, where you stood *five years ago*. Finally, mark *F* on the scale to indicate your goal aspirations for the future, where you want to be in the *next five years*. After you have done this for each scale, review the entire set of dimensions to evaluate where you have been, where you are now, and where you want to be in the future. The list is certainly not inclusive, so space is left for you to add additional items you feel are important life values, goals or concerns.

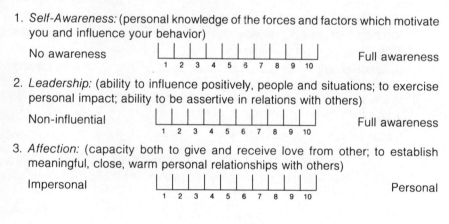

1. *Self-Awareness:* (personal knowledge of the forces and factors which motivate you and influence your behavior)

   No awareness   1 2 3 4 5 6 7 8 9 10   Full awareness

2. *Leadership:* (ability to influence positively, people and situations; to exercise personal impact; ability to be assertive in relations with others)

   Non-influential   1 2 3 4 5 6 7 8 9 10   Full awareness

3. *Affection:* (capacity both to give and receive love from other; to establish meaningful, close, warm personal relationships with others)

   Impersonal   1 2 3 4 5 6 7 8 9 10   Personal

Continued

---

*I consider wellness to be a critical factor in high performance. It is not discussed in this text, but a detailed discussion since can be found in Chapter 10 of *Management in Transition,* by P. R. Harris (1985). The principal publisher of stress and wellness learning materials is Whole Person Press, 1702 E. Jefferson St., Duluth, MN 55812 (1-800/247-6789). An excellent newsletter is Executive Health Report, P.O. 27287, San Diego, CA 92128.

Exhibit 2.9   Human Resources Inventory (HRI), *cont'd.*

---

4. *Independence:* (ability to control one's life space; to be autonomous; to make one's own decisions; freedom to act according to one's own conscience)

Dependent   1 2 3 4 5 6 7 8 9 10   Independent

5. *Self-Appreciation:* (valuing your own uniqueness and abilities; seeing yourself as a positive self; accepting what you are and can become, as well as your limitations)

Self-depreciation   1 2 3 4 5 6 7 8 9 10   Self-appreciation

6. *Self-Congruence:* (being comfortable with yourself and sensitive to your impact on others; being your *real* self regardless of the situation; being authentic and acting with integrity)

Incongruent   1 2 3 4 5 6 7 8 9 10   Congruent

7. *Responsibility:* (ability to persevere; to be responsible; to be dedicated to the pursuit of personal values and ideals; to be committed to the goals of your profession or organization; to stick to a job and get it done)

Irresponsible   1 2 3 4 5 6 7 8 9 10   Responsible

8. *Competency:* (capacity for excellence in chosen vocation or profession; adequate up-dated knowledge and skill in your role or specialized field or endeavor)

Less competent   1 2 3 4 5 6 7 8 9 10   Most competent

9. *Initiative:* (ability to motivate and actualize self to be a self-starter; ability to accomplish things, to move energetically)

Non-initiative   1 2 3 4 5 6 7 8 9 10   Initiative

10. *Acceptance:* (understanding and accepting other people for what they are and can become; respecting the dignity of others and valuing their uniqueness; unconditional regard for others)

Non-accepting   1 2 3 4 5 6 7 8 9 10   Accepting

11. *Trust:* (ability to have confidence in others versus being suspicious and controlling; capable of being trustworthy)

Suspicious   1 2 3 4 5 6 7 8 9 10   Trusting

12. *Creative:* (ability to be innovative; to experiment with new approaches; to generate original thought)

Uncreative   1 2 3 4 5 6 7 8 9 10   Creative

Exhibit 2.9 Human Resources Inventory (HRI), *cont'd.*

13. *Cooperativeness:* (ability to work with others in a collaborative fashion; to be an effective member of a team)

    Uncooperative   1 2 3 4 5 6 7 8 9 10   Cooperative

14. *Helpfulness:* (capacity to give and receive help; to be concerned about others and render assistance; to share generously of one's self)

    Helpless   1 2 3 4 5 6 7 8 9 10   Helpful

15. *Recognition:* (ability to achieve; to have one's abilities known and used in a meaningful fashion; to be seen as a valuable person in a group or organization)

    Non-recognition   1 2 3 4 5 6 7 8 9 10   Recognition

16. *Risk-Taking:* (ability to take risks to accomplish what one feels is necessary; to dare to be different; to follow one's conscience; to be creatively deviant)

    Cautious   1 2 3 4 5 6 7 8 9 10   Risk-taking

17. *Facilitating:* (ability to reconcile or mediate, to foster and develop, to resolve conflict and bring together people who differ; to heal interpersonal hurts; to be a peacemaker and relieve tension)

    Non-facilitative   1 2 3 4 5 6 7 8 9 10   Facilitative

18. *Sociability:* (ability to be with and to work with people; to be friendly, gregarious; to enjoy social relationships)

    Unsociable   1 2 3 4 5 6 7 8 9 10   Sociable

19. *Joyfulness:* (capacity to really enjoy living; to be happy with self and others; to experience fulfillment in one's experiences and life situation; to bring joy to others)

    Sad   1 2 3 4 5 6 7 8 9 10   Joyful

20. *Human Service:* (to seek to serve the welfare and advancement of mankind in a meaningful fashion; to serve humanistic goals; to serve community and country; to make the world better for your presence in it)

    No Human service   1 2 3 4 5 6 7 8 9 10   Human service

21. *Self-Realization:* (degree to which one is presently maximizing his own human potential; working toward being the person he can and wants to be; seeking self-fulfillment)

    Non-realizing   1 2 3 4 5 6 7 8 9 10   Realizing

Continued

Exhibit 2.9 Human Resources Inventory (HRI), *cont'd.*

22. *Others:* (in your own words list any other values or concerns which are strong motivations for you in your present situation)

_____

_____

_____

Re-examine the above list of personal value dimensions to evaluate yourself in terms of past, present and future. Identify below some areas in which you would like to change and enumerate some strategies for achieving such personal change and analyze factors that will block these personal growth plans.

Areas

_____

_____

_____

_____

_____

_____

Strategies

_____

_____

_____

_____

_____

_____

Obstacles

_____

_____

_____

_____

_____

Exhibit 2.9   Human Resources Inventory (HRI), *cont'd.*

Individual Competencies:

Each person possesses unique skills, and accomplishments. Identify some of these special strengths and talents as revealed in the past in your relationships, your work, your family or your hobbies. Also list those areas in which you find you have personal limitations. Such enumeration may help you group your personal assets and liabilities.

A. *Professional Attainment:* (list in the first column major vocational and professional successes, and then in the second column your objectives or potentials, both in terms of wishes and opportunities, based upon life experiences to date)

Attainments

_____

_____

_____

_____

Objectives

_____

_____

_____

_____

B. *Educational Attainment:* (list here educational accomplishments and needs; major areas of interest you wish to pursue; ask yourself if further or continuing education is desirable or necessary)

Attainments

_____

_____

_____

_____

Continued

Exhibit 2.9 Human Resources Inventory (HRI), *cont'd.*

Objectives

_____

_____

_____

_____

C. *Intellectual Competencies:* (analyze your unique rational or mental abilities—intelligence or capacity to apply knowledge; ability to conceptualize and to perceive relationships, etc.)

Attainments

_____

_____

_____

_____

Objectives

_____

_____

_____

_____

D. *Judgement Competencies:* (ability to abstract essences and make reasonable decisions; capacity to differentiate between fact and fiction; ability to weigh ideas, discriminate and to solve problems)

Attainments

_____

_____

_____

_____

Exhibit 2.9 Human Resources Inventory (HRI), *cont'd.*

Objectives

_____

_____

_____

_____

E. *Social Competencies:* (skills in interpersonal and human relations; capacity to deal with people on a one-to-one, group or organizational level, etc.)

Attainments

_____

_____

_____

_____

Objectives

_____

_____

_____

_____

F. *Physical Competencies:* (physical prowess and appearance; athletic/ outdoor abilities; skills to construct with hands, etc.)

Attainments

_____

_____

_____

_____

Continued

63

Exhibit 2.9   Human Resources Inventory (HRI), *cont'd.*

Objectives

_____

_____

_____

_____

G. *Aesthetic Competencies:* (responsiveness and appreciation of beauty in art or nature; good taste; capacities in arts, crafts, music, literature, etc.)

Attainments

_____

_____

_____

_____

Objectives

_____

_____

_____

_____

_____

H. *Actualizing Competencies:* (ability to make decisions and to perform; to act effectively upon judgement; to cope effectively; to motivate self beyond present level of accomplishment; opposite to procrastination; apathy and immobilization by fear)

Attainments

_____

_____

_____

_____

Exhibit 2.9 Human Resources Inventory (HRI), *cont'd.*

Objectives

_____

_____

_____

_____

I. *Personal Competencies:* (security within self, confidence and congruence; emotional strengths; personal integration, character, etc.)

Attainments

_____

_____

_____

_____

Objectives

_____

_____

_____

_____

Now that you have examined your present and past situation, your strengths or assets, and your personal directions for growth, you can examine strategies to maximize your potential. Analyze those factors in yourself, in others, and in the work situation which both *support* and *block* your personal growth goals. Secure feedback on your self-evaluation from others to check for discontinuities. Experiment with new behaviors to maximize your own personal growth tendencies and then seek continuous feedback to assess how you are doing.

Hopefully, this instrument may emphasize that you are a unique, dynamic, changing person. There is no one else alive now—or in the past or future—quite like you!

3
Improving Leadership Communication Skills

INTRODUCTION

Effective communications is essential to high performance. Yet in several surveys of corporations conducted by the American Management Associations during recent decades, management communications was consistently identified as the number one difficulty in business life. This chapter will focus upon the important issue of human interaction at work. Our capacity to communicate in diverse and complex ways sets humans apart from other species. Since communication is the key to organizational excellence, special attention will be paid to this subject.

Our primary objective is to better understand what is involved in the process of human communication so that we can improve our interaction skills. By comprehending, for example, what is involved in perception, coworkers should become more sensitive to each other's viewpoints and meanings, and ideally, better relations and exchanges will result. Specifically, we will analyze the all-important matter of self-image and how it impacts communications (i.e., the concept of behavioral communication).

Our second major aim here will be to examine organizational communications and how it affects performance and productivity. We will review some of the physical and psychological barriers to such communication, as well as some of the characteristics of effective communication within human systems.

INPUT

As human beings, we all see our worlds differently. Reality is unique for each of us since we were not raised in exactly the same way. Apart from the general differences inherent in our cultural backgrounds, we each have had special inputs, imprints, and experiences. This realization helps to explain the differences between the generations, and why sometimes people have difficulty communicating with each other even when they are raised in the same family. Exhibit 3.1 illustrates the concept of the perceptual field and shows how some of its influences affect communication between two persons. Consider interpersonal communication in terms of two partners in business or marriage, or two people who are brought together on the job and begin to interact for the first time.

Humans are symbol-using creatures with the power of abstraction. That is, the developed human brain permits us to ascribe meaning and

Exhibit 3.1 The Influence of Perception on Communication.

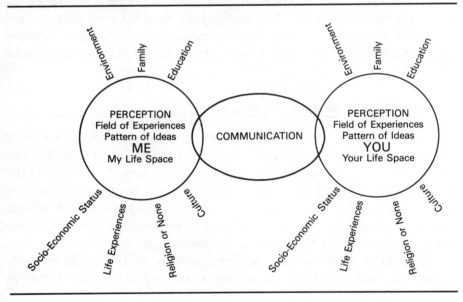

value to words, gestures, actions, experiences, and things, so that we have a rich capacity to communicate. Although some communication symbols are universal in meaning, the meanings of many others differ by culture—thus, sex symbols such as the female's breasts or the nape of the neck or hand-holding may connote entirely distinct intents according to the country. Furthermore, even within a culture, agreed-upon symbols are subject to continuous up-dating as the culture changes. Our point is that communication, especially in business, is a complex process and that would-be leaders have to increase their awareness of what is involved before they can improve their communication skills.

During the past 50 years we have probably doubled the number of communications accomplishments that humans had achieved in the prior 5000 years. With new technologies offering unlimited opportunities for global exchanges through mass media, computer interaction, communication satellites, and other innovations, we are truly forming an information society.

Communication is our most important tool and is at the heart of all organizational operations. Communication can be the basis for understanding, cooperation, and positive action; without it, such goals would be undermined. The vitality, creativity, and productivity of organizations depend on the content and character of their communications. Through the interaction process, information and knowledge are transferred between people. When the process is inadequate, messages are distorted, frustrations develop, and people or their organizations are rendered ineffective. Failures in communication contribute to management problems, and the cost of miscommunication may be incalcuable.

COMMUNICATION AS A HUMAN PROCESS

It may help to consider the communication process in terms of circular interaction between a sender and receiver of messages. The message is the *what* of communication, the content. The media is the *how* of the communication, the means or mechanism used to convey that message. The reason, or *why,* may be personal or professional, social or organizational. The sender may or may not be consciously aware of the motives for initiating a conversation or exchange.

Although humans are able to communicate with animals or commune with nature, let us focus now upon our formidable talent to interact with other people. There are some general observations to note before we get into details:

Every person operates from within his or her private world or perceptual field. As defined in Chapter 2, this perceptual field is our life space, and we can view it from in a personal and organizational context. Every individual or institution communicates from that perspective. We take in and give out information through the filter of our perceptions. These influence both the context of our messages and the media utilized to send them.

From time to time, effective communicators check out whether their perceptions of reality generally match what is commonly and currently held "outside" in the larger world or collective reality—is our subjective view in synchronization with objective actuality? Although two generations may share the same "outer" world, their "inner worlds" may be vastly different. The more we are aware of our past conditioning and understand the forces influencing our own behavior, the more successful our communication will be.

Every person projects self into human communication. Each of us communicates an image of self, including a system of needs, values, standards, expectations, and ideals, as well as our perceptions of people, things, and situations. We can sense this self-concept in others if we pay attention to their body movements, bearing, tone of voice, and choice of language, as well as the content of their message. The more we can understand their "world," where they are coming from, the better our chances for improved communication.

Every person is a medium or instrument of communication. We are not just senders and receivers of messages, but the medium can be a message also. Thus, if an individual is uncomfortable with self, then others are likely to become uncomfortable with that person. The more self-confidence or congruence conveyed by the communicator, the more likely the receiver is to accept the message.

Every person is a versatile communicator. We communicate verbally and nonverbally, orally and in writing. Our communication capacities are more than language—we communicate through gestures, signs, shapes, colors, sounds, smells, pictures, and other communication symbols. The artist, for instance, expresses thought and feeling in paintings, sculpture, music, dance, and architecture. Business communicates through its products and services, as well as through systems and procedures. Technologists communicate through their constructions and ever changing creations. The diversity of our communication media is evident in the past use of smoke signals and drum sounds and in the present use of television and videophones; this diversity will probably be apparent in future innovations, as well.

Exhibit 3.2 illustrates the process of circular interaction—the sender and receiver exchanging messages. Both occupy unique psychological environments, or perceptual fields, in which they receive, translate, and analyze input, and from which they send information to another. In technical terms, each *decodes, interprets,* and *encodes.*

Essentially, we selectively perceive new data and determine if it is relevant and consistent. That is, does it fit into our perceived way of thinking? Two people may receive the same message at work, but derive two entirely different meanings from it because of perceptual background differences. Each decodes and interprets the same input differently.

Consider a manager communicating to a colleague or subordinate about work performance. The messages are simultaneously being *transmitted* at different levels, intended and unintended; that is, we transmit information at a conscious, verbal level and subconsciously, through a so-called silent language. At the same time, messages are being *received* at two different levels, cognitive and affective; that is, thinking and feeling, the intellectual and emotional. The simultaneous, multilevel nature of transmittal and reception very often results in mixed messages—the

Exhibit 3.2 A Model of Communication.

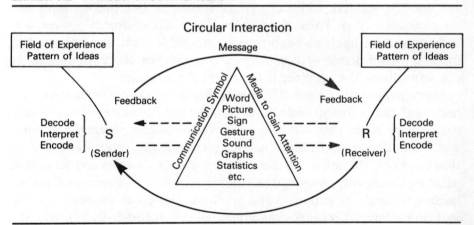

words, for example, do not match the feelings being conveyed. When the message is incomplete or ambiguous, the receiver has to try and fill in the meaning. The receiver's interpretation of the sender's intentions or motivations may or may not be accurate.

Understanding communication is important to everyone, but particularly to those who would exercise high-performance leadership. Because we transmit our self-image in the course of human interaction, we can influence—more often than not—the kind of reception we get from others. Usually, if we have confidence in ourselves, people sense this and respond more positively to us and the messages we send. On the other hand, if we lack confidence and convey inferiority feelings, we undermine the reception of our messages. Similarly, if a sender has a distorted self-perception, such as unwarranted feelings of superiority, these can be communicated intentionally or unconsciously and can produce hostility or resentment in the receiver. Talking down to fellow workers can lead to rejection of both the sender and the message.

So, if we wish to improve our human relations and communications, let us begin by examining our self-image. How do we answer the big question, "Who am I?" Filling out the *Human Resource Inventory* and the *Leadership Motivation Inventory* (Chapter 2) can help. These provide data for revising or improving our concept of self. The better our self-appreciation, the better our chances of improving our communications with others. Again, more often than not, we influence the response of others to us. If we are loaded with inferiority feelings, others will probably "dump" on us. If we project a positive image, people will be more likely to accept us and our messages.

One exception to this rule occurs when the receiver has prejudice against some kinds of people—tall or short, white or black, native or foreigner. Thus, an Eskimo meeting someone for the first time might project a very positive self-image yet be rejected. The problem is in the bias of the receiver against Eskimos. There are some persons we may never effectively communicate with because they close their minds to us, dismissing us as women, intellectuals, or whatever group in which they place us.

Usually, though, we can influence others by the way we communicate ourselves. Thus, it is vital for communicators to be comfortable within themselves and congruent, that is, with the inner and outer selves in harmony. Even if we have paid public relations or image consultants to improve our dress, appearance, and message delivery, people will eventually sense if we are inauthentic persons—not true to our own selves and beliefs. In real communication, two persons share themselves—their way of thinking, their values, their hopes and aspirations. That is why communication, in the deepest sense, is both the establishing of a relationship and an exchange of human energy.

ORGANIZATIONAL COMMUNICATIONS AND HUMAN PERFORMANCE

These insights on interpersonal communication can be applied to people in groups and organizations. Those who would exercise leadership in both personal and group communications need to take a systems approach, that is, analyze the communication systems within their organizations. The Instrument on page 85 provides one way of making such an analysis.

There are usually both formal and informal communication systems within a corporation, association, or agency. The former involves the official lines and media of communication. Information is sent or received in the form of letters, memoranda, reports, briefings, meetings, and conferences. The media employed include word processors, computers, telephones and teleconferencing, bulletin boards, newsletters, manuals, and even posters. In this manner, corporate policies, plans, programs, and procedures are transmitted. The formal aspects of what an organization wants to communicate may be seen both in its management information system for data processing, analysis, and distribution, and in its public information programs for communicating outside the organization.

There is also the unofficial system of communication. It is evident in work relationships, where people come together because they labor in the same organizational unit or because they are members of a project team, which may be made up of employees from various departments. Sometimes these occupational relationships also occur because people share a carpool, sit together in the cafeteria, attend the same union meeting, or serve on the same company recreational team. These interactions become opportunities for workers to exchange information, to spread rumors, to affect productivity. People within organizations may group together informally for a variety of reasons—they have compatible line or staff positions, they graduated from the same college, they share the same profession, they have the same interests or skills. It is in these relationships and settings that one can study the informal communication system of an organization—at the refreshment breaks, hobby or sport meetings, and even in the rest or fitness rooms. Extensive research is being done on this subject (Mcphee and Tompkins, 1985).

To be effective leaders, managers should be aware of both systems and be able to use them as appropriate. To rely on one and to ignore the other can be fatal. The two systems overlap and intertwine.

Another way to examine organizational communication is to classify it as internal or external. There are many messages and media that are intended only for use within the enterprise, for instance corporate handbooks, in-plant closed-circuit TV, task force meetings, and field visits to factories or offices. External communication may include executive participation in community organizations, press releases, advertising, and marketing strategies. The internal system is directed to the stakeholders in the organization—owners, stockholders, management, and other personnel, and sometimes suppliers and contractors. The external system is aimed at the public at large, government officials, customers, competitors, investors, and the media. Of course, many kinds of communication are not clearly external or internal, such as those aimed at workers' families, corporate bankers, and suppliers.

Perhaps managers can best appreciate the interplay between these four systems in the matter of organizational image. The behavioral communication concept described above applies equally to institutions and individuals. Since the organization is a collection of people, how does it see itself? If a company's perception of itself is inadequate or distorted, its representatives may behave inappropriately and cause negative reactions in others outside the organization. If a corporation really knows what business it is in and has energized its people to carry out the organizational mission, it is likely to positively influence its clientele.

Many executives are concerned that the firm portray the proper image through its logo and letterhead, its annual report and other such publications, and its advertisements or commercials. Executives sometimes seek to generate good will and positive community relations by demonstrating corporate social responsibility. Are they equally aware, however, of the effect on corporate image made by the appearance of corporate buildings, offices, and employees? They should be concerned about the informal communications about the corporation transmitted by

- Employee attitudes, manifested, for instance, in the way telephone operators or receptionists treat callers
- The quality of service by employees to customers
- Product appearance, packaging, and quality
- The appearance of company-owned vehicles and their operators
- The facilities made available for the safety and comfort of employees and visitors
- The creativity and tastefulness of illustrations used for media advertising and promotion.

Organizations perform well and gain credibility with their own people and the public when they make effective use of all four communication systems. Organizations must involve all personnel and their families, as well as board members and stockholders, in projecting a positive organizational image; it is not enough to rely on specialists in public relations or employee relations. Effective leaders should think of the four systems as a matrix of four equal parts. All of them—formal, informal, external, and internal—interact and together make up the full range of organizational communications.

For high performance, leaders make it easy to receive their messages. They can do this by helping their hearers broaden their perceptions or fields of experience as a result of new information. If the communication symbols are obsolete or inadequate, substitutes must be found so the message is more relevant and better received. If the media does not reach or inform for maximum coverage, then perhaps new communication technologies should be used. Leaders are sensitive communicators, capable of listening and meeting the needs of their receivers. Leaders are flexible in their communication styles, shifting to accommodate differences in time, place, and audience. Leaders accept the responsibilities of communication—to enter into the private world of the other by trying to see things as that person does.

Leaders understand that communication may fail not because of the message's content or because of the choice of media, but because of the manner in which the message is delivered. Psychologist Jack Gibb has developed a helpful communication model for this purpose which is replicated in Exhibit 3.3. Managers would do well, for example, to avoid words and behavior on the left side of the model, while speaking and acting in a way more like the descriptions on the right side.

The organization assigns roles and often defines work relationships in order to accomplish its mission. Just as we may have outdated

Exhibit 3.3   The How of Communication. (From "Defensive Communication Model" by Jack R. Gibb, *Journal of Communication* 11:3 (Sept. 1961), 141–148. Reprinted by permission of the *Journal of Communication* and the International Communication Association.)

THE HOW OF COMMUNICATION

Communication Channels

CLOSE   OPEN

Evaluative ....vs.......................	Descriptive
Controlling	Problem-oriented
Strategic	Spontaneous
Neutrality	Empathetic
Superiority	Accepting
Dogmatic	Provisional

Threatens Ego   Promotes Collaboration

images of ourselves and our organizations, so we need continually to revise our images of our roles. For example, what is the contemporary role of manager in a corporation or agency, particularly in relation to a work unit or team? If a manager acts according to the image of management developed in the disappearing industrial age, that person will increasingly be in difficulty with today's knowledge workers. If, on the other hand, we create an image of a metaindustrial manager, such as this author has previously described (Harris, 1983, 1985), communications will be effective now and into the future.

In the closing decades of the twentieth century, the role of manager is increasingly one of coach, consultant, coordinator, facilitator, and, above all, sensitive communicator. The latter role requires giving and receiving feedback to subordinates, colleagues, and others. The how of such communication will in part determine whether the message is perceived as offensive or inoffensive, acceptable or unacceptable, meaningful or irrelevant, helpful or hurtful. Managers who hope to have a high performing unit, therefore, adopt the strategies listed on the right side of the Gibb model in Exhibit 3.3, so that their feedback promotes collaboration. If we are sensitive to the subtle cues and feedback others give to us, then we will adapt our behavior and modify our messages accordingly.

Managers who would like to be leaders also communicate acceptance of their people, rather than rejection. We can respect a fellow worker's inherent dignity as a person, even when the performance may be less than adequate. We can recognize another's being, rights, needs, and feelings. We can demonstrate capacity to separate the unique person from actions that may displease us. We can convey this acceptance by demonstrating confidence in our people and their performance potential, permitting them thereby to have confidence in themselves. High-performance managers not only provide behavior models, but encourage others to emulate them through continuing positive reinforcement. A spoonful of honey still produces more with people than does a barrel of vinegar!

For the manager to fulfill the role of sensitive communicator, there are barriers to be overcome or pitfalls to avoid. Exhibit 3.4 lists some hindrances and Exhibit 3.5 lists some helps for effective management communications.

Exhibit 3.4   Hindrances to Management Communications.

Organizational

COMMUNICATION is a complex process, especially because different perceptions of those involved in human interaction may cause difficulties in the transmission of thoughts and ideas. However, there are some roadblocks to communications at meetings which managers can avoid or try to minimize. In this way, the message can be sent or received more effectively.

1. **Overload:** a barrier to communication may exist when talking is too long, too complex, or even too loud. Present the message so people can process it.
2. **Bias:** distortions can creep into communication when the message is not authentic, edited or reflects the prejudice of the sender. Be authentic and tell it like it is!
3. **One-sided:** that is interpreting the message from your own point of view, without trying to put yourself into the frame of reference of the receivers. Promote dialogue.
4. **Passive:** merely sending or passively receiving the message undermines two-way or circular communication. Only an active, dynamic process involves people.
5. **Assumptions:** communication cannot be based solely on the sender's assumptions about the realities connected to the message. You must check out assumptions and inferences to see if they are shared by others in the meeting. You must also explore what assumptions may underlie the message from their perspective.
6. **Suspicion:** avoid expressing, verbally or non-verbally, suspicion and dislike. Instead endeavor to build up trust among the audience.

Exhibit 3.4 Hindrances to Management Communications, *cont'd.*

7. **Imposition:** people are alienated when the meeting coordinator tries to impose personal ideas and values on them failing to take into consideration their opinions and feedback.
8. **Inattention:** both leaders and participants may not get their message across when their attention is not focused upon the subject of the communication or if they listen selectively. Keep the mind on the message, and avoid preoccupation with outside interests or concerns.
9. **Bad timing:** acceptance may be blocked when an important message is presented at a poor time, such as just prior to lunch. People must be prepared and "psychologically" ready to receive a vital communication.
10. **Insufficient explanation:** people are inclined to reject proposals or messages when they are not given adequate facts or reasons for the desired course of action. Gather data, present the case with the necessary information on its validity and allow for questions.

Some barriers to communication may be of a physical nature—such as, poor hearing on the part of a receiver, faulty microphone or audio system, inadequate chair arrangements, or too much noise. Other obstacles may be psychological in either sender or receiver—such as emotional handicaps, mental illness or inferiority feelings. All the manager can do is to be aware of such possibilities and minimize as many as feasible.

The communication doors, on the other hand, can be kept open by the manner in which the communication is delivered—the "how"! Body language may facilitate human interaction, or hinder it. If people are threatened, literally or psychologically, they may close the communication channels. When one is judgmental or evaluative, such as when giving feedback or discussing another's performance, the individual may get defensive. When the communication is given in a way that is descriptive and objective, the message is more likely to be accepted. When one attempts to control or dominate the conversation, for instance, the receiver may become resistive; but the cooperation is likely to be forthcoming if the communication is problem or issue oriented, and allows for exploration and exchange of ideas.

When meeting coordinators engage in "game playing" with participants, in the negative sense, the group becomes wary of being manipulated. But when the communication is spontaneous and authentic, they react favorably. When communicators are cold, neutral or equivocal, they turn the receivers off. They can reverse the situation when they are empathetic. When you indicate superiority in the communication, people may become resentful or hostile. However, if you treat others like equals, they are more likely to respond. Remember, stay on the right side of Exhibit 3.3!

When the communicators are dogmatic, people do not want to engage in conversation; but when those same individuals are tentative or provisional in communication, they are more apt to enter in an exchange of ideas or views. Thus, the "how" of the communication can also distort the message, no matter how valid its content may be.

Exhibit 3.5 Helps to Management Communications.

In effect, a leader should be like a consultant or facilitator. A sensitive communicator should check up on the following:

availability—involve as many human senses or powers as possible in the process.

contrast—let the message stand out, be vital and relevant, not colorless or indifferent.

reward—meet people's needs; let them know "what's in it for them" if they act on the message.

appropriateness—use communication symbols and content that are suitable to the people and circumstances.

efficiency—give maximum information in minimum time; be concise and precise.

flexibility—be resourceful, creative, and able to adapt your message to the changing situation.

High performance will result when these communication guidelines are observed.

INTERACTION

The manager who wants to improve a group's performance should take time out from task achievement to work on group maintenance, for example, by causing a project team to examine the communications among its members or with other units in the organization. A staff meeting or a training session might be devoted to such issues. To stimulate discussion, a management-development film on organizational communications might be shown. The following two group techniques have also be found useful for this purpose.

ANALYZING MEETING BEHAVIOR

When personnel gather for a group encounter, for instance, at a project team meeting, they operate at different levels of communication, as previously noted. Two such patterns of communication are called task behavior and maintenance behavior. Some of the members' input, actions, or activities contribute to the accomplishment of the team's mission; this is task behavior. Others' actions contribute to improving communication and building morale; these are maintenance behaviors.

It might be beneficial to show the distinction between these two behaviors while demonstrating the value of each. To do so, the leader sits in as an observer, rather than a participant, at a group meeting. (Alternatively the group can choose two of its own to assume the observer role, or invite two persons from outside the group to attend the session as observers.) The observers use check sheets, such as those shown in Exhibits 3.6 and 3.7, to track the communication behaviors during the session. One check sheet lists five categories of task behaviors; the second check sheet lists five categories of maintenance behaviors. The observers place the names of each team member across the top column and place a check in the appropriate row under that person's name when that person performs one of the listed functions. This method works best when the group consists of eight or fewer, and there is one observer to note task behavior and one to note maintenance behavior.

Before the meeting is concluded, a break is taken from the normal business of the day, and the observer(s) totals the number of checks in each category for each person. For the last 10 or 20 minutes of the meeting, the observers share their findings with the group and members discuss the implications of this data on their meeting performance. Another variation is to videotape the whole session, then distribute the check sheets to the members. During the replay, they could then analyze their group's communication with the aid of the task/maintenance forms.

What emerges from this exercise is a profile of individual interaction in the group that can then be used by a facilitator for diagnostic or feedback purposes. Team members then become more aware of what they have been doing in meetings to help or hinder performance. Those who have been too task oriented should be encouraged to experiment with some maintenance functions in future sessions, and vice versa. Actually, both functions illustrate something of the person's leadership style.

Chapter 8 fully covers issues of high performance by leaders at meetings. A unique and valuable guide to successful meeting management is cited in the resource section on page 92.

IMPROVING LISTENING SKILLS

Another group process can increase communication skills and member participation. The technique is best used with a large audience, such as at a major conference, annual meeting, or training session. Perhaps the members of a team can use this approach while listening to a formal presentation at a technical or professional meeting.

Exhibit 3.6 Functional Analysis: Task Behavior.

Name of Group: _____ Date: _____

Instructions: Write names of individuals in spaces below; make a check under the name of that person closest to acting out those items listed on the left; when the group has completed its work, the chart can give a picture of how each individual contributed to the group task.

Member Behavior Required for Doing Group Work

	Names of Individuals Observed			
1. Initiating: Proposing tasks or goals; defining a group problem; suggesting a procedure or ideas for solving problems.				
2. Information or opinion seeking: Requesting facts; seeking relevant information about a group concern, asking for suggestions and ideas.				
3. Information or opinion giving: Offering facts; providing relevant information about group concern, stating a belief, giving suggestions or ideas.				
4. Clarifying or elaborating: Interpreting or reflecting ideas and suggestions; clearing up confusions; indicating alternatives and issues before the group; giving examples.				
5. Summarizing: Pulling together related ideas; restating suggestions after group has discussed them; offering a decision or conclusion for the group to accept or reject.				

Exhibit 3.7 Functional Analysis: Maintenance Behavior.

Name of the Group: _____ Date: _____

Instructions: Write names of individuals in spaces below; make a check under the name of that person closest to acting out those items listed; when the group has completed its work, the chart can give them a picture of how each individual contributed to the group task.

Member Behavior Required for Building and Maintaining the Group as a Working Unit

	Names of Individuals Observed			
1. Encouraging: Being friendly, warm and responsive to others; accepting others and their contributions; regarding others by giving them an opportunity or recognition.				
2. Expressing group feelings: Sensing feeling, mood, relationships within the group; sharing his own feeling or affect with other members.				
3. Harmonizing: Attempting to reconcile disagreements; reducing tensions through "pouring oil on troubled waters"; getting people to explore their differences.				
4. Compromising: When his own idea of				

Continued

Exhibit 3.7 Functional Analysis: Maintenance Behavior, *cont'd.*

status is involved in a conflict, offering to compromise his own position; admitting error, disciplining himself to maintain group cohesion.				
Gate-keeping: Attempting to keep communication channels open; facilitating the participation of others; suggesting procedures for sharing opportunity to discuss group problems.				

In the first step, group members assume assigned listening roles. Each individual (or group) listens to the speech or the information being transmitted from a specific perspective, such as: *agreeing, disagreeing, seeking clarifications,* and *seeking applications.* After the presentation, these "designated listeners" present their perspective to the total group. As an alternative, the listening teams meet separately to arrive at a consensus on what they have heard (for example, those listening from the perspective of *seeking applications* discuss how to apply the speaker's ideas to their own work situation).

A variation that permits greater audience participation is "buzz groups." The audience is encouraged to listen carefully, taking notes or outlining, because later they will be asked to join a small group to discuss the speaker's ideas in greater depth. Following the presentation input, the audience divides into subunits of six to twelve people who sat near one another. These subunits meet for 10 or 15 minutes to react to the speaker's ideas. If time permits, each group selects a spokesperson. The spokesperson presents to the group as a whole the consensus achieved by the subunit, or perhaps a question for the speaker (subunit reports should be kept to 1 to 3 minutes). If a speaker has divided his or her address into logical themes or parts, sometimes the sub-units are chosen in advance and assigned to report on specific topics. With imagination, a leader can do much with group dynamics to stimulate both attention and involvement of the audience and achieve a meaningful learning experience for all.

INSTRUMENTATION

My 1985 book, *Management in Transition,* contains two instruments related to the organizational communications. *Group Maturity Analysis* (GMA)* enables an observer to evaluate a group's ability to work together effectively for the accomplishment of its tasks. The observer rates, on a scale from 1 (lowest) to 5 (highest), the group's effectiveness in ten categories, including mechanisms, decision-making, togetherness, flexibility, use of resources, communication, goals, interdependence, participation, and acceptance of minority views and persons. The second instrument is *Team Synergy Analysis* (TSA)†, designed for individual self-rating on fifteen critical team skills, such as cooperation and collaboration, feedback and synthesis, which contribute to improve group performance.

MANAGEMENT COMMUNICATIONS INVENTORY (MCI)

This inventory (Exhibit 3.8) is a check-list for self-appraisal of communication skills by a manager or team members. Respondents record the frequency (seldom, occasionally, often, always) with which they perform twenty-one listed behaviors. This inventory deals with such interaction issues as image projection, receiver's perspective, communication symbols, emotionality, and openness. The findings help create awareness of the complexity of communication and alert people to the need for further training.

---

* © Philip R. Harris/Harris International, 1985. Quantity copies of GMA (#503), TSA (#514), and the following MCI (#509) and OCA (#511) instruments are available from: Management Research Systems/Talico Inc., 2320 S. Third St. #7, Jacksonville Beach, FL 32250.

†See W. R. Reddy's *Team Building Blueprints for Productivity and Satisfaction* (San Diego: University Associates, 1988).

In a work unit or team, the inventory can also be adapted so that a member can analyze the communications competence of a project manager or another coworker; the results can then be compared with that individual's self-study. The insights gained from using the MCI can be the basis of discussion at a staff meeting or be used during performance appraisals.

Exhibit 3.8 Management Communications Inventory.

Here is a check-list for an appraisal of yourself as a communicator. Simply place a mark next to the category which best describes your present approach to the communication process.

You may wish to share your evaluation with a colleague or relative to ascertain if your assessment is confirmed or not. When you have identified areas of improvement, develop a strategy to increase your communication skills.

1. In communicating, I project a positive image of myself (e.g., voice, bearing, appearance, etc.)
   _____ Seldom
   _____ Occasionally
   _____ Often
   _____ Always

2. I try to understand and enter into the receiver's frame of reference (e.g., empathetic, restate his point of view, etc.)
   _____ Seldom
   _____ Occasionally
   _____ Often
   _____ Always

3. I establish eye contact with the receiver
   _____ Seldom
   _____ Occasionally
   _____ Often
   _____ Always

4. I communicate respect for the receiver of my message (e.g., listening carefully, not making him feel inferior, etc.)
   _____ Seldom
   _____ Occasionally
   _____ Often
   _____ Always

Continued

Exhibit 3.8 Management Communications Inventory, *cont'd.*

5. I use as many media as necessary to get my meaning across (e.g., communication symbols that appeal to several senses)

——————— Seldom
——————— Occasionally
——————— Often
——————— Always

6. I am aware of my own inner state which conditions my communication (e.g., feelings, needs, motives, assumptions, prejudices, etc.)

——————— Seldom
——————— Occasionally
——————— Often
——————— Always

7. I try not to let emotionally loaded words used by the other person distort my responses.

——————— Seldom
——————— Occasionally
——————— Often
——————— Always

8. I try to listen not only to facts and ideas (cognitive data), but to the feelings which the other reveals

——————— Seldom
——————— Occasionally
——————— Often
——————— Always

9. I try to be open to new ideas and constructive criticism regardless of the source

——————— Seldom
——————— Occasionally
——————— Often
——————— Always

10. I am willing to share the other person to the point of personal change if it is warranted

——————— Seldom
——————— Occasionally
——————— Often
——————— Always

Continued

Exhibit 3.8 Management Communications Inventory, *cont'd.*

11. I try to be authentic in my communication and level with others when it is appropriate
    _____ Seldom
    _____ Occasionally
    _____ Often
    _____ Always

12. I try to reduce the physical and psychological distance between me and my listeners
    _____ Seldom
    _____ Occasionally
    _____ Often
    _____ Always

13. I check to ascertain if my real meaning is understood
    _____ Seldom
    _____ Occasionally
    _____ Often
    _____ Always

14. I allow the other person to ask questions and seek clarification regarding my message-sending
    _____ Seldom
    _____ Occasionally
    _____ Often
    _____ Always

15. I ask questions and seek clarification during the communication exchange
    _____ Seldom
    _____ Occasionally
    _____ Often
    _____ Always

16. In speaking, I try to project my voice clearly
    _____ Seldom
    _____ Occasionally
    _____ Often
    _____ Always

17. In speaking, I try to vary the tone of my voice
    _____ Seldom
    _____ Occasionally
    _____ Often
    _____ Always

Exhibit 3.8 Management Communications Inventory, *cont'd.*

18. In speaking, I try to say what I really mean
    _____ Seldom
    _____ Occasionally
    _____ Often
    _____ Always

19. In speaking, I try to use a vocabulary that is understandable to the receiver
    _____ Seldom
    _____ Occasionally
    _____ Often
    _____ Always

20. In speaking, I try to be concise
    _____ Seldom
    _____ Occasionally
    _____ Often
    _____ Always

21. I follow up on the communication to see if agreements or instructions are carried out
    _____ Seldom
    _____ Occasionally
    _____ Often
    _____ Always

_____

Participant's initials

ORGANIZATION COMMUNICATIONS ANALYSIS (OCA)

This instrument (Exhibit 3.9) offers a way to analyze competence in the four systems of organization communications. Respondents (managers or employees) check the items appropriate to their company or agency in each of the quadrants related to the four interacting communication systems—formal, informal, internal, and external. The first purpose is to create awareness of the scope and subtlety of these systems, but the real learning occurs as an individual or group seeks to provide "other" examples in each category. In a work unit, this part of the exercise can lead to interesting discussion as to what is the

Exhibit 3.9 Organizational Communications Analysis.

Analyze the communication systems in your organization by checking the appropriate boxes if you utilize the practice.

system A   □ letters   **FORMAL**

EXTERNAL ORGANIZATION COMMUNICATION

- □ letters
- □ telephone
- □ advertising
- □ mass media
- □ press releases
- □ publications/reports
- □ public relations/marketing
- □ community relations program
- □ visits/field work
- □ teleconferencing
- □ products/services
- □ other _____

- □ plant/office appearance and atmosphere
- □ employee contacts (outside participation)
- □ grapevine/rumors
- □ visitor/guest relations
- □ networking
- □ other _____

system C   _____ **INFORMAL**

system B   □ letters/forms   **FORMAL**

INTERNAL ORGANIZATIONAL COMMUNICATION

- □ letters/forms
- □ memoranda/reports
- □ signs/posters
- □ bulletin boards
- □ telephone
- □ computer/electronic mail
- □ closed circuit TV/radio
- □ office visits
- □ staff or other meetings
- □ organization chart for "hierarchy" communications
- □ task forces/committees
- □ other _____

- □ work relationships
- □ social relationships
- □ geographic relationships
- □ union/trade professional relationships
- □ client/customer relationships
- □ economic/status relationships
- □ cultural/religious relationships
- □ grapevine/gossip
- □ internal networking
- □ other _____

system D   _____ **INFORMAL**

Exhibit 3.9 Organizational Communication Analysis, *cont'd.*

The previous conceptual model is simply a useful means of quickly reviewing the diversity of your organization communications. By completing the following questions, you may gain a greater understanding of the status of your communications system and what you can contribute to its improvement:

1. Image

(a) What is your perception of your organization's image?

_____

(b) What is your perception of your division's (department or work unit) image?

_____

(c) What do you feel is the perception of your unit's image of those *outside* your immediate organization/division?
(Consider this from the viewpoint of those people without the organization, such as the public, as well as those who are in the organization but are not a part of your unit—for example, members of other departments.)

_____

_____

II. Publics

(a) Who are the various publics to whom you communicate your organizational messages? (Remember to include such varied recipients as suppliers, politicians and family.)

_____

_____

(b) What could be done to project a better organizational image to these people?

_____

_____

III. Communication Flow

Describe the direction of your formal communication systems:
(a) Internal:
☐ Downward (one-way) _____

_____

☐ Upward _____

_____

☐ Circular (two-way or participative) _____

_____

Continued

Exhibit 3.9 Organizational Communication Analysis, *cont'd.*

(b) External:
☐ Outward _____

_____

☐ Inward _____

_____

☐ Circular _____

IV. Organizational Relations

(a) List the names (titles or categories) of those persons with whom you are in *most* frequent communication in the course of your work week:

_____

_____

_____

_____

_____

_____

(b) Review this list and put a check next to the person or groups with whom it is vital you maintain good relations to do your job effectively.

(c) As a result of your learnings in this conference, what steps can you take next week to improve your relations with these people? Be specific.

1. _____
2. _____
3. _____
4. _____
5. _____
6. _____
7. _____
8. _____
9. _____
10. _____

V. Organizational Environment

(a) The improvement of both formal and informal communications can contribute significantly toward bettering the organizational atmosphere. What other recommendations can you make in this regard next week?

_____

_____

Exhibit 3.9 Organizational Communication Analysis, *cont'd.*

(b) What strategy or procedures will you utilize to accomplish this? (To whom and how will you direct your observations?)

_____

_____

appropriate classification for such matters as facsimile transmission, electronic mail, and other new forms of communication technologies.

In addition, there are five sections dealing with questions of organizational image, publics, communication flow, relations, and environment. These require descriptive statements to be written. When a team, for instance, has completed individual analysis, members can compare their opinions and attempt to arrive at some consensus on the issues.

SPECIALIZED RESOURCES

We recommend three books for the reader's review:

- *The Information Imperative: Managing the Impact of Information Technology on Businesses and People* by C. F. Gibson and B. B. Jackson (Lexington, MA: Lexington Books/D. C. Heath Co., 1987)
- *We've Got to Start Meetings Like This!—A Guide to Successful Business Meeting Management* by R. K. Mosvick and R. B. Nelson (Glenview, IL: Scott, Foresman, 1987)
- *Handbook of Organizational Communication: An Interdisciplinary Review,* edited by F. M. Jablin, L. L. Putnam, K. E. Roberts and L. W. Porter (Newbury Park, CA: Sage Publications, 1987).

Leaders will find useful publications and audio tapes on language, words, and meaning from the International Society of General Semantics (P.O. Box 2469, San Francisco, CA 94126). Particularly recommended for use with employees is an inexpensive monograph by Don Fabun, *Communications The Transfer of Meaning.*

You may wish to consult *The Video Source Book,* which lists over 51,000 videotapes/cassettes available for training, and which is regularly updated: National Video Clearinghouse, 100 Lafayette Drive, Syosset, NY 11791. If you or your employees require computer updating, consider *Computer User's Training Program* and audio/visual system by Learning Consultants, Inc.: Masterico Press, Box 7382, Ann Arbor, MI 48107. If you are interested in telecommunications, you may wish to subscribe to the magazine for communications management, *TPT—Telecommunication Products & Technology* (available without charge from TPT, The Penn Well Building, 119 Russel St., Littleton, MA 01460); the newspaper *Tel-Coms* on teleconferencing (also free from Parker Publications, 2801 International Lane, Madison, WI 53701); or the free newsletter *GRG News* (from Gordon R. Gordetsky Consultants, 11414 Windy Summit Place, San Diego, CA 92127).

4
Influencing Work Culture at Home and Abroad

INTRODUCTION

Culture has a critical effect on the behavior and performance of people, individually and in groups. International traders can see this clearly. Only in the past decade, however, have executives and managers begun to appreciate the significance of corporate culture. This chapter will offer insights to leaders about this vital subject in the context of the work environment, so that we may better understand ourselves and provide leadership in a more diverse work force.

What is Culture? Culture is a coping mechanism, a tool of survival to deal with the circumstances in which people find themselves. People create a social environment out of the biological, physical, historical, and other aspects of our surroundings. This "culture" is the "communicable knowledge" that is transferred from generation to generation to help group members live in a time, place, or situation. Culture is the human coping mechanism, the tool that separates our species from other animals. In conjunction with biological evolution, culture has not only helped the human species to survive, but to grow and develop on this planet and even in outer space.

Culture is learned behavior and knowledge that are integrated by a group, shared among group members, and passed along to descendents. These group beliefs and practices become customs and traditions that distinguish one group (civilization, country, or organization) from another. Certain behaviors, for instance, arise from peculiar circumstances of climate, geography, danger, ignorance, or discovery; group members in time become "conditioned," and although the reason behind the behavior is forgotten, the behavior persists—it is part of the culture.

In this chapter we will look at culture and its diverse ramifications, especially in terms of the work environment. We will also examine *cultural conditioning* and see how it affects communication and performance.

Finally, we will review the influence of culture on work and organizations. We will show that the role of leadership is to design and sustain a more creative and productive work culture, one that helps personnel to achieve their human potential.

INPUT

Human performance is dependent upon culture; that is, the social environment strongly influences people, either to strive and excel or to be resigned and apathetic. Some cultures are dynamic and spur members to be creative and productive. Other cultures inhibit creativity and trap the mind or spirit, repressing human aspirations and efforts to improvement. Such cultures, whether national or organizational, overburden people with ritualism, legalism, defeatism, and fatalism. Leaders can change their group's culture so that it enhances worker productivity by removing obsolete norms, practices, and procedures and by introducing more relevant standards, operations, and technologies. Leaders can induce a society or a company to capitalize on its human assets.

CULTURAL INFLUENCES ON BEHAVIOR

Culture provides us with a framework for analyzing human behavior, especially in terms of people in groups. Because human beings are so complex and diverse, what we know about the effect of culture on behavior is relative and tentative—a series of generalizations subject to many exceptions. Furthermore, each of us tends to view others' behavior in terms of his or her own background, so that actions that may appear to us as bizarre or reprehensible may be acceptable and normal in another part of the human family. For example, some affluent societies find extreme poverty appalling and seek to eradicate it, while in other, Third World nations, it is accepted as one way of life and ignored. A society's shared values determine individual response on many issues (Fisher, 1988).

Anthropologists have called culture *created designs for living*. In addition to the customs and traditions mentioned, culture is manifested by a tribe, an organization, or a nation in the group's beliefs, rites, myths, symbols, morals, habits, thought patterns, language, standards, laws, art, architecture, artifacts, and technologies (Exhibit 4.1).

These manifestations of a culture, its guidelines, may be rational or irrational, explicit (spelled out and evident) or implicit.

The tenets of a culture—its "truths"—are expressed in its behaviors or its taboos—what members do and don't do. Culture members strongly identify with their culture's beliefs and practices. They are usually reluctant to question or change beliefs or practices commonly held within their society. Traditions evolve as to what are proper behavior and dress, what foods or people are to be considered desirable or to be avoided. In traditional or simple societies, daily life is somewhat smooth and predictable because of such observances—peasants, for instance, do not question the validity of these beliefs or practices because "That is the way we always did it!" Unfortunately, culture can also be the means for perpetuating ignorance and misinformation as well as prejudices and bigotry.

Culture is marked by both diversity and unity. Although we all belong to a culture, its manifestations differ by place and circumstances.

Exhibit 4.1 Cultural Characteristics

1. Identity and purpose: sense of self, space, mission
2. Communication and language: transmission, interaction, exchange
3. Dress and appearance: look, style, image, reputation
4. Food and feeding customs: preparation, serving, eating habits
5. Time and time consciousness: sense of duration intervals
6. Relationships and sexuality: associations, kinship, gender, rank and status, reward and recognition
7. Values and norms: need/priority system, behavior standards
8. Beliefs and attitudes: myths, philosophy, outlook, religion, rites, rituals
9. Mental habits and learning: thought processes, education
10. Work habits and practices: labor focus, work patterns and procedures, management and leadership

Cultural differences are so wide, and so compelling, that what one person consider's food is poison to another. There are numerous *universals,* however—behaviors common to all cultures and human nature everywhere. They include age-grading, sport, and adornment of the body; language, law, and luck; magic, marriage, and mourning; and visiting, weaning, and predicting the weather.

Different human groups, however, differ even in the ways they practice universal behaviors. Hand-holding, for instance, occurs in almost all cultures, but in some societies, it is permitted between men and women, while in other societies, only between persons of the same sex. The marriage customs and laws of certain societies favor monogomy, while in other circumstances polygamy/polygyny, or polyandry is preferred. We must be sensitive to these differences in cultural universals—whether in humor or hygiene, greeting or gift-giving—and, when outside our own cultural group, respect and observe (if possible) local custom. In seeking to interpret the behavior of a worker from another culture, be careful not to be fooled by appearances. What we consider phlegmatic others may think of as respectful. Americans are expressive; Asians generally cloak their feelings—a matter of cultural conditioning.

Actually, it is cultural differences that add spice to life and make people so interesting. If we were all the same, life might be quite boring. When we are sensitive to the differences in meaning attached to communication symbols, then we watch for subtle signs, such as body language, gestures, symbols, even color. In India, for example, people shake their heads back and forth to say "yes" and nod their heads to say "no"—exactly the reverse of U.S. practice. Similarly, here in North America, we usually associate black with bereavement and white with joy; doing so in an Asian nation could result in a *faux pas.* Mourners wear white, in Japan, blue in Iran, and purple in Latin America. A sensitive leader should check local customs when abroad and be aware of minority cultures at home.

To raise cultural awareness, look for patterns and themes in whatever culture you are studying. Some Asian cultures, India, for instance, instill in their members a belief in reincarnation, and their people are very fatalistic. Ruth Benedict pointed out that the Pueblo Indians of the American Southwest have an integrative culture that could be described as "middle of the road," that is, they avoid any form of excess or conflict in order to arrive at the value of existence. In the Far East, there are many cultures in which people follow a similar, consistently summative theme in their lives. We could search for distinctive themes in American culture in general or in minorities within our society such as Latin American or black American culture. Such world views, declared or implied, usually control behavior or stimulate activity within that group. In the American business subculture, one such theme is the importance of profit—the "bottom line." Many corporate cultures in our society differ however, place the emphasis on profitable service, quality, or excellence.

Within a group, organization, or nation, there are majority and minority cultures. The behaviors and attitudes shared by most members can be said to make up the *mainline* or *macroculture* (the term I prefer). Within any society, regardless of size, there are distinguishing characteristics that differentiate people by sex, age, race, class, or some other classification. Anthropologists call groups made up of people who share these distinguishing characteristics *subcultures*; I prefer the term *microcultures*. Thus, within the macroculture of the United States, there are many microcultures, that is, segments of American society such as criminals, drug users, the defense establishment, teenagers, surfers, senior citizens, blue-collar workers, college students, yuppies, Jews, Chicanos, immigrants, and refugees. In terms of business, a Canadian company represents the macroculture of that country and the microculture of that particular corporation; furthermore, within the organizational culture of the Canadian Broadcasting Company there are microcultures grouped around subentities such as subsidiaries, divisions, or departments. The offices of CBC operating in the province of Quebec differ somewhat from those in other provinces because of the dominance there of the French-speaking inhabitants.

People within national cultures, such as Mexicans or Romanians, may share a common microculture of Catholicism or Communism. Similarly, countries may share the subcultural traits of poverty, their particular stage of agricultural or industrial development, or of being urbanized or rural. So, too, groups of people across the world may share the traits of a microculture with which they have more in common than they do with their fellow citizens. Thus, globally, this could prove true within the microculture of managers, police officers, rock musicians, or computer addicts. A Japanese and an American manager often share more with each other in terms of occupation and class than they may share with a fellow national on their company's assembly line.

Realizing that we are all members of many cultural groupings both macrocultural and microcultural can help us understand the behavior of others. As a result, we become more tentative in our judgments, more tolerant in our attitudes, and more effective in coping with the pecularities of cultural differences. Perhaps awareness of culture can make us less simplistic and more sympathetic, for instance to a microculture of alcoholics, unemployed people, or welfare recipients.

By appreciating the impact of cultural conditioning on people, we may be less inclined to blame, to castigate, to express hostility toward those who are different from us. Instead, we may be more inclined to enrich life experience by including in our relationships those who are less like us in terms of ethnic background, customs, dress, thought patterns, or communication. The more we comprehend the concept of culture, the more able to develop cross-cultural skills and to manage change we become.

Today's global managers use a high performance strategy to manage cultural differences and promote cultural synergy. Harris and Moran (1987, 1982) have written two volumes on such strategies.

THE CHARACTERISTICS OF CULTURE

Leaders need a relatively simple method for analyzing a culture, that is, a logical way, when going abroad to do business, to examine the various dimensions of a national culture, or, when at home, to consider minority and organizational cultures. Anthropologists have many such schemes for studying the various parameters of cultures. One, for example, is a systems approach, by which the investigator examines the many subsystems that make up the whole of a society, such as, kinship, education, economics, politics, religion, health, recreation, and associations (Miller, 1978).

One way to analyze any macroculture or microculture, is to consider the way the group works. During the course of human development, societies and institutions have been created around the dominant work prevalent at that point in time. Early human culture, for instance, was organized around hunting; there are aboriginal tribes still living that way today. The mainstream of humankind moved beyond that stage of development to a work culture built around farming or ranching; this agricultural life-style still lingers on in preindustrial nations or in rural sections of America. For the last three hundred years, the dominant work style has been industrial, centered around the factory system and an urban way of life. Now we are undergoing a transition to a postindustrial work culture focused on "information processing and services" (Harris, 1983, 1985).

In *Managing Cultural Differences,* (Harris and Moran, 1987) some basic classifications were proposed for analyzing a group's life-style. Exhibit 4.1 lists these.

Note that, in each category, there are two related but distinct features of culture to be observed. These features can serve as ten benchmarks to categorize the various aspects of a culture, whether a national or organizational culture, a work or team culture. For each category, we will provide an illustration in terms of human behavior and performance within one of the following aspects of culture:

- A national culture (NC)—either a foreign country or a minority in this country
- An organizational culture (OC)—a corporation, agency, or association
- A work culture (WC)—specifically the metaindustrial society now emerging
- A team culture (TC)—either athletic or corporate

1. *Identity and purpose.* Culture helps to give people a sense of identity with reference to a group, and to some extent determines their life space (both physical and psychological). The borders that mark off and define the group can be concrete or abstract, explicit or implicit; drawing the lines is the way the group defines itself and exercises its territorial imperative. Culture also contributes to the group's rationale for being together: its sense of mission and goals.

   NC. The people of some nations express pride and confidence, while those of other nations are of humble bearing and more respectful of others. The American sense of space requires more physical distance between individuals, while people of some other countries tend to get much closer during interpersonal interaction.

2. *Communication and language.* A group distinguishes itself by its communication systems, both verbal and nonverbal. Unique interaction processes develop, with special vocabularies, terminologies, and codes. Within the major language groupings, further differen-

tiation occurs through dialects, accents, slang, jargon, and other variations. (Chapter 3 discussed this dimension in some depth.)

OC. The Department of Defense employs acronyms extensively, not only with its own members, but with its many contractors, so as to facilitate communications with the myriad DOD components. It also employs much of the jargon common to a bureaucratic government agency.

3. *Dress and appearance.* Whether as a whole or through its members, a culture delineates itself through garments, decorations, and other adornments or the lack thereof. Hair length or the lack of it, facial markings, jewelry, and body markings can set a tribe or unit apart—remember the pirates of old or the terrorists of today. Think of the Japanese kimono, African headdress, British bowler, Polynesian sarong, and the military or police uniform. The appearance of its members, equipment, and institutions sometimes conveys the nature of a culture or its business; consider an American Airlines flight attendant, the IBM personal computer, or the McDonald arch.

WC. In the new, metaindustrial work culture, high technology firms often require workers to wear white sanitary garments to prevent contamination (e.g., in computer microchip production). These knowledge-centered factories often look like college campuses—they are usually set in modern industrial parks that feature eye-catching buildings, attractive landscaping, and open spaces, as well as recreational facilities for worker fitness programs.

4. *Food and feeding customs.* The manner in which food is selected, prepared, presented, and eaten differs by culture, as every visitor to a Chinese or French restaurant knows. One person's pet may be a delicacy to someone in different culture. Religious observances forbid certain foods, such as beef or pork, while dictating the manner of their preparation: kosher cooking distinguishes the world's Jews. Feeding customs may determine the use of hands, chopsticks, or cutlery: an American uses a knife in the dominant (usually the right) hand to cut his or her food, then puts down the knife to wield the fork with the same hand; Europeans don't switch implements. In some subcultures, ladies prefer the tea room, soldiers use a mess, executives have separate dining rooms, and vegetarians have their own restaurants. Feasts and banquets in various forms, from luau to retirement dinners, are used to celebrate important events.

TC. NASA keeps its shuttle crews happy by permitting them to order their preferences for steak, fish, or whatever, but then has to package everything in special plastic containers to deal with the reality of eating or drinking in zero gravity when in outer space.

5. *Time and time consciousness.* The study of that aspect of human behavior called "time" is *chronomics*—keeping, telling, and measuring the duration of intervals. Our biological and circadian rhythms are affected by nature, climate, and speed—air travelers through time zones know of this and experience "jet lag." Cultural factors cause some people to have a more exact or relative sense of time. In some cultures, time is told by sunrise or sunset, rain its lack, or other seasonal variations: consider Daylight Saving Time. In the far north and on the lunar surface inhabitants cope with time disorientation caused by extreme variations in the periods of light and darkness.

WC. Like the military, who use the 2400-hourly system, the new technological work culture often functions on a round-the-clock schedule, either as standard operating procedure or to meet special project deadlines. The industrial-age approach to a 12-hour day with an 8-hour work day is disappearing. Chronobiologists are concerned about drastic changes in time and labor schedules, such as those brought on by night-shift work, which alter both performance and personal life and may contribute to accidents and illness.

6. *Relationships and sexuality.* Cultures fix human and organizational relationships by age, sex, status, and degrees of kinship, as well as by wealth, power, and wisdom. Studying sexual practices (clan, sibling, marriage, and familial groupings, as well as sex roles) is one way to map a culture. The family is a key manifestation of this characteristic. Families vary widely in size and in form; there are nuclear families, as in the West, or extended forms, such as the Hindu joint family. In these households, membership extends from parents and their children to uncles, aunts, and cousins, but the living areas separate the sexes. Depending on whether the culture is patriarchial or matriarchial, the authority figure is male or female. In some cultures, the elderly are venerated; in others, youth holds supreme. Culture can dictate equal opportunity for women, or force females to wear veils, appear deferential, and give up many rights to the dominant males. In addition, in human systems, customs and poli-

cies, organization charts and structures, role definitions, and even security clearances determine relationships. Protocol and rank can inhibit human interaction, even segregating minorities or the non-commissioned.

OC. In a successful multinational corporation, Schlumberger, multicultural relationships are that of global engineering and technical fraternity, male-dominated and family-oriented. Among the largely knowledge-based workers, personal and electronic networking is normal behavior. However, there are contradictions: outside of North America, the company discourages assignments to their remote sites of engineers who are married; wives of employees find it difficult to pursue their own careers because of their husbands' frequent transfers, often to Moslem countries. Customer relations are prized, and the emphasis is on service and honesty with clients. Relations with people in developing countries are deliberately cultivated in a company spirit of equality. Human-machine relations are encouraged through the widespread corporate use of automation, robotics, and artificial intelligence. In their global relationships, Schlumberger personnel tend to be more cosmopolitan and less ethnocentric, valuing human relations.

7. *Values and norms.* Culture influences what people perceive as their needs, and, as a result, what they set as their priorities. Those functioning at the survival need level value such basics as food, clothing, and shelter; those at the security need level value material things, law and order, and titles and other symbols that maintain their position; those with higher ego and actualization needs value recognition, quality of life, and self-fulfillment.

Based on what the culture values, behavior norms are overtly or covertly expressed in that society. These acceptable standards of behavior may take the form of a work ethic, principles of etiquette, codes of conduct, regulations, and laws. The process begins in the family, and the norms range from absolute obedience to permissiveness; the process continues into organizational life, where employee standards are formally or informally stated.

NC. Macrocultures start from different sets of premises in setting down what behavior is pleasing, annoying, embarassing, punishable, or rewardable. In some countries, one is expected to be truthful only with one's friends and family and not with strangers. These conventions differ; consider that in some Pacific Islands the higher status one has in the community, the more one is expected to share personal belongings. An extreme example of culture-based norms can be seen in the fundamentalist Islamic movement in Iran, which today teaches the population to value and seek death through martydom for their cause.

8. *Beliefs and attitudes.* Every cultural group has beliefs that shape member aspirations and attitudes, regardless of their rationality or objective truth. In national cultures, this can take the form of belief in the supernatural or a god and can be associated with the adoption of a religious system, so that the country and its people may be described as Christian, Jewish, Moslem, Buddhist, or Hindu. In this way, the culture seeks to provide guidance to fundamental life questions: the character of human nature; the relationship of humans to nature; the temporal focus of life (past, present or future); the modality of human activity (spontaneous expression, self-development, measurable accomplishment); the relationship of one person to another.

Within organizational cultures, the dominant business philosophy permeates policies, procedures, personnel, and publications. Corporate beliefs, for instance, may originate with a founder or company hero; that person's ideals and principles affect employee attitudes, so that they all want to make profits, innovate, provide service, or excel. Organizational beliefs and attitudes determine recognition and reward systems—rites and rituals that range from parties and ceremonies to prizes and the establishment of clubs for excellent performers. Furthermore, the culture's beliefs and attitudes are incorporated into its myths, those traditional or legendary stories about the group's heroes and events of exceptional character.

WC. The beliefs of a culture are manifested in many ways, for example, in the position and role of women in that society. In some societies, women are enshrined; in other societies, they are considered equal to men; in still other cultures, they are subservient and sometimes treated as chattel. In the disappearing industrial work culture, women were frequently denied entry or promotion to certain job classifications or activities, relegated to performing what was considered "women's work," and paid less than men for doing the same work. In the emerging metaindustrial work culture, competence, not sexuality, is the issue. Therefore, women (and minority members) are to be given equal employment opportunities, and organizations are expected to take affirmative action to aid, not interfere with, their career development. Compensation is to be based on performance and results, not on gender, race, religion, or other such irrelevant factors.

9. *Mental habits and learning.* Because the mind internalizes culture, the way people think, learn, and organize and process information is unique and often different. Some cultures may emphasize whole-brain thinking, others right- or left-brain development. For instance, in some countries logic is prized, while in others intuition is emphasized. As one travels abroad, it becomes evident that some people excel in abstract thinking and conceptualization, while others prefer rote memory and quantification. Although reasoning and learning are cultural universals, education and training are manifested in diverse and distinctly different ways.

TC. Many aerospace companies involved in space programs use *matrix* or *project* management. Engineers, for instance, are trained in both technical and interpersonal skills for effective performance on project teams. This instruction makes use of modern communication and educational technology, with the latest media and combinations, such as computer-assisted learning, videocassettes, and teleconferencing. Too often, the behavioral aspects and group dynamics involved in team building are neglected or deemphasized by those with an engineering education. NASA technicians, in preparing crews for the space shuttle and station, generally have not focused on the human dynamics involved in that work environment.

10. *Work habits and practices.* Cultures differ in the perceptions of and attitudes to work; they vary in the types of work they favor, in the manner of dividing work, and in work practices. Hall (1985) examines both the horizontal (division of labor) and the vertical (occupational gradations) dimensions of work. Cultures, especially through economics, determine what work is considered necessary and valuable to that particular group. In some cultures all members are expected to engage in desirable and worthwhile activity, but their members do not measure the work's value in terms of money; instead, they focus on the work's value to the community. Culture defines the terms, scope, and segmentation of vocational

activity—labor or toil, laborer or professional, job or career. As we have already noted, we can even analyze work cultures dominated by hunting, farming, machine production, or information processing. Today we are experiencing a change from a "work" ethic to a "worth" ethic, which emphasizes the quality of work life. More advanced, technical work cultures use technology to assist or replace workers, share work through team management, and value informal and comfortable work enviroments. Work also is the context for exercising power, authority, and leadership. Some organizations are formed as hierarchies with power concentrated at the top, while other work cultures distribute power and authority and encourage member participation and collaboration (Greiner and Shein, 1988).

NC/WC. In the American culture, the orientation is toward the future, free enterprise, and achievement. The emphasis is on focus innovation, entrepreneurialism, and high performance. Contemporary corporate recognition and reward systems support people who demonstrate such qualities in their work. (The Instrument on page 116 uses the American model for cultural analysis.)

SYNERGY AND HIGH PERFORMANCE CULTURES

Today's leader wants to do more than cope with cultural differences, domestically or internationally; it is more appropriate, as well as profitable, to promote cultural synergy, that is, through cooperation or collaboration, to capitalize upon cultural differences to produce something that is more than merely the sum of its parts.

Thus, when Japanese (Theory Y) and American (Theory X) management philosophies and practices are combined in "Theory Z" management, the result can be better than either approach can achieve individually (Ouchi, 1981). By interviewing Japanese business leaders, Thurow (1985) has debunked American businesspeople's myths about Japanese management and demonstrated that the Japanese are open to change and new experience, not locked into specific frameworks. For instance, the success of a bicultural manufacturing process with Toyota in Fremont, California, is having a dramatic impact on General Motors' thinking. The New United auto plant demonstrates the "best of both worlds," as the advertising for the new Novas proclaims. It is state-of-the-art, but is not crammed with robots; the high productivity is being achieved by adapting the Japanese approach to quality, employees, and effective management. With the enormous trade shift to the Pacific Basin, greater synergistic relations are desirable not only with the Japanese, but also with many other Oriental peoples.

A joint venture between First- and Third-world corporations based on principles of synergy, rather than on exploitation of one at the expense of the other, can prove mutually beneficial, with each organizational culture adding to and supplementing the other. It was evident when a Canadian consulting firm entered into an agreement to assist a Mexican company use advanced technology; this is but part of a larger deal between the governments of both countries in which Mexico supplies energy in return for Canada's supplying information, know-how, and equipment. These undertakings fuse both national and organizational cultures so that both peoples are enhanced in the exchange.

Synergy is combined action in which diverse or disparate peoples or groups work together, and it is a norm of the new work culture. The objective is to increase effectiveness by sharing perceptions, insights, and knowledge, so as to build on the strengths of each cultural entity. The very complexities of global problems and markets demand such cross-cultural collaboration, as is evidenced in the European Common Market or Airbus Industrie. The latter is a European consortium, a synthesis of national and corporate cultures to produce a successful and profitable series of jet airplanes. It involves French, German, and Spanish firms working together to create a superior aircraft that utilizes either an American or British motor. Technocrats have jumped traditional trade and cultural barriers in Europe, and choose personnel not on the basis of passport color but on the basis of ability to do the job.

Whether leaders are dealing with reorganization or relocation, acquisition or merger, or structural or environmental changes, synergistic strategies improve performance and promote productivity. The overly competitive and individualistic approaches of the industrial work culture are giving way to teamwork and team management. Within the context of national, organizational, or team cultures, synergistic groups are found to be more friendly, helpful, secure, and comfortable with themselves, and high in morale and performance. (Refer to Kraus [1980] for further insight.)

Personal and electronic networking is another example of how synergy pays off, especially when intercultural interactions are involved. International networks are being established among practitioners of the same occupation or profession. Material-handling or training managers within the same multinational corporation or within the same industry group together in cooperative exchanges to enhance both knowledge and skill. Leaders would do well to use such networks for their own professional development and to accomplish tasks and objectives. The network concept is based on shared superordinate goals, power, and self-interest; influence is by competence, not by position. It is an open system featuring not only collaboration, but changing and participative leadership, consensus decision-making and goal-setting, and multiple use of multicultural resources.

Synergy, then, is an idea whose time has come because it builds upon cultural uniqueness while promoting peaceful cooperation instead of divisiveness and conflict. Learning about cultural differences and synergy should be a part of all management development but is essential for those going abroad (Harris and Moran, 1987).

Leaders will find it advantageous to receive the free newsletter, *Issues & Observations* (Center for Creative Leadership, P.O. Box P-4, Greensboro, NC 27402). The November 1985 edition was devoted to "The Use of Culture in Strategic Management." The major theme of researchers Leonard Sayles and Robert Wright is that cultural awareness is a managerial instrument for reshaping the organization. They remind us that behavioral scientists have known for decades what today's executives are rediscovering: What employees do, in contrast to what they are told, depends on the norms, values, and unstated beliefs of the corporation, as well as on the infrastructure of procedures, incentives, and division of labor. An organization's culture can be the key to high performance, as IBM, Allied Chemical, and General Electric discovered. Vibrant work cultures are marked by diversity and synergy, not necessarily homogeneity.

Managers and human resource development practitioners are beginning to recognize that in this postindustrial period a new work culture is emerging (Johnson, 1987). The author devoted two volumes to this subject to help managers make the transition to a new work reality (Harris, 1983, 1985). Perhaps the special report excerpted in Exhibit 4.2 best highlights the cultural changes underway which alter employee behavior and the work environment.

Exhibit 4.2   The Changing Nature of Work. (Reprinted with permission of *TRAINING, The Magazine of Human Resource Development,* December 1987 (80 South Ninth St., Minneapolis, MN 55402, USA). Page references are to that section of the report by Chris Lee, managing editor, entitled "The New Employment Contract.")

---

*Today, few—if any—companies can assure current or future employees of career stability, advancement, or even a job. (45)

*Over the past five years, at least 13 million jobs have been eliminated in the United States, according to a *Forbes* magazine estimate. The Bureau of Labor Statistics puts the toll of lost executive, management, and administrative jobs over the same period at 500,000. (46)

*"The key issue in American industry today is not just downsizing as such, but the effect of downsizing has on the consolidation of a company, the decentralization of authority, on management systems, and on the morale and performance of the streamlined work force." (J. M. Rostrow, President, Work in American Institute, 46).

*Control Data Corporation is examining its changing employment contract against the backdrop of deeply held principles that emphasize its commitment to employee security and development. (45). . . . It also plans to create a career-management center that will help individuals map out their options—examine their values, update their skills, anticipate career shifts in the future—before they are displaced or simply decide they are simply misplaced in their current jobs. (49)

*As a result of survey on "Supervision in the 80's: Trends in Corporate America," The Opinion Research Corporation recommends that organizations

- understand employee work values. . . .
- let employees know what the standards of job performance are
- tie performance to reward and clearly communicate the links between them to employees
- provide effective performance evaluations
- give supervisors and managers the tools they need to manage, namely, train them in communication and appraisal skills, support from management for their actions, authority consistent with their responsibilities and reasons to be committed to the organization. (48)

*"Our national resource, which is also our national problem, is an almost unbelievably large number of educated, motivated and competent people striving to achieve both traditional and non-traditional kinds of success. Traditionally, they want increasing amounts of responsibility, money, power, status—all the things that come with promotion. Nontraditionally, they also want their work to expand their minds, fulfill their souls, and encourage personal growth—all the things that come from unending challenge." Judith Bardwick, *The Plateauing Trap.* (48)

SUCCEEDING THROUGH HIGH PERFORMANCE CULTURES

Recently, the author received a unique confirmation of the above observations in the form of a current article by John Sherwood, a San Francisco-based organizational consultant. His "Creating Work Cultures with Competitive Advantages" (*Organizational Dynamics,* Winter 1988, pp. 5-26) is the first such discussion I have discovered of high-performance, high-commitment *work cultures.* Sherwood makes a compelling case for such a strategy, citing many progressive companies, such as General Electric, Procter and Gamble, Digital Equipment, and Ford, that are innovating in the redesign of work and organizational structure. As a result, he maintains that personnel exhibit energy because work is then challenging and significant; in such firms, continuous "learning" is emphasized and rewarded to produce quality performance. He recommends, as a tool for this purpose, design teams to redesign sociotechnical systems (Passmore, 1988).

Sherwood believes that management will only succeed in gaining a competitive advantage when leaders change their views about people and the design of work, linking human and technical resources in a collaborative work *system.* He advocates many of the same approaches suggested in this text, emphasizing that *leaders inspire and articulate the organization's vision*—that is, its mission and a set of values for achieving its goals. For Sherwood, this is the foundation of an organization's work culture that anticipates the future and encourages high performance.

INTERACTION

Leaders who wish to increase the cross-cultural effectiveness of work units can employ a variety of group process, including case studies, critical-incident analysis, and role playing and dramatics (see Chapter 7). One source of helpful learning materials for this purpose is the Intercultural Press (P.O. Box 768, Yarmouth, ME 04096). Here we will focus on two interactive techniques useful to managers—simulation and the quality circle.

SIMULATIONS FOR CULTURAL UNDERSTANDING

Simulations are powerful training tools; through role-playing with actors or the use of computers or games, what might happen on a

Exhibit 4.3 Bafá Bafá—a Cross-Cultural Training Simulation. (Interview with R. Garry Shirts, Ph.D.)

What happens in Bafá Bafá?

Participants live and cope in a "foreign" culture and then discuss and analyze the experience. There are two cultures in the simulation. The Alpha culture is a warm, friendly, patriarchal society with strong in-group out-group identity. The Beta culture is a foreign speaking, task oriented culture. Once the participants learn the rules, customs and values of "their" culture they visit the other culture. The visitor is generally bewildered and confused by the strangeness of the foreign culture. Bewilderment often turns to intolerance and hostility once the visitor returns home. "They're strange, real strange, that's all I can say. They're making funny sounds and weird gestures. Just be careful when you go over there." But in the post-simulation discussion they come to understand that there were reasons behind the behavior they observed. With this realization their attitudes change from one of hostility to understanding. Through discussion this experience is then generalized to attitudes towards other groups in the real world.

Who is it for?

Anthropologists, sociologists, psychologists, instructors of communication skills, minority studies, language, women's studies, as well as any training program, course or situation in which it is important for the participants to have an experiential understanding of the meaning of culture. For example, the game is used by the Peace Corps, the Civil Rights Commission, American Field Service, the Census Bureau, and many other government and business organizations.

What is the unique feature of Bafá Bafá?

Probably the most unique feature of BAFÁ BAFÁ is that the interest and involvement reaches a climax in the discussion after the simulation rather than during the simulation itself. It is during the discussion that the mysteries of each of the cultures are unraveled and the participants compare perceptions of one another's culture.

What does Bafá Bafá teach?

BAFÁ BAFÁ simulation is often used to introduce the notion of cultures then followed up with a discussion and analysis of specific cultures and the way they are formed.

Exhibit 4.3   Bafá Bafá—a Cross-Cultural Training Simulation, *cont'd.*

Betans speak a "foreign" language made up of combination of vowels and consonants. It is easy to learn and use but difficult to understand if one doesn't know the rules governing its use. When Alphans hear the language, they often won't even believe that anything is being said, 'It's gobbledy gook." Others feel intimidated by it and withdraw from the culture, creating an impossible communications barrier. Some are able to make themselves understood very easily with gestures, sign language and facial expressions. Each of these reactions creates excellent opportunities to discuss and analyze the communication process: the use of body language, feelings created by language, language snobbishness, and the attitudes one must have to learn a foreign language.

Many instructors use BAFÁ BAFÁ to help students understand how stereotypes of other groups and cultures get formed and perpetuated. "They're cold, greedy, all they do is work," are some of the words which Alphans use to describe the Betans. The Betans, on the other hand, come to believe that the Alphans are "lazy, unfriendly to outsiders, and don't like females."

As in life, these stereotypes become so strong and useful during the game that many students do not want to give them up. Unlike life, however, there is an opportunity during the analysis and discussion of the simulation to examine the stereotypes in a non-threatening and constructive manner. The fact that the students are not only the perpetrators of stereotyping but also the victims, makes it possible to confront the students with a mirror image of their own behavior. This mirror image allows them to see and understand the negative effect of stereotypes in a way that is not possible with lectures, films and readings.

By the end of the discussion on stereotyping the students can see the value of description over evaluation. The importance of asking, "In what ways are they different from us?" and "What ways are they the same?" rather than "What is good or bad about their way of life?"

What does Bafá Bafá teach?

After playing BAFÁ BAFÁ, participants report that they learned that:

1. What seems logical, sensible, important and reasonable to a person in one culture may seem irrational, stupid, and unimportant to an outsider.
2. Feelings of apprehension, loneliness, lack of confidence are common when visiting another culture.
3. When people talk about other cultures, they tend to describe the differences and not the similarities.
4. Differences between cultures are generally seen as threatening and described in negative terms.
5. Personal observations and reports of other cultures should be regarded with a great deal of skepticism.

Continued

Exhibit 4.3 Bafá Bafá—a Cross-Cultural Training Simulation, *cont'd.*

6. One should make up one's own mind about another culture and not rely on the reports and experience of others.
7. It requires experience as well as study to understand the many subtleties of another culture.
8. Understanding another culture is a continuous and not a discrete process.
9. Stereotyping is probably inevitable in the absence of frequent contact or study.
10. The feelings which people have for their own language are often not evident until they encounter another language.
11. People often feel their own language is far superior to other languages.
12. It is probably necessary to know the language or a foreign culture to understand the culture in any depth.
13. Perhaps a person can accept a culture only after he or she has been very critical of it.

How long does it take?

It can be played in one 50 minute period and discussed the next. It is best, however, to allow one and one-half hours for playing the game and a half hour minimum for discussion.

How many participants does Bafá Bafá accommodate?

The lower limit at which the simulation can successfully be played is 6 persons in each culture, but it probably would work, although with less impact with 5 or even 4. The maximum number is less fixed, but it would probably become unmanageable when the number gets larger than 40.

How much preparation is required?

Approximately 30 to 40 minutes.

Are any consumable forms or special equipment needed?

Everything is included in the kit with the exception of the two cassette players and a chalkboard or newsprint pad. It is necessary to have an additional space besides the classroom such as a hallway, another classroom, a stage or patio.

NOTE: The author has successfully used this game with managers all over the world, including the U.S. Customs Service. That is why this and other Simile II games are recommended.

job in days or weeks can be telescoped into one or more hours. In a management or sales game, a life or work experience is recreated in a shorter time frame, according to established rules. People can practice behaviors in a simulated experience, just as a pilot trainee might do in an aircraft simulator. As people get more involved in such intensive learning experiences, their reactions are akin to their behavior at work. Simulation uses trial-and-error experimentation for problem-solving, learning, and research—it is better to fail in a job simulation than in real life.

Simulations, for instance, can be used to prepare a group of managers assigned overseas to deal with the culture they will face. Simulations can also be used to better human relations among minority groups in the workforce. Simulations can be purchased in the form of games or software or created to meet specific needs. Exhibit 4.3 summarizes an interview by the author with Dr. R. Garry Shirts, president of Simile II (P.O. Box 910, Del Mar, CA 92014) about the most popular of the simulations he has produced. This game about cultural understanding comes in a box containing a facilitator's manual, audio cassettes, and learning materials for practicing two simulated cultures, an imaginary Alpha and Beta.

SIMULATION MOON XXI

A leader can create a simulated situation from real life, from fiction, or from a likely future event that will promote learning among a work team, such as in the following example. This is a popular training game that can be used to instruct participants not only about cultural influences but about decision-making.

All members are informed that they have been appointed to a NASA Task Force to assist with an emergency related to the first work crew to return to the Moon since the last Apollo mission in 1972. However, the trip is now made in two stages—the space shuttle to the space station, then a second orbiter vehicle, called New Apollo XXI, to the lunar surface. All this is to prepare for the construction of a lunar base in 2010, where NASA expects to establish a permanent human presence on the Moon. It is the stepping stone for exploration of the universe, beginning next with Mars.

The Incident. The crew of six landed safely in this first mission of the new orbiter transfer vehicle (OTV). However, the New Apollo XXI developed a power problem during its landing, and the crew is unable to depart for the space station as scheduled when their work is completed. Because this is the early stage of the lunar return, there is only one other functional OTV now docked at the space station; another is nearing completion on Earth, and two others are in production. The available OTV, in lower geosynchronous orbit at the space station, is still experimental, like its counterpart on the Moon. Its chances for a successful rescue mission are calculated by Houston Control at one in six. The six lunar astronauts have enough food, water, and support services to last them for only two more days. If an attempt is made and is successful, six lives will have been saved, as well as national prestige. If an attempt is made and fails, then the lives of the second OTV crew may also be jeopardized. If no other solution is forthcoming, and no attempt is made, the Moon return mission will be a failure and the lives there are likely to be doomed.

The Problem. Should the second experimental OTV be launched to recover the Apollo XXI work crew? To ensure optimum conditions, the timing of the rescue orbit requires a decision within 35 minutes.

The Analysis. When the group or subgroups have reported their decision and their reasons, the facilitator should then raise these issues for further learning:

1. How does the American culture influence this decision? Were this to have been a decision of the USSR regarding stranded cosmonauts, would the outcome be the same? The same question might be rephrased for missions under the sponsorship of the European Space Agency or the Japanese Space Agency.
2. Would the decision change if two of the lost lunar astronauts were women or black? or if this had been an international mission with nationals of other countries aboard Apollo XXI?
3. Did the group really explore other alternatives for solving the problem? For example, did this NASA Task Force consider seeking assistance from the Soviets?
4. What process did the group go through in making this decision or arriving at a consensus? Was this culturally influenced?
5. How does one's culture affect the choice-making process, especially when the outcome involves the value of human life?

QUALITY CIRCLES ON WORK CULTURE

The concept of a quality circle was developed originally in the United States and transported to Japan by an American consultant. The Japanese adapted the technique so successfully that it was imported back to North America for further application and refinement. Westinghouse, for example, uses the strategy to transform its corporate culture. Quality circles are useful to bring about planned change in a work culture, to promote worker participation, to increase performance, and in general to improve the quality of working life. Quality circles have been used by human resource specialists as a strategy for organizational renewal; a whole professional society has developed around the method (International Association of Quality Circles, 801-B West Eighth St., Suite 301, Cincinnati, OH 45203).

Exhibit 4.4 What is a Quality Circle? (Reprinted with permission of: American Society for Training & Development, 1630 Duke Street, Alexandria, VA 22313.)

A Quality Circle is a voluntary group of workers who have a shared area of responsibility. They meet together weekly to discuss, analyze and propose solutions to quality problems. They are taught group communication process, quality strategies, and measurement and problem-analysis techniques. They are encouraged to draw on the resources of the company's management and technical personnel to help them solve problems. In fact, they take over the responsibility for solving quality problems, and they generate and evaluate their own feedback. In this way, they are also responsible for the quality of communications. The supervisor becomes the leader in the circle and is trained to work as a group member and not as a "boss."

A Quality Circle is a small group of employees doing similar work who voluntarily meet for an hour each week to discuss their quality problems, investigate causes, recommend solutions and take corrective actions.

A circle is primarily a normal work crew—a group of people who work together to produce a part of a product or service.

Circle leaders go through training in leadership skills, adult learning techniques, motivation and communication techniques. The Quality Circle itself is trained in the use of various measurement techniques and quality strategies, including cause and effect diagrams, pareto diagrams, histograms and various types of check sheets and graphs. More advanced circles move on in their training to learn sampling, data collection, data arrangement, control charts, stratification, scatter diagrams and other techniques.

A typical Quality Circle includes five to 10 members. If the department requires more than one circle, then a second leader is trained, and a second circle is formed. The circles then call on technical experts to assist in solving problems.

Circle meetings are held on company time and on company premises. Where companies have unions, the union members and leaders are encouraged to take an active role in the circle, to attend leader training and to become fully aware of circle principles.

This interactive process could be inaugurated by having the QC groups examine the existing work culture and propose what changes the participants would like in their work environment. Then management would be challenged to cooperate with their own personnel in planning, enhancing and implementing these changes with QC members. Exhibit 4.4 provides a summary of the QC process.

INSTRUMENTATION

The two data-gathering instruments presented here may be used by leaders to deal with cultural issues from two different perspectives. With the first, Cross-cultural Relations Inventory (CRI) (Exhibit 4.5), an individual may contrast his or her cultural background with another person of a differing culture. The second, Organizational Culture Survey Instrument (OCS) (Exhibit 4.6), may be used by an executive or consultant to analyze the principal cultural dimensions of a particular human system.

Exhibit 4.5 Cross-cultural Relations Inventory (CRI). (Quantity copies of CRI are available in a slightly different version entitled *Intercultural Relations Inventory*; also *Organizational Culture Survey Instrument* from Management Research Systems/Talico Inc., 2320 S. Third St. #7, Jacksonville Beach, FL 32250. ©Philip R. Harris/Harris International, 1985.)

Cross-Cultural Relations Inventory (CRI)

This inventory can be used for culture contrast purposes in two different ways, depending on whether one wishes to deal with a macro or a micro-culture. It can be employed to contrast one's own national heritage with another foreign culture, such as when an American is sent abroad as a manager, technician or professional and wishes to analyze similarities and differences of home and host cultures. Or it can be used by an administrator or supervisor to compare their own cultural influences with a person they supervise or serve who comes from a distinctly different subculture. Thus, a white manager might utilize the instrument for self-learning about black or Hispanic workers who report to that individual. Or, a Canadian health professional of English heritage might employ the process to better understand clients of the same nationality who come from a French-Canadian background. The instrument may even be used as a basis for contrasting cultures between institutions or organizations, especially during mergers or acquisitions. Within a company, for instance, it can be used to contrast the cultures of subsidiaries, plants, divisions, departments, and teams. The aim

Exhibit 4.5 Cross-cultural Relations Inventory (CRI), *cont'd.*

is to increase cultural awareness and sensitivity, while stimulating the respondent to obtain more accurate information about the two cultures under study.

This inventory is based upon the ten principal characteristics of culture suggested in the model provided in the Input section. Although the inventory is filled out on an individual basis, it is best employed as a learning experience in a small group situation. For example, a project manager of a multicultural work team might have the members complete the form in terms of each other's cultural backgrounds; then they could share and discuss their analysis with the group as a whole. Or perhaps a group of engineers is being relocated into an Asian country—as part of their pre-departure training, a valuable learning experience could be conducted by comparing the engineers' national culture with that of the target land to which they have been assigned.

When working with a group, the facilitator may wish to follow this procedure:

1. Everyone fills out the inventory privately as directed.
2. Individuals then share their insights on each of the ten principal characteristics of culture and try to arrive at some consensus as to the accuracy or inaccuracy of their perceptions.
3. Summarize the consensus visually for the group by means of two columns with ten classifications which may be displayed on a blackboard, flip chart, or overhead projector.
4. After editing, have this information transcribed and reproduced for distribution to participants.

Directions: In the blank space provided, contrast your understanding of your own culture (left column) with the one under review (right column) on the basis of the ten principal characteristics below. Please be brief and only outline with words, your ideas and illustrations on each point in terms of your relations with people from the target culture.

(Note—if you are doing this learning exercise with other members of a group, then allow no more than 30 minutes to complete the form. Then participants will be asked to share their information and insights with the whole group, correcting any gross inaccuracies in the process, and trying to arrive at some consensus for each of the key categories.)

YOUR NAME: _____

DATE OF ADMINISTRATION: _____

NAME OF YOUR CULTURE (this may be your own home majority or minority culture (e.g., Canadian, Black American, etc.), or an organizational culture, as desired): _____

NAME OF TARGET CULTURE (this may be a host culture in a foreign country, a differing minority culture within your own society, or another organizational/team culture): _____

Continued

Exhibit 4.5   Cross-cultural Relations Inventory (CRI), *cont'd.*

Your Culture   Target Culture

1. IDENTITY & PURPOSE (generally speaking, how do these people envision and project themselves as a group; how do they express their sense of space and purpose?)

_____

_____

2. COMMUNICATION & LANGUAGE (generally, what are the styles and systems for interacting, transmitting, and exchanging messages, both verbally and non-verbally? For example, what is the language of business and do any special media dominate the society?)

_____

_____

3. DRESS & APPEARANCE (generally, what is the look, style, and appearance of this group of people, both in terms of adornments as well as the image or reputation created? For example, is there anything distinctive about their clothing and its color, especially at business or work?)

_____

_____

4. FOOD & FEEDING CUSTOMS (generally, what distinguishes this people in terms of what and how they eat, including their preparation, serving and eating habits? What is distinctive about their diet or their use of meals to express themselves?

_____

_____

5. TIME & TIME CONSCIOUSNESS (generally, how do these people measure duration intervals, differing in their time sense? For example, is there anything different about meeting times and arrivals?)

_____

_____

6. RELATIONSHIPS & SEXUALITY (generally, how do these people differentiate

Exhibit 4.5   Cross-cultural Relations Inventory (CRI), *cont'd.*

their associations with one another and strangers, whether in terms of kinship and gender, age and rank, position or status, rewards or recognition. Is there anything different about their family and marriage arrangements? Particularly note matters of bisexuality, and the status of either male or female in society.)

_____

_____

7. VALUES & NORMS (generally, what distinguishes the need and priority systems of this people in terms of importance. And as a result, what behavior standards or expectations do they establish, explicitly or implicitly? For example, what about business ethics?)

_____

_____

8. BELIEFS & ATTITUDES (generally, what is the philosophy of life of this particular group? What is the dominant force, such as religion or myths, that dominate their outlook and possibly is expressed in various attitudes, rites and rituals?)

_____

_____

9. MENTAL HABITS & LEARNING (generally, what distinguishes the thought processes of this people—such as the method of learning, emphasis upon logic and intuition, whatever? Is there anything special about their systems of educating and training?)

_____

_____

10. WORK HABITS & PRACTICES (generally, what is the primary vocational focus of this people—hunting, agriculture, industrial, post-industrial or high technology? Is there anything distinctive about their view of the nature of work and the ways of organizing themselves for work, such as patterns, policies and procedures? For example, are there peculiar attitudes or arrangements about caste, color pigmentation or race, minority or foreign workers?)

_____

_____

_____

Continued

Exhibit 4.5 Cross-cultural Relations Inventory (CRI), *cont'd.*

Participants are encouraged to add any other dimension of culture which is considered significant to distinguish the two cultures.

Exhibit 4.6 Organizational Culture Survey Instrument

Organizational Culture Survey Instrument (OCS)

The 99 items in this survey can be used by a leader to assess the culture of one's own organization, including one's own managerial perceptions. (With adaptation, the instrument can be used to study another organization's culture. Further, with slight changes, the survey can also be extended to a managerial group or the whole workforce so as to obtain more comprehensive data for analysis.)

Unless instructed otherwise, the respondent generally provides an effectiveness rating for the items by selecting a number on a 7 point scale from 1 (lowest) to 7 (highest). The inventory is divided into 7 major sections—overall analysis, organizational communication, management team, work group, managerial self-perception, organizational relations, and organizational change.

The results can then be used to diagnose the health of an organization and its need for change. If used with others, such as among various subunits (e.g., a department or division), the findings can be tallied by section and group comparisons made. Within an organization, local norms may be developed. Among a management group which has filled out this form, individual results and differences in perception can be a basis of discussion, further learning, and action planning.

Instructions

This questionnaire should be as complete and authentic as possible. It provides you with an opportunity for: (a) giving feedback *anonymously* to foster your organization's development, (b) evaluating its key management, including yourself, and (c) understanding better your organizational environment, whether at home or abroad.

There are 6 major sections to this inquiry, and a total of 99 items seeking your opinion. A maximum of 50 minutes should be allowed for thoughtful completion of this inventory. Please consider your answers carefully for each point. Your first effort at responding should reflect your spontaneous reactions and thoughts on how you view your organization's culture from your position if time permits, review your replies, and make changes if necessary.

Exhibit 4.6   Organizational Culture Survey Instrument, *cont'd.*

Please check the appropriate categories that best depict your response to the inquiry. Where necessary, *fill in* the information requested:

This analysis will be for the total organization ( )
or for the subsystem of which you are a part   ( )
(e.g. division, department, subsidiary)

The majority of questions are to be answered by checking one column in a 7-point scale, with the lowest evaluations on the left or low side of the continuum, average in the middle area, and higher assessments on the right side. The exceptions are questions 23, 68, 69–81, which require a checking of the appropriate category provided.

Organizational Diagnosis

On a scale of *lowest* (1) to *highest* (7), circle your rating of your organization's effectiveness or ineffectiveness on the following items. On question 23, simply mark the appropriate category for your response.

Overall Analysis

1. The goals/objectives of this organization are clearly defined and regularly reviewed.
   Effectiveness 1 2 3 4 5 6 7
2. Managers and supervisors at all levels have the opportunity to participate in this process of setting goals/objectives.
   Effectiveness 1 2 3 4 5 6 7
3. The organization has mechanisms for periodic evaluation of its achievement of goals/objectives.
   Effectiveness 1 2 3 4 5 6 7
4. Key management devotes adequate time to advanced, dynamic planning, and involves subordinates in the process as appropriate.
   Effectiveness 1 2 3 4 5 6 7
5. Key management in this organization supports high achievers among employees.
   Effectiveness 1 2 3 4 5 6 7
6. Management regularly reviews the assignment of roles and responsibilities, as well as the delegation of authority for performance.
   Effectiveness 1 2 3 4 5 6 7
7. Key managers ensure that adequate personnel development and training are available for employees to carry out assigned tasks.
   Effectiveness 1 2 3 4 5 6 7

Continued

Exhibit 4.6   Organizational Culture Survey Instrument, *cont'd.*

8. Management has an adequate system for regular and meaningful performance evaluation of employees.
   Effectiveness   1   2   3   4   5   6   7
9. The organization emphasizes cooperation as an operational norm.
   Effectiveness   1   2   3   4   5   6   7
10. The organization demonstrates commitment to providing satisfactory service to its clients/customers.
    Effectiveness   1   2   3   4   5   6   7
11. The organization utilizes well the human energies of its workforce.
    Effectiveness   1   2   3   4   5   6   7
12. The organization rewards personnel on the basis of merit and performance, encouraging competence.
    Effectiveness   1   2   3   4   5   6   7
13. The work climate encourages employees to do their best and to perform as well as they can.
    Effectiveness   1   2   3   4   5   6   7
14. The atmosphere in the organization encourages people to be open and candid with management.
    Effectiveness   1   2   3   4   5   6   7
15. The organization treats employees equally, regardless of their sex or race.
    Effectiveness   1   2   3   4   5   6   7

Organizational Communication

16. The present state of organizational communications is satisfactory.
    Effectiveness   1   2   3   4   5   6   7
17. The communication between management and yourself is adequate.
    Effectiveness   1   2   3   4   5   6   7
18. Organizational communications between central headquarters' staff and field personnel are satisfactory.
    Effectiveness   1   2   3   4   5   6   7
19. In your area of responsibility, communication is satisfactory between you and your subordinates.
    Effectiveness   1   2   3   4   5   6   7
20. There is adequate written communication in the organization.
    Effectiveness   1   2   3   4   5   6   7
21. There is adequate oral and group communication.
    Effectiveness   1   2   3   4   5   6   7
22. Adequate communication is provided about organizational changes.
    Effectiveness   1   2   3   4   5   6   7
23. Communication with various levels of management around you is *largely* downward (   )   upward (   )   circular (   )

Exhibit 4.6 Organizational Culture Survey Instrument, *cont'd.*

Management Team Evaluation

In terms of upper-level management, the emphasis as I evaluate it is.

24. Clear organizational objectives and targets.
    Effectiveness 1 2 3 4 5 6 7
25. Competency in themselves and their subordinates.
    Effectiveness 1 2 3 4 5 6 7
26. Providing a leadership model for subordinates.
    Effectiveness 1 2 3 4 5 6 7
27. Continuous, planned organizational renewal.
    Effectiveness 1 2 3 4 5 6 7
28. High productivity standards.
    Effectiveness 1 2 3 4 5 6 7
29. High service standards.
    Effectiveness 1 2 3 4 5 6 7
30. Experimenting with new ideas and approaches.
    Effectiveness 1 2 3 4 5 6 7
31. Encouragement of human resources development.
    Effectiveness 1 2 3 4 5 6 7
32. Coordination and cooperation in and among the organizational work units.
    Effectiveness 1 2 3 4 5 6 7
33. Conducting meaningful and productive meetings.
    Effectiveness 1 2 3 4 5 6 7
34. Confronting conflict directly and settling disagreements rather than avoiding or ignoring it.
    Effectiveness 1 2 3 4 5 6 7
35. Promoting creative thinkers and innovative performers.
    Effectiveness 1 2 3 4 5 6 7
36. Always *trying* to do things better.
    Effectiveness 1 2 3 4 5 6 7
37. Equal employment opportunity and affirmative action.
    Effectiveness 1 2 3 4 5 6 7
38. Creating a motivating environment for employees.
    Effectiveness 1 2 3 4 5 6 7
39. Open, authentic communications with each other and their subordinates.
    Effectiveness 1 2 3 4 5 6 7
40. Seeking suggestions and ideas from employees and the public (feedback).
    Effectiveness 1 2 3 4 5 6 7
41. Clarifying organizational roles and responsibilities so there is no confusion or overlap.
    Effectiveness 1 2 3 4 5 6 7
42. Teamwork and collaboration within and among upper-level management.
    Effectiveness 1 2 3 4 5 6 7

Continued

123

Exhibit 4.6 Organizational Culture Survey Instrument, *cont'd.*

43. Effective concern for training subordinates to perform competently.
Effectiveness 1 2 3 4 5 6 7
44. Willingness to consider innovations proposed to increase organizational effectiveness.
Effectiveness 1 2 3 4 5 6 7
45. Sharing of power, authority, and decision making with lower-level management.
Effectiveness 1 2 3 4 5 6 7
46. Policies and procedures that counteract absenteeism, slackness, and unproductivity.
Effectiveness 1 2 3 4 5 6 7
47. Management of responsibility on the part of employees they supervise.
Effectiveness 1 2 3 4 5 6 7
48. Problem solving and confronting issues.
Effectiveness 1 2 3 4 5 6 7
49. Constantly improving working conditions, both physical and psychological.
Effectiveness 1 2 3 4 5 6 7
50. Consistency in organizational policies and procedures.
Effectiveness 1 2 3 4 5 6 7

Work Group Assessment

Please answer this section in terms of the work group you manage. That is, respond in terms of personnel who report to you or for whom you are responsible.

51. The atmosphere and interpersonal relations in my group are friendly and cooperative.
Effectiveness 1 2 3 4 5 6 7
52. The members encourage one another's best efforts, reinforcing successful behavior.
Effectiveness 1 2 3 4 5 6 7
53. The group organizes and problem-solves effectively.
Effectiveness 1 2 3 4 5 6 7
54. The members maintain adequate standards of performance.
Effectiveness 1 2 3 4 5 6 7
55. The group is open to and ready for organizational changes.
Effectiveness 1 2 3 4 5 6 7
56. The members work effectively as a team.
Effectiveness 1 2 3 4 5 6 7
57. The group communicates well within our work unit.
Effectiveness 1 2 3 4 5 6 7
58. The group communicates satisfactorily with other work units.
Effectiveness 1 2 3 4 5 6 7

Exhibit 4.6   Organizational Culture Survey Instrument, *cont'd.*

59. The members provide group input and may participate in the management process as appropriate.
Effectiveness 1 2 3 4 5 6 7
60. The group makes effective use of available equipment and resources (both material and human).
Effectiveness 1 2 3 4 5 6 7
61. The members generally demonstrate pride in themselves and in their work.
Effectiveness 1 2 3 4 5 6 7
62. The group actively seeks to utilize the skills and abilities of its members.
Effectiveness 1 2 3 4 5 6 7
63. The members do not feel constrained by rules, regulations, and red tape in accomplishing their work.
Effectiveness 1 2 3 4 5 6 7
64. The group is dynamic in its approaches and activities; that is, the work environment "turns people on."
Effectiveness 1 2 3 4 5 6 7
65. The members of this group are *not* characterized by conformity and dependency.
Effectiveness 1 2 3 4 5 6 7
66. The group has a record of consistent accomplishment in the organization.
Effectiveness 1 2 3 4 5 6 7
67. The members in my work group generally exercise responsibility and achievement.
Effectiveness 1 2 3 4 5 6 7

Managerial Self-Perception

68. As a leader in this organization, check the words or word combinations that best describe your management approach:

( ) idealistic	( ) realistic
( ) innovative	( ) pragmatic
( ) cooperative	( ) individualistic
( ) task-oriented	( ) sensitive
( ) change maker	( ) change reactor
( ) hard-nosed	( ) imaginative
( ) inspiring	( ) participative
( ) traditional	( ) futuristic

(Check appropriate category)

69. Do you seek out and use improved work methods?
Rarely ( ) Sometimes ( ) Usually ( )

Continued

Exhibit 4.6 Organizational Culture Survey Instrument, *cont'd.*

70. Does your managerial performance demonstrate sufficient skill in:
    *administration   Rarely( ) Sometimes( ) Usually( )
    *human relations   Rarely( ) Sometimes( ) Usually( )
    *obtaining results   Rarely( ) Sometimes( ) Usually( )
71. Do you reinforce and support positive behavior and performance in your subordinates?
    Rarely( ) Sometimes( ) Usually( )
72. Do you actively encourage your subordinates to make the most of their potential?
    Rarely( ) Sometimes( ) Usually( )
73. Are you willing to take reasonable risks in the management of your work units?
    Rarely( ) Sometimes( ) Usually( )
74. Do you take responsibility to ensure that the employees you manage make their best contribution toward achieving organizational goals and production targets?
    Rarely( ) Sometimes( ) Usually( )
75. Do your key subordinates really know where you stand on controversial organizational issues?
    Rarely( ) Sometimes( ) Usually( )
76. Do you demonstrate by example personal standards of competence and productivity?
    Rarely( ) Sometimes( ) Usually( )
77. Are you generally objective, friendly but businesslike in dealing with employees?
    Rarely( ) Sometimes( ) Usually( )
78. Are you doing something specific for your own personal and professional development?
    Rarely( ) Sometimes( ) Usually( )
79. Do you take responsibility to seek change in organizational norms, values, and standards when these are not relevant and need updating?
    Rarely( ) Sometimes( ) Usually( )
80. Please read back to yourself the above twelve statements. In light of the demands of modern management and employee expectations, how would you rate the above evaluations of your leadership role?
    Please check one: Inadequate( )   Adequate( )
81. A study by Michael Maccoby describes the new postindustrial organizational leader in this way: A gamesman, "in contrast to the jungle-fighter industrialist of the past; is driven not to build or to preside over empires, but to organize winning teams. Unlike the security-seeking organization man, he is excited by the chance to cut deals and to gamble." The author also states that such new leaders in top management are more cooperative and less hardened than the classical autocrats, as well as less dependent than the typical bureaucrats. This sociologist suggests that the new leader is more detached

Exhibit 4.6 Organizational Culture Survey Instrument, *cont'd.*

and emotionally inaccessible than his predecessors, yet troubled that his work develops his head but not his heart.

How does this description of the emerging executive fit you? (check one)
This is comparable to the way I am/feel   (   ).
I do not identify with this new type of manager (   ).

Organizational Relations

Please check the category that best describes the present situation for you.

82. Employees generally trust top management.
Effectiveness   1   2   3   4   5   6   7
83. Employees usually "level" in their communications with management, providing authentic feedback.
Effectiveness   1   2   3   4   5   6   7
84. Employees usually are open and authentic in their work relations.
Effectiveness   1   2   3   4   5   6   7
85. If employees have a conflict or disagreement with management, they usually work it out directly, or seek mediation.
Effectiveness   1   2   3   4   5   6   7
86. When employees receive administrative directives or decisions with which they do not agree, they usually conform without dissent.
Effectiveness   1   2   3   4   5   6   7
87. Older managers are not threatened by younger, competent staff members or subordinates who may have more knowledge, information, or education.
Effectiveness   1   2   3   4   5   6   7
88. Managers are able to interact effectively with minority and female peers or subordinates.
Effectiveness   1   2   3   4   5   6   7
89. Managers really try to be fair and just with employees, using competence only as their evaluative criterion of performance.
Effectiveness   1   2   3   4   5   6   7
90. Many managers have generally not "retired" on the job, and are not indifferent to needs for organizational renewal.
Effectiveness   1   2   3   4   5   6   7
91. Employees have opportunities to clarify changing roles and relationships.
Effectiveness   1   2   3   4   5   6   7
92. Organization is concerned about the needs of people, as well as getting the task done.
Effectiveness   1   2   3   4   5   6   7
93. Organization encourages and assists employees in the development of community relations.
Effectiveness   1   2   3   4   5   6   7

Continued

Exhibit 4.6 Organizational Culture Survey Instrument, *cont'd.*

Organizational Changes

94. Organization is able to adapt to the dramatic shifts and changes under way in society and the larger culture.
    Effectiveness 1 2 3 4 5 6 7
95. Organization is able to handle the new demands made upon it as a result of the changes in top administration and management emphasis.
    Effectiveness 1 2 3 4 5 6 7
96. Organization does seek adequate input from employees on those changes that affect them, or that they are to implement.
    Effectiveness 1 2 3 4 5 6 7
97. Organization is able to deal effectively with the new kind of person coming into your workforce and management.
    Effectiveness 1 2 3 4 5 6 7
98. Organization has changed its management priorities and approaches with regard to scarce resources, as well as environmental and ecological concerns.
    Effectiveness 1 2 3 4 5 6 7
99. Organization is innovative in finding ways to improve the institutional environment.
    Effectiveness 1 2 3 4 5 6 7

Note: Please recognize that cultural factors influenced the way the above questions were constructed, and the way in which you responded. However, this evaluation can provide insight into your organizational culture in terms of Western perspective and future trends.

Enhancing Organizational and Team Relations

Human relations affect the performance of the people in an organization. Such relations can be viewed from three perspectives: interpersonal (between individuals), intragroup (among members of a group), and intergroup (among groups that make up the organization or with external groups). Leaders should be aware of how these relationships affect their own behavior and may be used to enhance or undermine productivity. Awareness of and skill at human relations, applied to clients, customers, suppliers, and contractors, as well as government and community officials, increase good will and profitability. Finally, in the global marketplace, these insights have cross-cultural applications to improve the organization's international relations. Our first objective in this chapter is to understand relationships in terms of human systems in general and of organizations in particular. Leaders who truly appreciate the importance of organizational relations in achieving high performance devote time and energy to the following concerns:

- Group characteristics, space, and change
- Group goals, norms, and values
- Group style, leadership, and influence
- Group roles, relationships, and responsibilities
- Group image, communication patterns, and feedback
- Group decision-making and problem-solving

We will also examine organizational relations, focusing on the team. Because team management is one of the characteristics of the new work culture, leaders have to become more skilled in team formation and building. We will determine how to make teams productive, how to promote a helping relationship, and how to use conflict to achieve objectives. Many of the previous chapter insights can be applied here to a team's culture.

INPUT

Relationships are the key to successful individual and institutional performance. Career development, increased productivity or sales, organizational effectiveness—all depend to a great degree on positive human relationships. The Random House dictionary describes *relationship* as a connection, such as that of an individual with another individual or group. Apart from kinship through birth or marriage, relationship can refer to a special affinity, alliance, or association with one's fellows, such as with coworkers or professional colleagues. In a deeper sense, however, people confirm and express themselves in terms of their relationships with other human beings and creatures. The profoundest expression of relationship is love—between parent and child, husband and wife, friends, and even business partners. Our focus will be on work relationships.

Two primary forms that relationships can take are:

- *Dyad.* Two people interacting (e.g., two peers working together or a supervisor and a subordinate). The dyad is the basis of interpersonal relations. Partners are important, for example, in police work.
- *Triad*—Three people interacting; the beginning of group or intragroup relations. Triads affect morale and performance. Work teams may be three or more in number.

SYSTEMS APPROACH TO ORGANIZATIONS AND GROUPS

In the Prologue, I described the organization as an energy exchange system. A *system* is defined as the regular interaction or interdependence of parts in a more complex, unified whole. It can be an ordered and comprehensive assemblage of facts, principles, and doctrines, for instance, a system of philosophy; of tissues and organs, for instance, the reproductive system of the human body; a perceived arrangement of heavenly bodies associated and acting together, for instance, solar system; or a coordinated body of methods, schemes, classifications, and procedures, for instance, management system.

Miller (1978) describes seven levels of living systems: cell, organ, organism, group, organization, society, and supranational. We will consider here two of these systems, the group and the organization. Miller offers helpful explanations of these terms: A *group* is a set of single organisms, commonly called members, that over a period of time or multiple interrupted periods, relate to one another face-to-face, processing matter-energy and information. An *organization* is a system whose components and subsystems may be subsidiary organizations, groups, and persons; it is also a subsystem of one or more societies.

We can use a systems approach to analyze functional interrelationships in a group or organization. People in organizations enter into a "psychological contract"; they contribute their energy and information in return for role definition and compensation, which may take the form of money, benefits, or other types of rewards. In the modern corporation, for example, management is permitted to exercise power and authority over workers, but the employees enforce their expectations by giving or withholding work effort and energy. It is the quality of management relationships with personnel that influences performance and determines the success of organizational outcomes such as products and services.

In Chapter 2, we discussed the concept of life space, and in Chapter 4, we examined how culture contributes to the sense of space experienced by a whole people. Organizations, and work units or groups in organizations, are also set apart by and identified by physical and psychological space. Again, organizational culture contributes to this process of delineation and demarcation. Individuals who belong to a group, must integrate their life space with the life space of the group.

There are forces in both the individuals and institutions that influence behavior: image, needs, values, ideas, principles, standards, and expectations. Sometimes these may be in conflict and cause "binds" or frustrations for members, for instance, when individual values conflict with organizational values, or when employee norms are not in harmony with group standards. When managers are facilitators, they lead in resolving such conflicts and in promoting synergy between people and the enterprise. When organizational or group change is sought, these same forces may be seen as driving or restraining. Exhibit 5.1 shows this interplay of forces on behavior and relationships in terms of the system, the individual, and other significant people (e.g., coworkers, family, customers, suppliers). It is based on an analogy of taking pictures with a camera where we may get different images, so the operator seeks to bring these into focus by adjusting the lens. The four circles represent four differing life spaces and images which need to be synchronized.

The leader, like all group members, has a self-image and an image of the organization. The system, too, has an image of itself and of the individual. Other significant people related to the organization, such as managers or consultants, also have images of both the institution and its employees. As these images and spaces become more compatible or focused, performance is likely to improve. Thus, if an organization is committed to the value of quality work and excellence, the role of the leader is to focus the energies of followers so that they will be equally committed to that value, individually and as a team. By understanding organizational and group dynamics, leaders can synthesize differences and create consensus. For example, the *esprit de corps* and training system of the U.S. Marines has made it possible for countless drill sergeants to weld raw recruits from diverse backgrounds into successful fighting units.

The interplay of organizational relations influences the attitudes and

Exhibit 5.1 Conflicting Forces Affecting Work Relationships.

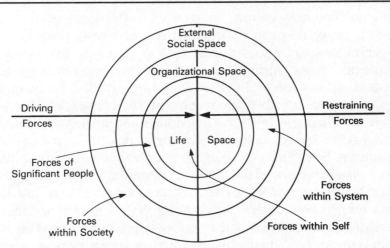

behavior of members. Leaders should learn not only how to cope wi. these forces in every individual or institution, but how to control and manage them, so as to actualize the person and the organization's potential. Leaders must do more, however, than exercise human relations skills to improve organizational relationships. The challenges to group leaders today are:

1. To provide for role enlargement, so that individual participation in the group and organization becomes more meaningful and effective.
2. To create temporary and supportive networks, groupings, and arrangements that cut across traditional divisions and promote cross-fertilization of ideas, knowledge, and specializations.
3. To increase the span of control, to increase employee participation in management controls, in order to enhance individual initiative and responsibility.
4. To decrease distance between people at various levels within the organization, removing barriers to organizational communications.

In essence, metaindustrial managers aim to dismantle hierarchies and to decentralize, so as to increase membership participation. With regard to organization relations, they behave as facilitators rather than as order-givers.

CHARACTERISTICS OF EFFECTIVE GROUPS

As social beings, humans take readily to group affiliation and formation. Some groups form naturally out of common interests or concerns. Others come into being because of a common task or assignment; for example, a product team. It is possible to study a group's behavior—that is, its personality, culture, interactions, relationships, and performance. Our discussion of groups will be in terms of such a work unit. A successful leader should understand his or her behavior in relation to the team, being able to observe the process and activities of the group.

Groups have ten characteristics that leaders may analyze. For instance, to assess team performance, a manager can ask the questions suggested in each category below.

1. *Group Background.* Every group develops a history. Individually, members contribute to the group's character by reason of their own attitudes, interests, feelings, and competencies. When a group

forms, each member has preconceived ideas and attitudes that influence directly the life and work of the group until that individual leaves it. What a group has experienced in the past affects its present and future. For example, technicians who work on a project team develop over time some unwritten agreements as to who does what and when; newcomers must discover these arrangements.

What is the team's history?

What traditions has it developed?

How does this affect relationships within the team and with other groups or the total organization?

2. *Group Participation Patterns.* Participation in group activities and accomplishment is one way in which power is exercised— members influence the behavior, direction, and work of the team. Teams develop patterns of member interaction, which frequently change. Some of these patterns show the high emphasis placed on status, politics, forcefulness, and competence. Participation patterns affect what members do in a group; for instance, an overly dominant member who talks 85 percent of the time reduces the participation possibilities for the others. On the other hand, when there is free and democratic exchange within the group, the opinions and input of all are sought and expressed equally.

Is there sufficient opportunity for participation in this team, so as to bring out what various members are able to contribute?

How do leader and members share participation and involvement?

3. *Group Communication Patterns.* The system of verbal and non-verbal communication within a group can be objectively analyzed. Who talks to whom? What do they say? What are the effects? In analyzing oral communication, leaders should look for clarity of expression, common vocabulary, and the results. The body language of members—posture, facial expression, and gestures—can also be studied. Top management should communicate quickly and easily with employee groups.

How clearly are the group's leader and members expressing their ideas?

Does everyone understand the group's mission and what is going on?

Are the verbal and nonverbal messages the same, and do they both aid communication?

4. *Group Cohesion.* When a group is working well together, it is attractive to members. Usually, cohesion is evident when elan or morale is high; members like one another, and are interdependent. Teamwork happens when people feel free to invest themselves in the group and contribute fully to the accomplishment of its tasks. Cohesion means that members work as one or as a unit for the common cause, and are concerned about the welfare of each member as well as that of the whole team.

How well does this collection of people work together as a team?

Do members help each other?

How willing are members to accept and act readily on group decisions?

5. *Group Atmosphere.* Cohesion depends in large part on atmosphere. To what degrees does the group permit informality, freedom of expression, and acceptance of individual differences? In an unfriendly, formal, and rigid situation, members are unwilling to be open and to express themselves, especially when authentic feelings and ideas may seem to be in conflict with the group's directions. Instead, members tend to say what authority figures want to hear, and group energies may be wasted. When the group climate encourages frankness and participation, it facilitates sharing, leveling, and creative exchange.

Do members really feel free to express themselves in this group?

How willing are members to listen and to share personal feelings or beliefs?

How would you rate the group on its friendliness and informality?

6. *Group Standards.* As a group, members adopt, formally or informally, norms of behavior. This results from the need to coordinate group effort and activities toward a common goal. Such standards provide a guide for adjusting individual needs and resources to the group's requirements. These norms stabilize group energies and contribute to cohesiveness and improved performance.

Has this group developed standards on member responsibilities or team discipline?

Are group expectations clear on such matters as ethics, operational behavior, protocol, dress (i.e., what distinguishes this team's culture)?

135

7. *Group Procedures.* Every group needs to define ways to get its work done. Whether formally set down or just commonly understood, procedures should help team effort; they should be adequate and appropriate, not burdensome. The job is made easier when procedures allow for flexibility and innovation. For example, procedures that allow quick and effective group decision-making are critical for high performance.

What kind of procedures does this group use to get its job done?

How appropriate are these in relation to the type of this job?

8. *Group Goals.* Members must agree on and accept the group's primary purposes. This is necessary, whether management has assigned the mission, or the group has established its own objectives and priorities, and whether the goals are long-range or immediate. When goals are clear and all endorse them, members tend to be more supportive and committed. Goals must also be realistic; when they are, group members are more enthusiastic. Group goals motivate the membership when they are compelling, offer mutual advancement, include interim objectives that are attainable, and are subject to alteration when the situation requires it.

Do members have a clear understanding of the group's goals?

Are the goals attainable given the group's resources?

Are members supportive of these goals?

9. *Group Leadership.* A group may have an appointed leader or an elected leader, or group members may share leadership functions. Sometime the designated leader, such as the project manager, is not the real leader; a "natural" leader may emerge. The trend today is toward democratic and participative, rather than authoritarian, leadership. Group leaders should be flexible and responsive to situations and people, able to use both formal and informal structures and communications. With knowledge workers, for instance, those in leadership roles must be helpful, open to experimentation, and capable of resolving conflict and attaining consensus. Much of what we discussed about organizational leadership in Chapter 1 also applies in terms of group leadership.

How is leadership influence exercised in this group?

How are leaders chosen and held accountable?

10. *Group Alignments.* Groups usually have subgroups and affiliate with other groups with similar concerns. How many and what

kind of subgroups form depends on the group's size and make-up. Subgroups form because members have mutual needs or interests or because of shared friendship or antipathy toward other members or the group's direction. These subgroups change as tasks, forces, or issues change. Although subgroups are a normal occurrence, in the interest of healthy group relations, leaders should be aware of them and ready to respond creatively. For example, the formation of cliques based soley on race, gender, sexual preference, harmful habits (e.g., substance abuse), or resentment of some perceived exploitation, may undermine group effort unless confronted. Similarly, groups interface with other groups, and may form coalitions or working relations, so as to be mutually helpful.

What subgroups exist?

Do they tend to work together as a whole, or do they dissipate group energies?

What are the needs, issues, or forces behind the formation of these subgroups?

How does this group deal with other groups, and for what purpose?

These ten categories provide a handy way for leaders to assess group performance; later we will provide instruments for this process (page 158).

IMPROVING GROUP PERFORMANCE

In the emerging high-tech work environment, executives and those in leadership positions will have to know more than finance, marketing, and technology. They will be leading workers into uncharted waters, and they need skills to transform the work culture. We have already indicated what some of these skills will be, including knowledge of group dynamics.

Consider, as a case in point, the challenges to group interaction and group leadership that will be posed by establishment of a lunar outpost and space colonies. NASA's 1985 report, *Living Aloft: Human Requirements for Extended Spaceflight,* examines such issues as habitability, performance, organization, and management. What concerns us here is the section on small groups. Space crews are becoming larger and more heterogeneous, and space missions are longer. Living together in what amounts to a microsociety, astronauts depend for survival on cooperation. The isolation and confinement spacefarers must face has prompted space scientists to study the behavioral science research literature of the past 40 years on group process and performance.

The following summary of some of the insights that Connors, Harrison, and Atkins provided for that NASA report on NASA small group behavior may prove useful to managers on Earth concerned about high-performance teams:

- Social compatibility is a key ingredient in group member selection, because incompatibility severely hurts morale and performance; members need interpersonal, as well as technical, competence.
- Groups with members of both sexes offer the advantage of greater social diversity but may face conflict on issues such as gender stereotyping and sexual harassment. These and other issues involving sexual prejudice and gender roles, such as leadership and command, must be resolved beforehand.
- Groups with a broader age range and mix not only can work together effectively, but may possess greater human resources and experience.
- Multicultural groups may have a broad outlook and a wide range of skills, but they present special challenges for consideration in training regarding differences in perceptions and communications.
- Work groups benefit when members possess task competence, emotional stability, and cooperativeness (sensitivity to other people's needs and concern for other people's welfare).
- Work group members should be selected and trained for such desirable attitudes and skills; an important goal of selection and training is member compatibility (members have different but complementary needs and skills).
- Work groups should be composed with a concern for acceptable size and homeostasis (group equilibrium). The balance between group responsibilities and the number of members may even favor slight understaffing, so that people stretch themselves to perform, as long as health and safety are not jeopardized in the process.
- Group leadership and followership involves mutual influencing and task-sharing, and social and emotional interaction.
- Group cohesiveness or solidarity results from the rewards and satisfactions of group membership; it is high when members experi-

ence intrinsically satisfying group activities, goals of importance, social support, and emotional gratifications.

- Group harmony should not be sought at the expense of performance; "groupthink" may lead to undermining critical thought and result in poor decisions, false optimism, fear of disapproval for expressing new alternatives, denial or rationalization of warnings or ill omens, and illusions of unanimity.
- Group management of conflict should include dealing with deviancy, including reintegrating deviants into the team.
- Group performance involves an interaction process dependent upon three variables: the knowledge and skills of members; the amount of energy and effort members apply; and performance strategies and procedures followed (e.g., manipulating social standards—norms favoring conformity might undermine problem-solving, while those favoring innovation might favor creative risk-taking).
- Group continuity depends upon whether goals are long-term or short-term; effective long-term group relations require strategies and methods for introducing and assimilating newcomers so that they are not disruptive but learn to share the group's history and knowledge base.
- High performing teams develop a delicate balance between the independent action of individual members and the social influence of the group.

LEADERSHIP IN HIGH PERFORMANCE TEAMS

In the industrial age, organizational relationships tended to be long term; today, the new work culture often features intense, temporary relationships with colleagues. The high-performance business environment, for example, emphasizes team management and ad hoc relationships formed for task forces, product teams, and other time-limited work arrangements. Such groups come rapidly into being, function for a period, and then are phased out. Personnel must, therefore, learn to jump quickly into such task-oriented situations, establish connections and communications with coworkers from different disciplines or work units, and then disengage when the mission is accomplished. All this may happen while one maintains a dual relationship with another group that serves as one's base in manufacturing, marketing, finance, or information systems. This type of organization may be formalized through some type of matrix management system that involves reporting to two supervisors, one from the functional group and another who coordinates a special project. Once the special project is over the worker may be assigned to another temporary group, and the cycle repeats itself.

Organizational realities such as these make new demands upon leaders and knowledge workers to develop team skills. In previous volumes, the author has more extensively reviewed the phenomenon of team management (Harris, 1985, Chapter 8; Moran and Harris, 1982, Chapter 7). In the Interaction section of this chapter we will deal with the need for team-building. But what should our aim be in team development?

My research indicates that there are certain behaviors practiced by team members that help their relations with others in the group and with other groups in the organization. These behaviors include:

- Taking an interest in both individual and team accomplishment
- Tolerating ambiguity and the seeming lack of structure at times
- Giving and receiving feedback sensitively and nondefensively
- Creating a team atmosphere or culture that is informal, comfortable, and nonthreatening
- Encouraging team participation, joint-decision making, and consensus-seeking
- Being open to planned change, risk-taking, and innovation
- Valuing listening and circular communication
- Being concerned about strengthening team morale and commitment
- Clarifying roles, relationships, and responsibilities
- Fostering trust, supportive norms, and shared leadership
- Resolving conflicts and using this energy constructively
- Promoting cooperative and collaborative relations (synergy) among members and with other work units
- Being (as a team) goal-oriented, self-evaluating, and linked to other organizational groups.

Such behaviors not only improve organizational relations, but also the organization's effectiveness as an enterprise. A culture in which people act in this manner encourages positive social exchange and interpersonal interactions. The very differences in the perceptions of team members then become a source of strength for the team, enriching the mix of the inputs and insights. Realistically, individuals may disagree on such issues as team strategies, problem-solving, accountability, resources, and scheduling, but with synergistic attitudes, such differences can be resolved and built upon. As Andre Van Dam, director of planning for Corn Products Company-Latin America, once said to me:

> Admittedly, cooperation requires trade-offs between rival ideas or interests—trade-offs imply negotiation. Cooperation hinges upon the recognition of common as well as conflicting interests.

The above characteristics can enhance team relations and performance particularly in regard to two critical factors, decision-making and conflict management. Leadership ensures that such collaborative teams function in this manner (Reddy, 1988).

IMPROVING TEAM DECISIONS

The character of a group is influenced by the way the group makes decisions; this process can foster or undermine the entity's progress. Ideally, decision-making should be integrative, that is, it should advance the common good of the group. Psychologist Eric Fromm maintains that the more one learns through making choices, the more one becomes truly free (instead of being limited by acting upon instinct, cultural conditioning, or provincial interests). When people are given the opportunity to exercise control over team choices, the group becomes a democratic laboratory for people to grow in decision-making skills. When those who must implement the decision are involved in the choices, not only is the decision likely to be better, follow-up on the decision is likely to be more thorough.

If freedom of choice is a prevailing norm, personal growth takes place as group members become aware of possibilities, alternatives, and consequences of following a specific course of action. Teams now have added technological resources to help with this process, for instance, improved information retrieval, system and program analysis, computer simulations, and decision-tree methodology (Gerstein, 1988; Schein, 1987, 1988).

Team decisions are further enriched when other, previously discussed characteristics of effective groups are present, such as com-

141

petent members, mutual trust, and shared leadership. Poor communications within the team, conflicting loyalties, and internal ego struggles, on the other hand, weaken a group's resolve and undermine the decision process. A too-rigid decision-making procedure may also inhibit imagination and thus group problem-solving. Premature decisions based upon inadequate information can also prove fatal.

If team decisions that improve performance are to be made, then members have first to consider the quantity and quality of the information available upon which to base a choice. Obviously, if it is inadequate, further data-gathering and analysis are called for. The next step is the adoption of the problem-solving method. This may range from the (less desirable) parliamentary procedure to (more useful) consensus approach. Scientific models, such as PERT (Program Evaluation and Review Technique), can be effective.

Exhibit 5.2 discusses strategies for problem-solving in groups devised by the late behavioral scientist, Gordon Lippitt. It is an eight-stage procedure for team members to follow when major decisions are at stake. As people increase in awareness and knowledge through the group decision experience, their potential grows for making better, informed, intelligent choices. When leaders are autocratic and make the decisions for the followers, they cut off these development prospects and endanger the organization's future growth. (Refer to Lippitt, Langseth, and Mossop, 1985.)

TEAM CONFLICT RESOLUTION

There was a time when leaders considered conflict a negative factor within organizational life, something to be avoided at all costs. This "happy ship" approach to conflict has given way to a more balanced strategy, in which a reasonable amount of conflict is permitted, to maintain a healthy tension and excitement in the group. Conflict management should be considered in the context of corporate industrial relations policies (Bomers and Peterson, 1982), and should become part of a "win-win" strategy of negotiations (Jandt, 1985). When conflict is viewed as energy, to be used instead of abused, its proper management can stimulate group action in place of boring conformity. Limited conflict among team members, for instance, may contribute to optimizing satisfaction and performance efforts.

Exhibit 5.2   Team Problem-Solving Strategies.

1. Clearly *define the problem:* Set the limits of group responsibility and provide necessary clarifications. Analyze resources available for solutions and conditions involved in the problem.
2. Define the *responsibility for decisions:* Who has the ultimate authority to make the decision? If the group is to assume this responsibility, then the degree of its freedom to act should be understood.
3. *Communicate ideas and alternative solutions:* Consider a wide variety of creative and innovative ways to resolve the problem without evaluation; here is where brainstorming may be an effective technique.
4. *Examine the group size:* Should the group be too large for effective decision-making, it may be preferable to break into subgroups to consider the problem and then reassemble to consider the data developed in the smaller groups.
5. *Test alternative solutions:* Through simulation or projection into the future, the group can imagine results based on certain courses of action; trials or pilot projects may be made of selected alternatives, to provide data for appropriate decisions at a later time. Consider the demands various solutions will make upon individual and group resources.
6. *Responsibility and delegation:* During the planning, the group needs to think about how various decisions are to be carried out. What commitment will be required of various members for a decision to become effective?
7. *Method of decision-making:* Before the issue is resolved, the group must first reach agreement on the procedures to be used in arriving at a decision. What criteria and standards will be used in choosing one alternative over another?
8. *Action and evaluation:* When the group has made final its choice then it must organize itself to carry out the decisions. Individual or committee or project assignments need to be made and accepted. Finally, a means to evaluate the decision is necessary in case it should prove to be unwise.

When conflict is properly managed, it may bring more input, wider consideration of alternatives, and improved solutions. In its positive aspects, conflict can identify issues that have not been confronted or problems that are not recognized. Had the crew of Skylab 4 not gotten into conflict with their ground controllers, those astronauts might have remained saddled with a work schedule that could have undermined their morale and impaired their performance (NASA, 1985). If conflicting views with other groups or within a team are synthesized, not only may a better solution emerge, but participants are more committed to making it work. Such disagreements, when professionally handled, can force the contending parties to identify mutually beneficial goals or arrangements (Walton, 1987).

Obviously, conflict, whether in an individual or institutional situation, can prove dysfunctional and can undermine peak performance. To contain the destructive elements in conflict energy, social scientists have developed two models of conflict management—structural and process (Thomas, 1976).

The structural model traces conflict to four sources:

- Behavioral predispositions related to individual inadequacies, in turn related to attitudes, needs, motivation, competence, and other personality qualities. Conflict can arise when the person with these problems projects them onto the group.
- Social pressures from within a group or with other groups, or from outside persons or systems.
- Incentive structures. The distribution of rewards to both cooperative or noncooperative actions, or the existence of a conflict of interest, can cause conflict.
- Procedural arrangements manifested in rules, regulations, customs, and conventions which may be open to differences in interpretation or become inoperative and ineffective.

The process conflict model, on the other hand, focuses on five variables related to specific episodes of disagreement:

- Perceived frustration in the satisfaction of a need or achievement of a goal.
- Conceptualizations based on individual perceptions that may be distorted and magnify one's frustrations.
- Behavior that maximizes or minimizes the conflict.
- Behavior by the other party (reaction) that may escalate, contain, or deescalate conflict.
- Outcomes, including resolution and future cooperation, compromise and accommodation, and mistrust and hostility. (Refer to Schein [1987] for insight on process consultation.)

As we understand more about conflict and its causes, team members can learn to cope with it better and not to react with panic. A staff meeting or group training session can be devoted to examining this issue. Exhibit 5.3 provides eight points for stimulating meaningful analysis. Conflict can be managed, rather than denied or dealt with by flight-or-fight behavior. When conflict in groups is not confronted

Exhibit 5.3 Dimensions of Conflict. (This material can be used for Input Bombardment—for details on this group process see page 45; each group member might then be assigned one point to read, react to, and report upon to the whole team or training class.)

The following ideas are presented to stimulate small group discussion about the subject of conflict, whether it is between individuals or groups.

1. *Conflict is a Relationship:* It takes at least two persons, groups or even nations to have a conflict. Do we permit the experience to develop so that issues, not personalities, can be confronted? Exploring differences can result in useful insight and information IF we do not cut off the relationship before data is sufficiently generated for analysis.
2. *Conflict is Energy:* Human effort is necessary to maintain it, so the critical question is whether we can use this energy constructively or permit it to be wasted. Conflicts cannot always be resolved when their source, for example, is a sick sense of self. Sometimes the individuals have to be honest with one another and "agree to disagree" while respecting one another.
3. *Conflict Can be Defused or Unfused:* If we do not deliberately seek and promote conflict, there are strategies which a leader can pursue to minimize unnecessary conflict in the organization or community. When the situation that can lead to conflict is not yet critical, when it is still simmering, an innovative supervisor can "head it off at the pass!" Like the bomb detection squad that deactivates weapons of potential destruction, a manager can confront or resolve situations that might end up in serious conflict. He or she can keep combustibles apart and can deal with differences of opinion before they get out of hand.
4. *Conflict is Aided by Hardening of Positions:* When people become inflexible and rigid out of a sense of fear or threat, they tend to set hard boundary rules, to draw lines and dare anyone to step over, to polarize in their positions. In periods of profound transition, like today, conflict seems to be growing as people experience "future shock." Pluralistic societies require cooperation rather than dogged adherence to past traditions and positions.
5. *Persons are in Conflict:* Human relationships are strained, tension is increased and emotions run high during conflict situations. Reason can work only when the situation is "cooled," objectivized rather than subjectivized. Keep in focus that "feelings" are involved, and try to shift discussion to the issues. Yet it is just as bad to over-emphasize the inter-personal elements in conflict as it is to de-personalize inter-group conflict.
6. *Conflict Involves Perception:* The apparent conflict may sometimes be caused by misunderstanding or misperception of the situation. Clarify each persons true position, and you might discover that there is no real conflict, or at least it is not so great that it cannot be handled.
7. *The Opposite of Conflict is Collaboration:* One way to reduce undesirable conflict in organizations is to encourage team building, consulting skills and the development of a "helping relationship" among staff.
8. *Conflict happens because people are different:* People come from different cultural, social, educational backgrounds, which form or condition their unique viewpoints and opinions.

---

and resolved, members may resort to fantasy or delusion in its regard. Leaders learn to understand conflict in themselves or others, deal with its symptoms and sources, and make use of resources for mediation.

Those who would exercise leadership need to remind themselves that people make up groups and institutions. In *Managing for Excellence,* Bradford and Cohen (1984) point out that motivated employees undertake even routine jobs creatively, and become candidates for greater responsibility and productivity. Management relationships can either turn people on or off—people may feel they are being manipulated or imposed upon or they may be inspired and energized. For truly high performance, leaders give high priority to organizational and team relations that are positive and supportive.

INTERACTION

Among the many group process opportunities for improving organizational relationships, team building is among the most valuable. Team building is most effective when it uses an internal or external consultant familiar with the process, although a concerned manager who is a good facilitator can conduct such sessions with the help of management development texts, instruments, and films. (See Appendix A, Directory of Human Resource Organizations and Publications.) Team building can improve team relations among group members and improve intergroup relations among various teams or work units. Team building meetings aim at group maintenance and consider such performance issues as

- How do we work together?
- How do we resolve conflict?
- How do we solve problems and make decisions?
- What are our roles and relationships on this team?
- What are our relationships with other groups?
- What changes are needed in how we function?

TEAM-BUILDING CONFERENCE

Who. Members of a work team or teams who must relate to each other and a facilitator from outside.

What. A series of intensive learning experiences about team structure, process, and relationships.

When. With the start-up of a team, when a group's performance level drops, or when the group is having difficulties with other teams.

Where. Begin away from the work site, for instance at a conference center, or weekend resort; continued with monthly meetings in an on-site company meeting room or training facility.

Why. To improve team collaboration and performance by

- Clarifying team expectations, goals, resources, and potential.
- Analyzing interpersonal dynamics.
- Confronting and clarifying issues that block mission accomplishment.
- Examining team relations with other work units or external groups.
- Developing leadership skills in communication, cooperation, problem-solving, and conflict resolution.

How. By structured exercises, role playing, data-gathering, and analysis, as well as problem-solving, the group learns how to work together more efficiently and effectively. Members are urged to

- Be experimental—test out new styles of behavior, communication, participation, and leadership.
- Be authentic and open—tell it like it is and avoid game-playing, while considering others' viewpoints.
- Be sensitive—express feelings while emphathizing with others; be attuned to nonverbal cues and communication.
- Be spontaneous and helpful—respond creatively to here-and-now data shared in the group, warmly receiving people's revelations of themselves and sharing yourself while assisting other members.

The team-building conference not only develops meaningful relations among members, but enables them to become more trusting and congruent (comfortable with themselves and their capacities). It is a challenge to participants to revise their self-images and to actualize their potential through personal and group change. The learning experience aids members to gain control over their own team space and to risk becoming what they are capable of becoming. If a company or agency does not have a competent facilitator on its staff to conduct the team building, external consultants in organization development or transformation are available. (Refer to Dyer, 1987; Greiner and Schein, 1988.) Dr. Ray Forbes of Northwest Airlines calls such resources "organization services."

THE HELPING RELATIONSHIP EXERCISE

People have many opportunities to promote organizational effectiveness by practice of the "helping relationship," for example when a manager gives feedback to a subordinate, when a coworker seeks assistance in solving a problem, or when a customer or supplier needs information or service. Despite the best of intentions, our "help" is seldom really helpful, particularly with colleagues or team members. To enable people to grasp this important concept and become skillful in its application, I recommend the S/H/O method. This method involves a triad of team members—a seeker of help (S), a helper (H), and an observer (O). They decide among themselves who takes what role, and they may later switch roles until all members have played all three. Although this strategy can be used with actual or simulated issues, I urge the "seeker" to bring a real problem related to a team or work unit. The manager or facilitator sets the ground rules for the process, such as a time schedule (e.g., 5 to 15 minutes for each role—for S to present the problem, H to counsel on solutions, and O to offer analysis and comments upon observations made). If the length of the staff meeting or training session permits, then the process can be repeated twice more until all three experience all roles.

While S presents the problem, H carefully listens to comprehend its scope and may ask questions for clarification purposes. When the sequence shifts to the helping time frame, H then assists, consults, or counsels. The observer is both a time-keeper and note-taker for the process. Exhibit 5.4 provides the criteria to be read and used by O in his or her evaluation of the helping relationship underway. Later, when O shares findings with the other two, a copy of these guidelines can be distributed and discussed among the triad. O can begin the feedback session by asking the seeker if that person actually received any help from H. The principal learning outcomes for the members involved should be to learn the nature and importance of an interpersonal relationship, which are:

- *Accepting*—An unconditional, positive regard of the other person's worth is manifested
- *Authentic*—the helper is genuine in approach and does not play games at the expense of the seeker of help
- *Empathetic*—the helper expresses understanding, is neutral, and places himself or herself in the other's life space

Exhibit 5.4 Criteria for a Helping Relationship.

Guidelines for Observers

The helper is in effect a consultant who provides added resources and a means for permitting the one in need to reflect more objectively upon his problem. The helper seeks to assist the other person to mobilize his own capacities to resolve the issue at hand or to develop his potential. The helper must first check his own reasons for wanting to give help; is it merely to gain recognition? to demonstrate superiority? to exercise power over another? to be a do-gooder? or to make the other person dependent upon him? Whose needs does he seek to serve—his own or the other person's? Furthermore, he should be able to listen and to let the other person exercise some responsibility in developing solutions.

On the other hand, the receiver of help must be ready and willing to accept assistance from another; he must face up to those inadequacies which make it necessary for him to obtain outside help. The receiver must be able to lower his own defenses if help is to be effective and to offer an open mind to the communication of the helper. The receiver must avoid undue dependency on the helper while realizing that the particular competence of the helper may enable the receiver to tap unused inner strengths in resolving the problems he faces.

Individuals can best give help to one another when the atmosphere in an organization permits expression of true feelings, when intimacy and flexibility are possible in behavior and when change is an accepted norm. Unfortunately, many systems today are in need of renewal, and such an organizational environment is more ideal than real. One of the greatest means for personal growth within organizations is the process of feedback. It is a manifestation of real help when feedback or authentic communication is given and received freely in a sensitive, caring manner.

Feedback is that aspect of the communication process which allows for the expression of feelings, attitudes and thoughts so that behavior is affected.

In describing the feedback process, one authority states that feedback is a "device which makes an effort to carry out its given aim. The differences between the real and ideal effect are transformed into energy which is fed back into the mechanism and tends to cancel out the original differences which set the system in motion." Feedback, in a sense, is a system of messages or cues which are sent and received. When a message has been sent from the originator and received by another, and a second message returned to the originator, and the originator reacts to the feedback, the process has been completed. The implication in human relationships is that "feedback is a way of helping another person to consider changing his behavior." It can be seen as a mechanism for helping a person to learn how his behavior matches his intention. Thus feedback is more than just a mechanical process but rather a means to learn, to grow, and to "become." It can aid or abort organizational relations.

- *Nonevaluative*—the helper avoids being judgmental of the person with a problem and making that individual feel defensive.

The exercise encourages members to seek help from one another and to be collaborative.

INSTRUMENTATION

Management in Transition (1985) provides three instruments by the author related to the topics of this chapter. They and the one shown in Exhibit 5.5 are available in quantity.*

Organizational Roles and Relationship Inventory. To be used by a work unit or team to clarify each member's role in relationship to the other worker; during these times of rapid change in job functions and descriptions, this can be used in a team building exercise so as to better manage responsibility and conflict (#I 513).

Group Maturity Analysis. To be used by those observing group behavior and performance; it is a ten-item checklist for evaluating key factors in team development on a 5-point rating scale. It can also be employed by team members to evaluate themselves as a group, and results can be compared with observer's assessment (#I 503).

Team Synergy Analysis. To be used by supervisor, managers, and other professionals for self-assessment or synergistic attitudes and skills within a work unit, team or group. The self-evaluation is upon twenty-one items by means of a 4-point rating scale (#I 514).

INDIVIDUAL BEHAVIOR ANALYSIS (IBA)*

This instrument is designed to help in the diagnosis of the level of a person's interpersonal performance skills within a work unit, team, or group. The range of inquiry goes from ascertaining the extent to which that individual helps others express their ideas in group communication to determining how conflict is managed. The inventory

---

*Quantity copies of all instruments described in this section may be obtained from Management Research Systems/Talico Inc., 2320 S. Third St. #7, Jacksonville Beach, FL 32250. © Philip R. Harris/Harris International, 1986.

can be for self assessment or for evaluation of another. A 5-point rating scale is employed on thirty-six items in which the respondent is to choose the word which best describes the individual's performance— always, often, occasionally, seldom, or never. With the exception of items 10, 12, 18, and 22, selection of the last three rating possibilities usually indicates a need for improvement. The instrument can be used for self-improvement purposes, for use during performance evaluation between a leader and team member, or for group discussion during team building.

TEAM PERFORMANCE SURVEY (TPS)*

TPS can be used for data gathering before or after a team-building session. Members of project teams or other work units can use the survey to evaluate a group's progress and problems from an individual perspective. Then the participants can compare their selection on the twenty-five items for further discussion, clarification, and learning.

To record total group scores, a matrix can be drawn on a blackboard or flip chart with the four columns on which the headings or choices are written horizontally across the top; yes, sometimes, no, uncertain. Vertically on the left side, insert the numbers 1 to 26. Each team member would then be invited to place their personal rating checks for all items on the display matrix for other members to see. By tallying up the results for the group on each item, trouble spots in team relations then could be identified. For example, with reference to item 1, in a team of eight persons, if four of them marked "no" and 1 checked "uncertain," the majority indicate that the group's goals are uncertain. In this way, a leader and team can diagnose the healthiness of the group's development and where improvements are desirable for increased performance. (Refer to Exhibit 5.6).

SPECIALIZED RESOURCES

Regarding the three key themes in this chapter, you may wish to consult these volumes: *Team Building: Issues and Alternatives* by W. Dyer (Reading, MA: Addison-Wesley, 1987); *Creative Problem Solving: A Guide for Trainers and Management* by A. B. VanGundy (Westport, CT: Greenwood Press, 1987). Other books and learning materials on these topics are available from University Associates, Inc. (8517

Exhibit 5.5 Individual Behavior Analysis (Team Member).

Group ————————
Date ————————

Name of person you are describing:

The person you are describing is: (Check one)
————— myself
————— my superior
————— my subordinate
————— my peer
————— other
Please specify ———————————————————————
———————————————————————————————
———————————————————————————————

Instructions: Following are listed thirty-six descriptions of ways in which people participate in group meetings. For each item, choose the alternative which comes closest to picturing how the person you are describing performs in meetings.

Answer the items by marking an "x" on the line in front of the alternative that best expresses your feelings about the item. Mark only one alternative for each item.

Keep in mind that you are describing this person's behavior in meetings and not how you have seen him/her perform in other settings.

1. Helps others express their ideas.
————— always
————— often
————— occasionally
————— seldom
————— never
2. Tries to understand the feelings (anger, impatience, rejection) which others in the group express.
————— always
————— often
————— occasionally
————— seldom
————— never

Exhibit 5.5   Individual Behavior Analysis (Team Member), *cont'd.*

3. Shows intelligence.
   _____ always
   _____ often
   _____ occasionally
   _____ seldom
   _____ never
4. Sympathizes with others when they have difficulties.
   _____ always
   _____ often
   _____ occasionally
   _____ seldom
   _____ never
5. Expresses ideas clearly and concisely.
   _____ always
   _____ often
   _____ occasionally
   _____ seldom
   _____ never
6. Expresses own feelings (for example, when he/she is angry, impatient, ignored).
   _____ always
   _____ often
   _____ occasionally
   _____ seldom
   _____ never
7. Is open to the ideas of others; looks for new ways to solve problems.
   _____ always
   _____ often
   _____ occasionally
   _____ seldom
   _____ never
8. Is tolerant and accepting of other people's feelings.
   _____ always
   _____ often
   _____ occasionally
   _____ seldom
   _____ never
9. He/she thinks quickly.
   _____ always
   _____ often
   _____ occasionally
   _____ seldom
   _____ never

Continued

Exhibit 5.5   Individual Behavior Analysis (Team Member), *cont'd.*

10. Is angry or upset when things do not go his/her way.
    _____ always
    _____ often
    _____ occasionally
    _____ seldom
    _____ never

11. Is persuasive, a "seller of ideas."
    _____ always
    _____ often
    _____ occasionally
    _____ seldom
    _____ never

12. You can tell quickly when he/she likes or dislikes what others do or say.
    _____ always
    _____ often
    _____ occasionally
    _____ seldom
    _____ never

13. Listens and tries to use the ideas raised by others in the group.
    _____ always
    _____ often
    _____ occasionally
    _____ seldom
    _____ never

14. Helps others in the group to express their feelings (for example, when they are irritated or upset).
    _____ always
    _____ often
    _____ occasionally
    _____ seldom
    _____ never

15. Demonstrates high technical or professional competence.
    _____ always
    _____ often
    _____ occasionally
    _____ seldom
    _____ never

16. Is warm and friendly with those with whom he/she works.
    _____ always
    _____ often
    _____ occasionally
    _____ seldom
    _____ never

Exhibit 5.5   Individual Behavior Analysis (Team Member), *cont'd.*

17. Is able to get the attention of others.
    _____ always
    _____ often
    _____ occasionally
    _____ seldom
    _____ never
18. Communicates feelings. He/she doesn't have a "poker face" front.
    _____ always
    _____ often
    _____ occasionally
    _____ seldom
    _____ never
19. Is quick to adopt new ideas.
    _____ always
    _____ often
    _____ occasionally
    _____ seldom
    _____ never
20. Encourages others to talk about whatever is bothering them.
    _____ always
    _____ often
    _____ occasionally
    _____ seldom
    _____ never
21. Comes up with good ideas.
    _____ always
    _____ often
    _____ occasionally
    _____ seldom
    _____ never
22. Pride is hurt when feels has not done his/her best.
    _____ always
    _____ often
    _____ occasionally
    _____ seldom
    _____ never
23. Pursues his/her points aggressively.
    _____ always
    _____ often
    _____ occasionally
    _____ seldom
    _____ never

Continued

Exhibit 5.5 Individual Behavior Analysis (Team Member), *cont'd.*

24. You usually know where you stand with him/her.
_____ always
_____ often
_____ occasionally
_____ seldom
_____ never

25. Encourages others to express their ideas before he/she acts.
_____ always
_____ often
_____ occasionally
_____ seldom
_____ never

26. Tries to help when others become angry or upset.
_____ always
_____ often
_____ occasionally
_____ seldom
_____ never

27. Tries out new ideas.
_____ always
_____ often
_____ occasionally
_____ seldom
_____ never

28. Is competitive. Likes to win and hates to lose.
_____ always
_____ often
_____ occasionally
_____ seldom
_____ never

29. Presents ideas convincingly.
_____ always
_____ often
_____ occasionally
_____ seldom
_____ never

30. Responds frankly and openly.
_____ always
_____ often
_____ occasionally
_____ seldom
_____ never

Exhibit 5.5 Individual Behavior Analysis (Team Member), *cont'd.*

31. Is willing to compromise or change.
    _____ always
    _____ often
    _____ occasionally
    _____ seldom
    _____ never

32. If others in the group become angry or upset, listens with understanding.
    _____ always
    _____ often
    _____ occasionally
    _____ seldom
    _____ never

33. Offers effective solutions to problems.
    _____ always
    _____ often
    _____ occasionally
    _____ seldom
    _____ never

34. Tends to be emotional.
    _____ always
    _____ often
    _____ occasionally
    _____ seldom
    _____ never

35. Talks in a way that others listen.
    _____ always
    _____ often
    _____ occasionally
    _____ seldom
    _____ never

36. When feelings run high, deals directly with them rather than changing the subject or smoothing the problem over.
    _____ always
    _____ often
    _____ occasionally
    _____ seldom
    _____ never

Exhibit 5.6 Team Performance Survey.

Directions:

Please consider each item relative to a specific work team or unit with which you are associated (e.g., a project or product team, or a task force).

Name of the Group you are describing: _____

Date: _____ 19_____

Please check for each item in the box which best describes your feelings or opinions about this group at this moment:

	YES	SOME-TIMES	NO	UNCER-TAIN
1. This group's goal or mission is quite clear to me.	____	____	____	____
2. The group's charter in terms of mandate, parameters, and time frame is evident to me.	____	____	____	____
3. My role and relationship to team members and other functional units is clearly understood by me.	____	____	____	____
4. The team shares with me a sense of being accountable individually for the group's results.	____	____	____	____
5. From my perspective, the material and human resources available to the group's tasks are adequate.	____	____	____	____
6. My competencies are sufficient to help this team accomplish its goal.	____	____	____	____
7. In my opinion, this team lacks some members in the organization who are vital to its success.	____	____	____	____
8. The team works well together and has cohesion.	____	____	____	____
9. The members of this group do not feel free to level with one another, hiding true opinions and feelings.	____	____	____	____

Exhibit 5.6   Team Performance Survey, *cont'd.*

	Y	S	N	U
10. Some members of this team seem to be psychologically threatened by me.	___	___	___	___
11. To be effective, this group has to deal with the differences within it, instead of ignoring or smoothing over them for task accomplishment.	___	___	___	___
12. This group has the skills within it to deal effectively with its differences and disagreements.	___	___	___	___
13. This group communicates at both the cognitive (I think) and affective (I feel) levels of interaction.	___	___	___	___
14. This team provides individual support to members when needed.	___	___	___	___
15. This group regularly gives recognition and encouragement to me.	___	___	___	___
16. This team facilitates member involvement and seeks their opinions.	___	___	___	___
17. This group fosters my participation and positively re-inforces my contributions.	___	___	___	___
18. The leadership in this team is shared.	___	___	___	___
19. Members play a variety of roles in this group, and no one person dominates.	___	___	___	___
20. This group welcomes my input and feedback.	___	___	___	___
21. This team is committed to cooperation and collaboration among members and with other groups.	___	___	___	___
22. This group values competence and high performance.	___	___	___	___
23. This team inspires my best effort.	___	___	___	___
24. Our members work well together.	___	___	___	___
25. This team pauses occasionally from pursuit of its tasks to improve group maintenance and functioning.	___	___	___	___

Production Ave., San Diego, CA 92121). Films and videos on these subjects may be obtained from CRM Films (2233 Faraday, Suite F, Carlsbad, CA 92008). The latter include offerings on "Team Building," "Group Productivity." In addition to obtaining catalogs from the above sources, you may wish to write for research reports (#110, "Power, Influence and Authority; #122, "Trade Routes: The Manager's Network of Relationships;" #124, "Fixing Relationships Through Joint Action." These are available from the Center for Creative Leadership (5000 Laurinda Drive, Greensboro, NC 27402). The Whole Person Press (1702 E. Jefferson St., Duluth, MN 55803) has book/tape series worth examining, such as: *Working with Men's Groups* by R. Karsk and B. Thomas and *Working with Women's Groups* (2 volumes) by L. Y. Eberhardt. The same publisher also offers practical handbooks (2 volumes) on *Structured Exercises in Stress Management* by N. L. Tubesing and D. A. Tubesing (1983 release). Other materials may be obtained from the Directory of Human Resource Organizations and Publications (Appendix A).

Leading in the Management of Change

In these turbulent times of transition, a high-performance work environment requires continuous planned change by both the organization and its people. Change must be built in to both institutional and individual systems, so that we learn to operate on the basis of a new work norm—*ultrastability*. Whereas the maintenance of stability was characteristic of the more static industrial age, the metaindustrial work culture demands a more dynamic leadership, which establishes innovation as standard operating procedure.

Coping with, that is, planning and controlling, is one of the most important skills required of modern management. Change happens at all levels—social, technological, financial, and individual forces are altering the way we live and do business. Consultants such as Tom Peters (1987) maintain that tomorrow's winners learn to deal with chaos and learn to thrive on it, while Robert Waterman (1987) echoes his colleague but focuses upon renewing institutions so they can more effectively serve human needs. To meet the challenge, transformational leadership, including effective management of change, is necessary.

Our first objective in this chapter is to look at the why and what of planned change. Managers need the "big picture" of what is happening to work and culture as we create a new information society in preparation for twenty-first-century life. As management expert Peter Drucker (1985) warned:

> If the big companies and big institutions do not innovate, change, and acquire entrepreneurial competence, the social costs of their obsolence and eventual failure may be un-bearable to society.

We will examine the transitional experience connected with major life changes and the relationship between culture and change, and we will look at some of the new methods of future research and technological forecasting.

The second objective is to consider planning for change: how to develop the skills of a change agent. It is impossible to review all of the various techniques for managing change, so we will focus on *force field analysis,* a strategy for analyzing the driving or resisting forces of change within the organization or individual. We will also discuss *organization development (OD)* and *organizational transformation (OT),* strategic planning and management, and ways to renew systems and position a company on the competitive edge. The outcomes should include some definite action plans for both organizational and personal change.

INPUT

Contemporary executives are confounded by such trends as the corporate mania for mergers, takeovers, and joint ventures. Leaders in established industries try to cope with the forces unleashed by deregulation and divestiture (McManus and Hergert, 1988). Managers struggle to adapt in a new business climate in which traditional procedures of managing, manufacturing, and marketing give way to such applications technology as automation and robotics.

In the new work culture, innovation and creativity are now norms of organizational behavior (Harris, 1987, pp. 555-566). Exhibit 6.1 summarizes the generally accepted role of leadership in managing change. Books, training programs, and business school courses now abound on this theme. Among the excellent references on change and transformation in Appendix B at the end of this book, I recommend: Kilmann and Covin (1988); Beckhard (1987); Gerstein (1987); Lippitt et al. (1985); and London (1988).

Researchers in future studies also are producing works on the subject, among them *Mastering Change: The Key to Business Success* (Martel, 1986) and *Vanguard Management* (O'Toole, 1985). In fact, visionary scholars are reminding organizational leaders of their emerg-

Exhibit 6.1   Leadership in the Management of Change

The Challenge

Because of acceleration in the rate of change, critical factors in modern management are to:

- ☐ be proactive—rather than reactive—to change;
- ☐ develop the means for planned change;
- ☐ utilize proven procedures for controlling change.

The Definition

Since change is characteristic of all life and growth, it is:

- ☐ dynamic—the word is synonymous with "evolution" and the opposite of "static";
- ☐ an alteration in relationships because of *new* information, inventions, situations, people;
- ☐ a shifting in the present equilibrium or balance (the current status quo).

The Organization

The organization is a system, and relative to *change,* it:

- ☐ allocates and plans changes in energy efforts by human and material resources;
- ☐ innovates to survive and develop—this involves retooling, redesign, reassignment, retraining, and review;
- ☐ is neutral, in that change is neither good nor bad in itself, but depends on surrounding factors and circumstances.

The Manager of Change

The manager of change:

- ☐ stimulates innovation and creativity in the achieving of goals;
- ☐ is concerned with being proactive in regard to both personal and organization aims;
- ☐ anticipates needed, constructive changes for increased effectiveness;
- ☐ subjects goals, objectives, and targets to continuous reevaluation and possible change;
- ☐ plans and controls change by creating mechanisms for continuous, dynamic change;
- ☐ makes choices about which changes can be realistically undertaken, given the limitations of time and resources;
- ☐ initiates the selected changes with the maximum of employee cooperation and the minimum of destructive disturbance.

ing role, for instance, in *Transformational Management* (Kozmetsky, 1985) and *Information Payoff: The Transforming of Work in an Electronic Age* (Strassman, 1985). Also see *An Agenda for the 21st Century* (Kidder, 1988); *The Information Imperative: Managing the Impact of Information Technology on Businesses and People* (Gibson and Jackson, 1987); and *Handbook for Creative and Innovative Managers* (Kuhn, 1987). The case for change to gain or restore an organization's competitive edge can be made best by key executives. They seek to comprehend the baffling changes in the business environment, which require them to rethink every aspect of their operations—from how many workers are needed to where to invest hard-earned profits. Some companies shrink while others expand; some dump unprofitable activities while others invest in automation or entrepreneurial ventures (Brandt, 1986). The acceleration of change demands speedy critical decisions and unprecedented risk-taking; to meet these demands, leaders must foster a faster-reacting, entrepreneurial culture in the organization. Listen to these recent observations of corporate leaders in the *Los Angeles Times* (Loden, 1985; Broader, 1985; Whitefield, 1985) about their "forced strategic self-analysis":

- Corporations are going through wrenching change because you are experiencing a revolutionary era when critical decisions are being made to preserve the future of American industry. (Richard M. Cyert, President, Carnegie-Mellon University)
- The company has to be concerned about future life of the institution. . . . You either make strategic adaptations or go the way of all flesh . . . The transformation of Motorola has made the company more dependent upon technology and less on human labor, particularly in the United States. (William J. Weisz, Vice Chairman, Motorola Corporation)
- Restructuring is a euphemism for struggling to adapt. This is business Darwinism—the dinosaurs didn't survive because they couldn't adapt. (Irwin Kellner, Chief Economist, Manufacturers Hanover Bank).
- The smart managers are redeploying assets and cutting their costs. . . . They're taking advantage of emerging technologies because they realize if they don't plan and invest for the future, there won't be one. (Carl Shrawder, management consultant, Coopers & Lybrand)
- Companies have always been interested in the new venture. But what makes the romance so much more serious is that all the pieces—entrepreneuring, decentralizing, venturing, restructuring—

are finally coming all together. (Rosabeth Moss Kanter, Professor, Yale University; author, *The Change Makers*)

Such insights into American industry result in the abandonment of the pyramidal and paramilitary style of organizations; corporate giants like GE, for example, are becoming leaner as they cut layers of management. Simultaneously, innovation, entrepreneurialism, and new venture incubators are "in," along with many other forms of creative change. It is important, however, to put this transition into some context, and for leaders to have the larger perspective. It is necessary to understand the why and what of such change.

Exhibit 6.2 provides an overview of changes in human development, and Exhibit 6.3 illustrates the model in terms of human activities at various stages in that evolution. The diagram is based on data from U.S. Bureau of Labor statistics and includes this writer's forecasts of the postindustrial or metaindustrial stage of development underway now and proceeding into the twenty-first century. The latter stage is summarized in the description of the Cybercultural Person. I foresee a dramatic increase in time spent in creative leisure and lifelong continuing education. The term *cyberculture* was coined by MIT physicist Norbert Weiner to describe the emerging society dominated by cybernation (the science of communication and control in man and machines). Cyberculture is the unfolding information culture centered around advanced automation and communication technologies, including the widespread use of computers, robotics, and artificial intelligence.

THE MEANING FOR MANAGEMENT

The "rural" mindset, values and ideals must give way to the realities of superindustrial life. The "industrial age" management philosophy, assumptions, policies, practices, and technologies, as well as rules, regulations, and traditions must undergo scrutiny and some elimination. They must be replaced by more tentative, relevant approaches that speak to the more informed, technologically/ecologically oriented worker in cyberculuture. The vocational shift is away from involving people in the production of things to more personnel in research, education, service, and new career and recreational activities. To this, add improved capabilities in transportation and communication, and management is in a "whole new ball game." It requires learning about *new* players, rules, plays, and operating in a wholly different "ball park."

Exhibit 6.2   Change Implications for Management

The Scope of Human Development

One way of viewing history is to conceive it in terms of four major stages and three significant turning points—all of which impacts on our culture, society, world of work, and way of working. Such happenings imprint themselves on human attitudes and thinking processes. Furthermore, human experiences in past and present provide the input for future planning.

□ *First stage, hunting*—survival level of human existence; the primitive hunter operates on a day-to-day basis in tribes and as a nomad; took millions of years for main body of humankind.

Agricultural Revolution   First major turning point in human history.

□ *Second stage, farming*—plant seed, domesticate animals, save up for to-morrow; settle down, cluster, build villages and civilization; security level of human needs; took thousands of years.

Industrial Revolution   Second turning point, from about the 17th century onward.

□ *Third stage, industrialization*—machines and assembly line replaces brawn; factory worker largely displaces the farmer; the population shifts from rural areas to the city—urbanization; present living generations are largely influenced by the social legislations, institutions, and mindset of this industrial age which is only an introduction to what is happening now; greater movement upward on the need hierarchy toward socialization, recognition, reward; took only a few hundred years, but has produced periods of affluence and abundance.

Cybercultural Revolution   Third major turning point since end of World War II; now in early stages of impact and already causing "future shock": the beginning of the post- or superindustrial age resulting from a scientific/technological revolution.

□ *Fourth stage, cybernation*—links computer to machines to create advanced automated systems; knowledge workers and technicians displace traditional farmers and factory workers; cybernation speeds up quantity and quality of production, with less people; life more complex and interdependent; sharp increase in leisure time and in recreational/cultural pursuits; roles and institutions faced with crises and challenge of rapid change and renewal; individuals and society in state of profound transition to a new state of being; needs, value, norm systems in process of transformation; movement toward highest levels of need hierarchy of self-actualization; humans no longer perceive selves as "earthbound" and begin to explore and consider colonization of the universe; cyberculture may only take decades to accomplish. Mankind may be well into this fourth stage of human development by the beginning of the 21st century. This has been also described as the metaindustrial or new work culture.

Exhibit 6.3 Changes in Human Development Activities

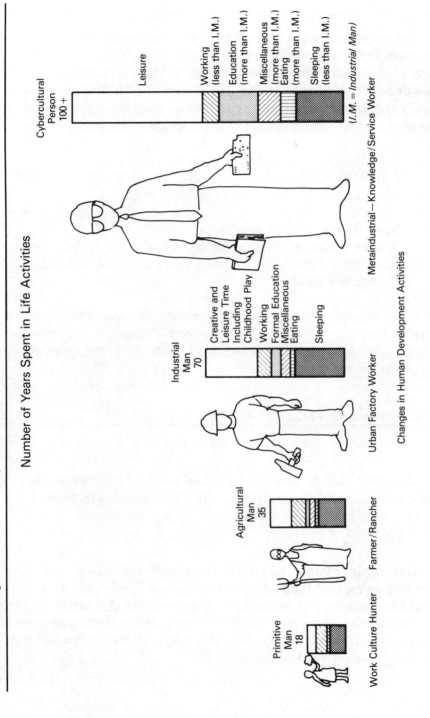

Number of Years Spent in Life Activities

THE ISSUE

The acceleration in the rate of change has caused time to condense, so that what once took a long period to accomplish can now be achieved in a far shorter time span. The twentieth century in particular has provided a remarkable example of intensified growth, development, and expansion in every aspect of human endeavor—from electronics to population. For management, the implications are:

- Rapid change is a reality of modern life
- A more positive philosophy of life toward change is needed
- An openness to continuous change is required
- An ability to project ahead and get the "big picture" of what is happening in society is essential
- A sense of history as to what has happened and why is necessary
- An ability to provide leadership in coping with, and planning for, change is a must

Are you managing in an industrial age context, using a leadership style that is increasingly archaic? Or are you changing to cope with the realities of this new time of the world—the meta or superindustrial, information society?

FACTORS INVOLVED IN PLANNING CHANGE

TIMING

Change should be introduced before the crisis occurs and at a time when the atmosphere is most conducive to implementation.

PSYCHOLOGICAL CONSTRUCT

This is the system that individuals and institutions construct to read meaning into their life space—to make "sense out of" the events and experiences that occur in their private world; change requires a reassessment or review of this traditional way of interpreting situations; essentially, it involves an "attitude change" before actual change in policy, program, or procedures.

PHILOSOPHY TOWARD CHANGE

Either one is consistently open to, or opposes, change and becomes a world-maker or world-squatter. The following rationale is proposed.

THE MANAGEMENT OF CHANGE

To live is to change! The very word "change" is synonymous with evolution, for the whole universe and all creature life are in a constant flux. Until recently, such change has been slow, almost imperceptible. Today humans live in a period of accelerating change. We have unprecedented technological and scientific power to accomplish change and to shape our own future. We are not only agents of change in the world, but are changed in the process of creating the future. The landing of men on the moon, for example, not only produced great changes in human society, it caused mankind to change its very image of the species—human beings are no longer earth-bound.

Men and women's ability to cope with such rapid change and to control it may very well determine our ability to survive as a species. Both individuals and organizations must learn to plan and regulate change so as to ensure growth and development. New skills can be learned so that persons can become agents of *planned change* within their life space.

Change alters our relationships with each other and the world as we perceive it. It is caused by new information and knowledge, by new insights and discoveries, by new situations and happenings. It challenges each person to reeducate self and to modify our psychological constructs—the way one reads meaning into the events and experiences of his life. Since the pace of change has risen so astronomically in this century, change must be managed if it is not to cause disastrous dislocation in individuals, organizations and society. Not all change is good, so careful choices must be made relative to which changes are to be inaugurated. Nor is it advisable to merely react to change, but to be instead pro-active—to plan for it. Haphazard change can sometimes be worse than no change.

Perhaps the first change to be considered is in one's *attitude toward change*. How do we feel about change? Most people fear it, for they are comfortable and secure with the status quo. The real issue is whether

169

one will permit fear of the unknown to paralyze us into inaction or to withdraw from necessary personal change in our life style or approach.

If a person or corporation is to survive in the future, these attitudes will be necessary: (a) openness of mind to consider new perspectives and more creative solutions to problems and other challenges; (b) adaptability and flexibility in reference to the many new changes with which one must cope and (c) development and use of methods for the management of change. (Refer to Exhibits 6.5 and 6.9 "Change Inventory.")

HUMAN FACTORS IN CHANGE

Each of us has a set of highly-organized constructs around which we organize the world in which we live. By these constructs, a person mentally puts order into the world as he or she perceives it. This intellectual synthesis of sense perceptions relates to our image of self, family, religion, nation, job, etc. Each individual develops a system of constructs that serve as anchor points for our mental functioning. This system exerts a pushing/pulling effect upon all other ideas we encounter. It gives meaning and order to the multiple sensations and perceptions that bombard us daily.

Not only do all individuals have a unique set of constructs through which they filter experience, but groups and organizations develop a construct system through which they interpret information coming from their environment. These result from a set of intense interactions of segments of various populations organized to achieve certain goals. Thus, organizational or group styles emerge as people share themselves and their perceptions converge. In a sense, members of groups and organizations link up their perceptual fields; they act and perceive according to their common, shared sets of relationships (for example, the objectively impassive face of a man in a picket line looks "threatening" to a representative of management, but "determined" to a representative of labor).

Since human interaction is normally dynamic, pressures for change build up in people and systems because of altered relationships. These forces for change can be avoided, resisted or incorporated into the person's or organization's perceptual field with the result of restructuring one's constructs. Generally, people react to new information, especially data inconsistent with their present constructs, in a way that tends to be resistive. Exhibit 6.4 illustrates the struggle.

But when one encounters new information or experiences inconsistent with old constructs, and they are of such a nature that they cannot be avoided, resisted or otherwise defended, the resulting pressure or dissonance will usually motivate the individual to change his or her construct system. During this phase there is within the person a temporary confusion or disorganization until equilibrium or order is restored to a relative state of congruence or harmony. Obviously, there are many factors which influence the direction or nature of this change.

GUIDELINES FOR CHANGE—THE HOW

With some knowledge of the psychological factors affecting behavior within the individual or group, the potential change agent is in a position to inaugurate planned change and to stabilize a new situation. The following are some guidelines which a change agent should utilize in the process of planned change:

A. Create a Climate for Change

The proper climate for change often makes the difference between successful change and disruptive, stress-producing chaos. A change agent must strive to create an emotional atmosphere in which people feel the situation is nonjudgmental and empathic toward their needs. We must not only make clear our own purposes and the extent of the projected change, but those affected must feel free to express openly their feelings and resistances with assurance that this input will be taken into full consideration.

The readiness for change can best be developed by first opening the system of organizational communications. One-way or downward systems of communication need to be replaced by two-way or circular systems, which permit feedback to the person proposing change.

Closed channels of communication foster dissatisfaction in a group or organization. Lack of knowledge about the expected change by those affected often creates organizational "paranoia" whereby people throughout the corporation express deep anxiety about the change by imagining every possible calamity and raising every conceivable objection as to why the proposed change won't work. Such expression often

Exhibit 6.4 Forces Affecting Human Behavior

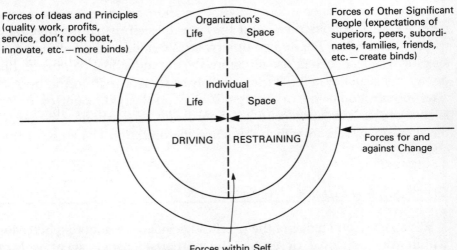

Forces of Ideas and Principles (quality work, profits, service, don't rock boat, innovate, etc.—more binds)

Forces of Other Significant People (expectations of superiors, peers, subordinates, families, friends, etc.—create binds)

Organization's Life Space

Individual Life Space

DRIVING | RESTRAINING

Forces for and against Change

Forces within Self
(self image, needs, expectations, values, standards, ideals)

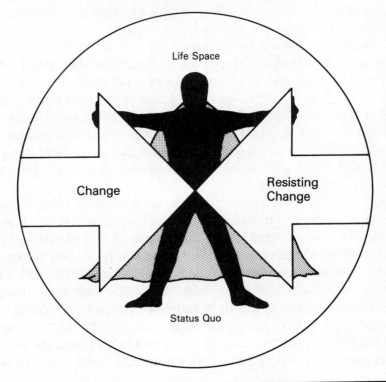

Life Space

Change

Resisting Change

Status Quo

gives rise to disruptive and vicious rumors which have the potential for creating widespread organizational damage.

B. Involve Those Affected by Change Efforts

People can adequately respond to change efforts only when they have some understanding of the purposes and consequences of the proposed change. Lack of knowledge, understanding, and involvement in planning for change only feed the forces for resistance. Therefore, change agents must allow for some participation by those affected by change in the preparations, decision-making and implementation. This may range from "brainstorming" about the change at a staff meeting to appointing a task force to make recommendations concerning the change.

People can be persuaded to reduce their objections, but they should not be treated arbitrarily. By practicing human relations skills, the change agent can help people to cope with fear of the change. When they have ample opportunity to affect the nature and extent of the suggested change, individuals may become self-motivated toward problem solution. When employees, for example, have some measure of control over the forces that influence their organizational life space, they are more apt to implement the change than to resist it.

Furthermore, participation by those who must implement the proposed change often results in better effort. It is often with these people that the more creative and realistic solutions lie. Change agents may often assume they have adequate knowledge of what is involved in the problem area requiring change to design its solution. However, those affected by such planning usually share unique perspectives, which more often than not contribute substantially to the overall problem solution.

C. Develop a Change Strategy

If change in individual and organizational lives is to be planned and controlled, the agent of change must employ an orderly problem-solving process. However, there are various methods for effecting change. One developed by the social psychologist, Kurt Lewin, has been designated *force field analysis.* In this conceptual approach, one proceeds with change on the basis that behavior is the product of a field of interdependent factors, such as action, thinking, wishing, striving, valuing, achieving and so forth. For each individual, this perceptual field encompasses one's life space or psychological environment. Groups, too, have a life space or organizational environment, which results from the merging of each member's perceptual field. The "private world" or life space involves (1) "existence"—anything having demonstrable effects on the individual or group whether conscious or not; (2) "interdependence"—various parts of this life space are to some degree dependent on each other; (3) "contemporaniety"—only determinants of behavior at a given point in time are properties of the life space at the same time.

With knowledge of these factors in the individual or group, one is able to analyze what forces drive the members in a particular direction and what restrain them (see Exhibit 6.10). A way of analyzing these factors influencing behavior is to consider one set of forces at work in our life spaces—the forces *for* and *against* a change in the current condition. These forces, for instance, may be people within an organization or economic factors (a recession) or social factors (a war or riot). Once the present situation has been determined, then the change agent is in a position to inaugurate the changes and stabilize a new situation.

Here are some of the questions a change agent must answer in the process of effecting planned change:

1. What *kind of change* is planned? Is it in attitude, behavior, policy, structure or process? Determine the nature and properties of what is being changed—customs, beliefs, opinions, principles, operational procedures. Define change in terms of the total system. Spell out the objectives of the change.

2. What are the number and strength of the *driving forces* in favor of the change? Once ascertained, concentrate on increasing these forces supporting the change; get these forces mobilized to create a climate for change (see Exhibit 6.6 which uses an analogy of a "tug-of-war" game; the center line is the status quo). For example, when these forces are people, interest them in promoting the change once they have been given sufficient information. Involve them in the communication of well thought-out reasons for the change, or enlist their help in doing the research necessary to develop a solid case for the change. Thus, the change agent helps to unfreeze the status quo and to provide a basis for growth within the group. Begin with those in the system most open to change who can provide leverage.

3. What are the number and strength of the *resisting forces?* Diagnose the opposition and the reasons or emotions behind the resistance. Systematically, counteract the arguments against the change; remove or isolate the obstacles to the change. To what degree is the group ready for change and what changes are realistic in the light of the resistance? How much power do the change agents possess to overcome the change resisters? What are the difficulties in inaugurating and maintaining the change? Each person who is a potential resister must be analyzed as to why he or she will take this position. If it is simply a question of ignorance, then adequate information must be supplied to enlist support. If one has a closed mind and is against any change in principle, then that person should be bypassed and effort should be concentrated on those most amenable to change. If one has a vested or conflict of interest, then the reasons for the opposition may have to be exposed. Coercion and repression of opponents of change are not in order; people have a right to disagree.

4. What *action* do the change agents plan? Who is to do it? How is it to be done? Where is it to be done? When is it most appropriate? (Timing is important in inaugurating change.) A strategy must be developed in the light of the situation and the abilities of the group. This means the change agents must know the resources of the group for promoting and maintaining the change.

5. How can the change agents *stabilize* the change when introduced? Once a new level of change has been brought about, it must be "refrozen" until it becomes an accepted and habitual practice. This means the change agents must stick with the change before moving on to new projects or changes. It implies "reinforcement" of the new balance established between the driving and resisting forces in the group. A force for stabilization occurs when those who must implement the change are involved in the decision-making about the change.

6. Are the change agents open to *continuous change* and have they a plan for re-evaluation of the change inaugurated after a trial period? This means that in the light of accelerating change, the change agents must be willing to accept improvement and further changes on the plan or program they espoused. Sometimes such follow-up studies can be accomplished by the change group itself. Large-scale changes, on the other hand, may require "action research" by outside consultants to objectively determine standards by which to measure

progress. Realistic fact finding and evaluation is a prerequisite for any learning from the change experience.

RESISTANCE TO ORGANIZATIONAL CHANGE

Need for change is often brought about in situations characterized by high levels of stress or tension within an organization. When organizations cease to function well, when the people in them are put under a great deal of stress and frustration, when tension is high, the time for planned change is evident. Paradoxically, these conditions can also mitigate against its success. The overwhelming evidence from the behavioral sciences is that heightened drive, tension and stress make people more rigid and inflexible in perceiving and interpreting events. Under tension our perspective and foresight become severely restricted. Individuals tend to see things in terms of our most probable expectations and to decide things along the most habitual lines. Our capacity to solve problems can be severely reduced. If change efforts are to be successful, they must be carried out in an atmosphere most conducive to it. Change efforts must be planned well ahead of any crisis and carried out in a climate in which stress, frustration and anger are at a minimum.

In assessing resistance to change, change agents must be aware of the fears of disorientation because of the unknown factors involved for the people affected by the change. We must be conscious of threats to existing vested interests, power and status ties to existing conditions and the resulting potential for personal loss when conditions change. We must be alert to the defenses of past tradition, standards, values and beliefs.

Attempts by the change agent to meet resistance with defensiveness, advice-giving, premature persuasion, censoring, controlling or punishment will only engender greater resistance. Rather, dissent should be valued in its own right as it represents a legitimate point of view. As previously indicated, when the people affected by any given change are involved in its planning and implementation, restraining forces against the change can be reduced and successful change can be accomplished (Rubenstein, 1987).

Because of the rapidly rising rate of change within the life spaces of individuals, organizations and communities, the thesis of this presentation has been that such *change must be managed* (Exhibit 6.5). Merely reacting or coping with accelerating change is unsatisfactory. Leaders in families, business and society need to view themselves as potential agents of change. Managers, especially, should not be dragged "kicking and screaming" into the twenty-first century; rather, they should develop the skills now available for planning and controlling change.

Applied behavioral scientists describe change as a process within a system of initiating, diagnosing, implementing, and maintaining a new level of performance in the group or organization. By viewing the organization as a total system and a department or division as a sub-system, one begins to appreciate the interrelatedness of all the parts. Thus, when a change agent attempts to bring about an alteration in one aspect of the system, he or she takes into consideration its effect on the other parts of this whole. Planned change involves the creation of a new environment in which people function. The force field analysis method can be a powerful means for bringing about changes with a minimum of dislocation and a maximum of collaboration. (Refer to "Force Field Analysis," in next the Instrument section.)

Here is one more thing to think about. Among scientists, there is a growing belief that many of the primitive hominid species disappeared not because they merged to form one larger family of man, but because they failed to meet the challenges of their time and so became extinct. They also think it possible that those hominids may have vanished without having contributed to the evolution of the species that did adapt and survive: *Homo sapiens*. Today, in an information society, the survival of the wisest depends upon managing change.

Exhibit 6.5 Managing Change.

Driving	Resisting
1. Analyze types of change.	1. Diagnose the resistance.
2. Respond sensitively and creatively to influences on change.	2. Channel the resistance constructively.
3. Provide adequate data on the change	3. Counteract the arguments against change.
Refreeze the driving forces of change at a new level.	Respect the freedom of dissent.

STRATEGIES FOR ORGANIZATIONAL TRANSFORMATION

THE CHALLENGE

Having considered in general *why* it is necessary to plan and control change, the manager relates these trends in society and the world of work to his/her current experience in organizations. In other words, a leader is challenged to consider why it is vital to become an agent of change in organizations.

THE ORGANIZATION

An organization:

- Defines human objectives, expectations, obligations
- Structures human roles and relationships
- Provides processes, procedures, technologies
- Develops human and material resources
- Goes through growth stages—(1) formation; (2) survival; (3) stabilization; (4) image projection; (5) rendering unique products and services; (6) cooperating in achieving goals and satisfying needs

THE REORGANIZATION

Reorganization is necessary when the organization:

- Diminishes in its uniqueness or satisfaction of relevant needs
- Begins to operate ineffectively and is financially threatened
- Must redefine its objectives, policies, structures
- Must eliminate traditional roles, procedures, products, services
- Must create *new* roles, procedures, products, services
- Must acquire *new* specialists and markets

Then it is time for planned change or renewal. Otherwise, "organization shock" will be experienced in varying degrees.

ORGANIZATION SHOCK

"Organization shock" is characterized by:

- The superindustrial stage impacting upon traditional modes of operating
- Resistance to organizational change at all levels
- High degrees of stress, tension, and frustration among its people
- Positive or negative results, such as increasing job satisfaction, or threat and defensiveness
- Symptoms such as a drop in members/clients/customers; declining loyalty, attendance, and productivity; increasing turnover, absenteeism, tardiness; decreasing income or profit; increasing dissatisfaction and charges of irrelevance about operations; decreasing communication and increasing conflict; increasing alco-

Exhibit 6.6 Altering the Equilibrium of Forces.

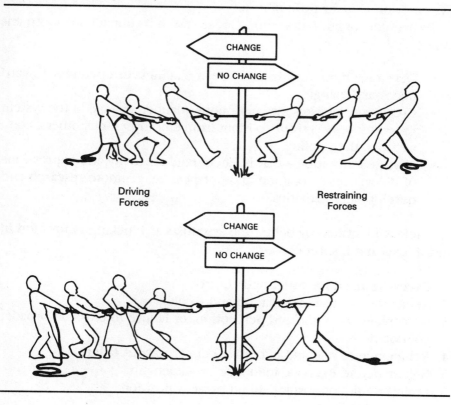

Driving
Forces

Restraining
Forces

holism, drug abuse, nervous breakdowns, and even suicides among workers; take-over target by others.

ORGANIZATIONAL MODEL

The organizational model known as *bureaucracy* is disappearing, while a new modus operandi called the *ad-hocracy* is emerging. (See the profile of characteristics for these two models in the Interaction section under the heading "Trends In Organizational Change"—the shift in emphasis is from the left side of the chart to the right side.) The management style in the old "factory-like" organization of the past has been called, by Douglas McGregor, *Theory X* or *traditional management*; the more appropriate style for the superindustrial system of the future has been called *Theory Y* or *participative management*. In terms of organizational characteristics, Rensis Likert has described the former as either System 1 or 2 while the latter would be more System 3 or 4. Refer to Exhibit 6.6.

To prevent "organization shock" or to lessen its impact, management must

- Develop a more positive attitude, a readiness or openness, toward necessary change
- Create mechanisms for continuous, planned change in the system
- Listen more effectively to input from employees, customers, competitors, the public
- Manage innovation—that is, encourage creativity and expressions of differences in opinion and perspective, promote research and development activities

Six factors identified by behavioral scientists as blocking innovation in individuals and institutions are:

1. Excessive need for order and control
2. Reluctance to use imagination and to play
3. Narrowness of vision and perception, or failure to envision broader connotations
4. Reluctance to risk and excessive concern about failure
5. Reluctance to exercise influence or leadership
6. Overcertainty or absolutism on present position

Exhibit 6.7 Preventative Measures Delimit.

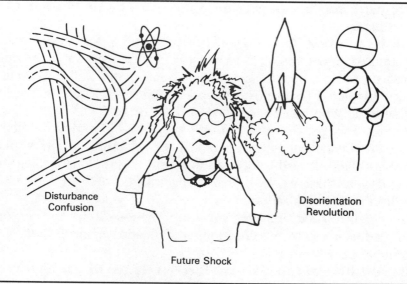

Disturbance
Confusion

Disorientation
Revolution

Future Shock

If your organization is to survive and develop, it must not only be willing to inaugurate the change processes, but also to project ahead with imagination and anticipate the future. In fact, it must learn to create the future (Exhibit 6.7).

THE STRATEGY TO AVOID FUTURE SHOCK

Managers who wish to promote a planned change should

1. **Become aware of the psychological environment,** the factors at work in the individual or organizational life space which may further or hinder the projected change.
2. **Examine the communication system:** Evaluate the managerial communication style of you, yourself, as the agent of change or of the organizational communication system. If the style is open, two-way, circular, and participative, then you are ready to promote the change. If it is a closed, one-way, authoritarian style, then the communication system must first be opened before the change can take place.
3. **Encourage participation in the change planning process.** Identify and involve those (a) who are open to the proposed change

and (b) who must implement the change once it is adopted. Utilize participative management in the very process of planning for the change.

4. **Develop a case for change.** Begin by doing the background research and investigation as to why the change is desirable. Assemble data on the reasons the change is advantageous. Build up a file on your projected change. At the appropriate time, communicate this case to all who will be involved in the change.

5. **Keep a low profile as a change agent:** Avoid having the change identified with you or your personality. Seek collaborators who can provide the outward leadership in promoting the change, and feed the data to these persons. Real change makers are often not visible within their organizations.

6. **Be prepared for changes on your proposed change:** Be open to feedback and to modification, amplification, and revision of the original plan for change.

7. **Be sensitive to the pro/con forces relative to the change:** Be alert to the varied forces at work within the individual or the system that promote or restrict the anticipated change. Assess these driving and resisting forces.

8. **Unfreeze the present equilibrium:** Unlock or unstick the status quo by eliminating or weakening the restraining forces and strengthening or increasing the driving forces.

9. **Be prepared to take risks:** The agent of change must be ready to take wise and calculated risks, to expose himself or herself to ridicule, and to live with the consequences of initiating change. Progress is not made by "playing it safe."

SUMMARY: THE MEANING FOR MANAGEMENT

Because accelerating change is a reality in most life spaces during this superindustrial age, change must be managed. To accomplish this, the leader needs to acquire skills to better plan and control change. In human systems this implies initating, diagnosing, implementing, and maintaining a new level or performance within a group or organization. Change is an altering of energy priorities within that energy-exchange system called "the organization." This alteration can be *begun* by following the above nine strategies. By eliminating the archaic and obsolete, by experimenting with the innovative and unknown, the agent of change insures the organization's survival, so it can develop. Such managers help to renew their organizations and create a new psychological environment in which people can function more effectively.

INTERACTION

In this section we offer three forms of group process that a manager can use with staff or team to improve their attitudes and skills in the management of change. "Imagineering" is a creative means to involve the group in planning and preparing for change. "Trends in Organizational Change" (Exhibit 6.8) is a diagnostic tool for assessing the need for system change. "Creative Risk-Taking" is an exercise in evaluating the risks involved in implementing a change.

IMAGINEERING

In the new work culture, people will be expected to make more use of their imagination and intuition, as well as to be more future oriented. To stimulate capacities in this regard, I recommend regular reading of two periodicals by leaders: *The Futurist* (World Future Society, 4916 St. Elmo Ave., Bethesda, MD 20814) and *New Management* (John Wiley & Sons, 605 Third Ave., New York, NY).

Imagineering has been successfully used with managers all over the world and from all types of systems. It is useful to preface this process with the showing of a short educational film on change or future shock. Having stirred up the participants' imaginations, invite them to project themselves into the future of their organization, industry, or profession. Since the turn of the century is just ahead, leaders may like to use the year 2000 as the point of reference. For example, with a large audience considering the future of a specific multinational corporation at the beginning of the twenty-first century, the facilitator can divide up participants into smaller groups representing various operations, such as a particular subsidiary, division, or product line. Another way is to assign groups to consider the future of the company in terms of only one dimension, such as human resources, personnel policies and practices, technology, marketing, manufacturing, and customers. Before the exercise begins, each group is instructed what their frame of reference is to be in the year 2000, and asked to base their projections on what they know of present trends.

With an audience of representatives from an occupation or career, the imagineering procedure is simpler. Instructions for management information specialists might begin: "Given what you know about changes in your field, about developments in a distributed information environment, growth in the use of personal computers by line managers, the emergence of information resource managers, and similar trends, what will happen to your MIS role by the year 2000? Will systems programmers and analysts disappear? What is the likely function of information professionals by the end of the twentieth century? What will be the impact of advances in artificial intelligence? Take off your perceptual binders and use your imagination."

The steps for conducting an "imagineering" session are outlined below. Final reports should be recorded on audio- or videotapes, or the flip-chart reports should be edited, for feedback to key executives and planners. The process fosters participative management.

PROCEDURES FOR IMAGINEERING

Managers are challenged to expand the horizons of their subordinates and to assist them in developing new psychological *constructs*. Everyone views reality through the perspective of his/her own private world or life *space,* as Kurt Lewin called it. Personal and professional development requires the subordinate to revise his/her *construct,* or the way in which he/she has read meaning into his/her world. Staff input and discussion should encourage a change in opinions, attitudes, and thinking.

To help participants become more future-oriented, rather than past-oriented, use the group technique called *imagineering.* This method is especially helpful in sessions dealing with management of change, forecasting, and planning. This technique can be used for predictions relative to a career field, such as selling, to a department or division, such as marketing, or to the whole organization. The approach helps to get the group out of the rut of *status quo* or *the way we always did it,* using imagination to anticipate tomorrow's realities based on today's trends.

Consider how much better-prepared salespeople might have been for their changing role in an economy of scarcity if five years ago they had done some "imagineering"! This technique encourages trainees to *think unthinkable thoughts* and to take risks in stating their prognosis.

Steps in this process are:

1. The audience is invited to take a fantasy trip into the future and to let imagination flow freely. The manager might dim room lights to provide a setting for this forecasting exercise.
2. Next, the trainees are asked to close their eyes and to project ahead one, five, ten, or thirty years. For example, the manager might comment: "Imagine it is now 19XX. Place yourself in that time frame and consider what kind of world will be likely."
3. Specifically, ask the group to fantasize in terms of their occupation (or some specific subject, industry, or company) and to identify four or five changes that are probable in the time frame of the assignment. For instance, if considering changes within the field of sales over the next decade, participants would be encouraged to think creatively about the near future of their occupation—to loosen their perceptual and psychological "binds." Three or four minutes might be devoted to this task. One minute before the end of the exercise, the manager reminds the group again: "Now it is 19XX, and you should have identified some specific changes that have occurred in your field."
4. If the lights were turned off or dimmed, they may be readjusted to normal functioning. Trainees are asked to jot down three, four, or five of the changes that they have predicted for the time period ahead. The staff is then broken down into small groups of six or eight and encouraged, as groups, to sit in a circle with no table between the members. An easel or newsprint sheet is provided to each group, along with a large felt-tip marking pen.
5. Each member is asked to take turns and to share with the group his/her insights without elaboration; the group is requested to hold back comments until every participant in that group has provided his/her input. Based on these projections, the whole group is asked to arrive at some consensus concerning five to eight major trends in their field.

   Instruct the group to summarize findings on the newsprint sheet, using the marking pen. The group should name a recorder for this purpose. Allow twenty to thirty minutes for this portion of the assignment. Meanwhile, the facilitator takes marking tape and puts two pieces for each group on a wall in front of the class where reports can be displayed. A five-minute warning reminds the group recorder to place sheets up front where the tape has been provided.
6. Each group then gives a five-minute oral report on the written outline to explain the reasoning behind the selections.

The manager notes any pattern which emerges from the group reports—for example, a similar idea mentioned by more than one group; such concepts might be underlined or starred.

In conclusion, the manager might inquire what the participants are doing now to plan ahead for the changes in their field which they have identified as likely to occur. A general discussion on the implications of the data might be undertaken.

TRENDS IN ORGANIZATIONAL CHANGE

This exercise is an opportunity for a leader to interact with a work unit or a group of managers on issues related to organizational transformation. The whole undertaking can be accomplished in one three- to four-hour session as part of a training experience or in a series of three or four staff meetings. There are four sections of individual readings and instrumentations each followed by group discussion. Beginning with organizational change in general, the participants are asked to diagnose the situation in their own company, agency, or association:

1. Read, "Trends in Organizational Change (TOC)" (see Exhibit 6.8); discuss its implications regarding your organization—any instances of bureaucracy being replaced by "ad-hocracy." Fill out "Stages of Organizational Growth" to ascertain by group consensus where your organization is in its development.
2. Using the input from TOC, make "Your Organizational Diagnosis"; in the first section this means rating yourself in regard to certain organizational characteristics, and in the second section it means evaluating how far organization shock has progressed. The participants then share their assessments and attempt to arrive at a group consensus in their evaluations.
3. The final diagnosis comes from "Systems Analysis" based on the research of behavioral scientist Rensis Likert and relates to the insights gained from TOC. Using six major characteristics of organizational management, the individuals rate for twelve items whether the organization is still traditionally authoritarian or emerging participative in its style of management. Then the data is shared with the group, and some consensus on evaluations is sought for all items. When there is no agreement, simply add up the scores of each person, and circle the majority rating.

Exhibit 6.8 Trends in Organizational Change

Disappearing Bureaucracy	Emerging Ad-Hocracy
(Industrial age—factory system)	(Post-industrial age—cybernation)
1) *Old Systems*—Characteristics: permanence, hierarchy, and a division of labor; traditional organization sometimes called Theory X or Systems 1/2.	1) *New System*—Characteristics: fast-moving, information-rich, a kinetic organization of the future, filled with transient cells and extremely mobile individuals. Sometimes referred to as Theory Y or Systems 3/4.
a) workers in sharply defined slots for a division of labor; narrow specializations—each in own niche.	a) workers' roles more hazy and temporary; convergence of talent and disciplines to accomplish a task.
b) vertical hierarchy—chain of command from top down.	b) fluid, participative arrangements; organizational redesign is a continuous function.
c) permanence of organizational relations and structures; intractable departments and divisions.	c) temporariness of organizational relations and structures— disposable divisions, task forces, ad-hoc committees.
d) slow to change, often by external influences static	d) self-renewing; constantly changing in response to changing needs, dynamic.
e) operates well in stable society when problems are routine and predictable; needs highly competitive, undifferentiated environment.	e) functions best in a super-industrial society of accelerating change.
f) concerned primarily about organizational self-interests, board, and stockholders.	f) concerned about community and ecological implications of organizational actions.
2) *Old Power/Authority*—Vertical, power concentrated in a few.	2) *New Power Authority*—Horizontal, power disbursed.
a) those at top make all important decisions for lower echelons; managers share a monopoly on decisions.	a) shift of decisions "sideways" and to lower levels of responsibility; workers share in decision-making; sharing may include consumers.
b) organizational communication vertical; information flow slow; delay normal.	b) organizational communications circular or lateral, information flow fast; delay costly.

Exhibit 6.8 Trends in Organizational Change, *cont'd.*

Disappearing Bureaucracy	Emerging Ad-Hocracy
c) simple problem-solving mechanism ideal for routine issues at moderate pace; low speed decisions.	c) complex problem-solving; capable of meeting increasing number of non-routine, novel, unexpected problems; high-speed decisions.
d) staff/line arrangements between support and operative units.	d) specialists and advisors more involved in planning and decisions; convergence of specializations; team approach.
e) requires masses of moderately educated workers to perform routine operations.	e) requires limited numbers of skilled technicians and self-regulating cybernated systems.
f) emphasis on efficiency and profitability.	f) emphasis on effectiveness and profitable service.
g) focus upon plant equipment maintenance and capital expansion.	g) focus on people maintenance and development; human resources development.
3) *Old Organization Man*	3) *New Superindustrial Person*
a) executives and managers are the "brains" and workers are the "hands."	a) executives and managers are coordinators of varied and transient work teams.
b) people differentiated according to rank and role in hierarchial pyramid.	b) people differentiated flexibly and functionally according to skill and professional training.
c) personnel have more permanent work relationships.	c) people need to develop human relations skills for quick, intense relationships on the job and disengagement from enduring relationships.
d) organization man looks within the corporation for approval, rewards and punishment; conditioned to subservience and paid to conform; deviancy and creativity discouraged.	d) superindustrial person looks within one's self and profession for approval and fulfillment; an agent of change and non-conformity; unorthodox, creative and venturesome.
e) factory system produces the industrialization of the skills and profession into narrow specializations.	e) techno-societies foster the professionalization of industry; the reaching beyond narrow disciplines.
f) free-swinging rugged individuals built vast enterprises unafraid of defeat and adverse opinions became the leaders of industry	f) emergence of entrepreneurial groupings within large organizations affluent independent men and women unafraid to rise and venture into new fields

Exhibit 6.8   Trends in Organizational Change, *cont'd.*

Summary

Old Bureaucratic Man
employs his skills and energies for the good of the organization to whom he is loyal and committed; concerned about economic security and hierarchial status; subordinates individuality for good of the organization; emphasis on competition and quantity production; fears change and advocates status quo, by his past orientation, he is ripe for future shock; usually a white male.

New Associative Person
employs his or her skills and energies for self-actualization in temporary groupings committed to personal and professional development; mobile self-motivated people who take economic security for granted; find transience liberating and never permanently submerges individuality while working on the team; emphasis on cooperation and quality service; change is a challenge for new learning and adaptability is advocated; future-orientated; prevents or lessens future shock; varied; competent people; including women and other minorities at all levels.

Step 1

Stages of Organizational Growth

Using as the model the company or agency that employs you, **Identify** in terms of dates in the past and present the stages of growth it has gone through; that is, **Insert** dates or the approximate number of years in the allotted spaces.

Name of the Organization _____

Stages of Growth—	Time Period (Dates/Years)	**Example**
1) **Formation**	_____	Company seeks to establish.
2) **Survival Period(s)**	_____	Company seeks to meet expenses.
3) **Stabilization**	_____	Company seeks to make profit and develop workable systems.
4) **Image Creation/ Projection**	_____	Company develops a brand and/or public relations program.

Continued

189

Exhibit 6.8   Trends in Organizational Change, *cont'd.*

5) **Renders Unique** _____ Company becomes
   Products/Services distinctive in its output.

6) **Cooperates in** _____ Company matures
   Achieving Goals/Needs and is involved with
   Satisfaction community.

Step 2

Your Organizational Diagnosis

Review the special insert, "Trends in Organizational Change." Then, take an objective look at your organization: specifically, your work unit and your subordinates. George DeMare reminds executives of the need to hear, observe, sense, and apprehend change—"the whisper of the future." Only when the manager has such a sensitive inner ear to catch the voice of change can he/she avoid obsolescence and business disaster.

Observe, Sense, and **Apprehend** the need for change in your situation.

Identify some of the symptoms of "organization shock" which might be present in your organization. **Note** some needed changes that yet have to be considered.

A) **Organizational Characteristics**

Analyze your organization's present state in terms of the following characteristics:

Rate your organization as *adequate* (+) or *inadequate* (−) for each characteristic.

	Rating	
Competency Level	(+)	(−)
Managers	☐	☐
Staff	☐	☐
Subordinates	☐	☐
Training of new entries	☐	☐
Human-resource development at all levels	☐	☐
Employment of new specialists	☐	☐
Effectiveness Level		
Productivity standards	☐	☐
Useful meetings	☐	☐
Utilization of human potential	☐	☐
Clarity of job roles, functions	☐	☐

Exhibit 6.8 Trends in Organizational Change, *cont'd.*

	+	−
Encouragement of creativity/innovation	☐	☐
Resolution of conflict	☐	☐
Motivating work environment	☐	☐
Rewarding of high performance	☐	☐
Job enrichment/redesign	☐	☐
Involvement in problem-solving/decision-making	☐	☐
Job advancement/mobility	☐	☐
Time management	☐	☐
Organizational relations	☐	☐

Step 3

System Analysis

In light of the preceding organizational change diagnosis, which described the "disappearing bureaucracy" and the "emerging ad-hocracy," do now a more in-depth analysis of your organization based on a systems approach. That is, evaluate your organization's communication, goal setting, control motivation, and leadership style. Decide if your organization is either Traditional Authoritarian or Emerging Participative in each of the six areas, rating each of the 12 points below as High, Medium, or Low in your opinion. For example, if organizational goals are *always* set at the top, the management style is "TA" and you might rate it **Low.** If middle management are permitted input into organizational objectives, then you might mark it **High**. On the other hand, if a Management by Objectives system has been introduced throughout the organization at all levels, it is likely your company or agency is in the "EP" or emerging participative style of management, and you might decide to rate it **Medium** or **High.** If MBO only exists at the division levels, you may give it only a **Low** rating under "EP." . . . or if you look at Item 7 on direction of information flow and it is largely downward, an appropriate rating under "TA" would seem to be in order, whereas if it is circular—two way in direction—the mark would be placed under "EP" in the appropriate evaluation, depending on how open you consider the organizational communications to be.

Now **do the rating** for the twelve items. Then **plot a graph** by connecting the points with a line. (Then turn the page sideways to view your "highs," "mediums," and "lows" more graphically.) This will indicate the current trend of your organization's management style as you perceive it.

Continued

191

Exhibit 6.8 Trends in Organizational Change, *cont'd.*

Organizational Characteristics	Traditional Authoritarian			Emerging Participative		
Goal Setting						
1) Establishing organizational goals/objectives	L	M	H	L	M	H
2) Amount of resistance or collaboration to goals set	L	M	H	L	M	H
Control						
3) Unity of purpose/activity of formal/informal organization	L	M	H	L	M	H
4) Use of control data	L	M	H	L	M	H
Decision-Making						
5) Levels of delegation/involvement	L	M	H	L	M	H
6) Contribution to worker motivation	L	M	H	L	M	H
Communication						
7) Direction of information flow	L	M	H	L	M	H
8) Accuracy of information flow	L	M	H	L	M	H
Motivation						
9) Cooperation and teamwork	L	M	H	L	M	H
10) Human energy productivity utilized	L	M	H	L	M	H
Leadership						
11) Confidence shown in subordinates	L	M	H	L	M	H
12) Freedom to discuss job with superiors	L	M	H	L	M	H

B) Test Spots Signs of Organization Shock

This test will help you determine if some of the typical symptoms of organization shock are present in your institution. Simply check the appropriate box.

	Some	Little	Much
1) Substantial drop in membership, clients, or customers.	☐	☐	☐
2) Gradual loss of chapters or local units, plants, or subsidiaries	☐	☐	☐

Exhibit 6.8   Trends in Organizational Change, *cont'd.*

3) Drastic reduction in attendance at conferences, conventions, meetings, or exhibits.	☐	☐	☐
4) Decreasing financial income/drop in profits.	☐	☐	☐
5) Declining loyalty of adherents.	☐	☐	☐
6) Increasing dissatisfaction with program content or process; white/blue collar "blues."	☐	☐	☐
7) Charges of irrelevance of program topics and activities; or decline in productivity.	☐	☐	☐
8) Widening communication gaps between younger and older members/workers.	☐	☐	☐
9) Inability to attract or involve younger members; recruitment difficulties.	☐	☐	☐
10) Polarization of activists and traditionalists.	☐	☐	☐
11) Increased conflict or confrontation between professional staff and volunteer members, or between labor and management.	☐	☐	☐
12) Growing dissatisfaction of younger staff with older management or administration.	☐	☐	☐

Step 4

Action Planning

A) As a result of reading the input section and engaging in this learning exercise, identify two personal changes which you might undertake to advance your professional development:

_____

_____

B) What specific targets will you establish to accomplish these changes and in what time frame:

_____

_____

C) What specific steps will you undertake to achieve these targets:

_____

_____

Continued

Exhibit 6.8 Trends in Organizational Change, *cont'd.*

D) From the above analysis of your organization, what changes should be planned immediately:

_____

_____

E) What strategies would you propose to implement these changes:

_____

_____

F) What personal contribution could you make to fostering these changes in your organization:

_____

_____

4. On the basis of the learning experience, the group engages in "Action Planning" to identify what organizational changes should be sought and what could be done to accomplish these.

CREATIVE RISK-TAKING

Regardless of the change being planned, an individual or group may engage in an introspective process to identify the risks involved and to assess what may happen if one does/does not facilitate the change. Weighing the pros and cons in this regard may help in the decision to proceed or not with the innovation or alteration. The following example demonstrates how one management team uses this approach to consider changes in their management style.

Undue resistance to change is caused by fear, particularly hesitancy to take risks. There are two types of people in the world—world-makers and world-squatters. The critical factor distinguishing the two seems to be risk-taking; the former will take reasonable risks, while the latter sit back, play it safe, and observe from the sideline.

A reasonable risk-taker weighs alternatives, makes decisions, and assumes responsibility for control of his or her own life. Living involves risks, many of which are taken unconsciously. Those who accomplish great things in their personal and professional lives are aware of the risks, consider them carefully, and are not afraid to make judgements. In other words, they are not afraid to stick their necks out.

Risk-taking can be creative. To illustrate this creativity, here is a creative risk report by a group of supervisors on the risks involved in adopting a "Theory Y" or an emerging participative approach to management. This example will underscore the insights that can be obtained by a group dynamic approach.

Risk	Reasons
1. Lack of time to meet deadlines by using this management style.	1. Personal needs interfere with accomplishing task and prevent lack of mutual understanding.
2. Inability of subordinates to work together and arrive at a timely decision.	2. Perhaps the composition of the group is inadequate and the wrong members are participating.
3. Having to change is painful. The old way is easier.	3. Threat of the unknown, loss of traditional controls, initial confusion in learning new approach.
4. The authority of middle and upper management is compromised.	4. Lack of information and training in new concepts and practices.
5. Inefficiency because it takes too much time and involves too many.	5. Preliminary inefficiency may result in long-term commitment and greater productivity because of involvement.
6. Some of the traditionalists will resent it, and the dependent types will be afraid to participate	6. No Risk—too big an issue for compromise, those who can't be retrained will have to take their chances

The challenge in the creative-risk exercise is to have the whole group examine and weigh the risks, as well as the alternatives, if participative management is not adopted. The above data can be "massaged" and new learning stimulated. Based on this input one can conclude with five principal points:

1. Primary responsibility of the manager is to define the area of freedom relative to the new leadership style.

2. Greater personal growth can be possible in this new participative mode, and this can contribute to greater organizational growth.
3. With proper planning, time problems can be minimized; initial time loss by this method can be regained by improved organizational relations and cooperation. Success is not measured by getting things done but by getting them done better.
4. New approach permits expression of diversity of opinion in the discussion stage and may prevent costly mistakes.
5. Training is required for subordinates to gain new skills in cooperative group action.

INSTRUMENTATION

In *Management in Transition* (Harris 1985), two data-gathering instruments related to the subject matter of this chapter were provided by this author:

- *Transformational Management Skills Inventory.* To assess leadership skills at bringing about planned change and renewal. The twenty-five items are divided into four sections that deal with self-appraisal of leadership style, change skills, communication skills, and managerial performance. The evaluation is based upon the assumption that in the transition to a new work culture, transformational management skills such as these are critical. A group of managers can compare scores and engage in discussion on the implications of their findings.
- *Manager's Quality of Life Index.* For leaders seeking change in the quality of their life. This personal assessment is based on thirty items. The five sections allow for an appraisal of self-care on physical, philosophical or spiritual, and social well-being or life-style. The basic assumption is that staying well and fit gives the individual greater control over one's life space, and is preferable to the costs of rehabilitation necessitated by illness or substance abuse. Self-health management or wellness also contributes to the developing of our potential. This instrument may also be used for lively group discussion.

These two instruments and the next two to follow may be ordered in quantity from Management Research Systems/Talico Inc., 2320 S. Third St. #7, Jacksonville Beach, FL 32250, USA.

CHANGE INVENTORY FOR LEADERS

The Change Inventory (Exhibit 6.9) is a two-part checklist for determining a leader's attitude toward accelerating change. There are fifteen statements of attitude, and participants indicate how often they feel that way—"usually," "sometime," or "never". The first eight items deal with the qualities required in an agent of change—openness, flexibility, sensitiveness, creativeness, person-centeredness, and goal-oriented planning. The second part examines the capacity to cope with personal and organizational change relative to changing image, construct, values, role, society, goals, and life-style. The inventory takes about 15 minutes to fill out. If desired, participants may share findings or enter into a group discussion on their significance. The instrument can be used to create self-awareness and to stimulate thinking about planned change, or to delimit "future-shock". As an organization development survey, it can provide insight into managerial attitudes toward change.

FORCED FIELD ANALYSIS INVENTORY

Based upon the groundbreaking research of Dr. Kurt Lewin, this instrument (Exhibit 6.10) helps analyze driving and restraining forces in people or organizations. It could be used, for example, with each of the changes identified through the previous imagineering or organizational diagnosis. There are 18 questions, ranging from analysis of the type of change and one's relationship to it, to the resources available to implement the change and the case that can be made to get others to support it. Item 7 requires use of the accompanying worksheet for in-depth consideration of the driving and resisting forces to this alteration of the present equilibrium or status quo. Thirty minutes is required for a thinking manager or professional to answer the inquiries and to delimit the trauma of transitioning away from the "way we always did it." The inventory is suitable for group analysis, especially on organizational changes.

For example, suppose a department group has identified likely changes to occur over the next ten years within a specific market. Force field analysis can be applied to study which human or non-human forces push for each change, as well as the forces likely to restrain these forces from having their fullest impact.

Essentially, human behavior is the product of a field of interdependent factors which motivate or energize individuals and organizations. These have been designated *energy forces* (physical or psychological),

---

Exhibit 6.9 Change Inventory for Leaders.

Do you have a positive or negative attitude toward change? Most people fear change, but the issue is whether you let such concern paralyze you into inaction. Some persons merely react to change; others are pro-active—they plan and control change.

Part 1

The following check list includes some characteristics of effective change agents. Perhaps the reader will be aided if he analyzes himself as an agent of change in his organization or community by evaluating himself on these criteria, checking his present life style in terms of one of the following: "usually," "sometimes" or "never."

1. *Openness*—willing to consider new ideas and people of differing opinions; tentative in communications, rather than dogmatic or closed-minded in one's approach.
   _____ Usually
   _____ Sometimes
   _____ Never
2. *Flexibility*—adaptable to new people, situations, information and developments; able to handle the unexpected and to shift position; spontaneous in responding to the "here and now" data and experiences.
   _____ Usually
   _____ Sometimes
   _____ Never
3. *Sensitiveness*—conscious of what is happening to oneself and others in the communications about the change and its effects; aware of the needs and feelings of others because of the proposed change; able to respond empathetically.
   _____ Usually
   _____ Sometimes
   _____ Never
4. *Creativeness*—respond with resourcefulness to new people and situations; avoid stereotype answers and solutions; exercise initiative, imagination and innovativeness.
   _____ Usually
   _____ Sometimes
   _____ Never
5. *Person-centered*—concerned more about people than task or mere progress; care what happens to the people involved in the change; support, encourage, inform and involve people in the decisions for change which they will be expected to implement; respect the right of dissent.
   _____ Usually
   _____ Sometimes
   _____ Never

Exhibit 6.9 Change Inventory for Leaders, *cont'd.*

6. *Goal-oriented planning*—develop a case for change with others which takes into account long-range objectives, while developing a plan with different stages or targets and short-term steps to accomplish the planned change; communicate these purposes and plans to all involved; state goals in terms that have positive value to those affected by the change.

_____ Usually
_____ Sometimes
_____ Never

7. *Group understanding*—possess knowledge of the group process and skills in team dynamics; analyze the driving and resisting forces within the group relative to proposed change; understand the character, structure, needs and wants of the group or organization to be affected by change; involving entire group in change process.

_____ Usually
_____ Sometimes
_____ Never

8. *Communicativeness*—promote open, circular interaction; able to analyze and clarify the problem and reasons for change; motivate members to desire to change and to use the available resources; develop a helping relationship with others so they can accept and live with the change.

_____ Usually
_____ Sometimes
_____ Never

Part II

Relative to your capacity to cope more effectively with rapid change in your own personal and organizational life, indicate your present typical response by checking the category in the right-hand columns which is most appropriate for each descriptive item in the paragraphs on the left. Be self-critical in your appraisal, for no one will receive these results but you, and it is intended as an exercise in "mind-stretching."

9. *Changing image*—possess the capacity to re-evaluate my concept of self based on new feedback, so as to expand my self-image; fluid in my self-conception, amplifying my sense of identity as a result of new encounters and experiences.

_____ Usually
_____ Sometimes
_____ Never

Continued

Exhibit 6.9   Change Inventory for Leaders, *cont'd.*

10. *Changing construct*—willing to review periodically the way I read meaning in my life; flexible in my attitudes and perceptions, so as to make "new sense" out of added inputs and insights; able to break out of "old mindsets" and to develop new rationale; able to accept, at times, inconsistencies and discontinuity in my life.

_____ Usually
_____ Sometimes
_____ Never

11. *Changing values*—able to sense new needs in myself and others, to develop new and changing life values, to abandon past, readymade values and ideals, to revise my expectations of self and others; and as a result, willing to re-examine the norms or standards which I have set for myself and others and to develop new ones as appropriate.

_____ Usually
_____ Sometimes
_____ Never

12. *Changing role*—willing to have an unclear, hazy role in life or an organization—one that is dynamic and responds to current relevant needs; able to live with a role definition which is open-ended and subject to continuous clarification; accept new role definitions for women, for parents and spouses, for colleagues, for professionals and other career people.

_____ Usually
_____ Sometimes
_____ Never

13. *Changing society*—able to be comfortable with impermanence or a lack of structure; capable of coping with constant alteration and perpetual transition; willing to live in changing times, without the traditional stability and reference groups; able to make the most of the present moment—the "here and now"— to be "existential" or to "hang loose," ready to combat unwarranted resistance to change in myself and the communities in which I participate.

_____ Usually
_____ Sometimes
_____ Never

14. *Changing goals*—concerned about actualizing my own and others' potential, as well as increasing the levels of awareness and consciousness in both; seek improvement in my capacity for feeling, and intuitiveness, for creating and risk-taking; desire more knowledge and education for personal and professional development; willing to provide cultural leadership by experimenting with new life styles of adaptation to the demands of rapid change.

_____ Usually
_____ Sometimes
_____ Never

Exhibit 6.9   Change Inventory for Leaders, *cont'd.*

15. *Changing life style*—willing to be more transient and mobile within and among organizations; able to change jobs and locations when appropriate; capable of abandoning old relationships when necessary, and to search for new, more meaningful ones; willing to reject past stereotypes of other people, especially various minorities or foreigners; able to participate in team efforts to solve increasingly complex problems; able to cope with stress and urban crowding, lack of privacy, noise, pollution and other modern discomforts, while seeking to improve these situations; capable of enduring discontinuities and disconnections in my life.

_____ Usually

_____ Sometimes

_____ Never

NOTE: The above inventory items are offered with a view to stimulating your thinking about planned changes within your personal and organizational life space if "future shock" is to be avoided or minimized. There are no "right" or "wrong" answers. Research indicates that people who check "usually" are moving in the direction of developing those qualities which make for a more healthy personality in today's and tomorrow's fast-changing world. Those who check only "sometimes" or "never" are challenged by such items to set new personal goals which enable them to move in the future to a state of mind or behavior whereby they can mark "usually" if they were to retake the inventory.

---

such as action, thinking, wishing, striving, valuing, achieving. These forces may be human (some person who is pushing for the change), or non-human (like a drop in the stock market or a tornado). Forces may be ideas, principles, other people, or within oneself (self image, needs, standards, perception).

Exhibit 6.10   Force Field Analysis Inventory.

This exercise is based on the theories of the late Kurt Lewin, a behavioral scientist who did "pioneering" research on the subject.

Exhibit 6.10   Force Field Analysis Inventory, *cont'd.*

1. Describe the change you wish to initiate _____
   _____

2. Analyze the type of change (check one or more):
   (   ) Policy;   (   ) Structure;   (   ) Attitude;
   (   ) Program;   (   ) Procedures/Methods; Others
   _____

   _____

3. Self-analysis (describe your relationship to the change and analyze your
   needs and motives for promoting it)
   _____

   _____

4. Organization analysis (describe briefly why the organization—or the larger
   society—will benefit from this planned change)
   _____

   _____

5. Related effects (describe the related effects this change may have on the
   socio-economic system in which it may be introduced)
   _____

   _____

6. Identification of change agents (note the names of those people who can
   collaborate with you in the promotion of this planned change)
   _____

   _____

7. Analysis of forces (on the pages 205–207 list the driving and resisting force in
   your life space which will promote or retard the introduction of this intended
   change. Within your perceptual field, analyze these forces which may be
   persons, events, situations, customs and traditions, etc.)

Exhibit 6.10 Force Field Analysis Inventory, *cont'd.*

8. Counter Arguments (anticipate objections which might be raised by those resistive to the change and how you may deflect its force)

   ARGUMENT _____

   _____

   _____

   COUNTER _____

   _____

9. Analysis of creative dissent (listen to the valid objections to the change as you intend to promote it. If you are satisfied that the change is still worthwhile, what modifications should be made in your plan as a result of these observations? How would you revise the plan?)

   _____

   _____

   _____

10. Channel resistance (what steps can be taken to convert some resistance into a constructive force for the change?)

   _____

   _____

   _____

11. Inventory Resources (what other resources are present in the organization which can be utilized in initiating and carrying out this change?)

   _____

   _____

   _____

12. Develop your case (summarize the case for change which you will later develop in detail)

   _____

   _____

   _____

Now do the investigation or research which makes the change worthy of support.

Continued

Exhibit 6.10   Force Field Analysis Inventory, *cont'd.*

13. Communicate your case (your reasons for the change must be properly conveyed to those who will be affected by the change; create a climate of readiness).

a) How? What media will you use to communicate this message? _____

_____

b) To whom will you primarily direct this communication? _____

_____

The above should not only include names of individuals, but divisions and departments within the organization.

14. Other strategies (in addition to what has already been done, what other steps could you take to insure the general acceptance of this change?) _____

_____

_____

15. Project ahead (if you understand your goal in this change, as well as the means for achieving it and your expectations if it is inaugurated, then you are in a position to predict the probable outcomes when this change is under way)

_____

_____

_____

16. Action plan (list the immediate steps to be taken to get the change accepted and functioning. You may wish to include a testing or pilot project phase) _

_____

_____

Use additional sheets of paper if more space is needed. Such a plan should include *what* is to be done, *how* it is to be done, *who* is to do it, *when* it is to be done. It should include a datagathering stage before communication.

17. Alternative plan (if the plan you propose is rejected, you should have done adequate thinking on other alternatives to the change as described) _____

_____

_____

_____

Exhibit 6.10 Force Field Analysis Inventory, *cont'd.*

18. Participative provisions (if the change is to be successfully introduced, then some provisions must be made to involve those who will be expected to implement the change or who will be affected by it. What have you done with regard to planning and decision-making to insure that this has been accomplished?) _____

_____

_____

_____

Worksheet for Item 7
Analysis of Forces

DRIVING (D)

(List all the promoting forces for the CHANGE)

1. _____
2. _____
3. _____
4. _____
5. _____
6. _____
7. _____
8. _____
9. _____
10. _____
11. _____
12. _____

ADDITIONS:

_____

_____

Continued

Exhibit 6.10 Force Field Analysis Inventory, *cont'd.*

_____
_____
_____
_____
_____
_____
_____
_____
_____
_____
_____
_____
_____

RESISTING (R)

(List all the restraining forces against the CHANGE)

1. _____
2. _____
3. _____
4. _____
5. _____
6. _____
7. _____
8. _____
9. _____
10. _____
11. _____
12. _____

Exhibit 6.10   Force Field Analysis Inventory, *cont'd.*

ADDITIONS:

_____

_____

_____

_____

_____

_____

_____

_____

_____

_____

_____

_____

_____

_____

_____

_____

_____

CHECKLIST   (In identifying the above sets of forces, did you list those which might be found under these headings? If you missed any, then note them under D or R)

( ) Goal/objectives problems
( ) Power/authority problems
( ) Communication problems
( ) Role/relationship problems
( ) Decision making problems

207

THEME REVIEW

High-performance leadership is achieved mainly through people skills. Certainly, today's executives have to know how to manage technology, to take advantage of scientific advances to reduce costs. But that is not enough to ensure outstanding organizational effectiveness—it is in the arena of human resource management that the real payoff will come over the long term. In a *US News & World Report* feature (December 23, 1985, p. 46), James Kouzes, director of the executive training center at the University of Santa Clara, contrasted the leadership of two recent national presidents—Jimmy Carter, an engineer, sought to master details, but Ronald Reagan, a master communicator, was effective because of his people skills. To streamline bureaucracies and function well in a high tech-environment, managers will have to exercise judgment and communicate more easily and quickly with employees. As Ford official Nancy Badore observed in that same article, the rise in foreign joint ventures and overseas manufacturing also requires managers to deal with someone not only from another company, but another culture. Therefore, our emphasis in this text is on leadership development of all such human relations skills.

The media is filled with stories about American management waking up to the new work realities, especially regarding the critical human factors. The messages of behavioral scientists to management for the past 40 years are finally being heard and practiced as these few quotations from the *Los Angeles Times* (November 29, 1985, p. 20) confirm:

> Everybody from the high-level manager to people at the hourly level like to feel they are participating in the decision-making. If people don't feel like they own a piece of the action, then they're not going to act like entrepreneurs; they're going to act like paid help. (Lodwrick Cook, Chief Executive, Atlantic Richfield)

> As incentive for our employees in GE's small business ventures, we hold out the promise of company stock if the project gets their products out on time and meet specific growth targets. But workers have to be convinced they won't be fired or demoted for speaking out or tackling something that fails. If GE is to continue to put distance between itself and the bunters of the business world, it must take the big swing with increasing frequency. That may mean some strikeouts along the way. But the prospects of hitting a home run make the risks worthwhile. (John F. Welch, Jr., Chairman, General Electric)

> Measurable improvement in the quality of GM products is oc-
> curring because of greater worker involvement over the past
> two years. (Roger Smith, Chairman, General Motors)

A later *Los Angeles Times* story (March 28, 1988, p. 4/IV) provided another side to the above observation with this story under the
headline, "GM's Smith Ignored the Human Side." It described a 1988
book, *Call Me Roger,* by Albert Lee, a former aide to Roger Smith,
which claimed that the Chairman is destroying morale in the world's
biggest corporation by not including the "human equation" in General Motor's sweeping modernization program. The author—once a
GM speechwriter—maintained that in addition to public relations blun-
ders, the GM chief fails to consider the roles played by the company's 3
million employees, dealership, and suppliers. After the loss of director
Ross Perot, Lee claimed, 'By almost every measure of management . . .
his (Smith's) *leadership* had failed."

That same newspaper carried another feature under the banner,
"U.S. Firms Wasting Prime Asset: People." The message was simple:
If America is to boost its position in the global market, then adversarial
relationships between managers and unions must end. CEOs must view
workers as essentially expendable. Arrogant American chieftains were

Exhibit 6.11 Developing Human Potential through Change.

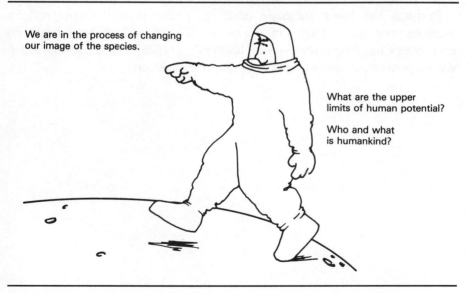

We are in the process of changing
our image of the species.

What are the upper
limits of human potential?

Who and what
is humankind?

criticized for not valuing employee relations and talents, and for putting profits before quality products and service. Executives must relearn that their primary resource is people: Power and profit reside in personnel, not property.

We have completed our review of the six major human relations themes that dominate the behavioral science management literature. We began by examining the issue of *leadership* in a high-performance work environment. We then examined *motivation* and related factors of human performance at work. Then we concentrated on the *communication skills* necessary for both personal and organizational excellence. Furthermore, we linked these insights to culture and its impact on behavior at work. We also focused upon *relationships* in terms of both organizations and teams, demonstrating their importance, particularly with reference to decision-making and conflict management. Finally, we concluded with *change* and why it is so vital to manage it for personal and organizational transformation. Throughout these previous chapters, the emphasis has been upon these six dimensions for developing human potential. Perhaps Exhibit 6.11 best illustrates the leadership challenge.

Throughout the input, interaction and instrumentation sections, creative ideas and methods have been suggested for the leader to share these learnings with colleagues. However, the last two chapters will focus specifically on presentation skills for managers or trainers who wish to transmit these key insights to co-workers or customers.

Perhaps the basic message of these pages is best expressed by management guru Tom Peters, who calls for an *alliance* between employers and employees so that leadership is shared at all levels. Thus, we empower personnel to renew our organizations.

7
Developing People through Learning

In an information society, in which knowledge is power, a large part of the work force is engaged in acquiring, analyzing, processing, distributing, or otherwise servicing this precious resource. Data are pieced together to form information, and information is shaped to create knowledge. When knowledge provides enlightenment, it then can be profitably applied to improve performance or to increase productivity. This happens as a result of study, of sharing the knowledge. The process is called learning—the systematic acquisition of knowledge, for instance, as in the mastery of a specific scholarly field or a new technology. In the emerging metaindustrial environment, the new work culture emphasizes lifelong learning, either formally or informally (Harris, 1985, Chapter 4). Today those who would be leaders must first and foremost be learners. They must create a learning environment in the human systems in which they lead, so that learning may be fostered among others.

To capitalize on an organization's human assets, leaders must develop people. In Chapter 1, I described the emerging role of the manager as an agent of change. For career development, such planned change begins with oneself and extends outward to include those for whom one is directly responsible. This human resource management and development function includes the promotion of learning. (The Epilogue after Chapter 8 will develop this theme even further.)

Such learning can happen through:

* Attendance at classes outside the organization, for instance, universities, colleges, adult education centers, or through confer-

ences and seminars sponsored by professional and trade associations
- Self-learning endeavors, such as correspondence or television courses, video or audio cassette programs, and community service activities
- In-service training opportunities, such as varied programs for personnel development sponsored by a corporation or agency

The last method is the one that concerns us in this chapter. Human resource development—simply put, learning—can occur at weekly or monthly staff meetings, (see Chapter 8) or in formal training sessions, annual conferences or retreats, programmed instruction, job rotation or exchanges, or international assignments, which make cross-cultural learning possible. If an organization operates a formal "assessment center," then action learning research should occur there (London, 1985).

As a case in point, take the major themes of behavioral science management that we have discussed in this book. How can a reader share these insights with coworkers? The professional development strategy proposed in this chapter will help the manager or trainer improve human resource development skills through:

1. The concept of action learning, an approach to adult education involving variety of input, interaction, and instrumentation
2. Planning and designing action learning to improve personnel performance
3. Action research in training sessions for data-gathering and evaluation
4. Action learning methods for group dynamics

INPUT

ACTION LEARNING STRATEGIES

The human resource development (HRD) function includes recruiting, selecting, counseling, training, and evaluating people. In regard to the last two concerns, action learning requires acquiring and applying new insights and information, changing attitudes, and gaining knowledge (Mumford, 1987; Revens, 1982). To foster high performance and to actualize the potential of knowledge workers, action learning provides a rationale and system for planning, designing, implementing, and evaluating adult education or organizational training. It is a strategy to promote learning by doing, a means for accomplishing *andragogy* (the art and science of helping mature people learn). Action learning encompasses a variety of methods of learning and requires maximum participation by the learners (trainees). To make the best use of resources, the action learning strategy is organized in modules; these are learning units, usually several hours long, that are independent in themselves but can be linked together, for instance in a seminar or workshop. The learning modules provides time for three undertakings:

1. *Input* from the presenter, facilitator, or trainer; from the trainees; from audiovisual aids or printed material (such as the material in the Input sections of previous chapters)
2. *Interaction* or group process opportunities (such as in the Interaction section of this and previous chapters)
3. *Instruments,* in the form of inventories or questionnaires that can be used with learners for data-gathering, analysis, and reporting (such as in the Instrumentation section of this and previous chapters).

Action learning sessions can be a mechanism for engaging in action research through interaction and instrumentation, thus contributing to organization development. All told, it is an intensive learning experience, both cognitive and experiential, that encourages action during the process and as a result of the training. Each day learners are expected to write "action plans" based upon the insights and information received. Sometimes their supervisors are given copies of these plans, so that they may follow-up on the outcomes of the learning or utilize them in performance appraisal.

Action learning is a strategy that a manager may use for staff training, team building, or to fullfill any HRD function. Action learning can be employed by anyone with a training responsibility. Action learning can be done within the organization, or outside, for instance, as a volunteer in community activities.

In general, action learning has these characteristics:

1. *Situational.* It is in-service education or on-the-job training that has as its target *change* in the work situation or in the person who receives the training in the work or therapy situation. It is most effective when it concentrates on training a work unit or team. By

providing time for practice in the learning session, the learner has an opportunity to internalize knowledge.

2. *Experiential.* It makes the prime focus of training data gathered by participants in the learning experience or provided by them from previous experience.

3. *Plural.* It emphasizes both affective and cognitive learning; its concern is for both feelings and ideas; it should be a balance of the "I feel" and the "I think."

4. *Problem-orientation.* It deals with issues for personal and organizational change and provides practice in problem-solving and decision-making; it aims for action not only in the learning process, but also in the follow-up as a result of training.

5. *Systematic.* It envisions the training effort as only a subsystem of a larger system for human resource development; it is given as a part of a total program for personal and professional growth; it is viewed as an essential component for broader organization development. The systems approach can also be applied to the actual training process itself.

6. *Personalized.* Although group process may be utilized, due consideration is given to individualizing the learning so as to make allowance for each trainee's unique needs, perceptions and expectations. Action-learning, furthermore, provides performance standards for the trainee by setting goals. It also offers a means for self-assessment by using feedback and group evaluation.

Action learning is based on certain assumptions about the learner and educational methodology. Dr. Malcolm Knowles (1984), the noted adult education specialist, proposed these assumptions:

- Adults enter a learning activity with an image of themselves as self-directing, responsible grown-ups, not as immature, dependent learners. Therefore, they resist situations in which they are treated with disrespect. Implication for methodology; if adults help to plan and conduct their own learning experiences, they will learn more than if they are passive recipients.
- Adults enter a learning activity with more experience than youth. Therefore, they have more to contribute to the learning activity and have a broader basis of experience to relate to new learning. Implication for methodology: those methods which build on and

make use of the experience of the learners will produce the greatest learning.

- Adults enter a learning activity with a different quality of experience and different developmental tasks than youth. Implication for methodology: the appropriate organizing principle for adult learning experiences is developmental sequence primarily and logical subject development only secondarily.
- Adults enter a learning activity with more immediate intentions to apply learning to life problems than youth. Therefore, adults require practical results from learning. Implication for methodology: adults will perceive learning experiences that are organized around subject topics.

Argyris (1982) proposes that such learning be used by a manager to

- Establish trust and cooperation with new members in a work unit
- Build a cohesive and effective work team
- Educate new people in corporate policies, procedures, and culture
- Deal with ineffective performance and improve productivity
- Encourage managers to change leadership style and accept greater responsibility
- Foster a participative group approach to problem-solving and planning.

The essential characteristic of action learning is that it seeks behavioral change in the learner. The impact of this learning experience can lead to a change in knowledge, understanding, skills, values, attitudes, interests, or motivations.

The conditions necessary for action learning to be effective are

1. Recognition of the learner or trainee's needs, as well as those of the organization
2. Ability of the learner to take an active role in the process
3. A threat-free learning climate of acceptance and freedom
4. Measurable criteria and means for achieving learning goals or module objectives
5. Skill on the part of the learning facilitator

PLANNING

There are many ways to meet the first criterion—identifying the learning or training needs of a group. One strategy is to bring together several knowledgeable and representative people from the organization to assist in planning the learning program. For example, suppose an executive wished to conduct a professional or management development institute based upon the content of this book. Having identified those for whom the project is intended, the executive establishes a planning task force with a representative sample of all those eventually to be involved (e.g., people from different levels or divisions of the organization). If the organization has an HRD or training department, obviously these specialists also would be invited.

The task force is asked to

1. Determine what the organization and the targeted training group need in the way of human relations skills
2. Review this text's ability to provide the information, instruments, and interaction methods needed, and ascertaining if additional learning materials are required
3. Use the method described in Exhibit 7.1 to further refine the planning process for the proposed institute;
4. Determine the objectives of the program, the number and topics of learning modules to be presented, dates and schedule of the institute, the learning materials necessary (such as audiovisual aids or film or video rentals), preferred instructional methods and resources (e.g., case studies or simulations, speakers or trainers), suggested action research during the sessions (e.g., forms of data collection, program evaluation).

The Planning Task Force may prefer to work together as one entity and follow the model in sequence (thus avoiding breaking up into subgroups). Exhibit 7.2 provides an overview of the five key steps in this planning paradigm, relating the proposed learning to the organization's human resources development strategies. There are other planning strategies. For example, Exhibit 7.3 is a planning flowchart used by a Sunbelt corporation to prepare for a training program. In this case, the corporate training staff identified the target audience, developed a questionnaire for obtaining information from the intended trainees

Exhibit 7.1   Action Learning Planning Model—Planning Task Force Procedure. (The initials stand for the major topics or tasks which make up this model: Needs, Goals, Methods, Contents and Resources.)

1. The planning group or committee should be divided into five subgroups for task assignments and formed into small circles.
2. Each group is given several sheets of large newsprint and a felt-tipped marking pencil for reporting purposes; it is asked to choose a recorder.
3. Each group is given a specific task as outlined in Exhibit 7.2; each group works on one of the five tasks within a definite time frame (e.g., 30–45 minutes).
4. The consensus of their findings should be summarized on a single sheet of large newsprint.
5. This is then posted in sequence (N/G/M/C/R) with the other reports on a wall using masking tape; each task force recorder then provides an oral summary for the group using the outline displayed.
6. When all sub-groups have reported, the entire committee reviews the results in order to modify and integrate the data into a meaningful whole.
7. The committee then decides whether (a) it can accept the information as edited as its training plan or (b) it should return for further group work to refine the reports in each of the five categories or (c) it should appoint an ad-hoc coordinating commission to synthesize the information and issue a formal training plan.

as to their needs on the job, and established an advisory committee to assist with the planning. The advisory committee was a task force of managers from the five geographical areas in which the firm operated. They helped in the analysis of the preprogram questionnaire data and interviewed key managers and supervisors in their respective regions about their opinions on the proposed training. Exhibit 7.4 outlines the six points of their inquiry.

The task force reviewed the results from the questionnaire and interviews, integrated the findings, and chose four topics for inclusion in the projected program: training in human relations, finance, planning, and safety. Some task force members monitored the actual learning modules, so as to ensure that they met the identified needs and the program objectives. The whole process involved participation by a wide range of people, including HRD specialists, especially those who were to be the recipients or beneficiaries of the learning.

Another way to plan for training with their clients is a performance-oriented job analysis of tasks and functions through interviews with

Exhibit 7.2 Planning Model Sequence.

I. Needs

The purpose of this session is to develop a *policy statement* which summarizes the training needs of the group you seek to serve by this educational program. In your discussion, please focus on the following issues, incorporating the decisions in the group report.

1. What are the over-all training needs in your field and facility?
2. What training is presently available to serve these needs?
3. What are the unmet training needs?
4. In terms of priorities, list the most important needs to which this training program should be directed. (Check the hierarchy of human needs to see if any level has been neglected—physiology, security, belonging, recognition, self-fulfillment.)

II. Goals

The purpose of this session is to develop a policy statement of goals for training in the area of your group's concern. In your discussion, focus upon the following issues:

1. What are legitimate broad *goals* for agencies or departments in your field and in your institution?
2. What are the *objectives* for training (staff or clients) in the proposed program?
3. How do these relate to organizational goals?
4. What specific targets should be set in this forthcoming training course? Describe behavior changes and consequences desired after training.

III. Content

The purpose of this session is to develop a *policy statement* relative to the *content* to be covered in the course of human resource development. In your discussion, please focus upon:

1. new knowledge to be acquired by the learners;
2. new skills to be developed as a result of the training;
3. new attitudes or insights to be attained by the trainees.

IV. Methods

The purpose of this session is to outline a *policy statement* regarding the *methodology* for the proposed training. In your discussion, focus upon:

Exhibit 7.2   Planning Model Sequence, *cont'd.*

1. a general pedagogical approach;
2. specific methods and techniques to be employed;
3. evaluation instruments and procedures to be utilized.

V. Resources

The purpose of this session is to develop a policy statement relative to the educational resources available for the projected training. In your discussion, focus upon:

1. the general support services and resource consultants in your community which could be used to enhance your training effort;
2. the overall resources—human and material—in your organization which could be tapped for the proposed training;
3. the specific resources in your center or training department that would actually be utilized for this training.

Check to see if you have neglected any person who can provide valuable assistance and whether the necessary facility and equipment is available.

Conclusion

When the total group reviews the five reports and pulls the data together into a comprehensive whole, ask these questions:

a. Have we adequately identified the needs of the organization and the training group?
b. Have we sufficiently detailed the training goals of this program to satisfy those needs?
c. Have we satisfactorily outlined the content to be covered and the methods to be used in the projected training endeavor?
d. Have we sufficiently identified the human and material resources available to conduct this training?

Now having reviewed the purposes, subject matter and means for satisfaction of the training needs, consider the following factors relative to IMPLEMENTATION of these policy statements:

a. *Action Plans*—the who, what, when, where and why relative to the training.
b. *Research Design*—how will we evaluate the training and measure its behavioral consequences? What plans should there be for follow-up study of the group after training?

Exhibit 7.3   HRD Planning Flowchart.

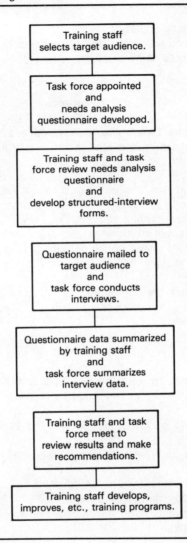

Training staff
selects target audience.

Task force appointed
and
needs analysis
questionnaire developed.

Training staff and task
force review needs analysis
questionnaire
and
develop structured-interview
forms.

Questionnaire mailed to
target audience
and
task force conducts
interviews.

Questionnaire data summarized
by training staff
and
task force summarizes
interview data.

Training staff and task
force meet to
review results and make
recommendations.

Training staff develops,
improves, etc., training programs.

experienced and successful performers in that role. Then, objectives and tests are created for the proposed training with emphasis on specific desired behaviors. The learning experience is designed to ensure such behavior results. The system is described in Exhibit 7.5.

The planning strategy should be appropriate to the specific situation, synthesizing the needs and concerns of both the organizational sponsor

Exhibit 7.4 Planning Interview Strategy.

Structured Interview Sample Questions

1. Think back to when you first started your present job. What type of training would have helped you at that time?
2. What training would benefit you now in your present job?
3. What training do you need to become a promotable candidate for the next position up? What job is that?
4. What would the prerequisites for your job be? What is the minimum experience level of a candidate for your job?
5. How should you receive training, i.e., seminars, on-the-job, etc.?
6. Where should we have training, i.e., resort, hotel, work location?

---

and the learners, while ensuring that the presentations and content will accomplish the desired objectives and results. Planning cannot be done in a vacuum and should be participative, including the intended learner.

For leaders who aim to develop high-performance personnel, there is an advantage in designing learning programs in terms of needs and functions related to specific job roles. Exhibit 7.6 amplifies on the previous systems strategy by proposing ten steps to follow in such a planning process.

DESIGNING ACTION LEARNING PROGRAMS

In a sense, all action learning is customized to meet the needs of a client. For an outside consultant, the client is the organization that hires that person, including the people in any training program or meeting. For an internal consultant employed by the corporation or agency, the client is the department, division, or subsidiary seeking that individual's services. In either case, it is valuable to obtain some understanding and agreement as to the program being planned. Exhibit 7.7 is a form which may prove useful for such clarification. The term *trainer* is used to indicate the one with organizational responsibility for planning, designing, and conducting the training; some may prefer *facilitator* or *instructor*. This person can be an HRD specialist or a manager (sales, operations, plant, or safety). For the manager who is

Exhibit 7.5 Training Systems Planning for Specific Performance. (For further information on this McBer learning strategy, consult Boyatzis, R. E., *The Competent Manager: A Model for Effective Performance.* New York: John Wiley, 1982.)

The blocks in each phase are:

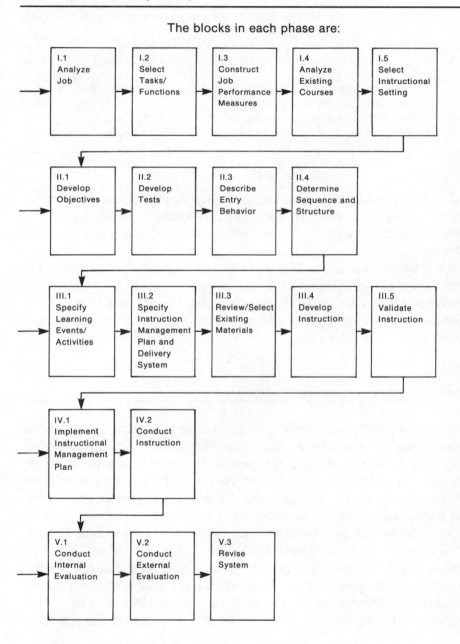

I.1 Analyze Job

I.2 Select Tasks/Functions

I.3 Construct Job Performance Measures

I.4 Analyze Existing Courses

I.5 Select Instructional Setting

II.1 Develop Objectives

II.2 Develop Tests

II.3 Describe Entry Behavior

II.4 Determine Sequence and Structure

III.1 Specify Learning Events/Activities

III.2 Specify Instruction Management Plan and Delivery System

III.3 Review/Select Existing Materials

III.4 Develop Instruction

III.5 Validate Instruction

IV.1 Implement Instructional Management Plan

IV.2 Conduct Instruction

V.1 Conduct Internal Evaluation

V.2 Conduct External Evaluation

V.3 Revise System

Exhibit 7.6   Ten Steps in Training-Needs Analysis for a Job Role.

1. *Analysis of the organization* as a human system particularly in terms of its training history, policies, and facilities
2. *Analysis of the particular job* in terms of tasks required to accomplish it well and its relationship to other positions
3. *Analysis of job restructuring* in terms of other alternatives for doing this activity, or for enriching the work experience on the job
4. *Development of measures for job proficiency,* or ways for determining how well the job is being performed if adequate training is provided
5. *Specification of knowledge and skills,* or the competencies involved in performing this job well
6. *Determination of training objectives,* or what needs to happen in the action learning experience for the trainee to succeed in this job?
7. *Synthesizing personnel policies with training objectives* by consultation with both personnel and training specialists
8. *Construction of the training program,* or design, creation, and conducting of the training for the job, choice or self or group learning
9. *Evaluation of the training,* or action research to assess program effectiveness.
10. *Consideration for retraining or redesigning,* that is, dealing with those who fail to achieve on the job after the training. Is it the fault of the individual? What should be done, if anything about retraining? Are their weaknesses in the training program? How can it be redesigned?

Exhibit 7.7   Preliminary Program Planning Agreement.

Organization/Division/Department _____ Date _____

Client Representative _____ Title _____

Address _____
                 (Street)   (City/State)   (Zip Code)

Telephone _____
                 (Area Code)

Description of Proposed Services

Program title _____

Purpose of program (goals) _____

_____

_____

Continued

Exhibit 7.7 Preliminary Program Planning Agreement, *cont'd.*

Type of trainees (if applicable) _____

Special needs of the group _____

_____

Services training consultant would provide _____

_____

Anticipated number of days for: Training ___ Consulting ___ Research ___

Anticipated number of: Trainers _____ Consultants _____
                        Researchers _____ Trainees _____

Preferred dates for the program _____

Number of sessions to be conducted ___ Number of Days to be in Session ___

Number of learning modules per session _____

Materials trainer would provide _____

_____

Materials client would provide _____

_____

Number and type of client staff available to assist with training/coordinating

_____

Place(s) program to be conducted _____

_____

Facility to be utilized _____

( ) Client to make arrangements
( ) Trainer to make arrangements

Acceptance can be indicated by signing and returning one copy of this agreement

Approved for _____   Accepted for _____

By: _____   By: _____
    (Trainer signature)   (Client signature)
                                    Date: _____

(one copy is retained by client; one by trainer)

undertaking such training with his or her own staff, the items may be useful as a checklist for preliminary discussions about the learning with the participants.

As part of the design phase, a leader in learning may wish to prepare a "prework package." Participants receive this handout material prior to the opening session of training. It contains advanced reading materials on the subjects to be discussed, or an inventory or questionnaire to be completed before the first learning module. This could sensitize the learners to issues to be considered and get them interested in the coming sessions. As an alternative, the completed instrument could be collected as part of the registration process for the training course. In that case, the information is feedback on trainee expectations to be used in both the design and preparing for presentations.

Some professional trainers prefer to wait until the initial meeting with the learning group to engage in an "expectations exercise," which is then included in the learning design. Following the general orientation to the program and introduction of the key resource personnel, the exercise is an opportunity to clarify why participants are engaged in this learning as they introduce themselves to the group. Each trainee at the opening session is invited

1. To write down three personal expectations regarding the learning experience
2. To join a small group to share those expectations and to come to some consensus on the principal expectations of that group
3. Finally, to put the group's mutual concerns down on newsprint or flip-chart paper and share them with the total class or seminar

The trainer or facilitator then posts these sheets around the room. In this first session, the trainer comments on his or her own expectations of the participants and the program. In the closing session, as part of the evaluation process, the trainer refers to the expectations on display and discusses with the learners whether they were fulfilled and to what degree.

Previously, we indicated that the planning should include setting forth both the organizational and individual program objectives. Eventually, this statement of objectives is distributed to the participants (along with the program format or schedule). At the same time, the trainer should set down specific behavior and performance changes

225

to be sought through the training. The design of the actual program should be developed with such changes in mind. For example, if the contents of this book were to be incorporated into a Professional Development Institute (PDI) for selected employees, the general program theme, "Increasing Organizational Effectiveness with People," might be included in the announcement or schedule. Each training session or learning module, then, might have a specific theme that aims at a particular behavioral change or performance improvement, such as Improving Management Communication Skills.

Some HRD professionals take a systems approach to the whole learning process. In Exhibit 7.8, this approach is further amplified in sixteen critical steps or stages.

Steps 1 through 7 are part of the preliminary planning, and steps 8 through 14 are the design phase, or final planning. In this phase, the schedule of "events to happen during the training" is finalized. Since the design phase is primarily for the benefit of the trainees, the trainer may wish to develop for his or her own use a "trainer's planning sheet." In one column list vertically each learning objective; the next three vertical columns are for the name of the learning module, the date/time of its presentation, and the specific activities that help to achieve the objective. If more than two persons make up the training staff, then it may be necessary to further clarify who does what and when. This can be accomplished by developing a "staging directions form," a four-column list with the headings Time, Activity, Participant action, and Staff action. This becomes a sequential guide for the staff as to their mutual responsibilities when the actual learning program unfolds.

Final planning includes selecting particular learning activities with the participants that contribute to the achievement of program objectives. Trainers or facilitators should limit their "on air" time during the sessions. In place of long lectures, for example, present illustrated "lecturettes" that last from 15 to 45 minutes. In the Interaction section of this chapter, some methods for group process are discussed. Exhibit 7.9 demonstrates some of the possibilities to ensure learning variety that will stimulate the learners.

To select just the right learning activity, the manager or trainer needs to know what resources are available. Standard sources for such information include Nadler (1984) *The Handbook of Human Resource Development*, Huczynski (1984) *Encyclopedia of Management Devel-*

Exhibit 7.8 Systems Approach to Action Learning.

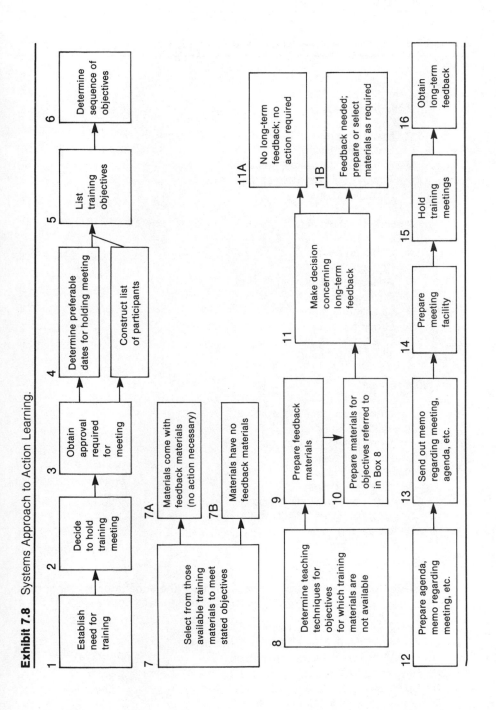

1. Establish need for training

2. Decide to hold training meeting

3. Obtain approval required for meeting

4. Determine preferable dates for holding meeting / Construct list of participants

5. List training objectives

6. Determine sequence of objectives

7. Select from those available training materials to meet stated objectives

7A. Materials come with feedback materials (no action necessary)

7B. Materials have no feedback materials

8. Determine teaching techniques for objectives for which training materials are not available

9. Prepare feedback materials

10. Prepare materials for objectives referred to in Box 8

11. Make decision concerning long-term feedback

11A. No long-term feedback; no action required

11B. Feedback needed; prepare or select materials as required

12. Prepare agenda, memo regarding meeting, etc.

13. Send out memo regarding meeting, agenda, etc.

14. Prepare meeting facility

15. Hold training meetings

16. Obtain long-term feedback

Exhibit 7.9 Selecting Alternative Learning Activities.

1. *General Sessions:*

   (a) Platform presentations

   □ Speeches, research reports, book reviews
   □ Group interviews
   □ Panels, symposiums, debates
   □ Audiovisual aids, dramatizations
   □ Demonstrations

   (b) Audience participation

   □ Listening teams
   □ Reaction panels
   □ Audience role-playing
   □ Buzz sessions
   □ Question and answer
   □ Group reports
   □ Open discussion
   □ Triad consultation

2. *Work Groups:*

   (a) Laboratory groups
   (b) Special interest groups
   (c) Problem-solving groups/task forces
   (d) Discussion groups
   (e) Planning groups
   (f) Instructional groups
   (g) Research and evaluation groups
   (h) Skill practice groups
   (i) Consultation groups
   (j) Operational groups
   (k) Leaderless groups

In designing learning topics and activities, the facilitator is concerned about:

□ Sequence (movement); logic
□ Continuity (line); build on previous knowledge
□ Unity (coherence); appropriateness
□ Rhythm (pace); variety
□ Color (spirit); excitement
□ Climate (feelings); atmosphere
□ Creativity (uniqueness); innovativeness
□ Involvement (ego-identification); participation

228

opment Methods, and Dartnell (1985) *How to Develop and Conduct Successful In-Company Training Programs.* For those with computer access, there is the Human Resource Information Network (Executive Telecom Systems, Inc., 9585 Valparaiso Court, Indianapolis, IN 46268). Today, those who are new to the training business have a host of aids to facilitate the learning process. These range from management games (Elgood, 1984) to video and computer learning systems such as those offered by Venicompass Business Systems (155 West Eighth St., Erie, PA 16501). At the end of this book, a resource section has been provided (Appendices A and B).

One critical factor in planning is the selection of the appropriate presenter for live input during the training program. If a manager or in-house trainer is not suitable, then speakers may be sought from elsewhere within the organization. It may be necessary to use an expert from a nearby university, a trade or professional association, or an industrial source. Speakers directories are available from the National Speakers Association (P.O. Box 6296, Phoenix, AZ 85005) and the American Society of Association Executives (1101 16th St., N.W., Washington, DC 20036). Consulting organizations also provide information on their members and their expertise. For example, annual registries are published by the International Consultants Foundation (11612 Georgetowne Ct., Potomac, MD 20854) and the Society of Professional Management Consultants (163 Engle Street, Englewood, NJ 07631). In addition, there are speakers services and agents, such as Success Leaders Speakers Service (Lenox Square Box 18737, Atlanta, GA 30326) and the International Speakers Network, Inc (Suite 4601, 176 East Deleware Pl., Chicago, IL 60611). Many national and international professional associations have membership directories that may be helpful in this search. A logical source to start with is the American Society for Training and Development (1630 Duke St., Alexandria, VA 22313), which offers a national *Who's Who in Training and Development,* as well as its affiliated International Training and Development Organizations, which issues a *Who's Who in International Human Resource Development.* Once a presenter has been chosen, invitations have to be communicated to that person, negotiations undertaken, and speaking dates and expections confirmed. The program planning agreement may prove useful in this regard (see Exhibit 7.7).

During the design phase, the trainer or manager will have to select or create instruments to gather data or to create awareness among the participants. Throughout this book, the Instrumentation sections have shown examples and possibilities. In addition to Talico Inc. (al-

229

ready cited), there are also commercial publishers that offer tested inventories, checklists, and questionnaires for this purpose, including Organizational Tests Ltd. (P.O. Box 324, Fredericton, N.B., Canada), or its subsidiaries International Publications Ltd. (Melbourn House, Parliament Street, Hamilton 5-31, Bermuda) and Teleometrics International (1755 Woodstead Court, The Woodlands, TX 77380). A central source for such data is a directory of suppliers published by Instrumentation Network (P.O. Box 87, Mound, MN 55364; 612/472-3573).

It is helpful if the participants receive a program schedule or agenda at least two weeks prior to the actual training event. Exhibit 7.10 is a sample of a schedule for a training institute on the contents of this book.

Exhibit 7.11 illustrates a form for ensuring that all necessary supplies and materials are on hand for the opening of the training session. Provision is made to include other learning aids, which could range from games to computers.

It is vital that the HRD planner order films, videotapes, slides, and other audiovisual aids in advance so that they are available at the time and place required. Just before the event, preview all audiovisual materials.

Similarly, arrangements must be made for adequate rest period facilities and for refreshments, possibly when trainees arrive in the morning or during the mid-session breaks. Sometimes this may include group meals for participants, which involves menu selection, luncheon speakers, or the showing of a film. Preparations also include supervising the reproduction and packaging of the learning materials, from textbooks to workbooks to name tags, to be distributed to participants.

Nothing should be left to chance if high performance is to occur during the learning. An organization makes a significant investment when it devotes time, energy, finances, and people to a training program, so HRD planners strive to ensure that people both enjoy and learn while the program moves along smoothly and produces the desired results. When dealing with external facilities, such as hotels, triple-checking with their representatives may ensure that arrangements proceed smoothly.

As we describe the planning process, it should be evident that those who take a professional approach to action learning effectively

- Use strategies in human resource development (Fombrun, Tichy, and Devanna, 1984)

Exhibit 7.10 Professional Development Institute Schedule.

AM 8:00	First Day	Second Day	Third Day
	Learning Module I	Learning Module III	Learning Module V
↓ 12:00 Noon	Dynamics of Human Behavior • Input: Human motivation • Learning aids: Slides; "Motivation of Human Resources," handout; "Management Motivation Inventory" • Group process—Input Bombardment	Improving Communication Skills • Input: A behavioral communication theory; perception and communication model • Learning aids: Slides; "Communication as a People Process," handout; "Communication Inventory" • Film	Creative Approaches to Conflict Resolution in Organizations • Imput: Conflict utilization theory • Group process: anecdotal reports • Learning aids: "Analysis of Conflict Utilization," handout • Film
PM 1:00	Learning Module II	Learning Module IV	Learning Module VI
↓ 5:00	Understanding Deviant Behavior • Group process: Critical Incidents • Film • Learning aids: "Motivation & Human Resource Development," handout; "Human Resource Inventory"	Overcoming Communication Obstacles • Group process: Communications laboratory • Learning aids: "Organization Communications Analysis"; "Communications Bibliography"	Insights from Client Feedback • Input: Utilizing feedback • Learning aids: Audio or videotape playback; administration of client profile—"The Helping Relationship and Feedback in Organizations," handout and exercise
AM 8:00	Fourth Day	Fifth Day	Sixth Day
	Learning Module VII	Learning Module IX	Learning Module XI
↓ 12:00 Noon	Cultural Influences on Client/Staff Behavior • Input: Concept of culture • Learning aids: Slides • Group process: "Understanding Culture," programmed learning exercise	Understanding Group Behavior in Organizations • Input: Group dynamics and organization relations • Learning aids: "Systems Approach to Groups and Organizations" • Group process: Task assignment	Managing Change and Changing Roles • Input: Why and how to plan change Learning aids: Slides and Film; "Management of Change Inventory" • Group process: "Force Field Analysis"
PM 1:00	Learning Module VIII	Learning Module X	Learning Module XII
↓ 5:00	Cultural Influences on Decision Making • Management game—Moon Twenty or Hollow Square • Learning Aid: Decision Making and Cultural Influences • Group process: "Intercultural Relations Inventory," or "Supervisor/Worker Relations" exercise	Interpersonal Skills for Human Resource Personnel • Simulation exercise: Kerner Commission Report • Learning aid: "Behavioral Science Management," handout; "Organizational Roles & Relationship Inventory" • Film	Behavioral Strategies within Organizations and with Clients • Learning aids: Brainstorming • Optional programs: Creative problem-solving • Closing ceremony • Distribution of certificates • Evaluations

Exhibit 7.11   Checklist for Training Materials and Supplies.

Project Manager:		Date:	
CLIENT AND PROGRAM:		SHIPPING/PICK-UP INSTRUCTIONS, INCLUDING DATES:	
ITEM		CHECK IF NEEDED	TO BE PROVIDED BY
A. TRAINING AIDS			
1. Overhead Transparent Projector			
2. 16mm Movie Projector			
3. Screen size			
4. Blackboard, Eraser, Chalk			
5. Newsprint, Easel, and Paper			
6. Podium Type			
7. 35mm Slide Projector			
8. Tape Recorder-audio ( ), video ( )			
9. Flannel Board			
10. Other:			
B. TRAINING MATERIALS			
1. Pencil Sharpener			
2. Stapler			
3. Name Tents			
4. Lapel Tags			
5. Pencils			
6. Yellow Tablets			
7. Punched White Bond			
8. Grease Crayons (marking pencils)			
9. Masking Tape			
10. Training Workbooks (number)			
11. Special Handouts (number of items)			
12. Other:			

- Prepare very carefully and leave nothing to chance before, during, and after the training session;
- Customize the design of the training to meet both organizational and trainee needs
- Seek to vary the learning experience, so as to maintain interest and involvement on the part of participants
- Use training sessions for data-gathering and action research, so as to achieve organization development (OD) aims.

If Nash (1985) is right when he contends that the whole human resource management effort is aimed at making people more productive, then this is doubly true for HRD planning and implementation.

IMPLEMENTING THE TRAINING PLAN

Those who are not amateurs at offering training programs, take steps to make certain that the plan is carried out effectively. That means working assidously with those in charge of the meeting facilities, whether internal or external (see Chapter 8). The meeting coordinator seeks to provide a comfortable facility with proper lighting, noise control, ventilation (air conditioning or heating as necessary), seating, equipment, and other amenities to facilitate learning. The details are important, for example, the question of smokers from nonsmokers, or banning smoking in the conference rooms, should be resolved in advance.

Twelve learning modules, as described in Exhibit 7.10, can be accomplished in six days, perhaps during a one-week session at a residential or resort facility. Adult workers are not use to sitting for learning purposes for six to eight hours a day for almost a full week. Even with the best action learning plan, to make the process more acceptable and to improve performance, the sponsor must do other things, such as scheduling a recreation hour after lunch, or a hospitality hour at 5 P.M. Perhaps the afternoon of the fourth day could be given over to golf or sightseeing or the evening devoted to a fiesta, luau, or banquet. If the same program is scheduled for six monthly meetings held in the company training room, such arrangements are unnecessary. The way the schedule is implemented influences the choice of site and the other arrangements.

Group size also influences the facility arrangements. Learning groups often consist of from twenty to forty people; the ideal for effective

233

participation is around thirty. If small rooms are used for such groups, then extra, break-out rooms or outdoor facilities may be necessary for subgroup meetings. A very large ballroom can also be used, with the training area in the center and circles of chairs on the sides for smaller group discussions. On the other hand, if there is a large audience, of several hundred or even several thousand, the seats must be movable, so people can move chairs to form small groups of from three to six persons for short assignments.

Room arrangements depend on program objectives, participant numbers, and facility possibilities or limitations. Assuming a group of thirty, it is often advantageous to set up the training room with tables forming a U; people can sit along the outside of the U, and the center is left open for a projection table and for the trainer to easily move among the participants. That same open area can also be utilized for role-playing or demonstration; a screen for visual aids, a lectern, a table for trainer supplies, and a blackboard or easel can be set up at the top of the U. Name plates or cards will help staff members identify participants.

The implementation stage begins at the training site when the trainer arrives well in advance of the trainees to ensure that all learning materials and equipment are in place and in working order. If necessary, an information or registration desk is set up and staffed. Food and refreshment arrangements must be finally checked out. Then the training coordinator warmly greets the participants either informally and personally, as they arrive, by circulating during a reception or registration hour, or by welcoming them as a group during the opening sessions.

Special guests, such as company officials, speakers, or panelists, have to be greeted and acculturated, so they integrate quickly and smoothly into the learning experience. Everyone, including learners, guest presenters, and company officials, should be made to feel wanted and comfortable by the HRD staff or manager.

Exhibit 7.12 lists some useful guidelines for adult education. The training coordinator needs to be especially mindful of timing and pacing, so that activities occur as scheduled and the program moves along in a lively manner. Learning can be fun as well as enlightening, and boredom can be avoided. Be aware also of "O'Toole's Law," which is a supplement to "Murphy's Law": Murphy says that if anything can go wrong it will; O'Toole claims that Murphy is an optimist. Despite all the detailed planning, be prepared not only with contingency plans, but to meet the unexpected, from power failure to a speaker's sudden unavailability.

Exhibit 7.12 Guidelines for Training Adults.

America is moving into the age of the "knowledge worker" in contrast to the laborer of the past. Increasingly, authority will be given to those with the information and skill to solve complex problems. Competing is becoming the true criteria for career advancement. Thus, there is a growing demand by adults for *continuing education.* Large numbers of personnel must be constantly retrained in new skills and occupations. Because of this expanding desire for learning, their instructors, too, must develop more dynamic methods for teaching them. If the interest and commitment of mature learners is to be maintained, then various instructional techniques must be used which personally involve the trainees.

Instructors in continuing education should take into account the following factors in preparing their course presentations:

1. The age, maturity and diversity within the trainee group.
2. Previous trainee education and the length of time since the trainee was involved in formal instruction.
3. The actual needs of participants for the content of the course (e.g., in adapting a particular course to a trainee group, some subject matter might be eliminated and other topics added).
4. The amount of time the trainees are devoting to an intensive schedule of classes (e.g., sitting for five or six hours over a one or two-week period will cause fatigue and limit efficiency of learning; it also reduces the available time for outside reading assignments which are usually expected.)
5. In residence programs, the trainees may travel long distances to a strange location and be separated from their families (this requires extra effort on the part of the staff to help them feel at home, overcome strangeness, facilitate their adjustment and assist in any problems; each instructor should be concerned about the human factors related to the participants' learning).
6. To make learning a pleasant experience, an informal classroom atmosphere is to be encouraged. The instructors can help the trainees appreciate the value of further education and the need for continuing self-development.
7. Adults are normally very grateful for any help offered and hold trainers in high regard. Frequently, the instructor will have great impact on adult trainees and their organizations. Therefore, flippancy and unsubstantiated generalizations are to be avoided; your words may be quoted to back-home organizations and your behavior imitated.
8. The trainees have interesting and varied experiences which they should be encouraged to share with the group (they may even present their own case studies).

The key factors in adult training are *variety* and *participation.* It is not always possible to have a variety of places at which the training is conducted

Continued

235

Exhibit 7.12   Guidelines for Training Adults, *cont'd.*

(e.g., change of classroom or setting). However, you can use different techniques in the sessions. While the lecture method might be acceptable with the class which meets two or three times a week for a short time period, it becomes wearing to sit in one place for long sessions with only one instructional method.

A varied approach to teaching is very helpful in maintaining interest. Furthermore, it is disconcerting to sit several hours simply listening and taking notes. The field of group dynamics provides many worthwhile ideas for improvement of adult training.

Finally, Exhibit 7.13 suggests some strategies for bringing the training program to a fitting and successful conclusion. The purpose is not only to bring the learning to a climax, but to send the learner away satisfied and motivated. The training cycle ends with program evaluation, which

Exhibit 7.13   Strategy for Concluding the Training Program.

I. Planning for the Closing Exercises

After the last learning module in a training course, some provision should be made for a formal ending to the program. This can be as short as one hour or as long as three hours, depending on how elaborate the trainer wishes to make the procedure. Since the participants have just finished an intensive learning experience, something should be planned which will summarize the course, reinforce the learning and motivate the trainees to apply their new knowledge and skills. Provisions might be made for the following:

A. *"Program evaluation"* or feedback from the participants on the total experience. (Forms as illustrated in the next section might be administered for 15–50 minutes.) It is also possible to use objective tests for some measure of content knowledge or to ask the trainees to write a short essay on "What was the most important concept I learned in this course," or "My plans for applying this new knowledge." A brainstorming session could be conducted on "What can I do to further the professional development of my subordinates/clients." (See Exhibits 7.19, 7.20, and 7.21.)

B. *"Guest Speaker":* Someone of prominence inside or outside the organization can be invited to make a "graduation" address for 20 or 30 minutes. Be sure to confirm the arrangements by writing/telephone as to when, where and why the event is scheduled. Brief the guest beforehand on the type of trainees to be present, the objectives and content of the course and request that his remarks be appropriate to the theme of "human service."

Exhibit 7.13 Strategy for Concluding the Training Program, *cont'd.*

C. *"Certificates of Achievement":* **Prepare a certificate to signify comple-**
tion of the course; printed, it can be adapted to suit your circumstances.
Before writing the trainees name on the document, have the participants
check the correct spelling of their names on a roster which is circulated to
them prior to the last class. A prominent official in your organization should
be invited to sign these and later distribute them personally to the trainees
at the closing ceremonies.

D. *Other possibilities:* Arrange for an opening and closing invocation by a
chaplain in your organization or the community; invite spouses and relatives
to attend; have the certificates inexpensively framed or placed in a plastic
folder; invite the class to elect a spokesman at the closing ceremonies; have
the ceremonies video-taped and transmitted to the staff's clients assembled
together elsewhere in the building; have some appropriate music played
before and after the event (organ, band, etc.); provide some refreshments
after the ceremony for all. Arrange for university credit for the course.

II. Outline of a "Graduation" Address

A. *Congratulations* on reaching another milestone in the development of your
own human potential—significance of the accomplishment.
B. *Praise* to all those who provided support services to you during this learning
experience—faculty, clerical/cleaning/food staffs, family.
C. Concept of *"professional" development*—what sets the "pro" apart from those
who take a mechanical approach to a job; the need for continuous, life-time
personal and professional growth.
D. Concept of *"change"* as a byproduct of learning—you should not be the same
people who came here on the first day of class. As a result of new information,
experiences, insights, dialogue and encounter with people in a new way
during this course, you should enlarge your "psychological construct" or the
way you read meaning into your life; your ideas, attitudes, needs and values
should change. Most importantly, you should change your IMAGE of yourself,
your role, your clients and your organization.
E. Concept of *action learning*—something positive should happen as a result
of this training; you are *challenged to apply* the new knowledge and skills
which you have acquired to improve the human condition. You learned much
about people and what makes them "tick;" hopefully you will benefit by all this
and utilize it for the benefit of those you seek to serve on your job. Learning
should make you both humble and curious—humble about how much you do
not know and curious to gain more knowledge.
F. Concept of *behavioral leadership*—you do not "tell" people what they must do
as a result of your new-found knowledge; you provide a behavioral model for
your subordinates and clients. You create your own future; you make things
happen for the better as a result of your presence. As a leader, you should
be an agent for planned, positive change in your organization.

begins during the closing session, when some time is devoted to filling out feedback forms. At this time, the participants might discuss what they have learned and assess the value of the training program. In the Instrumentation section, several examples of these forms are presented for the reader's convenience.

Typically, this is only the start of several strategies to appraise program effectiveness, determine what changes should be made before offering any future similar training. Ascertain what additional training may be necessary and why and how to undertake applied HRD research. This issue will be discussed next, but for further information on the subject, I recommend

- *Business Research: Concepts and Guides* (Murdick and Cooper, 1982)
- *Effective Evaluation: Strategies and Techniques* (Merwin, 1986)
- *Human Resource Accounting* (Flamholtz, 1986)
- *How to Measure Human Resource Management* (Fitzenz, 1985)
- *Nonextrapolative Methods in Business Forecasting* (Mendell, 1985)
- *Handbook of Training Evaluation and Measurement Methods* (Phillips, 1983)

ACTION RESEARCH FOR ORGANIZATION DEVELOPMENT

Behavioral scientists began to have impact on organizations with their research, writings, and interventions several decades ago. This took the form of an intensive learning experience called the human relations laboratory. Under the sponsorship of the National Training Laboratories, professionals and managers from various organizations met in "T groups" for sensitivity training. (Now called the NTL Institute, P.O. Box 9155, Rosslyn Station, Alexandria, VA 22209). Then, consultants began to conduct this "laboratory education" inside organizations—with "family" groups—to increase the effectiveness of people who work together. The behavioral science technology thus spawned was called *organization development (OD)*. (For further information contact OD Network, 1011 Park Avenue, Plainfield, NJ 07060, or read Burke [1987].)

Organization development is a system for planned renewal of institutions. French and Bell (1984) have defined OD in this way:

> Organization development is a top-management-supported, long-range effort to improve an organization's problem-solving and renewal processes, particularly through a more effective and collaborative diagnosis and management of organization culture—with special emphasis on formal work team, temporary team, and intergroup culture; with the assistance of a consultant-facilitator and the use of the theory and technology of applied behavioral science, including action research.

More recently, there has been emphasis upon *organization transformation* (OT). (For details, contact OT Network, 15 Garrison Avenue, Durham, NH 03824.) Its practitioners believe that OD is focused on fixing here-and-now problems, while they favor a more visionary, futuristic approach. OT seeks to transform not only organizations but work and management in the process. They wish to unblock people, to recharge their energies, and to stimulate their intuition and innovation. They concentrate on personnel relationships and group processes, on promoting a sense of purpose and more flexible responses.

Organizations are sometimes not in a position to benefit from the services of OD or OT consultants, either by contracting for external specialists or by hiring them as part of the HRD staff. However, most organizations do devote resources to training. This may be for professional development or personal growth, and may include learning about the people skills described in this book, or such issues as wellness, networking, high performance, and team or transformational management (Harris, 1985, Unit II). In-service education encompasses a wide range of concerns—from substance abuse and stress management to new technical or intercultural training. Use this existing vehicle and accepted mechanism for data-gathering and analysis. That is, managers or trainers can conduct action research during these learning sessions, and follow up with reports to executives as a means of promoting feedback and change. The strategy is to use the training as an opportunity to accomplish some of the aims of organization development or transformation. At least, it is a beginning, a way to work on turning an organization around until the experts can be employed.

WHAT IS ACTION RESEARCH?

The term "action research" is recent, and there are different perspectives on its meaning. French and Bell (1984) define it as a process of collecting research data about an ongoing system relative to some objective goal or need of the system; feeding these data back into the system based upon both the data and on hypothesis; and evaluating the results of actions by collecting more data (Exhibit 7.14). It is an approach to problem-solving that can be incorporated into the organization's human resource management and development. It is a form of fact-finding and experimentation that is on-going and can be integrated into the action learning endeavors. It is a synergistic effort that requires the collaboration of managers and workers and internal and external resource persons. It is pragmatic in that it seeks solutions that improve decisions, increase performance, and alter the status quo.

As a consultant, I have always been concerned with bringing about planned and significant change in the human systems that I serve. More often than not, I am employed by clients to design and conduct training programs to enhance personal and organizational effectiveness. Many times these clients understand and support management or executive

Exhibit 7.14 Organizational Relations.

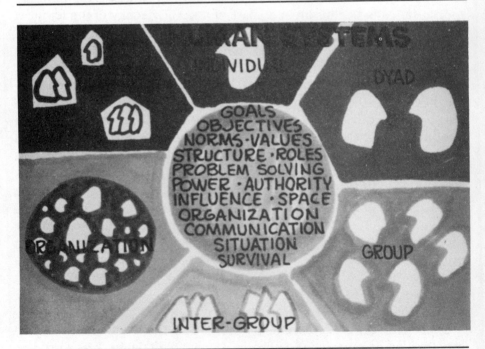

development, although they are not familiar with such behavioral science buzzwords as organization development or transformation. Therefore, I design my program interventions around this model: MD/OD or OT. That is, I try to use management or executive development to achieve some organizational development or transformation. Thus, when departments of Los Angeles County asked me to design a management development institute, I used data-gathering interviews and instruments to ascertain participant and organizational needs, as well as to design the training program. I used group process and survey instruments to collect data during the sessions. Then I summarized and analyzed the data and incorporated it into a written report and oral briefing of top management. With such action research, however, I only set the stage for organizational change; the wise consultant lets the information speak for itself, and merely offers recommendations based on the findings. This strategy has been successfully repeated with such diverse systems as the U.S. Customs Service and Control Data Corporation and has proven of value both nationally and internationally.

The learning process involves three entities: the learner or learning group—the immediate recipient of its benefits; the learning facilitator or trainer—the coordinator of the process; and the organizational sponsor or client—the investor and ultimate beneficiary of the learning when it is applied. As a result of the learning experience, all three parties should be positively changed. The purpose of action research is to discover if that has happened. Was the learning both informative and fun? Will it achieve the results intended? Does it improve both individual and institutional performance? These and other questions for evaluation are answered in the process of action research.

To determine the effectiveness of training efforts, some form of evaluation of the course design and its execution is important. An element of accountability is introduced when there is some attempt to measure the extent to which the educational objectives set down before the learning experience have been realized. An experimental, inquiring approach to the planning and analysis of training programs can insure more relevant courses. The training process is cyclical—design, train, evaluate, redesign, retrain, re-evaluate, etc. A systems concept of learning would require that so much "input" by the trainer would require feedback control of the next "output" by that instructor. Thus, some form of applied research should be built into the instructional system.

A previous statement on action learning pointed out that learning can take place best when it meets the trainees' as well as the organization's needs and goals, when it provides means for involving the learner in the process and for measuring criteria relative to learning goals. The "climate" must also foster learning, and the facilitator of training must possess competency and skill. An assessment program for a training course, for example, should be concerned about such factors. Furthermore, action learning emphasizes behavioral change in terms of knowledge, insight, understanding, attitudes, values, interests and skills. An evaluation of learning should focus on one or more of these elements with regard to the trainees.

Action research by human resource practitioners centers investigation on people problems, to which it hopes to contribute solutions. It is a form of applied research that deals with social issues in an on-going type of scientific analysis. Such research might center on a new technique for rehabilitating the alcoholic, drug addict or criminal offender. Or, it might consider new ways for furthering organizational staff development, such as through a training course. It is related to the daily activity of the practitioner and the desire for professional improvement of service. It seeks to measure the behavioral consequences of the innovative activity which is being tried out.

In its simplest form, it might be a survey of opinion from the trainees as to their general reactions to the learning experience.

In essence, the instructor invites the trainees to look at the learning experience together to see whether or not it was useful; the emphasis is on the "effect" of the training. The type and amount of feedback sought by the trainer can be expanded beyond this, depending on how he plans to analyze and use the data collected. Or specific segments of the training program can be the subject of evaluation.

From such initial data gathering, the trainer can expand the research efforts in a variety of directions. Here are a few possibilities which could be undertaken depending on the research capabilities of the training director and the degree of assessment sought concerning the program:

1. Design a pre/post instrument to ascertain attitudes or knowledge of the trainees before and after training. (See Exhibits 7.15, 7.16, 7.17, and 7.18.)
2. Utilize a control group which is comparable to those in training, but which is not exposed to learning experience. The same pre/post instruments can be administered to this control group, and the results can be statistically compared between the training and non-

training groups. In this way one can determine quantitatively the impact of the training upon the participants versus those who were not exposed to it.

3. Seek an evaluation from the supervisors, peers or subordinates of the trainees to discover if their behavior is any different as a result of the training. (See Exhibits 7.17, 7.18, 7.19, 7.20, and 7.21.)

4. Conduct a follow-up study of the training group sometime after the learning experience to inquire about the long-term effects of the program. It is one thing to collect data from the group at the end of the last training session in the heat of enthusiasm and another to obtain feedback three weeks three months or a year later when people have had an opportunity to test the application of the information and skills acquired in the training program.

Such action research efforts will help to gain greater credibility for the endeavors of a training division within an organization. By such an objective approach to educational efforts, management may be more inclined to support and expand programs for human resource development if it receives some evidence that the investment in training is having some "pay off." Furthermore, the data collected in such inquiries about training effects can be used to improve programs in their next administration.

Research is a valuable tool to determine if a full-scale rendition of a particular training design should be employed. For example, if the training coordinator makes a study of employee or member needs and organizational objectives, one may conclude that a particular type of training is in order. Before suggesting to the administration in the organization that the proposed educational program be undertaken with large numbers of trainees, however, try another strategy—design a pilot project in which part of the intended program would be tested on a limited sample of participants. Thus, the costs of the endeavor are scaled down to a reasonable proportion. If action research proves the training program to be effective, then a case has been made for further use of the "prototype training model."

This introduction has attempted to provide some rationale as to why a busy training coordinator should be concerned about a more objective assessment of his or her efforts in training. Now it might be helpful to review what are some of the basic elements involved in the research process.

STEPS IN TRAINING RESEARCH

THE QUESTION

Research is a systematic way of arriving at a new level of knowledge. Hopefully, it turns up something new and justifiable which can lead to improved thinking and action. It is more than mere fact-finding or experimentation or statistical analysis of data, though it may include all of these functions. It begins with a question(s) on what the investigator proposes to study. The stating and selection of this question(s) is of prime importance, for it indicates the whole purpose or direction of the research, as well as its scope. Thus, a question on how a live training program compares to a self-learning instructional program on the same subject may lead to an experimental design for research.

Development of a new training model may indicate theoretical postulates and experiential data which can be united into a prototype. Logical development of it may lead to the establishment of criteria for the interpretation of the ideas. But if the original question was not clear, then nothing that follows it in the research process will be clear. When research is begun, question(s) may be stated in the form of (a) a question(s), (b) a purpose(s), (c) an hypothesis or a series of hypotheses. The hypothesis is a tentative proposition suggested as a solution to a problem or as an explanation of some phenomenon. It presents the researcher's expectations which one proposes to test in the research study. It is a part of a "theory" to investigate and evaluate.

Hypotheses in the field of training research are often formulated around some innovation in methodology or content. Perhaps the matter was best stated by Alfred F. Smode in a study conducted for the Office of Naval Research on recent trends in training methods, materials and procedures.

> The discovery of ways for improving training comes about in two ways. One is by means of invention or induction. This relates to aspects of creativity and the discovery of new ideas. Another way is through experimentation and field tests to evaluate the soundness of the ideas and techniques. Experimentation, in turn, may be essentially empirical, or it may be based upon a rational-deductive approach.
>
> Specifically, new ways for training come into being in the following ways:

1. An individual conceives an idea for solving some training problem and develops it to the point where it can be introduced into a training program. Such ideas often are adaptations of innovations which have appeared in other areas, in relation to other problems.
2. Innovations may arise not only as inventions, but as a result of systematic analysis and evaluation of existing procedures and materials. Improvement may come about as a result of systematic manipulation of training variables (e.g., a new or original use of a training device or technique).
3. A specific theory or broad concept may lead to hypotheses and deductions for improvements in training.

It should be emphasized that only rarely are novel ideas subjected to careful tests or validation studies. Usually, they are either adopted or rejected without any real knowledge of their true value in training.

Perhaps these concepts can take on new meaning for the reader if we review the origins of the *Professional Development Institutes on Human Behavior*. The author first tried out his ideas for action research in a course titled "Police Development and Human Behavior" which he designed for the Philadelphia Police Department. Some years later he read a Congressional investigation report concerning the causes of the 1968 Camp Pendleton prison riots. One factor cited was "poor training and morale among the Marines assigned to staff the correctional facility." He then theorized that the behavioral sciences could perhaps alleviate the situation by means of an action learning program for staff and administrators of military correctional facilities. He formulated an unsolicited theoretical proposal which eventually received support from the Office of Naval Research and brought this investigation into being (refer to Harris, 1972/73). This book is an outcome of that research.

THE REVIEW

Lest we rediscover the wheel, one should, in the second stage of research, look into the roots from which the question has originated. What has been done in this area before? Who are the people, ideas and procedures in the background of this inquiry? A professional approach would review published literature on the subject and all that is related to it. In such a review lies the real justification for doing the present research. It reveals what has been done on the question and equips the investigator with knowledge of the field so he will recognize the innovative and the significant. For example, in preparing to undertake the research on correctional training previously referred to, this investigator reviewed literature on the following subjects: military criminal justice, correctional manpower and training, Naval correctional reports, police training, behavior modification and human relations training.

The library and other centers of information, especially college and university libraries, become the focus of attention for the trainer who wishes to do a thorough job in his action research. The main sources of related literature are (1) books, (2) periodicals, (3) research reports (such as graduate theses and dissertations) and (4) information retrieval systems. The average busy manager or trainer in the process of designing a new training program has limited opportunity to survey the literature related to a proposed project. One may delegate this task to a member of staff, and there are research tools available to help with the task. For locating up-to-date information in libraries, one might utilize various reference works which organize by topics that which has been written recently on the subject. A few examples of sources to be checked by trainers are: Education Index, Reader's Guide to Periodical Literature and the Annual Review of Educational Research on Psychology. The Dissertations Abstracts, published by University Microfilms, Ann Arbor, Michigan, can provide microfilms on unpublished doctoral studies.

As an aid in educational research, the U. S. Office of Education established ERIC (Educational Resource Information Center), 400 Maryland Avenue, S.W., Washington, DC 20202. By means of the computer, a clearinghouse of information is available to the investigator together with annotated bibliographies concerning a wide variety of topics dealing with education and training. Among the other such storehouses of knowledge, the Defense Documentation Center (Defense Supply Agency, Cameron Station, Alexandria, VA 22314) has special meaning for those trainers who work with government agencies. Its National Technical Information Service provides bulletins, reports, announcements, bibliographies and microfilm about government-sponsored research.

Another useful data bank for managers and trainers is RISS (the Remote Interactive Search System). It is a combination of hardware, software, and peopleware that originates with NASA. Through its regional industrial applications centers (NIAC), technology transfer from research and development of NASA and other government laboratories is possible. Through a subscription service, NIAC associates gain instant access to information on almost any topic and from a variety of scholarly disciplines. Many journals and periodicals are included on subjects ranging from biography and management to social sciences and humanities. Contact 1-800/872-7477 in the USA or 1-800/642-2872 in California for further information, or write NIAC (3716 S. Hope St. #200, Los Angeles, CA 90007). For annual "spinoff" publications of NASA technology transfer, write NASA Scientific and Technical Information Facility (P.O. Box 8757, Baltimore/Washington International Airport, MD 21240).

Local university libraries or computer centers can be valuable sources of information on the most appropriate reference or database for research on a topic. For example, for those with computer capabilities, there is the DIALOG Information Retrieval Service of Lockheed Missiles and Space Co., (Marketing Department, 3460 Hillview Ave., Palo Alto, CA 94304; 1-800/227-1727, or, in California, 1-800/982-5838). This provides access to over 100 databases, providing bibliographies and abstracts of periodical and scholarly literatures.

As the manager or trainer gathers data on what others have said or done relative to the subject under study, this information must be organized and stored for later reference. Again, a personal computer may be the means for setting up such document files; special software is available for this purpose. Sometimes an index file is the simplest approach for this purpose. Then it becomes a matter of sorting out the most pertinent data, and setting priorities as to which material will actually be referenced in one's own proposal or report. This helps to substantiate the case that supports the research questions and strategies.

A few tips on organizing such notes might be helpful at this point:

1. Begin by listing the most recent studies in the file and then work back to earlier references.
2. Read the abstract or summary of a report or article to find out if it is really relevant and worth reading in greater detail.

3. If the reference is worthwhile to include, skim over it first before taking notes.
4. Begin to make notations on the second reading of all that is significant for your purposes; 4×6 inch file cards are usually the best for this.
5. The first entry should be a complete bibliographic reference according to the format you plan to use in the bibliography of your own report; it should contain the full name of the author(s), title of the work, place of publication, publisher or source and date of publication, as well as the page numbers.
6. Indicate which parts of your notes are direct quotations and which are your own paraphrasing; make sure your abbreviations or shorthand will be understandable some time hence or that a typist can read them.

THE PLAN STAGE

The third stage in action research is to set down in some detail the systematic procedure you plan to follow in your investigation. You might start with a research design outline which can be expanded as warranted. Here you state the hypothesis or problem you wish to investigate, how you plan to test your hypothesis or seek solutions to the problem, a description of the procedures to be used, a description of the subjects or samples of population that will be involved, the logic or the criteria to be applied to the learning material or training model which you are proposing, the way you plan to analyze the data gathered (including statistical analyses) and the logistics of the research.

There are research style manuals which can assist you in organizing your thoughts in proper format. As much as possible, use a computer to record and analyze your data.

Sometimes a trainer has to seek moral or financial support from within or without the organization. In that case, one formulates a preliminary and/or final proposal. This can be simple or elaborate depending on the person for whom the proposal is intended and its purpose. The less complicated format might include the following: introduction, rationale, strategy and tentative plan. The more formal approach would include sections such as: Introduction, statement of the problem, scope of the work, research objectives, methodology, facilities, schedule and tasks, staffing, project costs, follow-up research possibilities and a statement of qualifications or biographical information on the researcher.

Back-up materials on the above can be included in the appendices. Essentially, then, what has been described in the previous paragraphs about a research plan has several applications: (1) it can be used as the researcher's own guidelines in pursuing the study; (2) it can enlighten those whose support one seeks for the investigation and be included in a proposal and (3) it can form the basis for parts one and two of a final report, namely, the description of the problem and the methodology.

The most frequent method used in action research by trainers is the survey technique. It is used to secure data in the behavioral sciences and in the field of education by means of questionnaires, the data from which is then analyzed and quantified. From this a report may be drafted, and conclusions and recommendations may be drawn about the experimental effort.

THE REPORT

The fourth stage of action research involves a report on one's findings after the data has been collected and analyzed. This information is presented and interpreted according to the plan set forth in the methodology. Findings must be related to the hypotheses the trainer set out to test. Were the findings statistically significant? Were there any strange, bizarre or unexpected findings not anticipated in the hypotheses? A researcher must be detached and objective about what he discovers through the investigation.

Ideas about preferred styles for reporting findings and analysis of data can be obtained from the various reference works suggested in this chapter. These suggestions will range from how to illustrate the data through figures and tables to writing style. Generally, the last stage of the investigation and report is a summary in the form of a section or chapter. It should include an abstract which pulls together briefly the statement of the problem, review of the literature, outline of procedure and the principal findings. In addition, the investigator may offer his interpretation as to what the experiment or data reveal. This is listed as "Conclusions."

With key executives who suffer from information overload, the following strategy may get their attention and ensure positive action on your recommendations. In addition to the full report, prepare an executive briefing of a few pages on the major findings and their implications (usually from the above summary). During oral briefings of top management, use this digest and refer them to the full report for details. If those in leadership positions do not have the time to read the complete version, they may have their staffs do it. Similarly, if the contents are not confidential, this digest may also be widely circulated within the organization in order to gain support for the necessary reforms.

To conclude, action research, especially of the human factor survey kind, should be regularly conducted for organizational diagnosis and improvement. However, the ongoing training programs offer an ideal situation to collect relevant data from the participants for their own benefit, as well as for the renewal of the system.

VALUES OF ACTION LEARNING AND RESEARCH

Action learning is a dynamic process that is appropriate to mature trainees because it involves adults in a variety of intensive, educational experiences. Its advantages are:

- It stimulates learning at both the cognitive and affective levels, that is, by rational thinking and through the emotions or feelings
- It is carefully prepared, timed, and paced to make optimum use of the training period
- It promotes individual and group learning through variety of input, interaction, and instrumentation
- It focuses on results and requires planning for action that occurs because of the training.

The principal value of action learning is that it promotes positive and constructive change in people and their systems through increased awareness, knowledge, and skills.

Action research compliments this approach by furthering an organization's effectiveness by gathering data from its membership on individual and institutional performance. Meetings and training sessions are viewed as opportunities for this information collection. With a systematic analysis of findings, the merits of action research are

- It aids organization diagnosis and development, helping to validate the need and the means for planned change

- It evaluates the effectiveness of the human resource development efforts
- It provides measures of performance, productivity, and profitability
- It improves the basis for decision-making, planning, accountability, and career development

With synergy, action learning becomes a means for action research. Combined, both are a powerful strategy for maintaining personal and organizational health. These are managerial tools suitable for an information age of knowledge and service workers. Many corporations have realized the value of marketing research and included such specialists on their staffs. The new work culture requires expansion of such inquiry to go beyond surveys of public preferences and customer concerns, so that the broadening of human factor research encompasses all employees or members.

Every manager has a responsibility to develop his or her people, and action learning and research enable leaders to do so. When technicians and other specialists are assigned a training task, action learning and research strategies permit them to be more professional in their approach. Action learning and research are a means for capitalizing upon human assets!

INTERACTION

Throughout these chapters, we have provided guidance in this section on various ways to involve trainees in the learning process. In addition to a dozen possibilities for group dynamics already reviewed, an overview is now offered of twelve more adult education methods that will enhance action learning:

ADULT EDUCATION GROUP METHODS

AudioVisual Aids

In an age of mass media, the imaginative group facilitator has numerous mechanical and technological aids, in addition to traditional means, of stimulating the senses and communicating more effectively by involvement of more powers within a person. The use of the new media not only conveys the message in a different, perhaps more startling way, but the medium chosen can itself be a message. Audiovisual aids may merely illustrate a point or serve as a catalyst for group discussion.

Such devices may be purchased, loaned, or created. If mechanical equipment is being used with a group, then it is important that it be checked beforehand to assure that it is in working condition. Any material to be shown should be previewed before a group assembles, so that the discussion leader is familiar with its contents and has devised questions or points for further analysis. The simplest visual aids are drawings or charts produced by the programmer or the group. For this purpose, a blackboard with both white and colored chalk is helpful. A flannel board with felt symbols is also attractive, while a flip-chart with plain newsprint or white cardboard may be employed with colored marking pencils. Sometimes groups find it useful to express themselves in this visual manner. Other materials, such as water and oil paints, paper cut-ups and wire and cloth, may be used by creative persons within a group to communicate a concept or design.

An added dimension to visual techniques can be the use of an opaque or overhead projector. Then you can project on a wall or screen printed or commercially produced illustrations or cartoons to stimulate group discussion. Materials from books or original slides can be projected for all to see.

Slides and filmstrips in one, two, or three dimensions help the viewer to put himself into a scene. Slides can be reproduced in black and white or color, in 16mm or 35mm, and in 8" or 10" size (as for use with a Vu-Graph). If desired, you can add audio by using a tape recorder or phonograph. The 35mm slides can be in the form of a strip (filmstrip) or shown separately; homemade or commercial cassettes or records can be played to accompany the visual presentation. Both slides and filmstrips permit concentration on one scene for any length of discussion.

Films in 8, 16, or 35mm—black and white and color—offer a unique way to involve the group. However, long films are not the best for group discussion purposes; usually 12 to 30 minutes are adequate to stimulate communication. Slow motion can be used in any playback, but many projectors do not permit you to hold a still scene in the film for discussion. Guidelines for instructors sometimes accompany films in order to foster discussion.

Audio tapes, cassettes, or discs are excellent with groups. A recording of the group's discussion can become a means of feedback for group analysis. The same approach can be used with videotape if one has access to such equipment. Videotape has the added value of presenting visual, nonverbal communication. The recordings can be analyzed by the group itself or by external observers. Of course, commercial audio- or videotapes with outstanding speakers or drama may be utilized as a group technique.

Television, live commercial, educational or closed-circuit, can be used as a unique learning tool. Since young people today are products of the television age, this media and other audiovisual devices are essential to keep the interest of youthful groups. *The One Minute Management System* of Ken Blanchard is one example of a video leadership series (Video Publishing House, 1011 E. Toughy Ave. #580, Des Plaines, IL 60018).

A group might watch a commercial or educational program and use it as the basis of discussion. The group might employ videotapes for the same purpose, or it might use them to record its own group interaction. The playback can have great impact on trainee growth. A group might observe another group through closed-circuit television or it might engage in a cooperative project—such as the production of a television program or tape.

The videocassette recorder (VCR) or disc player have provided new capabilities for trainers. Not only are films available in videocassette format (½" or ¾" size, Beta or VHS), but catalogs may be obtained describing the offerings for management development:

- *Video Bluebook,* Knowledge Industry Publications, Box 429, White Plains, NY 10602
- *Applied Management Series; Managing for Productivity,* Organizational Dynamics, Inc., 16 New England Executive Park, Burlington, MA 01803
- *Video Courses,* Time-Life Video, Box 666, Radio City Station, New York, NY 10019

However, it is in the area of "interactive systems" that real breakthroughs are being accomplished in educational technology. These systems link computers with video and other A/V capabilities. These innovations are useful for both individual or group instruction and will dominate the future of training.

Further, creative trainers may now use lightweight, comparatively inexpensive video equipment to record their own learning materials, customized to organizational needs. This video equipment can be used in training courses for skill development or to record high performers. To further tailor media to trainees, trainers may also program computers with the most appropriate learning for their groups. New educational media opportunities are constantly unfolding for those seeking to take full advantage of electronic aids (Harris, 1985, Chapter 4).

Other forms of audiovisual communication with groups are the puppet show, pageant, pantomime, model congress, mock convention and stereograph. These are all unusual ways to present concepts and involve group members. A new dimension of group involvement through audiovisual aids is being experimented with today through various multimedia projects. These involve immersing group members in a kaleidoscope of sound and color, using colored spotlights, films, filmstrips and other "psychedelic" media.

BRAINSTORMING

This technique can be used to stimulate creative thinking in a group and to permit members to participate in the decision-making process. Brainstorming promotes a maximum number of ideas from a maximum number of people in a minimum amount of time. This form of problem-solving can focus on one or more subjects for an hour, a day or a weekend. By following a sequence of timed steps, a pressure is created which forces intense involvement. The person conducting the sessions encourages an open, non-judgemental atmosphere so that innovative ideas can be expressed without evaluation or recrimination on the part of any member. There are different ways to conduct brainstorming (Osborn, 1963). One approach takes the following steps:

1. Have a short, warm-up session to "oil the brain"; practice on a light problem unrelated to the real issue. For example, "If you had a boatload of pipecleaners in a foreign country where there was no market for that product, what new uses or markets could you develop for the item?" Then allow the group to free-wheel solutions for one minute and have a recorder note how many replies come

forth. You may wish to have one more practice session, perhaps using paper clips as a theme this time and setting a minimum target of at least 15 good uses within one minute.

2. Clarify the real problem and expand the time period for responses (5, 10, 15 minutes). Arrange for some members of the group to record and number the answers on a blackboard, flip chart, or vu-graph projector. To remove constrictions and mental blocks, inform the group that no comment or evaluation about their ideas will be made as they are offered by the group.

3. Allow the group to spend a few minutes in screening the answers in order to note (by calling the number of the replies) whether there is any duplication or combining of similar ideas or a pattern of ideas to be observed in the responses.

4. Break into subgroups to work out various plans for solving the problem based on the ideas already generated; the group may eliminate or expand upon these ideas recorded. Twenty to forty minutes should be sufficient. The small groups are instructed to present their plans to the total group by using the blackboard or large sheets of plain paper or cardboard (record their results with marking pencil).

5. Reassemble the whole group so that subgroup reporters can orally and visually present their consensus on the problem. A few minutes might be allowed again for a preliminary evaluation by the total group of the ideas that they prefer or find most emphasized in the various group reports.

6. If desired, subgroups may meet again to integrate or synthesize into a final plan the above data.

SMALL GROUPS

- *Buzz Groups.* When a film, lecture, or presentation is made to the total group, the audience can be divided into small groups of six to eight people who meet in a circle for approximately 6 to 15 minutes to discuss the subject. A variation is to assign one question for the group to answer or prepare one issue in the presentation upon which they are to focus. The group discusses the subject freely after it has decided upon a recorder and spokesman. Groups should be given a two-minute warning that time is coming to a close and urged to conclude. The recorder or chairman then presents a summary or consensus of the group's reactions to the total audience.

Sometimes a variation of this method is referred to as the Phillips 66 plan. The important elements are (1) timing of the discussion period, (2) small groups and (3) understanding of what is to be discussed and reported. If you wish, the groups can receive specific assignments before the presentation (e.g., take only one point of the lecture or form listening teams which listen from different viewpoints).

- *Discussion Groups.* These task-oriented groups are assigned or select a topic or a series of related subjects for discussion. The whole group may investigate the same issue, or subgroups may be formed out of common interest or to analyze different facets of the question. The discussion may be based on a committee report, a book or magazine article, a television or radio program, an audio- or videotape, a lecture or sermon, a film or filmstrip. On the other hand, the subject may merely be announced and a free-swinging discussion permitted to ensue. The group may assemble for one meeting to discuss a single subject or meet for a series of sessions on the same, related or different subjects. If all viewpoints are tolerated, sensitive communication is encouraged, and critical issues are analyzed, group discussion can be a very valuable approach. It is helpful for the group to lay down some basic ground rules for the discussion, to clarify its purpose, and to determine if any action or follow-up is to flow from the discussion. The discussion is most meaningful when people are given time to prepare their thoughts about the subject rather than merely expounding on a subject about which they are uninformed. It can be a useful learning experience both from the perspective of content and human relations.

CASE STUDIES/CRITICAL INCIDENTS

To objectify a situation for group discussion, it helps if you set up the subject for discussion in the form of a case. The case may be printed for all members of the group to analyze or simply read to the others by the group leader. The issue or problem brought out through the case should be one with which most members can identify or be typical of the challenges they will have to solve themselves. By putting the matter in case style, you de-emotionalize the topic for a group solution. The study may center around a person who faces a common problem; it should include facts about the fictional or real individual and include something of his background and the surrounding circumstances relative to the problem. Or it may concentrate on a critical incident in the life of a person or a group of people.

On the other hand, the case may simply describe a situation that involves a whole group, institution, or organization. Enough facts are provided to raise issues, but no solutions are presented. The introduction of the case may include a few questions about the case or critical incident to provoke discussion.

The language used should be informal and familiar to the audience reading or hearing the case. Personalize the story by including local names and references. Depending on the time available for analysis of the case, the length of the case may vary from one to several pages. When the incident is tailored to a real challenge which faces a particular group, then the members can get very involved in the discussion. Although it is possible to purchase books of case studies, it is usually more effective to compose your own case or incident, so that it is quite real to the participants. This technique can encourage nondirective learning by inserting specific issues and questions in the case that will expand the group's thinking.

Cases are written descriptions of actual events or situations that the trainees may confront in their own organizations. Encourage groups analyzing the case to

- Identify key issues and problems
- Diagnose and evaluate the problems and situations
- Identify alternative viewpoints and solutions
- Come to consensus on preferred strategy for meeting the challenges or resolving the problems

DEBATES

Any subject of concern to a group can be viewed from opposite positions. The group can be divided into two teams with a single chairman or moderator. The groups preferably should prepare their position for or against the issue by outside reading, investigation and discussion. It is desirable to set ground rules for the debate as to time, procedure and possible scoring of points. The teams should select a captain before returning to the next meeting at which they or their representatives will defend their position on the question at hand. The more contemporary and meaningful the subject is to the group, the better will be the debate. Each side should be permitted a summation of their position at the end of the specified time period.

SOCIOGRAM

The sociometric test permits members to express their feelings about others within the group with whom they would like to be or work with in certain circumstances. It is designed to study the social structure of a group and its patterns of belonging. The basis for the choice must be real, not hypothetical, and members must know that action will follow the test results. The individuals are usually given three to five choices in order to show the relative position of a person in the group. Negative choices may also be added with the instruction that the purpose is not to pass judgement on anyone and that all the choices will be kept secret. The advantage is that members will reveal choices that they may not be willing to show in their group behavior. The results are plotted or pictured on a sociogram by drawing lines so that it is possible to analyze who is most frequently chosen, who is less frequently chosen, and what patterns of subgroupings exist. The group should then be given an opportunity to discuss the implications of this visual presentation of their preferred relationships.

FORUM/ASSEMBLY

A group can sponsor a forum to promote its ideas or can take part in one. This assembly procedure brings together large numbers of people for thought-provoking exchange on an announced subject. It may be conducted by a chairman, guest speaker, or discussion leader and may include questions from the audience. A panel of three to six persons can be appointed to discuss the speaker's points after his presentation. The procedure can be adapted to a symposium, in which several people present brief speeches on the subject to provide the audience with different perspectives on the topic. A question period usually follows the formal presentation.

Any large assembly can be broken down into smaller groups for more meaningful discussion by means of several techniques. One is listening teams, whereby the audience is divided into segments to listen to the presentation from a specific perspective or with a question in mind. For example, one group may be instructed to listen to the speaker from the viewpoint of "application" for his ideas, another from the viewpoint of "agreement," another for points of "disagreement" and still another for necessary points of "clarification." Each group meets after the speaker's address, compares its observations, and then appoints a spokesman to provide its reactions to the talk for the benefit of the whole assembly.

Another small group technique is circular response which may follow a formal speech or be used simply as a method of group discussion. Sitting in a circle of fifteen to twenty, the group takes up a point or question. After the first person speaks to the point, the next group member to the right expresses his or her views and so on until the discussion has gone around the circle. No member may speak out of turn until the whole group has provided input in sequence.

The buzz group (previously described) is another device to use before or after a speaker has made a presentation. When used to precede a talk, each subgroup may be given a quotation concerning the subject to discuss for six minutes in order to warm them up to the topic. When this method follows an address, the small groups of six to ten people are expected to discuss the subject matter for a limited time (10 to 20 minutes) and appoint a recorder to present the group's synthesis to the total meeting.

DRAMATICS

The dramatic approach may be utilized by a group to present a full-length play or a short skit of ten minutes or less. Essentially it involves role playing wherein the participant projects himself into another's position and acts as the other person would act in the situation created. In such a presentation, the script, the characters or the materials used highlight material or issues for later group discussion. The participants may follow a regular script, read their lines or converse extemporaneously. In the "sociodrama," the presentation stops at the climax, and the whole group is involved in the solution.

Sociodrama is a technique that employs the best of two methods— the case study and dramatics. It uses role playing, wherein participants project themselves into others' position and act as other individuals would in the situation created. In such a presentation, script, characters, and issues provide material for later group discussion.

259

This dramatic technique may be used to present a full-length play, a short skit of 10 minutes or less, or merely a critical incident.

Such a social drama on real work situations offers the trainer an opportunity to guide the group to new insights and learning. The facilitator may assign the group a topic or situation or let the class choose the subject of its drama. It is important that the problem be defined or the general situation be sketched. It could be the issue of salespeople not filing proper contact reports, a conflict between salespersons and their manager, or a shortage of materials to sell.

The point is that the subject matter should be familiar to the group, something they can identify with as real to their work environment. Human or organizational relations are always a fit topic for this purpose.

The presenters can be given a script which they read or act out extemporaneously, or they can be assigned the task beforehand with the freedom to develop their own script or situation. They should be urged to plan their presentation carefully, and to have a warm-up or practice run. Essentially, they are to create a situation just as it happens on the job, and then stop at the climax. They should discuss the characters, put themselves into their position, and use their language.

For example, suppose the issue is a salesman with much male ego who is assigned to a new female sales manager. His approach to women is typically chauvinistic; he uses them as playthings. Now how is he going to deal with this new situation? What are the manager's feelings likely to be? How will her judgments of his performance be influenced? What problems are likely to arise? How can he change his attitudes?

When the players have presented their drama, but provided no solutions, two alternatives are possible. The trainer may lead the problem-solving discussion or permit the presenters to continue the discussion period. In the latter case, they would then have prepared some questions and would consider ways to stimulate the audience's thinking.

One important consideration is to involve the whole class in the sociodrama—let them experience the emotions involved, the difficulties, the stresses, the possibilities. This is the time for analysis of the situation in depth, for behaviors to be illustrated, and for the issues at stake to be clarified.

Observers are challenged to seek the insights and understandings the actors try to convey. It is important to relate the discussion to the original problem under consideration. Players might be asked to comment on the characters they attempted to portray.

The trainer should keep the group from evaluating acting talent and concentrate instead on solutions to the problem presented.

Finally, the audience should be asked to summarize what they learned through the experience. It is important that the group members have the opportunity to discover if they can explore a problem dramatically, break it down into its causal factors, and construct methods for meeting the issue effectively. If it is feasible, have the players act out some of the alternative solutions for further evaluation by the audience.

A creative trainer can work various options on the basic technique. For example, the trainer might encourage people to use masks to portray characters or to reverse their role by this means. Thus, a black is asked to portray a white; a male is asked to portray a female; a subordinate is asked to portray a supervisor; a salesman is asked to portray a customer.

A common tendency on the part of amateurs is to let a scene go too long, so the facilitator may have to cut it off when (1) enough behavior has been exhibitied for the group to analyze the problem; (2) group can imagine or project what would happen if the action continued; (3) players have reached an impasse because of poor briefing or miscasting; (4) a natural closing point has arrived.

Sociodrama allows group to be objective about a situation which might be too painful for those concerned to deal with directly. Attitudes and feelings often unexpressed are brought out into the open. Dynamic factors in group process and human relations are brought out clearly. An artificial environment is provided within which a person may experiment with different behavior and attitudes, make mistakes and try new skills without risking the hurt of the real-life situation. And all this is accomplished in the presence and with the cooperation of colearners, not judges.

ROLE-PLAYING

Role-playing is a relatively new educational technique in which people spontaneously act out problems of human relations and analyze the enactment with the help of other role players and observers.

There are several values to this technique

1. New skills can be developed for dealing with human relations problems, because a participant not only hears or tells about a problem but lives through it by acting it out.

2. Understanding may be broadened since participants gain insight into their own and others' feelings.
3. Many new attitudes and feelings are brought before the group for review. Thus, role-playing helps illustrate and objectify many frequently ignored causal and dynamic factors in group process and human relations.
4. Most important, role-playing provides an artificial environment within which a person may experiment with behavior, make mistakes and try new skills without risking hurts that experimentation in real-life situations may involve; this in the presence of colearners, not judges.

Necessary to the role-playing process is a director, who is responsible for all procedures involved and who helps actors and other group members become emotionally involved with the situation to be acted out. The director is mainly concerned with helping actions' spontaneity in the presentation of characters and in helping audience-observers to analyze situation and behaviors presented so that insights into problems and effective knowledge of how to deal with them are increased.

Role-playing involves more than simple acting out of roles. It consists of a series of steps, which usually flow into one another quite naturally and have more or less importance in different role playing situations.

Steps in the role playing process:

1. *Defining the problem.* Role playing should be focused on a problem both meaningful and important to the entire group; chosen as a method only when particularly useful; concerned with clear, specific, valid problems in human relations.
2. *Establishing a situation.* The situation (design) of the role play is always dependent on learning outcomes desired or needed by the group. Planners must always work with the training purpose of the role play in mind. Some ways in which situations can be designed are:
   a. A subcommitte can plan a situation and bring it to the group.
   b. The total group can make up a situation on the spot.
   c. A member or a leader can suggest an actual case which illustrates a particular problem. (Be careful that the scene does not become clogged with details about what happened.)
3. *Casting the characters.* Responsibility for defining and casting characters may be taken by the whole group or delegated to certain

members. In general, persons should be chosen because it is thought that they can carry the role well. No one should be urged to take a role if he is unwilling to do so. (If forced, a person is likely to give a constructed, unspontaneous version.) When dealing with beginners, start with roles in which they feel at home and confident.

4. *Briefing and warming-up actors.* It is important to keep the problem to be studied before the group at all times and to remind members why they saw the problem as a significant one. No attempt should be made to use this process to structure what actors are to say or to do in the action. The director sets the tone by pointing out the job of observers: to look at actors in terms of their roles. It should be made clear that each actor is playing a specified role in a specific situation and is merely giving his spontaneous interpretation of a character's response in such a situation.

5. *Acting.* The mood of the play can be destroyed if the actors get out of character and talk about themselves.

6. *Cutting.* A common tendency is to allow scenes to last too long. Generally, a role play should be cut when:
   a. Enough behavior has been exhibited for the group to analyze the problem.
   b. The group can project what would happen if the action were continued.
   c. The players have reached an impasse because of miscasting or poor briefing.
   d. There is a natural closing.

7. *Discussing and analyzing the situation and behavior.* It is important to relate discussion to the original problem under study. Sometimes players are asked to comment first; sometimes discussion is begun by observers. (The advantage to the players' beginning the discussion is that it allows them to set the tone for constructive criticism.) If players show (by their own observations) lack of self-consciousness because they are analyzing characters portrayed and not themselves, observers are more likely to feel free to express their full reactions. Do not evaluate the acting ability of actors.

8. *Pinning down what is learned.* This involves making plans for further testing of insights gained or for practicing new behavior implied.

Some groups may be hesitant about role playing, either because of not seeing themselves as actors or out of fear that such spontaneous

expression and exploration of problems may come too close to personal anxieties. This type of group quickly learns to feel at ease when
role playing is begun with some very simple situation which enables
them to have a profitable discussion.

It is also important that group members have the experience of dis-
covering that they can explore a problem, break it down into casual
factors and construct methods of meeting the problem through changing their behavior in the role playing situation. A new group technique
for role playing is to use masks and to reverse people's roles. For example, when dealing with an incident about racial prejudice, the white
role player of a black person would use a black mask, while the black
person uses a white mask.

Field Trips

Group growth and cohesion can be enhanced by a visit to a public
place, institution, or industrial plant. Ideally, the group is presented
with an experience beyond its usual understanding and is given an
opportunity to meet and talk with people at the location of the field
trip. It may range from a visit to a newspaper plant or a museum
to a state park or Indian reservation. The purpose can be for career
information, social involvement, or enlightenment. It is one thing to
have a group discussion on poverty; it is another for the group actually
to visit the slums and talk with poor people. Some discussion precedes
the event as to the field trip's purpose and what to look for. The
group leader must make arrangements for an appointment and a guide,
transportation and food, and plan for an evaluation period following
the experience. The most valuable learning will come in the group
discussion after the trip when participants share their perceptions and
insights. Local service clubs such as Kiwanis or Rotary can be helpful in
arranging field trips, while the Chamber of Commerce and the National
Association of Manufacturers unit in your area may assist in such efforts.

Another variation is to break the group into smaller teams who then
go out on a field investigation to a competitor, a high-tech industrial
park, or a university to answer specific questions and then report back
to the main group on their findings. Within a multinational corporation,
for instance, the field trips could be to other plants, divisions, or
subsidiaries.

Exhibits

A group can find expression for itself in the joint task of developing an audio and/or visual display. This method not only provides training in working together, but it challenges the group to communicate its ideas to a larger audience. It permits the employment of creative talents within the group by the use of various media—art, sculpture, photography, film and slides, posters, cartoons, graphs, comic strips and other graphic expressions. The exhibit may be portable or permanent, stationary or mobile. In conjunction with developing this presentation, the group meets to discuss what thoughts it wishes to convey through this means, how to best display information and what assignments are necessary to get the project accomplished.

Projects

Like the exhibit or display, the project offers the group a task to accomplish which requires the exercise of skills of interpersonal relations as well as the special resources of members. The group determines the nature of these cooperative construction activities which may involve skills of painting, cooking, weaving, performing or building. Investigation and research may have to precede the actual construction; the planning period allows for group participation and thinking. The atmosphere in the group should be such as to encourage, not stifle, creativity.

Related to this approach is the report which may be conducted for the group by an individual or a committee. When the in-depth study is presented to the group, then discussion and decisions take place based on the information accumulated. The report may be written, oral or a visual presentation such as a mock-up.

The computer lends itself to special projects that pull various members of a team together. For example, a group can devise a new software program that will be of benefit to the total group or organization, or construct a computer simulation that will enable the group to test out a new theory or strategy, make better choices, or anticipate future problems. Scott, Foresman and Company (Professional Publishing Group, 1900 East Lake Avenue, Glenview, IL 60025) has a catalogue of computer books useful for such purposes.

Now that the readers know more than two dozen learning methods to use with trainees, what type do professional trainers consider to be the most effective? In a recent survey of its membership, the American Society for Training & Development* (1630 Duke Street, Alexandria, VA 22313) found the preferred techniques in the following six categories to be:

- *Knowledge acquisition:* programmed instruction, lecture, conference method, and case study
- *Changing attitudes:* role-playing, sensitivity training, conference and case study methods
- *Problem-solving:* case study, business games, conference method, and role-playing
- *Interpersonal skills:* role-playing and sensitivity training
- *Participant acceptance:* conference and case study methods
- *Knowledge retention:* role-playing, programmed instruction, conference and case study methods

Ninety-three percent of these respondents—all HRD specialists—ranked leadership training skills as the most important learning subject, while giving priority also to problem-solving skills, decision-making skills, performance appraisal, and time management. Note that some of these preferred methods can now be enhanced by the use of electronic technology, such as when the computer is used for programmed instruction or business games. Sterling Institute (1010 Wisconsin Ave. N.W., Washington, DC 20007) has a "Careers in Management Series," which puts case studies on videotape to obtain the best of both approaches.

INSTRUMENTATION

Previously, we have listed some publishers of commercial instruments, however, managers and trainers should not hesitate to construct their own data-gathering forms, questionnaires, and inventories to suit their specific purposes. This book contains many illustrations of such devices, devised by this author in the course of his action learn-

---

* Excerpted from *Bulletin on Training,* BNA Communications, January, 1982.

ing and research. Walter Mahler, a management consultant who heads up his own organization in Midland Park, New Jersey, has long used such tools for analytical studies of some of America's biggest corporations. Although Dr. Mahler wrote the definite work on the subject, *Diagnostic Studies* (Reading, MA: Addison-Wesley, 1973), it is out of print and difficult to obtain. Therefore, for those involved in survey and marketing research who seek to collect information from people, I recommend: S. Sudman and N. M. Bradburn's *Asking Questions: A Practical Guide to Questionnaire Design* (San Francisco: Jossey Bass, 1983).

Regardless of the format chosen, the manager or trainer wants to select a survey approach with these features:

- Ease of administration and collection of data
- Appropriate and understandable wording or questioning
- Convenience for scoring and interpreting the results
- Viability for validity and comparative studies

The computer now can be used to score responses, as well as to undertake statistical analysis of the results.

For example, one behavioral scientist who assisted me with the original Office of Naval Research studies upon which this book is based designed two interesting instruments (Harris, 1972/3). One was an "adjective rating scale," in which trainees were asked to respond (anonymously) to a dozen words. After each key term, such as "reward" or "punishment," the respondents checked the pair of adjectives that best described their personal reaction to the word cited. There were five pairs of adjectives from which to choose: good/bad, unimportant/important, strong/weak, inferior/superior, active/passive. The investigator was trying to gauge the group's attitudes toward certain topics before the training was undertaken. He also created a "modified polarity scale," consisting of 16 statements to assess opinions on matters related to the learning program. For instance, since one of the learning modules was to be on change, two items dealt with the "changeableness of human feelings": one described change making life more interesting; the second described change as a sign of weakness in human beings. Respondents reacted to such statements in one of five ways: "strongly agree, agree, don't know, disagree, and strongly disagree." The findings on both instruments were summarized and analyzed during the training program, then included in the project report for the benefit of management.

To improve the reader's efforts at action learning and research, I now will include seven samples of forms that I have used in leadership or professional development institutes based upon the contents of this text. Exhibit 7.15 is a demographic inquiry that can be modified and used as part of a preregistration process; it provides the manager or trainer with some insight into a group prior to the training experience. Exhibits 7.16 and 7. 17 are training inventories of 46 items that seek basically the same information; the program coordinator administers the forms before and after the training to assess the impact of the learning upon the trainee's attitudes and opinions. Exhibits 7.18 and 7.19 were used in the same project, but with training instructors before and after the seminar; it endeavors to evaluate their skills as trainers through pre/post inquiries. After the action learning, Exhibit 7.20 can be used to assist the learner to review what learning experiences were the most impactful, and Exhibit 7.21 is an example of a program evaluation rating sheet on the usefulness of various learning modules. All of these forms can be adapted by readers to suit their needs in training personnel more professionally. (Note: All forms were originally designed for a course to prepare trainers.)

Such data-gathering has several values:

- It creates awareness and sensitivity in the respondents relative to some of the key learning issues
- It provides information on the trainees that can be used in program design and preparation, or in post-project reporting for purposes of organizational development and HRD planning of future programs
- It helps in the evaluation of the program's effectiveness, particularly regarding change in the learning group as a result of the training.

Instruments, whether they take the form of questionnaires, inventories, or checklists, are diagnostic tools that facilitate the identification of people and program needs. They are also a means for assessing performance and contribute to organizational effectiveness.

Personally, over 40 years experience in education and training has convinced me that high performance can be achieved if organizations

Exhibit 7.15 Sample Demographic Information Form.

Directions: Please check the most appropriate answer or supply the information requested to the best of your ability.

1. Organization: _____ 2a. Division: _____
3. Age _____ 2b. Job Title _____
4. Length of Service ___ yrs. ___ mos.   5. Total years of schooling you have had_____
6. Indicate your highest academic achievement:
   a. High School Diploma (or equivalent) _____
   b. College Degree _____ (Major subject area _____
   c. Masters Degree _____ (Major subject area _____
   d. College level work (indicate number of years completed) _____
   e. Other educational credentials (certificates, etc.) _____

7. Are you currently enrolled in any of the following continuing educational programs (excluding this course)?
   a. Inservice Training   ( )   d. Correspondence Courses   ( )
   b. Non-Degree Course Work ( )   e. Video/Audio Courses   ( )
   c. Degree Course Work   ( )   f. Other (specify _____
8. Have you ever had any formal teacher training?   Yes ( )   No ( )
      If yes, specify: _____
9. Have you ever had any "Instructor" training?   Yes ( )   No ( )
      If yes, specify: _____
10. Are you presently engaged in teaching, training, or instructing?   Yes ( )   No ( )
      If yes, indicate the category below which best describes your work:
      Trainer ( )   Instructor ( )   Counselor ( )   Other (specify) _____
11a. If the answer to number 10 was "yes", please estimate the portion of your workday which is normally devoted to teaching (or instructing) and related activities:
      Full Time ( )   ¾ ( )   ½ ( )   ¼ ( )
11b. If the answer to number 10 was "no," do you *supervise* the training of personnel?   Yes ( )   No ( )
      Indicate the type of personnel for which you have a supervisory training responsibility:
      _____

12. In the field of human resource development what is your major area of concern relative to the training of personnel?
      Corrections   ( )   Drug Abuse   ( )
      Alcohol Education   ( )   Human/Race Relations   ( )
      Other (specify) _____

Continued

Exhibit 7.15 Sample Demographic Information Form, *cont'd.*

13. Please rate the assignment you now have in comparison to the other duties you have had:

    Worst ( )   Fair ( )   Good ( )   Very Good ( )   Best ( )

14. If you were required to develop a new title for your job what would you select?

_____

Upon completion of this course do you expect to be able to apply what you have learned in some type of educational work?   Yes ( )   No ( )

a. If the answer to the above was "yes," please specify the work you expect to do?

_____

b. If the answer to the above was "yes," will the assignment specified be:

    A new job ( )   An additional duty ( )   Change in previous duty ( )
    Same job as before ( )   Other _____

15. What are your expectations or hopes relative to participation in this Training Directors Seminar?

(1) _____

(2) _____

(3) _____

(4) _____

Exhibit 7.16 Pre-training Inventory: No. 1.

Date: _____

As you begin this training experience, how would you rate your behavior in relating to other people? Please make a check mark on the left hand side if you perceive that you now possess the inter-personal skill listed. Leave blank those items in which you feel you do not possess average ability. Your honest personal reactions will help significantly towards an overall evaluation of the performance of this group as it participates in these training sessions. Complete individual anonymity will be maintained. Your responses will be compared at the end of the course with a second administration of this questionnaire.

1. ___ I am attentive in listening to others.
2. ___ I take pains in putting my ideas across to others.

Exhibit 7.16   Pre-training Inventory: No. 1, *cont'd.*

3. ___ I am anxious to share information, both positive and negative, about myself with others.
4. ___ I usually understand what others communicate to me.
5. ___ I am concerned to be understood by others, in both big and small matters.
6. ___ I take a firm stand on matters or issues.
7. ___ I express positive feeling toward others.
8. ___ I often feel negatively toward others.
9. ___ I express honest feelings and attitudes about myself.
10. ___ I go out of my way to be helpful to others.
11. ___ I am willing to experiment with ideas coming from others.
12. ___ I am hasty with judgments on other people.
13. ___ I am able to negotiate easily with people who do not know me.
14. ___ I am able to control my temper and moods easily when others are not agreeing with me.
15. ___ I perceive myself as tolerant of others' shortcomings.
16. ___ I am patient with people who work and think slowly.
17. ___ I analyze others' actions and speech.
18. ___ I am usually able to accept others' negative criticism of me.
19. ___ I analyze my own shortcomings.
20. ___ I am conscious of my efforts to recognize and commend the potentialities and contribution of others.
21. ___ I recognize prejudiced attitudes in myself.
22. ___ I am willing to seek help and consultation in overcoming my shortcomings.
23. ___ I am willing to assume group roles.
24. ___ I am generally relaxed and at ease in group situations.
25. ___ I am consciously considerate and attentive in my relations with those who may be in somewhat subordinate roles.
26. ___ I take responsibility for things for which I know I will never get credit or recognition.
27. ___ I take responsibility for things I should have been taking responsibility for.
28. ___ In my relations with peers, I am consciously sensitive to the needs of others.

In Group Situations

29. ___ I find myself speaking up.
30. ___ I perceive myself as not dominating.
31. ___ I consciously give others time to think.
32. ___ I am irritated when people do not understand me.
33. ___ I consciously try to encourage the participation of the more quiet and shy members.
34. ___ I am conscious of how people are reacting to what I say.
35. ___ I consult frequently with my peers before making a decision.
36. ___ I am able to encourage a variety of action by group members.

Continued

Exhibit 7.16   Pre-training Inventory: No. 1, *cont'd.*

37. __ I consciously seek feedback to evaluate my performance.
38. __ I am willing to delegate functions.
39. __ I find myself able to stimulate others and to provoke discussion.
40. __ I am receptive to the contribution of others.
41. __ I am anxious to make contributions that are concretely helpful as opposed to being impressive.
42. __ I am anxious to resolve conflict rather than to accomplish a task.
43. __ I consciously try to analyze subcurrents in groups and group processes.
44. __ I am concerned with the personal development of the group members rather than with getting a particular task finished.

Open End

45. Would you characterize yourself as a person who is open-minded or close-minded?
46. What expectations do you have for this program?

Exhibit 7.17   Post Training Inventory: No. 2.

Date: _____

Over a period of time, people may change in the ways they work with and relate to other people. People may also change in their attitudes and insights in operational ways as a result of personally meangingful and organizationally structured experiences to which they may have been exposed. As a result of your experience in the groups so far, do you believe you have changed your behavior in relating to people in any specific ways?

Directions for Answering

Please make a check mark on the left hand side if you perceive a *noticeable* difference.
Do not make a check mark if *no noticeable* difference is perceived in any one item.
Complete anonymity will be maintained.

_____ 1. I am more attentive of listening to others.
_____ 2. I take more pains in putting my ideas across to others.

Exhibit 7.17 Post Training Inventory: No. 2, *cont'd.*

_____ 3. I am more anxious to share information, both positive and negative, about myself with others.

_____ 4. I understand others more frequently.

_____ 5. I am more anxious to be understood by others, in both big and small matters.

_____ 6. I am beginning to take a firm stand on matters more often.

_____ 7. I express positive feeling toward others more often.

_____ 8. I feel negatively toward others less frequently.

_____ 9. I feel less inhibited in expressing honest feelings and attitudes about myself.

_____ 10. I go out of my way, more often, to be helpful to others.

_____ 11. I am more willing to experiment with ideas coming from others.

_____ 12. I am much less hasty with judgment of other people.

_____ 13. I am able to negotiate more easily with people who do not know me.

_____ 14. I am able to control my temper and moods more easily when others are not agreeing with me.

_____ 15. I perceive myself as becoming more tolerant of others' shortcomings.

_____ 16. I am becoming more patient with people who work and think more slowly than I do.

_____ 17. I am becoming more analytical of others' actions and speech.

_____ 18. I am able to accept others' negative criticism of me more positively.

_____ 19. I am becoming more analytical of my own shortcomings.

_____ 20. I am more conscious of my efforts to recognize and to comment on the potentialities and contributions of others.

_____ 21. I recognize prejudiced attitudes in myself more easily.

_____ 22. I am more willing to seek help and consultation in overcoming my shortcomings.

_____ 23. I am more willing to assume group roles.

_____ 24. I am generally more relaxed and at ease in group situations.

_____ 25. I am consciously more considerate and attentive in my relations with those who may be in somewhat subordinate roles.

_____ 26. I am taking more responsibility for things for which I know I will never get credit or recognition.

_____ 27. I am taking more responsibility for things I should have been taking responsibility for.

_____ 28. In my relations with peers, I am more consciously sensitive to the needs of others.

Continued

Exhibit 7.17   Post Training Inventory: No. 2, *cont'd.*

In Group Situations:

_____ 29. I find myself speaking up more often.
_____ 30. I perceive myself as much less dominating.
_____ 31. I consciously give others more time to think.
_____ 32. I am less irritated when people do not understand me.
_____ 33. I more consciously try to encourage the participation of the more quiet and shy members.
_____ 34. I am conscious of how people are reacting to what I say.
_____ 35. I consult more frequently with my peers before making a decision.
_____ 36. I am able to encourage more variety of action.
_____ 37. I consciously seek more feedback to evaluate my performance.
_____ 38. I am more willing to delegate functions.
_____ 39. I find myself more able to stimulate others and to provoke discussion.
_____ 40. I am more receptive to the contribution of others.
_____ 41. I am anxious to make contributions that are more concretely helpful as opposed to being impressive.
_____ 42. I am more anxious to resolve conflict than to accomplish a task.
_____ 43. I consciously try to analyze subcurrents in groups and group processes.
_____ 44. I am more often concerned with the personal development of the group members than with getting a particular task finished.
_____ 45. As a result of this group experience, do you think you are more:
       ( ) open-minded   ( ) close-minded
46. Have your expectations of this program been fulfilled:
       ( ) Yes   ( ) No   ( ) Partially
Other comments:_____

_____

_____

Exhibit 7.18   Pre-Instruction Survey: Training Instructors' Seminar

1. When I review my career history, I would rate my abilities as an educator of adults (teaching, instructing or training) as: (check one)
   ( ) Inadequate ( ) Adequate ( ) More than adequate ( ) Does not apply
2. When I consider my knowledge and skill in the applied behavioral sciences, I rate my background as: (check one)
   ( ) Inadequate ( ) Adequate ( ) More than adequate ( ) Does not apply

Exhibit 7.18 Pre-Instruction Survey: Training Instructors' Seminar, *cont'd.*

3. Relative to my previous attempts at training in the field of human behavior, I would rate my efforts as: (check one)

( ) Inadequate ( ) Adequate ( ) More than adequate ( ) Does not apply

4. My present feelings concerning my capabilities to teach the staff course in the Professional Development Institutes on Human Behavior with its emphasis on the behavioral sciences are: (check one or more)

( ) I have the necessary preparation to teach this course.

( ) I do not have the necessary preparation to teach this course.

( ) I have a background which, with the additional training received in this course, should enable me to teach the institute successfully.

( ) I believe that sufficient learning resources presently exist in my organization for me to teach effectively the new Professional Development Institute.

( ) I do not have direct training responsibilities. This question is not applicable to my present job.

5. I feel I am qualified now to provide training on the following behavioral science topics:

Learning Module	Yes	Somewhat	No
(a) Human Behavior	___	___	___
(b) Communication	___	___	___
(c) Conflict Resolution	___	___	___
(d) Feedback Utilization	___	___	___
(e) Cultural Influences	___	___	___
(f) Group Behavior	___	___	___
(g) Interpersonal Skills	___	___	___
(h) Managing Change	___	___	___
(i) Behavioral Strategies with Clients	___	___	___

6. I feel I am presently qualified to utilize the following behavioral science methodologies:

Methodology	Yes	Somewhat	No
(a) Films for instructional purposes	___	___	___
(b) Slides/filmstrips in instruction	___	___	___
(c) Audio-tapes/cassettes	___	___	___
(d) Videotapes	___	___	___
(e) Resource Instruments (inventories, check-lists, etc.)	___	___	___
(f) Resource Papers on subjects of instruction	___	___	___
(g) Group process (small group exercises and problem solving)	___	___	___
(h) Action-learning techniques	___	___	___
(i) Action research and evaluation	___	___	___

7. In general, I feel I am qualified to design, conduct and evaluate training programs in the area of human behavior:

___ ___ ___

Continued

Exhibit 7.18   Pre-Instruction Survey: Training Instructors' Seminar, *cont'd.*

8. Other comments on my abilities as an instructor in the areas of human relations and group skills:

_____
_____
_____
_____
_____
_____

Exhibit 7.19   Post-Seminar Evaluation: Training Instructors' Seminar.

Date: _____

Your feedback on the general reactions to the Training Instructors' Seminar learning experience would be appreciated. Please refer to the seminar schedule, and check the categories which most appropriately reflect your state of mind and feelings upon completion of this instructors' course:

1. To what extent were your expectations in coming to this program fulfilled?
      ( ) Very well   ( ) To some extent   ( ) Very little
   Comments: _____
   Do you believe this program will assist you in improving your work in human resource development?
      ( ) Very well   ( ) To some extent   ( ) Very little
   Which part was *most* helpful? _____
   What part was least helpful? _____
2. Generally, how effective were the speakers and discussion leaders?
      ( ) Excellent ( ) Very good ( ) Good ( ) Fair ( ) Poor
   Comments: _____
3. What changes would you like to see in this program (parts dropped, additions made, etc.)?
   Comments: _____
4. In comparison to other training programs in which you have participated, how would you rate the overall program?
      ( ) Excellent ( ) Very good ( ) Good ( ) Fair ( ) Poor
5. What are your action plans to apply the learning and skills acquired in the seminar for the development of human resources?
   (a) _____
   (b) _____
   (c) _____
   (d) _____
   (e) _____
6. Relative to your abilities as an educator of adults, would you *now* rate yourself as:
      ( ) Adequate   ( ) More than adequate   ( ) Inadequate
      ( ) Does not apply-I am not directly involved in training.

Exhibit 7.19   Post-Seminar Evaluation: Training Instructors' Seminar, *cont'd.*

7. Relative to the *Professional Development Institutes on Human Behavior,* how would you now rate your capabilities to teach the staff course? (check one or more)

( ) I have the necessary preparation to teach the course adequately.

( ) I do not have sufficient preparation to teach the course adequately.

( ) The seminar has made me confident that I can teach human behavior subjects to the degree required by my organization.

( ) I do not have direct training responsibilities, but the information and insight obtained in the seminar will be helpful to me in my present job.

( ) I believe that sufficient learning resources were provided in the seminar to to enable me to do an effective job in teaching the staff course.

8. Do you believe that you are *now more qualified* to provide training on the following behavioral science topics?

Learning Module	Yes	Somewhat	No
(a) Human Behavior	___	_____	__
(b) Communication	___	_____	__
(c) Conflict Resolution	___	_____	__
(d) Feedback Utilization	___	_____	__
(e) Cultural Influences	___	_____	__
(f) Group Behavior	___	_____	__
(g) Interpersonal Skills	___	_____	__
(h) Managing Change	___	_____	__
(i) Behavioral Strategies with Clients	___	_____	__
(j) Other: _____			

9. Do you believe that you are *now more qualified* to use the following behavioral science methodologies?

Methodology	Yes	Somewhat	No
(a) Instructional films	___	_____	__
(b) Instructional slides/filmstrips	___	_____	__
(c) Audio-tapes/cassettes	___	_____	__
(d) Videotape	___	_____	__
(e) Resource Instruments	___	_____	__
(f) Resource Papers	___	_____	__
(g) Group Process	___	_____	__
(h) Action learning	___	_____	__
(i) Action research	___	_____	__
(j) Other: _____			

10. In general, do you *now* feel *more qualified* to design, conduct and evaluate training programs in the area of human behavior?

    ___ _____ __

11. Other comments on how you feel *now* about your abilities as a human relations instructor:

_____

_____

Continued

Exhibit 7.19   Post-Seminar Evaluation: Training Instructors' Seminar, *cont'd.*

12. Below are listed some of the demonstration lessons covered in this seminar. Please evaluate each in terms of their *usefulness* to you as a human resource practitioner. Use the following scale:

    5 = Excellent
    4 = Good
    3 = Average
    2 = Fair
    1 = Poor

No.	Training Module Title	Usefulness Rating No.
A	Communication	_____
B	Culture	_____
C	Team Building/Organizational Relations	_____
D	Management of Change	_____
E	Practice Lessons by Participants	_____

13. Below are listed some of the topics presented in special report and workshop sessions during the seminar. Please evaluate their usefulness in helping you to become a more effective trainer or in understanding the process of adult education. Use the following scale for this purpose.

    5 = Excellent
    4 = Good
    3 = Average
    2 = Fair
    1 = Poor

No.	Training Module Topic	Usefulness Rating No.
F	Orientation: Adult Education Approaches	_____
G	Philosophy and Methodology on Action Learning	_____
H	Report on "Team Building" Project	_____
I	Media Workshop	_____
J	"Behavior Management" Project	_____
K	"Action Research on Training"	_____
L	"Problem Solving"	_____
M	"Staff Training Needs and Models"	_____
N	"Seminar Review and Research"	_____

Exhibit 7.20   Post Session Evaluation.

Learning Analysis Form-Part I

Note: Please list below three learning experiences you have had in the course of this training program which made a difference in your thinking and behavior.	What was the major learning your gleaned for yourself from this experience?	In what categories would you put this new learning?
Experience Number 1:		(Check one or more) ___ New Knowledge ___ Improved Skills ___ Changed Attitudes ___ Changed Behavior
Experience Number 2:		(Check one or more) ___ New Knowledge ___ Improved Skills ___ Changed Attitudes ___ Changed Behavior
Experience Number 3:		(Check one or more) ___ New Knowledge ___ Improved Skills ___ Changed Attitudes ___ Changed Behavior

Post Session Evaluation-Part II

1. To what extent were your expectations before coming to this program fulfilled or not fulfilled?

   ☐ Very well   ☐ To some extent   ☐ Very little

   Comments: _____

   _____

2. Do you believe the program will assist you in improving your management practice?

   ☐ Very well   ☐ To some extent   ☐ Very little

   Which part was *most* helpful? _____

   _____

   Which part was *least* helpful? _____

   _____

Continued

279

Exhibit 7.20   Post Session Evaluation, *cont'd.*

3. How effective were the speakers and institute leaders?
   ☐ Excellent   ☐ Very good   ☐ Good   ☐ Fair   ☐ Poor
   Comments: _____

   _____

4. How were the facilities, meals, program arrangements, etc.?
   ☐ Excellent   ☐ Very good   ☐ Good   ☐ Fair   ☐ Poor
5. What changes would you like to see in this program (parts dropped, additions made, etc.)?
   Comments: _____

   _____

6. How would you rate the overall program from your point of view?
   ☐ Excellent   ☐ Very good   ☐ Good   ☐ Fair   ☐ Poor
7. Would you recommend that others from your organization participate in programs presented by MOD?
   ☐ Yes   ☐ No   ☐Not Sure
   Comments: _____

   _____

8. Please feel free to list any other comments or suggestions for course improvements on the back of this page. Kindly also note on reverse side one or two practices or ideas you intend to try out as a result of this learning experience. Your name on this form is optional.

   Date _____ Name of Program _____

   Name of Organization _____

Exhibit 7.21   Professional Development Institutes on Human Behavior

Date: _____   Code No. _____

Below are listed the titles of the lessons that have made up the program in which you have been participating. Please evaluate these lessons *individually* in terms of the potential (or current) usefulness to you in your work. Use the following scale:

   5 = Excellent   4 = Good   3 = Average   2 = Fair   2 = Poor

Staff Course

Learning Module—First Week	Usefulness Rating
I. Dynamics of Human Behavior and Organizational	( )
II. Understanding Deviant Behavior	( )

Exhibit 7.21 Professional Development Institutes on Human Behavior, *cont'd.*

III.	Improving Communications Skills	( )
IV.	Overcoming Communication Obstacles	( )
V.	Creative Approaches to Conflict Resolution in Organizations	( )
VI.	Insights from Client Feedback	( )

Learning Module—Second Week		Usefulness Rating
VII.	Cultural Influences on Client/Staff Behavior	( )
VIII.	Cultural Influences on Decision-Making	( )
IX.	Understanding Group Behavior in Organizations	( )
X.	Interpersonal Skills for Human Resource Specialists	( )
XI.	Managing Change and Changing Roles	( )
XII.	Behavioral Strategies Within Organizations and With Clients	( )

Module Evaluation—Administrators

Learning Module—First Week		Usefulness Rating
XIII.	Managment of Change	( )
XIV.	Behavior Modification	( )
XV.	Management by Objectives	( )
XVI.	Problem Solving Workshop	( )
XVII.	Improving Organizational Effectiveness	( )
XVIII.	Team Building	( )

Learning Module—Second Week		Usefulness Rating
XIX.	Behavioral Science Applications to Organizational Systems	( )
XX.	Management Simulation	( )
XXI.	Improving Administration/Staff Relations	( )
XXII.	Trends in Organizational Administration	( )
XXIII.	Staff Training Needs and Models	( )
	Closing Session	

Please feel free to list any other comments or suggestions for course improvements on the back of this page.

make better use of their personnel and training staffs to further action learning and use internal resources in market research or R & D departments to enhance action research on human factors. In our Chapter 8, the focus, will be upon the opportunities offered through conferences and meetings to actualize human potential.

OTHER SPECIALIZED TRAINING RESOURCES

Specialized training resources include: *The Technical Manager,* a video-based program for technical specialists who become managers. Addison-Wesley Training Systems, Reading, MA 01867. Inquire also about *The Trainer's Library; TR,* computer software for managing the human resource function. Random House, 201 E. 50th St., New York, NY 10022 Attn: 16-2; *Audit Handbook of Human Resource Management Practices.* American Society for Personnel Administration, 600 North Washington St., Alexandria, VA 22314; *The Trainer's Resource,* annual guide to packaged training programs by L. and Z. Nadler and E. Fetteroll, eds. Human Resource Development Press, 22 Amherst Rd., Amherst, MA 01002; *Resource Catalog,* annual. Training House, Inc., PO Box 3090, Princeton, NJ 08543; Train-the-Trainer Workshops, The Training Clinic, 645 Seabreeze Dr., Seal Beach, CA 90740; Workshops on Interactive Lesson Development and Executive Development, Learcom/Sandy Corporation, 215 Cambridge, MA 02142; *Journal of Management Development,* plus related journals and monographs, MCB University Press, 62 Tollner Lane, Bradford, UK BD8 9BY; Human Resource Outlook Seminars, The Conference Board, 845 Third Ave., New York, NY 10022; SyberVision, Fountain Square, 6066 Civic Terrace Ave., Newark, CA 94560 (Video on high performers/successful achievers); Cornet/MTI Film & Video, 108 Wilmot Rd., Deerfield, IL 60015 (Videocassette workshop on *Peak Performance* featuring Dr. Charles Garfield and based on his book); John Wiley & Sons, Ltd., Baffin Lane, Chichester, West Essex, UK PO19 IUD (Publish *Strategic Management Journal, Journal of Behavioral Decision Making,* and *Journal of Forecasting*); *Interactive Classroom Instruction* series by Dugan Laird and Ruth House (including *Workbook, Facilitator's Manual* and audio cassette). Scott, Foresman and Company, 1900 East Lake Ave., Glenview, IL 60025).

NOTE: The Directory of Human Resource Organizations and Publications (Appendix A) lists additional aids.

8
Energizing Personnel through Meetings

Are you wasting too much time in meetings? That is the question raised and answered in an article on "Successful Meetings" offered by the *Personnel Journal* (P.O. Box 2440, Costa Mesa, CA 92628). A survey conducted by Burke Marketing Research in Cincinnati discovered that the average executive spends 16½ hours a week or 21 of the 40-hour workweeks in a year in meetings (*Time,* December 16, 1985, p. 50). Another time management researcher estimated that the average worker spends 3 years of his or her lifetime in meetings! The investigators concluded that if such top managers earn a yearly average of $45,000 then they receive an average of $18,559 each just for sitting in meetings. Because many upper-level managers get paid more than the figure cited, the meetings may be even more costly, especially when nearly one third of those gatherings are considered unnecessary.

One of the ways that meetings waste time, talent, and money is the regularly scheduled sessions with no agenda. For example, an organization may have a tradition that certain key personnel meet once a week at 8:30 A.M., so everyone involved dutifully includes the time on his or her schedule whether there is any need for the meeting or not. Corporate headhunter Robert Half, who commissioned the study, laments that America does not lead the world in productivity, but in meetings!

Our concern in this book is for exercising leadership in high performance. One way to do that is by finding innovative substitutes for the standard, face-to-face meeting, whether we use videophones or electronic mail. Another is to make better use of people's energies when

283

they do gather for meetings. These two issues are the focus of our concluding chapter, which flows naturally from our previous commentary on action learning.

The Input section discusses improving meeting effectiveness, using new meeting technologies, and making meetings more fun, as well as more productive. The Interaction section offers two methods for increasing learning at meetings through simulations and creative thinking exercises. Finally, the Instrumentation section provides a meeting and conference management checklist, as well as an inventory of a leader's capacities to energize people's performance at work.

INPUT

If we look at our organizations as energy-exchange systems, then we as leaders have to be concerned that this energy flows properly and is channeled into the activities that will have the best pay-off. Looked at in these terms, meetings are major loci of energy expenditure, because they consume so much personnel effort in preparing, conducting, and following-up. From the perspective of energy conservation, there are several questions: Is there a better way to confer and communicate than in the person-to-person format? Should people's presence be required in a group encounter? If so, how can we meet more productively? Many of the insights and methods of action learning and research (Chapter 7) can be applied here, because a training session is a meeting. Similarly, what is offered in this chapter on meetings is equally applicable to education and training.

INCREASING MEETING EFFECTIVENESS

To find out what can be done to improve meetings in an organization, ask the people who work there. This topic is perfect for action research, as long as the replies are anonymous and personnel are free to tell it like it is. A properly conducted survey can be done with questionnaires or interviews to ascertain what meetings are considered boring or unnecessary, what bothers people about the meetings, and what can be done to make the affairs more productive.

The author was once a vice-president in a corporation which held a weekly executive meeting. A common pattern prevailed—the president presided, made small talk and jokes, and dominated the proceedings. Rarely would the others present contribute to deliberations, and no real decisions were ever made. No agenda was ever set, no meaningful business was ever transacted, and everyone left frustrated, except the CEOs obsequious cronies. Knowing the company was losing money and going nowhere, I resigned to start my own enterprise. A few years later, after the first mentioned corporation had gone bankrupt, I discovered that, at the time of the meetings in question, the former president was going deaf, yet would not admit that he was unable to hear the contributions of others or wear a hearing aid. Thus, that strange meeting behavior contributed to the business failure. This was an organization that did not welcome feedback from personnel, and when it was given tended not to act upon it. This company lacked what Gordon Shea (1987) defines as "trust," something that can be developed through meetings.

Bradford D. Smart, president of Smart and Associates in Chicago, did a study as to what meeting characteristics bothered executives, particularly in team sessions. The respondents (14 board chairpersons, 358 presidents, 142 vice presidents, and 121 general managers) complained about

1. Poor preparation for the sessions by meeting planners or participants
2. People drifting off the subject under discussion
3. Members not listening properly during the presentations and analysis
4. Participant wordiness during questioning or discussions
5. Lack of participation on the part of some
6. Emotional outbursts and conflicts
7. Ineffectiveness of methods or discussions
8. Excessive length

The same executives reached some consensus as to ground rules during business meetings, including training or team building:

- Each member must feel totally responsible for group effectiveness and team solutions, ensuring the maximum use of time and human resources available (e.g., invite silent ones to speak up and dominators to shut up).

- Telephone call interruptions should be banned except for serious emergencies of "life and death importance."
- Circular seating arrangements were requested, even without tables.
- Participants should contribute to structuring the agenda and priorities, usually in the initial minutes and always in team meetings.
- Participative decision-making achieved through group consensus is the desirable form of group action.
- Conflicts are to be confronted, used, and resolved, lest they hamper group effectiveness.
- Teams should learn how to diagnose and deal with problems of group process, including the appropriate use of instruments for this purpose.

The readers may wish to compare these groundrules with those I proposed for team building in Chapter 5 (page 140). Certainly these observations offer clues as to what to do and what to avoid if one's own performance at meetings is to be enhanced. As a means for upgrading a group's performance, a survey might be conducted within one's own organization on the same subject matter; the above executive report would provide a good basis for comparison of findings. In the Instrumentation section, a checklist is supplied for a more comprehensive diagnosis of meeting planning. Further, a review of the insights from Chapters 3 and 5 will offer guidelines for improving meetings. Related to this topic is the art of conference planning which requires a larger expertise (Nadler and Nadler, 1977).

TIPS FOR EFFECTIVE MEETINGS

1. Recognize that meetings have different purposes, requiring participants and methods suitable to the type of meeting proposed (e.g., meetings for regular staff business, for work programming, for unit feedback on progress, for problem-solving, for information sharing, or for training); therefore, plan accordingly.
2. Realize there are meeting skills to be acquired relative to planning, chairing, controlling, facilitating, and coping with problems or obtaining solutions; acquire these competencies.
3. Consult resources that can assist in improving the technical presentations during meetings (e.g., seek training in multimedia methods, production of slides or videotapes, group dynamics).

4. Use meetings to provide interaction opportunities for managers or supervisors of complex, interdependent operations.
5. Hold meetings, if possible, on one's own "territory," but ensure that the facilities are adequate for optimum performance, including all necessary supplies and equipment.
6. Seat participants for minimum conflict or collusion (e.g., divide antagonists and buddies) and maximum exchange (e.g., round tables, U-shaped table set-up, or other logistic arrangements to promote eye contact and interaction).
7. Agendas are normally helpful to focus efforts and save time, while excluding undesirable and irrelevant subjects (except in unstructured meetings, in which the group develops the agenda). Issues are who sets agenda, how to get items on the docket, and when agenda is distributed. Does the leader establish the agenda or delegate this? Is there a procedure for members to contribute points for discussion? Is the agenda published in advance for preparation purposes, or held until the actual meeting?
8. Control time in business meetings so that it is used productively (e.g., provide advance materials, set a time limit, use a timing device, limit individual input, establish meeting procedures).
9. Facilitate the meeting process (e.g., provide for notetaking and recording when desirable, invite and foster participation, encourage compromise and conflict management, replay people's ideas and synthesize input, use audiovisual aids, articulate clearly and nondefensively, divide the group into subgroups or task forces to study critical issues, obtain support beforehand on critical decisions, offer positive reinforcement of sound strategies and positions, seek and obtain consensus (possibly by calling for a vote).
10. Conclude meetings by clarifying action steps, establishing accountability, setting deadlines if necessary, confirming unusual contributions, encouraging feelings of accomplishment, and ending on time.

Andrew S. Grove, the founder and president of Intel Corporation, notes that in the course of a work day, he normally engages in twenty-five separate activities, but that two thirds of that time is spent in meetings. Obviously, then, this time must be used productively—meetings provide the medium for most managerial activity, and, when conducted effectively, provide managerial leverage. In his book, *High Output Management,* Grove (1983) describes two basic types of business meetings:

1. *Process-oriented.* Knowledge is shared and information exchanged; should take place on regularly scheduled basis and recorded on people's calendars for minimum interruption of production. Generally these are of three kinds:

   - *One-on-one,* such as supervisor–subordinate, for mutual information exchange, learning, coaching, and problem-solving; number and length may vary, but agenda is normally set by subordinate in outline form for note taking; usually is performance oriented; participants may "batch" together key issues for discussion together or establish a "hold" file for those that are less urgent and can be put off until another encounter; supervisor welcomes authentic communication and sees these meetings as an opportunity to build organizational relationships; the face-to-face encounter may be supplemented by telephone and note exchanges.
   - *Staff meeting,* in which supervisor and subordinates confer; opportunity for peer interaction and decision-making; leader plays multiple roles of observer, expediter, questioner, and decison-maker and may share authority with the group in this context.
   - *Operation review,* which brings together managers and peers from various parts of the organization to motivate, share progress and problems, and generally to inform of the larger operational activities; usually formal presentations, well-organized format; an opportunity for senior management to provide behavior models, to share the "big picture."

2. *Mission-oriented,* ad hoc affairs aimed at producing a specific output, such as a decision, in a short time-frame. The key is in the chairperson, who must understand why the meeting is necessary, what specific accomplishments are required, who must attend, and what logistic arrangements are critical. That person is also responsible for follow-up action—minutes of the meeting, commitments pursued. No more than 25 percent of time devoted to meetings should be of this occasional, emergency type.

Grove estimates that the manager's time is worth around $100 per hour, so that a meeting of ten managers may cost the company $2000. Thus, such meetings must be justified and expedited if the participants are really to be committed to them. When it comes to conferences of twenty or more persons, Leonard and Zeace Nadler (1987) believe they must be carefully and professionally planned and executed, and they have compiled an outstanding handbook for this purpose. Being a competent meeting coordinator means managing a whole range of activities from conference design and site selection, to exhibits and learning materials, to registration and presentation, and finally to evaluation and follow-up.

Meeting planners or facilitators need to use imagination and innovate in the manner in which people are brought together. I am indebted to a client, Dr. Martin Apple, president of San Francisco, Adytum Inc., for this case in point. As chief executive at one of the high-tech firms he founded, Apple held a daily stand-up meeting for all key researchers at 8:30 A.M.; normal work day for the plant began at 9 A.M. During the opening half hour, the group would brainstorm ideas for possible patents; the session was taped. In the course of the day, the CEO would play back the ideas kicked around by the group in a very creative manner. Before leaving work that day, each member had received a brief typed memorandum to the group from the president on what concepts seemed feasible to pursue further for patent filing. In this way, the knowledge workers were energized and enthused, knowing that each day they had an opportunity to meet with top management and contribute their creativity, and eventually they might be rewarded. As a result of these unusual meetings, the entrepreneurial activity prospered and a record number of patents were actually filed and recognitions given.

NEW MEETING TECHNOLOGY

Meeting performance can be enhanced by intelligent use of the many new electronic devices available to promote human interaction. In fact, the "children of the television" age expect innovation when they attend meetings, conferences, and conventions. They not only have high expectations on the use of various media for presenting knowledge and information, but they want it done professionally in terms of content, format, and technical expertise. Thus, sound tracks have to be clear and understandable; live commentary has to be dynamic, appropriate and stimulating; the visuals have to be crisp and the pace fast. Whether attending a seminar or listening to a sales pitch, today's audience, products of mass media, demand that both medium and message be informative, sophisticated, and entertaining. This applies equally to live meetings, teleconferencing, or combinations of both.

Such expectations place an added burden on meeting planners, to see that films, video, slides, audio, computers, synthesizers, and other such technology is carefully chosen and combined for maximum impact. Therefore, planners must ensure that

- The proper hardware and/or software has been identified and selected.
- The premeeting testing of this proves satisfactory, especially in terms of sequence and integration of equipment and presentations.
- The provision has been made for alternative programming in case of technical breakdowns, power failures, or other emergencies.
- The plan makes for optimum use of the senses of those in the audience—the more individual powers involved, the better the chance that the message will be retained.

People enjoy variety at meetings, change of pace, and opportunities to directly participate in what is happening. The new communication technologies make this all possible in dazzling ways. Live input can be alternated with mass media, group process, and even electronic involvement. Multiple projectors can now be synchronized for maximum impact. The planner might begin with a training film, supplement it by offering new dimensions of the same subject with two slide projectors, and then end the demonstration with live and active participation by actors or the audience; these methods can be used in sequence or simultaneously with multiple screens. Because annual corporate conferences may represent a considerable financial investment, a multidimensional transmission of a message may establish the right mood and learning environment. In addition to professional conference consultants, most professional conference facilities have personnel to assist planners with the use of meeting rooms, including colors, lighting, ventilation, seating, and sound or musical background. Then, it becomes possible to immerse a group in a maelstrom of sight, sound, and feelings, providing a stimulating and at times almost psychedelic learning environment. To summarize, in this era of mass communication, imaginative meeting facilitators have numerous mechanical and technical aids, in addition to traditional means, to stimulate the senses and transmit the message more effectively. Indeed, there can be a message in the media chosen, as rock concert promoters have demonstrated.

Educational media publishers now offer a variety of instructional kits, learning packages, and other seminar aids to assist the manager or trainer conducting the meeting. For example, some distributors use a training systems approach, supporting management development films with instructor's guides and supplementary materials from videocassettes to computer discs to case studies to diagnostic instruments. Longman Crown of Reston, Virginia, offers computer-based training. These user-friendly, interactive systems can be used on personal computers and include learning strategies for drill and practice, tutorials and inquiries, simulations and computer-managed instructional methods. The subjects range from time and project management to decision-making and management performance. When these capabilities are combined with television receivers and videocassettes, a learning system is created for individual or group training. Interactive video is the marriage of computer to videotape or videodisc, and represents a powerful new meeting and training tool. In the resource section at the end of this book, we have provided indications as to where some of this information is available.

Demonstrated Electronic Possibilities

The prospects for improving meetings through technology are staggering. These technologies include satellite communications, word processing systems, fiber optics, paging devices, and new uses of long lines. High technology offers exciting opportunities at meetings or conferences to present graphics and simulations, to survey an audience for rapid response or texting purposes, to promote interactive, individual, or group learning, and to encourage networking. The following successful examples of meeting technology use may inspire further management leadership:

- Instantaneous, multisite, two-way satellite meetings can be used for small groups or teleconferences of very large audiences; currently, there are three alternatives: (a) slow-scan video using standard video cameras and telephone lines for sound/video; (b) one-way full bandwidth video in which the audience may respond by two-way audio telephone link; (c) two-way full bandwidth for video and audio, so that participants both see and hear one another from remote locations and may exchange as if they were together at the same site. Major corporations, such as ARCO, TRW, and Ford, Westinghouse, Sperry, and Merrill Lynch, have their own telecommunication networks. Among the principal private enterprise communication network services are Satellite Business Systems of McLean, Virginia, and VideoNet of Woodland Hills, California.

- International hotel chains offer a combined service of meeting rooms and private satellite communications for conferencing purposes. For example, Holiday Inns, Intercontinental, and Hilton Hotels not only have electronic networks for this purpose, but offer ancillary services, such as story board development or exchange of hard copy across continents.
- Telephone conference calls for either audio or video meetings by combining the use of various visuals, computer video display terminals, and electronic mail exchange. The range of network applications extends from telemarketing and teletraining to mass calling and electronic order exchange. Among the several telephone utilities offering such service, AT&T (1-800/257-4636) has the most comprehensive training and support system (Network Exchange, Communications Consultant Liaison Program, Rm. 5355A2, 295 Basking Ridge, NJ 07920).
- Computer response system for live meetings enables the presenter quickly to profile the audience, customize input, control audience attention, stimulate discussions, and create more intimate groups within large gatherings.
- Electronic matchmaking between employers and potential employees eliminates the need for some job interviews or at least reduces the number of expensive meetings between the parties. The Corporate Interviewing Network of Fort Lauderdale, Florida, sends client companies videotaped interviews with candidates. Other firms now use satellite television to directly interview job applicants at remote sites, in preference to bringing them to corporate offices or sending out recruiters.
- Satellite Seminars is a new teleconferencing service which teams up the resources of the U.S. Chamber of Commerce, American Management Associations, and BNA Communications. Subscribers receive a variety of seminars from marketing to management (VideoStar Connections, 3390 Peachtree Road, Atlanta, GA 30326).

MEETING RESOURCES

For further information, managers and trainers may utilize:

- Periodicals and annual directories of suppliers and sites, such as *Successful Meetings* (633 Third Avenue, New York, NY 10017); *Meeting News* (1515 Broadway, New York, NY 10036); *Corporate Meetings and Incentives* (P.O. Box 6238, Duluth, MN 55606)
- Books, manuals and computer software, such as *The Successful Meeting Master Guide for Business and Professions* by B. Palmer and K. Palmer, 1983 (American Management Associations Book Club, 135 West 50th Street, New York, NY 10020); *The Teleconferencing Handbook: A Guide to Cost-Effective Communication*), annual, edited by E. Lazer (Knowledge Industry Publications, 701 Westchester Ave., White Plains, NY 10604); *Conducting Successful Meetings,* a computer software program by DSI Micro, Inc. (770 Broadway, New York, NY 10003); *Louder and Funnier: A Practical Guide for Overcoming Stagefright in Speechmaking* by R. B. Nelson, (Berkley, CA: Ten Speed Press, 1985); *We've Got to Start Meeting Like This* by R. K. Mosvick and R. B. Nelson, 1987 (Scott, Foresman and Company, Glenview, IL); *Managing a Difficult or Hostile Audience* by G. F. Shea, 1984 (Prentice-Hall, Englewood Cliffs, NJ); and *Robert's Rules of Order* by H. M. Robert et al. (Scott, Foresman and Company, Glenview, IL).

In this postindustrial age, information and learning are the means to establishing the authority of competence and furthering career development, as well as the solution to problems and challenges. Leaders who are sensitive to their human resource development responsibilities realize this, and make effective use of meetings to accomplish such purposes. Whether the situation requires a live or electronic meeting, innovators either master the professional methods or know where to obtain support services for achieving high performance through meetings.

INTERACTION

Frequently at meetings, a manager or trainer is asked to lead a discussion group. Exhibit 8.1 provides 15 guidelines.

293

Exhibit 8.1 Discussion Group Guidelines. (From Robert Letwin, Successful Meetings, July 1983, pp. 8–9.)

1. State the objective of the session to the group and the area of discussion.
2. Explain that everyone participates, but there are to be no speeches.
3. To get started, you put a sharply defined question to the group. If no one responds, have an alternate question that is easy for anyone to answer. Resist answering your own question and entering into a monologue.
4. Test for the audience's objective. Is it the same as yours? If the audience would like to steer the discussion in another direction, make sure there is a consensus. If there is, discuss what the audience considers to be more important. Good discussion follows when everyone agrees on what to discuss.
5. Keep in mind what you hope will be the outcome. Ask questions that will focus on the agreed upon objective.
6. Have a member of the group serve as a reporter to keep a running record of problems, issues, facts and decisions discussed. From time to time, have the reporter summarize. This is useful when the group starts to stray from the main topic.
7. Resort to easy-to-answer questions when discussion bogs down. For instance, ask a question about the time sequence, such as: "What comes first, and next?" You can also ask, "What is the biggest problem with . . . ?" or, "What has been your experience with . . . ?"
8. Ask for votes. Get a consensus on as many points as possible.
9. Don't rephrase what is offered by a group member. Repeat the statement exactly as it is given. (Resist inserting your words or editing comments. This can be intimidating. No one wants his or her words corrected in public. This also tends to stifle discussion.)
10. Don't feel you have to cover everything you know about the subject. That's not the purpose of discussion. Rather, the aim is to have everyone in the audience participate. It is better to have a lively, well-explored segment of a subject than breeze along quickly without deep reflections.
11. Summarize with the help of the reporter. Point out problems raised during the discussion. List bright ideas. Point out areas of agreement and disagreement.
12. If some members of the group do not have the courage to speak up, draw them in with non-threatening questions. Ask them to share their experiences.
13. It is best to toss questions to the entire group. But, if you want to ask a quiet person to speak, call the person by name before you ask the question. Say, "John, what did you think when you first heard about . . . ?" By starting with the person's name, you provide time for him or her to concentrate and think about an answer.
14. When someone tends to monopolize discussion, politely interrupt and ask someone else in the audience to comment on the monopolizer's statements. Allow the audience to straighten out its members instead of your doing it. Too tight a rein will cut off discussion.
15. Feel good about not covering all the points you had written in advance. This means you have led a wholesome discussion and were not prompted to inject your opinions in favor of those in the group.

MEETINGS CAN BE FUN AND PRODUCTIVE

The key to high performance is energized people who are interested and involved. One of the best ways to accomplish this at meetings is through play, games, and simulations (as discussed in the Interaction section on page 113). Further possibilities are now described. When people enjoy themselves at work, they tend to be more productive. The meeting, especially for training purposes, can be a useful mechanism for unleashing hidden creativity through play. It permits employees to reveal joyful, spontaneous, and even silly facets of themselves that is often restrained. Enlightened management takes advantage of this approach for creative problem solving and education, as well as for its mental health and recreational values.

Over many years in leadership development, I have personally found that management games are very worthwhile because they:

- Provide a change of pace in the training schedule or meeting schedule.
- Foster experiential or affective learning.
- Reveal behavior in a simulation that often occurs on the job.
- Entertain while teaching important lessons of teamwork.
- Build on the competitive spirit while demonstrating the disadvantages of unrestrained competition and the synergistic value of cooperation or collaboration.
- Offer opportunity for meaningful analysis and discussion after the play as to what happened and why.
- Give incentive to extra team effort which can thus be rewarded, literally or figuratively.

In a meeting simulation, a real life experience is simulated or replayed through a "game-like" experience, but in a condensed time span.

As in recreational games, a person acts out the situation according to established rules. A life experience that might require the passage of days or weeks can be telescoped into a short time-frame of several hours. Practice in planning, decision-making and communication can be obtained through a simulated experience. As people get more deeply involved in the game, behavior which is often common in their real life is also exhibited in the game.

Simulation uses trial-and-error experimentation with a model for re-

295

search, problem-solving, or training purposes. A simulated group technique permits learning and problem-solving to take place through a group experience. It enables a trainer to demonstrate, by a simulated model within a short time period, a larger human relations truth that the participant may eventually experience in a different setting. Frequently, in business and industry, these techniques of group dynamics are employed for the purpose of management development in a short-term laboratory demonstration. Principles are taught and insights gained which have application to the job situations.

Behavioral games involve developing strategy, resolving conflict and setting objectives. The most vital part of this action-learning experience is when the game ends and the participants analyze what they learned.

Simulated exercises are used to teach a number of things not easily taught by any other method. These include: (1) the importance of planned, critically timed decisions; (2) the need for flexible, organized effort; (3) the need for decision-assisting tools, such as setting objectives and establishing criteria for measuring and evaluating performance; (4) the significance of reaching a dynamic balance between interacting managerial functions and (5) the power of the modeling concept for providing a scientific approach to problems.

An interesting use of the simulation is to train personnel through this "practice session" to prepare for the "real thing." War games have long been used for this purpose.

Increasingly, the computer is being used for simulation purposes. Mathematical models of potential situations are programmed, and the trainees act out "live" work situations through the computer.

As previously indicated, a manager or trainer may purchase, borrow, or create a simulation game to meet a specific need (Eitington, 1984). Two examples of helpful commercial games for management development are "Starpower" and "Relocation," both distributed by Simile II (P.O. Box 910, Del Mar, CA 92014.) "Starpower" teaches a group about the realities of power and its influence on behavior. "Relocation" examines the issues involved in moving a corporate headquarters, both from the viewpoints of the community and the employees.

On the other hand, innovative trainers may use cardboard, sticks, glue, tinker toys, or other household items to create a structured learning experience that teaches managers the importance of cooperation or of "win-win." There are noncompetitive games based on the approach that both teams either win together or lose. Two of my favorite "homemade" games of this type for managers are "Hollow Square" and "Blue Green."

At the beginning of the Hollow Square exercise (Exhibit 8.2), two teams are given various pieces of cardboard, which they are to assemble within a specific time frame. Each group is further divided into subgroups of planners and operators. The planners are to prepare a plan, like a plan for a jigsaw puzzle, for the operators to assemble the pieces into the correct pattern; in this competitive game, the first team

Exhibit 8.2   Hollow Square Exercise: **A,** Overall Pattern, **B,** Detailed Assembled Pattern. (NOTE: **A** is the incomplete design given to planners/operators. When properly assembled, the pieces make up this following pattern. **B** is the completed design that the winning team must produce with the pieces.)

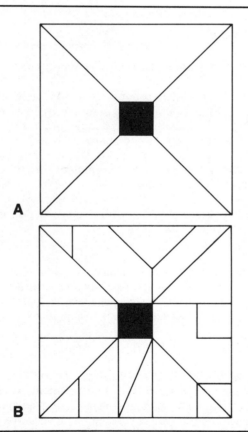

to correctly assemble the pattern wins. There are also observers of the process going on among the four groups of planners and implementers. Exhibit 8.2*B* shows how the pattern of cardboard pieces is properly assembled with its hollow square in the center. Following the simulation, the trainers hear reports from these observers on their own behavior and strategies. Exhibit 8.3 summarizes the instructions given to the planners, operators, and observers as well as learnings. After the observers' reports, participants contribute their own insights from the learning experience. Exhibit 8.3,*D* provides a synthesis of the lessons real people have learned from this "game"—the principal one is that only when planners and operators collaborate, when planners involve those who must implement their plans in the planning process, does the team succeed.

Exhibit 8.3 Hollow Square Exercise: Briefing Sheet.

Part A: Briefing Sheet for Planning Team

Note to Facilitator: There are two groups, each with two teams. For learning purposes, it is possible to influence the outcome by instructing one group to consider electing a team leader, while suggesting to the other group that they try participative management and share the leadership.

Each participant will be given a packet containing four (4) or more cardboard pieces which, when properly assembled with pieces from other participants, will make a hollow square design.

Your Task   During a period of 45 minutes you are to do the following:

1. Plan how these pieces, distributed among you, should be assembled to make the design.
2. Instruct your operating team on how to implement your plan so as to complete your task ahead of the other teams. (You may begin instructing your operating team at any time during the 45 minute planning period—but no later than 5 minutes before they are to begin the assembling process).

General Rules

1. You must keep all four pieces you have in front of you at all times.
2. You may not touch the pieces of other team members or trade pieces with other members of your team during the planning or instructing phase.
3. You may not show Sheet E (which contains the detailed design as shown in Exhibit 8.2*B*) to the operating team at any time.

Exhibit 8.3   Hollow Square Exercise: Briefing Sheet, *cont'd.*

4. You may not actually assemble the entire square at any time (this is to be left to your operating team).
5. You may not number or otherwise mark on the pieces.
6. Members of your operating team must also observe the above rules until the signal is given to begin the assembling.
7. When time is called for your operating team to begin assembling the pieces you may give no further instructions, but are to step back from the table and observe the operation only.
8. All members of the planning team must be involved in the exercise; also, *all* members of the operating team.
9. If you have specific questions which may affect the way you propose to go about your task, it may be preferable to ask them of the Resource persons privately rather than before the large group.

Part B: Briefing Sheet for Operating Team

1. You will have responsibility for carrying out a task for 4 people according to instructions given by your planning team. Your planning team may call you in for instructions at any time. If they do not summon you before _____ you are to report to them anyway. Your task is scheduled to begin promptly at _____, after which no further instructions from your planning team can be given. You are to finish the assigned task as rapidly as possible.
2. During the period when you are waiting for a call from your planning team it is suggested that you discuss and make notes on the following:
   a. The feelings and concerns which you experience while waiting for instructions for the unknown task.
   b. Your suggestions on how a person might prepare to receive instructions.
3. Your notes recorded on the above will be helpful during the work group discussions following the completion of your task.

Part C: Briefing for Observing Team

You will be observing a situation in which a planning team decides how to solve a problem and gives instructions to an operating team for implementation. The problem consists of assembling pieces of cardboard into the form of a hollow square. The planning team is supplied with the general layout of the pieces (Exhibit 8.2A). This team is not to assemble the parts but is to instruct the operating team on how to assemble the parts in a minimum amount of time. You will be *silent observers* throughout the process.

Continued

Exhibit 8.3 Hollow Square Exercise: Briefing Sheet, *cont'd.*

Suggestions for Observation

1. Each member of the observing team should watch the general pattern of communication but give special attention to one member of the planning team (during the planning phase) and one member of the operating team (during the assembling period).
2. During the Planning period watch for such behavior as:
   a. For planners:
      1) The evenness or unevenness of participation among planning team members.
      2) Behavior that blocks or facilitates understanding.
      3) How the planning team divides its time between planning and instructing (how early does it invite the operating team to come in?)
      4) How well it plans its procedure for giving instructions to the operating team.
   b. For operating team:
      1) What do members do with their time?
      2) What evidence is there of anxiety, boredom, and feelings about planners?
      3) What could the planners have done to alleviate the anxieties and/or negative behavior evidenced by the operating team?
3. During the instructing period (when the planning team is instructing the operating team) watch for such things as:
   a. Who in the planning team gives the instructions (and how was this decided)?
   b. What is significant about the management or leadership style followed in the group you are observing?

Part D: Learnings from Hollow Square Game

Problems which may occur when one group makes plans which the other group is to carry out:

1. Planners sometimes impose restrictions on themselves which are unnecessary.
2. It is sometimes difficult for planners to see the task from the point of view of the operators.
3. Sometimes in planning, more attention is given to details while the larger clues and possibilities go unnoticed.
4. Planners sometimes fail to apportion their time wisely because they plunge into the act of planning before they think through their entire task and the amount of time available to them.

Exhibit 8.3   Hollow Square Exercise: Briefing Sheet, *cont'd.*

5. Planners sometimes have different understandings of their task and the boundaries in which they must operate.
6. When members of a planning team fail to listen to one another, time is lost in efforts to clarify.
7. Sometimes planners fail to prepare a proper physical setup for the working team.
8. Sometimes planners become so involved in the planning process that they do not plan their method of instructing the implementers.

Common problems when planners instruct operators:

1. Sometimes planners do not consider the operators' anxieties when they orient them to the environment and task.
2. Planners may not allow enough time for instruction and help the operators to "get set" and feel comfortable for the job.
3. Planners may not encourage questions from the operators and therefore assume greater understanding than the operators have.
4. The planners' own feelings of anxiety or security are likely to be transmitted to the operators.
5. Planners sometimes give detailed instructions before giving the operator an "overall" feel of the task.
6. Planners sometimes stress minute problems which concerned them while ignoring more important points.
7. The instructions may be given in a way that discourages members of an operating group from working as a team.

Common problems when operators carry out the plans of others:

1. If instructions are confusing, operators tend to display irritation toward each other as well as toward the planners.
2. If instructions are unclear, considerable time will be spent in clarification.
3. Members of an operating team will often have different perceptions of their instructions.
4. The factor of pressure will influence different operators in different ways—the efficiency of some will go up and the efficiency of others will decline.
5. If members of an operating group do not feel themselves to be a team, they will usually perform less efficiently. (During some periods one person may be working on part of the problem all alone while the others wait inactively for him to complete the task.)

Note: Each of the above parts (A-D) should be reproduced and distributed as separate sheets when appropriate. Two sheets are produced with the drawings in Exhibit 8.2.

The simpler "Blue-Green" game drives home the win-win philosophy. Two groups are told they both are separate divisions or subsidiaries of the same organization. They are instructed on procedures for amassing points, and told that within the specified time period, their group scores will be totaled to determine the winner. Although there is nothing in the ground rules preventing their mutual cooperation, each usually proceeds to gain points at the expense of the other group in a mad competitive battle. Only in the post-game learning analysis do the participants realize that the whole organization stands to lose because of their failure to cooperate as parts within the same system. This game teaches a powerful lesson about how the competitive race for profits may have destructive effects on the common good. Management games are useful tools for communicating about the new work culture norm of collaboration or team effort.

There are many training resources available that provide details on how to formulate and facilitate such games for the development of personnel. For example, University Associates (8517 Production Ave., San Diego, CA 92121) issues an *HRD Resource Guide* describing publications available for this purpose (e.g., *A Handbook of Structured Experiences for Human Relations Training* and yearly workbooks of methodology listed in the *Reference Guide to Handbooks and Annuals*). Dr. Allen Zoll also produces *Dynamic Management Education,* which describes a variety of dynamic adult education techniques from cases and in-basket exercises to action maze and business games (Management Education Associates, 2003 33rd S., Seattle, WA 98144). Other major creators and distributors of management simulations are Didactic Systems, Inc., P.O. Box 457, Cranford, NJ 07016, and Education Research, P.O. Box 4205, Warren, NJ 07060.

Local computer software stores also can advise on what is available on the market in terms of computer simulations. A useful newsletter is *Simulation Today,* published by the Society for Computer Simulations (P.O. Box 2228, La Jolla, CA 92038).

CREATIVITY EXERCISES

An effective strategy at the end of a training session or meeting is to propose creative problem solving on the question: "How are we going to apply this learning, information, or technique back on the job?" Such an exercise can stimulate a group to produce action plans for performance improvement. In the Interaction section on page 254, we outlined one technique for this purpose, called "brainstorming." Four major steps in the creative thinking process are outlined in Exhibit 8.4 with examples. Such techniques can be used by a manager or facilitator at a meeting to "loosen up" the group's imaginative and intuitive capacities before turning them loose to creatively solve a real organizational problem (Exhibit 8.5).

Dr. Matt Weinstein has developed a whole company to teach adults how to play—Playfair, Inc., based in Berkeley, California, with offices in Dallas and New York City. His corporate clients use these services at meetings and conferences to help their employees decrease stress, increase productivity, and improve morale or camaraderie. As a replacement for the cocktail hour, he can engage a ballroom full of meeting attendees in free form play. There are no winners and losers; only celebration, bonding, and community results. When the meeting sessions are spread over days or weeks, it is essential to build into the conference design opportunities for physical and emotional release, so that participants are recharged for further intellectual effort. This

"re-creation" can serve as a learning experience when so planned, such as a team golf game using the rules of "Scramble," in which individual scores are replaced by a group tally (combining the best performance of each member for each shot on every hole). Many resorts catering to conference groups have a variety of silly games to relax tired registrants—water-balloon tosses, egg-carrying relays, sandcastle building contests, or creative theme parties. The resulting laughter is good for morale, encourages convivality and comradeship, and puts attendees on an equal footing. Meetings, a part of the whole work environment, can be made enjoyable in a variety of ways.

Exhibit 8.4 Creative Thinking Techniques.

I. Stating the Problem

Creative problem solving requires that the problems be stated in such a way that the thinking of those who are attempting to solve the problem is not *unduly* restricted. Example: The old saw, "Build a better mousetrap and the world will beat a path to your door." The implied problem, "build a better mousetrap," is inadequate. A better problem statement is, "find a way to eliminate mice from _____X_____ area." This latter statement permits us to think beyond an elimination that requires the presence of rodents. The former restricts us to thinking in terms of spring traps, gas, ultrasonic devices, and rodent-proof building construction.

The problem statement must not be unduly restricted nor must it be stated so broadly as to make it difficult to focus on constructive possibilities. Example: A problem solving team at one institute was to consider the problem of utilizing the knowledge gained about creativity at the conference. This is too vague, too broad, to handle effectively. A better statement was found when one of the group outlined his company's background and restated the problem: "How can we install an educational program on creative thinking in our company?"

Oftentimes mechanical methods, such as the following, are big helps to coming up with a "best" problem stated. It is worth the time it takes to settle on the problem.

Method 1. State the problem in ten words or less.
Method 2. State the problem in a specified number of ways—at least five and oftentimes, as many as ten.

The importance attached to problem stating cannot be overdrawn. The "old timers" and best technical men must be most wary that changing technology and conditions do not make yesterday's problems only apparent, but false, problems today. It is all too easy to work at solving problems

Exhibit 8.4   Creative Thinking Techniques, *cont'd.*

which have become irrelevant in the course of time, or just as bad, to deny ourselves the posing of certain problem statements *supposing* that solutions are beyond technical or human capability. In an age of increasing rates of technical and organizational capability, virtually all problems may be stated without stating a pre-judged case.

II. Analytical Operational Techniques

These techniques employ a logical step-by-step approach to the problem. These techniques include attribute listing, the input-output method, and morphological analysis. These techniques have two basic rules: (1) All judgment or evaluation is eliminated from the idea-producing step. (2) All ideas, *even the most impractical,* are considered.

A. *Attribute Listing* was developed by Professor Robert Crawford at the University of Nebraska. Its form is:

1. Isolate all the major characteristics or attributes of a product, object, or idea.
2. Consider each in turn and change them in every conceivable way. No attempt is made to limit the suggested changes in any manner.
3. After all the ideas have been listed, evaluate them in the light of the limitations posed by the problem and the situation.

Example: Consider design improvements for the common telephone instrument. The characteristics (attributes) are listed: Usually black; has a handset and base, a dial for indicating the number desired, and is constructed principally of plastic.
Possible changes include:

Black color—Could by any other color or transparent; could be two-tone; could utilize designs such as polka dot, abstract art designs, personalized designs (initials, names), or pictures.

Handset and base construction. Could design handset to fit hand (finger grooves); make it more square or more round in the base; oval base; higher or lower base; wall set; eliminate (use microphone and speaker.)

Dial. Could use a push-button system; design the dial differently (ex. numbers and letters outside the dial; lever system; abacus-type system; computer to interpret voice commands.

Plastic construction. Could be metal, glass, wood, hard rubber, stone, or lucite or other plastics.

Note: Unique attributes tend to produce the greatest opportunity for *original* variations. Attributes common to many products (i.e., color, shape, size, weight, etc.) tend to produce opportunities for fewer extraordinary original ideas.

Continued

305

Exhibit 8.4 Creative Thinking Techniques, *cont'd.*

B. *Input-Output Methods,* developed by General Electric Company, are useful where the problem involves the use of one or more forms of energy.

1. Establish the desired output, or end result. This "output" is the goal we are seeking to attain—the problem solution.
2. The input is the starting point. The input includes the various forms of energy which are available to provide the initial stimulus which sets in motion the dynamic system involved.
3. Analyze the input to determine how various forms of energy produced by it can be used to ultimately achieve the desired output.

Example (Problem): To devise a fire warning system within a given building.
1. Establish desired output—warning of the presence of fire.
2. Determine input—fire.
3. Analyze the input.
   a. Specifications: The warning must be received one mile away from the building site within a matter of seconds after the fire starts. Cost must be under $1,000. System must be operative 24 hours a day, 7 days a week. System must be relatively trouble-free and easy to maintain.
   b. Problem attack.
      (1) What outputs are produced directly by the input? Fire is characterized by the presence of a certain amount of heat and light and by the presence of the gaseous and solid products of combustion and smoke.
      (2) Can any of these factors be used to produce the desired output directly? (Without referring to the specifications, we can say that once the fire became large enough, a combination of its light and smoke would supply its own warning signal. But by that time the fire would have devoured a good part of the building, thus making a solution of this kind unsatisfactory.)
      (3) What reactions are caused by heat? light? smoke? Here a serious attempt should be made to list all the possible physical and chemical reactions. Those actions caused by heat include: expansion of various metals, liquids and bases; melting of metals and glass; changes in the composition of certain chemicals. Light and smoke can cause various chemical and physical actions and reactions.
      (4) Can any of these reactions be used to achieve the desired output? The melting of an alloy such as Wood's metal, which melts at a temperature below the boiling point of water, could be used to break a circuit or to open a valve. Actually, Wood's metal is used in sprinkler systems designed to extinguish undetected fires. The expansion of liquids is the principle used in the thermometer. The unequal expansion of bimetal strips when exposed to heat is the basis for the thermostat (a heat-actuated electric circuit breaker). Light can be detected by various chemicals.

Exhibit 8.4   Creative Thinking Techniques, *cont'd.*

Note: Only those problems that deserve extensive treatment would warrant use of the input-output method.

C. *Morphological Analysis* was developed by Dr. Fritz Zwicky of the California Institute of Technology to aid the determination of practical energy sources and engines for space flight. The problem is defined in terms of its parameters. For instance, if we are interested in determining all possibilities for our own chemical formula, a detergent in liquid form, and its possible uses, it would take somewhat the following form.

At least forty-eight possible combinations

	□ Clothes
	□ Dishes
	□ Walls
	□ Glass
	□ Floors
	□ Industrial
	□ Human skin
	□ Aerospace
	□ Etc.

Liquid Flake Powder Bar Spray Paste

By forcing ourselves to take a positive view of all possible combinations and by viewing the novel relationships that are bound to present themselves, we can often find solutions for previously "impossible" problems.

Additional parameters can be added to the two, illustrated in the example using detergents. The search for possible space engines provides an example of a three-dimensional, three-parameter morphological analysis. The parameters could include: energy source, medium of travel, and cargo. These three parameters could be arranged in three-dimensional form or all combinations of two could be tried against a third. Arrange the following possibilities and one can see where it became possible to find the useful machines for space, the solar sail and ion engines.

Energy Source	Medium of Travel	Cargo
Chemical	Space	Instrumentation only
Steam	Air	Plant life
Wind	Land	Animals—nonmammal
Electricity	Rail	Mammals—nonhuman
Water	Water	Human
Nuclear	Oil	?????
Moving belt	???	
Solar		
Stars		
?????		

Continued

Exhibit 8.4 Creative Thinking Techniques, *cont'd.*

Forced Relations Techniques

In most instances, the forced relationship is established arbitrarily—often by mechanical means.

A. *Catalog.* Open a catalog or other source of printed information and select any item or subject, or even a single word, at random without conscious effort. A second item, subject, or word is selected in the same arbitrary manner. These elements are then considered together, and the person using the technique attempts to create original ideas based upon this forced relationship.

B. *Listing.* List a number of objects or ideas which are all associated with a general subject. After all items have been listed, give each one a number. Consider each item in turn with each other item. Example: A manufacturer of office equipment might consider the following objects: desk, chair, desk lamp, filing cabinet, bookcase. He would consider such combinations as chair and desk, chair and lamp, chair and filing cabinet, and chair and bookcase—and others as possible marketable items.

As with all other operational techniques, no attempt is made to judge any of the ideas produced until all possible ideas are collected.

C. *Focused Object.* The elements in the relationship are pre-selected with a definite purpose in mind.

1. Select the fixed element in the forced relationship. This may be a product, an idea, or a problem statement.
2. Focus attention on some other element—usually something in the immediate vicinity. Once the fixed element and the element selected at random have been chosen, the forced or unnatural relationship has been established. This is then used as the basis for a free-flowing chain of free associations from which are to come new and original ideas. Usually the first ideas will come from a simple transfer of the attributes of the random to the fixed element. Example: A chair manufacturer might choose a chair as the fixed element and choose a light bulb as a random element. First level suggestions might be a glass chair, thinner chair, bulb-shaped chair, screw-plug construction, electrically operated chair, and chair with built-in reading light. Usually the most profitable ideas evolve from the second level ideas—ideas developed from free association of first level ideas.

D. *Checklists.* An accumulation of points, areas, or possibilities that should be covered in a complete examination of a problem are put in checklist form. The following checklist, developed by Alex Osborn, the author of *Applied Imagination,* can be used with the two basic rules of original thinking to develop many, many ideas.

Checklist

- Put to other uses? New ways to use as is? Other uses if modified?

Exhibit 8.4   Creative Thinking Techniques, *cont'd.*

- *Adapt.* What else is like this? What other idea does this suggest? Does the past offer a parallel? What could I copy? Whom could I emulate?
- *Modify.* New twist? Change meaning, color, motion, odor, form, shape? Other changes?
- *Magnify.* What to add? More time? Greater frequency? Stronger? Larger? Thicker? Extra value? Plus ingredients? Duplicate? Multiply? Exaggerate?
- *Minify.* What to substitute? Smaller? Condensed? Miniature? Lower? Shorter? Lighter? Omit? Streamline? Split up? Understate?
- *Substitute.* Who else instead? What else instead? other ingredients? Other material? Other process? Other power? Other place? Other approach? Other tone of voice?
- *Rearrange.* Interchange components? Other pattern? Other layout? Other sequence? Transpose cause and effect? Change pace? Change schedule?
- *Reverse.* Transpose positive and negative? How about opposites? Turn it backward? Turn it upside down? Reverse roles? Change shoes? Turn tables? Turn other cheek?
- *Combine.* How about a blend, an alloy, an assortment, an ensemble? Combine units: Combine purposes? Combine appeals? Combine ideas?

E. *Modification* is an individual operational technique which consists essentially of attempting to modify or twist a given idea in as many ways as possible. In actual practice a goal consisting of a certain number of modifications is usually set. For some people it is helpful to specify 25 or more modifications of one basic idea.

F. *"The Fresh Eye."* An ordinary object is selected and examined with a great amount of concentration. An attempt is made to find beauty in this common object. This close scrutiny of a familiar object permits us to see it in a new "fresh" light and so may be the source of new ideas. This method is often used by people working in the fine arts.

IV. Free Association Techniques

Free association techniques include brainstorming, the Gordon Method, buzz sessions, slip writing and others which put a premium on quantities of ideas.

A. *Brainstorming.* A typical brainstorming session consists of a group of from six to twelve people seated about a table and spontaneously producing ideas designed to solve a specific problem. There are five basic rules as follows:

1. Judicial judgment is not permitted.
2. "Free-wheeling" is welcomed. The wilder the ideas, the better, because it is easier to "tame down" an idea than it is to build an idea into something more novel.

Continued

309

Exhibit 8.4   Creative Thinking Techniques, *cont'd.*

3. Quantity of ideas is wanted.
4. Combination and improvement are sought.
5. Rule out the negative and traditional.

Note: By ruling out judicial judgment and making all ideas acceptable, an unusually psychologically safe climate is created. The pressures that one finds in an ordinary conference are removed by the conditions established. Because no time is devoted to discussion or criticism, a great many more ideas per conference hour are expressed than in the usual conference.

Choose people for a brainstorming session with as much diversity in background as possible. It is often helpful to include some people in the group who have little direct experience with the problem area—they are not aware of the do's and don'ts that experts may have developed. The expert can also be a valuable member of the group because he is a source of useful information. However, the expert must not be permitted to indicate any negative reaction—or positive reaction or, as a result, the implied disapproval or sanction will likely destroy the effectiveness of the session.

It is often useful to have mixed groups—men and women, highly active and relatively quiet people.

Do *not* mix widely differing ranks within the organization in the same group. The junior men are likely to hold back any ideas that are unusual because they feel that their superiors are judging them and that their future success depends upon their reputation for sound judgment. The boss is also restrained because he has a certain dignity and aloofness to maintain.

Equipment for the best brainstorming sessions will include:

1. A tape recorder. A secretary may take down the ideas, but she will often miss a few. A tape recorder can capture all of them for later review.
2. A blackboard. The participants can use the blackboard to help others in the group to visualize the problem and certain kinds of ideas.
3. A conference table, preferably round, permits easy communication between members of the group.

Brainstorming sessions may last from 40 minutes to an hour. This time range seems to be best for the better sessions.

The evaluation of the ideas may be conducted by the brainstorming group, by another group, or by an individual. If the same group that brainstorms the ideas is called upon to evaluate them, usually it is done several days after the session.

B. *Gordon Technique.* Professor William J. Gordon of Harvard University and of the Arthur D. Little Company developed this highly valuable method.

A group conference is held in which unevaluated free-flowing discussion is encouraged. No one except the group leader knows the exact nature of the problem under consideration. Example: The leader has in mind a particular type of fastener or, rather, he has a problem such as: "how to close and

Exhibit 8.4   Creative Thinking Techniques, *cont'd.*

open a space suit easily and quickly." The leader asks the group questions and receives answers similar to the following hypothetical circumstance:

Leader   "If we can't use our hands, how can we close things?"
           "Suppose we have *heavy* gloves on."
   Ans.   Wish it closed.
   Ans.   Have an insect close "it" on command.
   Ans.   Have a beetle with large pincers do the job.
   Ans.   Use steel loops that easily slip together and as easily can be taken apart even with heavy gloves on the hands.

Other methods of brainstorming and imagineering were provided on pp. 254–255. (For further information on creativity exercises, write for the free newsletter *Mindplay*, 6033 Gaines St., San Diego, CA 92110.)

   C. *Reverse Brainstorming,* developed by the Hotpoint Company, works somewhat opposite to brainstorming. Still the same, is the procedure, but the product, idea, or problem statement are subjected to a barrage of ideas as to why and how they are inadequate. The object of the group session is to think of all the possible limitations, shortcomings, and failings of a product or idea. After the session, the ideas are evaluated to find true problem areas. The new problems are then made the focus of standard creative problem solving methods.

   D. *Slip Writing.* This method is best described as brainstorming limited to a single person. The person formulates his problem statement and writes or tapes all the ideas on the problem that come to his mind. As with other methods, the goal is for a great quantity of ideas. The quality of each idea is to be judged in a separate session.

   Another form of slip writing, developed by Dr. C. C. Crawford, requires each member of a group or audience to perform as described in the preceding paragraph. The slips are then collected and the ideas are evaluated.

   Remember: Being creative and innovative is becoming a norm of the new work culture!

CONCLUSIONS

The principal conclusion to be drawn from both our Input and Interaction sections are that managers and trainers should invest more care and professionalism into meeting arrangements and implementation. Whether it is a weekly staff meeting, an annual stockholders' gathering, a regional sales conference, an employee retreat, an appraisal interview, or a regular meeting between supervisor and subordinate, performance can be enhanced. This can be accomplished first, by utilizing established guidelines and group dynamics in the planning, conducting, and evaluating of such events; second, by employing multimedia technology to interest and involve participants; and third, by remembering the human element—making provision for people's comfort and relaxation. The manager or trainer has many resources to call upon for assistance in improving meetings—the organization's HRD specialists, the staff at the meeting site, the external speakers or consultants employed as presenters, and the suppliers of meeting or game materials and services. (See Appendix A and B.)

INSTRUMENTATION

As indicated throughout this text, meetings can be used for data-gathering, especially by means of instruments. This same device can provide information during a meeting for group discussion and analysis of the findings. Apart from their feedback and other values, questionnaires, inventories, and checklists can be devised to improve the performance of the manager or trainer. Our last two examples, the Meetings Management Planning Inventory (Exhibit 8.5) and the Managing People Skills Inventory (Exhibit 8.6), will help leaders to assure that meetings are planned and conducted effectively, as well as to provide a means for further evaluating how people are managed in the workplace.*

Exhibit 8.5 Meeting Management Planning Inventory.

Meeting Management Planning Inventory (MMPI)

To assure an effective meeting, conference or seminar, this instrument provides thirty critical check-points for planners. Included are intercultural factors in case the meeting is cross-cultural or international in scope. Developed in the form of a rating scale, the meeting planner, or his/her supervisor, may evaluate the individual from 1 (lowest) to 10 (excellence). A wide range of planning activities are covered from meeting content input, objectives, site, and budget to site visitation, international protocol, detail preparations and arrangements. The scoring allows for skipping of some items which may not be appropriate in specific circumstances. The author, Dr. Philip R. Harris, has supplied a useful tool to accompany this inventory in his text, *Managing Cultural Differences* (Houston, TX: Gulf Publishing, 1987.)

---

* © 1988, Harris International—Dr. P. R. Harris. These two instruments may not be reproduced and are available in quantity from Management Research Systems/Talico Inc., 2320 S. Third St. #5, Jacksonville Beach, FL 32250 (904/241-1721).

Exhibit 8.5   Meeting Management Planning Inventory, *cont'd.*

Directions: Please supply the following information:

Name of the organizational sponsor: _____

Date of the Meeting: _____

Site of the Meeting: _____

Purposes of the Meeting: _____

_____

Number and function of attendees expected for the Meeting:

_____

Type of Meeting being planned: Conference (   ); Seminar (   );
Operational Review (   ); Regular Staff Meeting (   );
One-on-one Encounter(   ); Other: _____
In planning this meeting, please rate yourself on a scale of 10 as to how you have
carried the following functions. Use the box on the right column to place your
score: 1 would be lowest, 5 would be average, and 10 would be the highest
rating for excellence. If the item is not applicable, just skip it and move on to
the next number.

_____

	Rating
1. Input was sought from both management and potential partici-pants on this meeting's purposes and agenda.	[ ]
2. Objectives were clearly stated and circulated with schedule to the intended audience or attendees.	[ ]
3. Adequate and comfortable site/facilities selected, and successful negotiations concluded with operators.	[ ]
4. Proper budgeting or provisions were made for the meeting expenses (and income if any).	[ ]
5. Adequate arrangements were made for the selection and/or pre-registration of attendees, as well as on-site registration and/or welcome of meeting participants.	[ ]
6. Adequate negotiations and arrangements were completed for all guests, presenters, exhibiters, and other human resources required for this meeting.	[ ]
7. If meeting off site, adequate provisions were made for transportation and registrants were so informed.	[ ]
8. If residential meeting, adequate arrangements were made for housing and alternatives; registrants, guests, exhibitors and staff so informed.	[ ]

Continued

Exhibit 8.5 Meeting Management Planning Inventory, *cont'd.*

Rating

9. Adequate design planning as to program activities, variety, sequence, time, and pacing. [ ]
10. If appropriate, adequate provision included for relaxation and play. [ ]
11. Adequate arrangements ensured for ordering all program equipment, learning materials, and exhibits. [ ]
12. Adequate provisions ensured for on-site monitoring and management of external support service, meeting staff and procedures (e.g., registration and hospitality desk, refreshment and food services, exhibits, handout materials distribution, etc.) [ ]
13. Adequate pre-meeting briefing of registrants and resource staff, plus coordination with site management. [ ]
14. Arrangements made for special needs of participants (e.g., handicapped, non-smokers, session recordings, etc.) [ ]
15. If necessary, shipping or mailing arrangements completed for all material and equipment on site (or for their purchase/lease/ rental on-site.) [ ]
16. Final checking executed satisfactorily on functional logistics (e.g., the details and set-up of meeting rooms, media equipment, exhibits, food and beverage services, etc.) [ ]
17. Final confirmation of arrangements and site opportunities to all concerned (e.g., mailing of schedule or agenda with travel directions to participants, staff, presenters, and possibly entertainers, exhibitors, suppliers, and site managers.) [ ]
18. Provisions made for staff person or contractor to select, communicate and coordinate with resource persons (e.g., speakers, facilitators, panelists, entertainers, exhibitors, travel guides.) [ ]
19. Provisions completed for entertainment and informative program alternatives if spouse or family accompany attendee. [ ]
20. If appropriate, arrangement completed for public relations program in conjunction with meeting (e.g., press release, media coverage, follow-up stories). [ ]
21. Arrangement completed for recording the meeting or conference (in writing, stenotype, or audio/video); if appropriate, for editing and publishing the proceedings, and distribution and/or sale of recordings/proceedings. [ ]
22. Arrangements completed for evaluating the meeting as to its effectiveness and implementation of action plans set at the meeting. [ ]
23. Provision for payment of all gratuities and invoices for services contracted, including any reimbursements due the participants. [ ]

Exhibit 8.5 Meeting Management Planning Inventory, *cont'd.*

Rating

24. Provision for letters of appreciation or commendation to be sent
to appropriate persons connected with meeting's success (e.g.,
participants, presenters, suppliers, etc.)   [ ]

(NOTE: If this is an international meeting, then continue with the inventory.)

25. Prior to the meeting, personal visitation ensured that:
    —The overseas' facility and services were adequate;
    —Equipment and power incompatibilities were resolved;
    —Negotiations with contractors had achieved mutual cultural
    understanding and agreement as to what is being provided;
    —Problems of overseas' shipping and entry of materials/
    equipment had been resolved with customs in home/host
    countries (whenever possible, equipment leased or rented
    abroad, while contracting for local supplies).   [ ]
26. Observance of all the foreign formalities regarding international
    meeting amenities, such as:
    —Invitations and confirmations to government or corporate
    officials invited to receptions, luncheons, and banquets;
    —Selection of local representatives to welcome participants, give
    addresses or lectures, and bestow honors/rewards.   [ ]
27. Preparations made to facilitate intercultural communication with
    the locals or among participants from other countries (e.g.,
    business cards in both languages, proper use of titles and
    seating arrangements, multilingual presentation of learning
    materials and slides, interpreters and simultaneous translation
    equipment, etc.)   [ ]
28. Arrangement made for participants to enjoy the international
    resources, such as:
    —Extra group services and discounts of airlines and travel
    agencies;
    —Use of local stately mansions, grand estates or convention
    centers;
    —Optional offerings for local or supplemental sightseeing tours
    and appropriate field trips;
    —Incorporation into schedule of host culture's food/dress, as
    well as music/festivals;
    —Cultural briefings on the foreign customs, protocal,
    opportunities and dangers.   [ ]

Continued

315

Exhibit 8.5 Meeting Management Planning Inventory, *cont'd.*

Rating

29. Pre-departure briefings provided all participants by mail or in person on customs regulations, currency issues, tipping, security issues, and other relevant matters (e.g., host country cuisine "pros & cons," public safety and terrorism, cultural differences regarding meeting activities and participation, role of women in country.) [ ]

30. Arrangements made for translations of meeting/conference proceedings in the major participant languages, as well as editing, printing or recordings' reproduction, and distribution of volumes or cassettes. [ ]

(NOTE: to obtain a total score, among the 30 possible selections add up the number of items to which it was appropriate for you to respond; then tally up the number of rating scores. To attain an evaluation average, divide the total number of items into the total of ratings.)

Exhibit 8.6 Managing People Skills Inventory

Managing People Skills Inventory (MPSI)

For those concerned about the human side of enterprise and its impact on productivity, this rating instrument can be quickly used on one's self or by another colleague or subordinate. Twenty-four key questions are raised concerning people skills—the behavioral science management concerns which compliment technical proficiency of managers. A five-point rating scale is utilized for assessment ratings which range from poor to excellent. The content covers behavior and innovative management practices to human relations and communication. The totaling of ratings permits assessment in three categories—need for improvement, average, and high performance. The inventory is supplementary to the High Performance Management Inventory on page 18 (Exhibit 1.5), and its inquiries applied to meeting performance.

Instructions—For yourself or a colleague, use a five-point scale to evaluate one's effectiveness as a leader in the human relations competencies at work. In the column at the right, rate the manager by inserting the number which best describes his or her present performance or behavior at work:

5 = Excellent; 4 = Good; 3 = Average; 2 = Inadequate; 1 = Poor

The manager being assessed is (check one):

( ) Myself

Exhibit 8.6 Managing People Skills Inventory, *cont'd.*

( ) My subordinate named _____

( ) My colleague named _____

Since we are to be learning managers concerned about high performance on the job, I rate this person as follows:

Rating

1. Possesses and practices a positive management philosophy regarding people. [ ]
2. Is a behavior model to workers of the desired attitudes and performance on the job. [ ]
3. Is innovative in dealing with people, being quite open-minded and flexible. [ ]
4. Is sensitive to people and opportunities around him/her. [ ]
5. Is positive and encouraging with personnel, not given to falling back on negative statements. (e.g., "It can't be done;" "it's never been done before;" "it's not the way we do things around here"). [ ]
6. Is aware of the differences in people, capitalizing upon their uniqueness. [ ]
7. Understands the influence of culture upon individuals and institutions, but is able to change it or move beyond. [ ]
8. Is results, not task, oriented-places emphasis on accomplishments and rewarding performance. [ ]
9. Is goal oriented with self and subordinates—sets realistic objectives, targets, and deadlines. [ ]
10. Maintains high performance standards—values competence, professionalism, and measurable growth. [ ]
11. Operates on the principle of expect/inspect—each employee reporting to him/her comprehends the job expectations, is encouraged to ask questions, but is held accountable to achieve measureable standards. [ ]
12. Provides performance leadership by dynamic achievements, inspiring personnel to stretch and achieve their potential. [ ]
13. Trusts people by delegating, giving them freedom to perform in their own unique way, thus building self-reliance. [ ]
14. Fosters reasonable risk-taking and creativity in others. [ ]
15. Re-inforces cooperation and collaboration, rather than interpersonal or intergroup competition. [ ]
16. Seeks continually to learn, even from failure—promotes personal and career development for self and others. [ ]
17. Endeavors to capitalize on human assets, helping people to experience success and results. [ ]
18. Searches to understand his/her own, as well as others' needs and attempts to satisfy them through work. [ ]

Continued

Exhibit 8.6 Managing People Skills Inventory, *cont'd.*

Rating

19. Believes in positive re-inforcement, so confirms people's
    self-concept when it is healthy or assists them to gain in a strong
    sense of personal identity and confidence.   [ ]
20. Enables people to gain control over their work space, thus
    sharing in the exercise of power.   [ ]
21. Communicates authentically with co-workers, customers, and
    suppliers, giving and receiving appropriate feedback.   [ ]
22. Provides recognitions and rewards customized to the individual
    worker's needs and values.   [ ]
23. Arranges for training opportunities for employees so that
    performance may be improved or new skills acquired.   [ ]
24. Manages conflict constructively and acts as a facilitator.   [ ]
                                            TOTAL RATINGS _____

(NOTE: Tally up the rating scores and insert the total in the space provided. A
high performing manager would gain a score of 100 or more; and average
manager would obtain ratings of 75+, indicating a need for gradual
improvement. Scores below that level should raise questions about this
person's suitability for management. In developing goals for performance
improvement, go back over the items in which a score of 3 or less was recorded.
If this was a self-evaluation, one might ask a supervisor or colleague to rate
you, and then compare the assessment on each of the 24 items.)

Epilogue:
The Learning
Manager

To be a leader in this Information Society dominated by knowledge and service workers, a manager promotes a learning environment within the organization. As a thinking manager, he or she facilitates continuous self-development, both personal and professional. Beginning with oneself as the model, this responsibility is extended outward to all who report to the manager, as well as to one's own family members.

The rationale for this has been laid throughout this volume, particularly in Chapters 1 and 8. Selwyn Enzer, a research professor at the University of Southern California, offers further confirmation. In a report "Working Our Way to the Twenty-first Century," he notes that both students and workers have to prepare themselves for a radically different job market by the year 2000. (Report F60 is available without charge from Graduate School of Business Administration, USC, Los Angeles, CA 90089). Jobs in the future will be more demanding and tomorrow's workers will have to learn new techniques to maintain their marketability. Since *lifelong learning* is becoming a necessity, Enzer offers these guidelines for those who wish to prepare for the changing work environment:

- Master the basic principles underlying your discipline so as to be able to innovate, or face machine replacement.
- Cultivate creativity, learning how to analyze alternatives and open-ended problems.
- Recognize the limitations of current methods and products, being open to improved approaches.

- Keep abreast of changes in your field, and be ready to make career changes.

As a futurist, I naturally agree with these observations, but it may help to explain why our emphasis here in this text on learnings is related to these topics.

What organization development (OD) as a strategy does for the renewal of institutions, professional or human resource development (HRD) does for renewal of individuals. Because a learning manager exercises leadership in both processes, in this book we have highlighted some of the enabling skills required. Although there are also many technical competencies to be acquired by contemporary managers and their colleagues, we have focused here on human skills that can be learned in order to

- Increase performance through motivated personnel
- Use communication and culture for systems development
- Collect, analyze, and apply human data for the improvement of organizational relations and effectiveness
- Foster productivity through team building, monitoring, and management
- Plan for organizational changes that re-design and enrich the work environment, especially by employee participation
- Channel human energy in the organization toward more work accomplishment and goal achievement

In *Human Resource Management Trends and Challenges,* Walton and Lawrence (1985) maintain that the pressures of changing social expectations and foreign competition are forcing American corporations to reexamine the way in which they deal with employees. These editors report on the movement toward a system of mutuality in the workplace, the emphasis on learning and collaboration among workers, the trend to giving personnel more voice in job performance and goal setting. This results in a new commitment along with change in managerial control. These Harvard business professors sense a shift from a work model based on traditional American individualism to a paradigm that stresses more communitarian elements. Macromanagement challenges, such as renewing the Earth's infrastructure or building a space infrastructure in the high frontier, are but two dramatic cases that point to this need for cooperation instead of wasteful competition or conflict. The case has been well made for participative work systems that ensure employment quality and security (Rubinstein, 1987).

In a study and report on *The Learning Enterprise,* Carnevale (1986) underscores the scope of educational efforts by U.S. business and industry. This economist points out that financial investment in workplace training and development is equivalent approximately in size to that of the entire elementary, secondary, and higher education systems (employee training, informal, $180 billion; formal, $30 billion; plus government training, $5 billion). Corporate learning has itself become a $30-billion industry, and the training so provided, not prior education, more often determines what a person earns throughout a lifetime. Exhibit E.1, prepared for the American Society of Training and Development, illustrates who benefits and in what numbers. Carnevale discovered that about 62 percent of workplace trainees receive their learning in-house, with 38 percent going outside for training. The correlation between learning and performance was somewhat established

Exhibit E.1 Sources of Training by Occupational Group. Source: Anthony P. Carnevale, American Society for Training and Development, 1985. Based on data prepared by the Bureau of Labor Statistics, 1985.

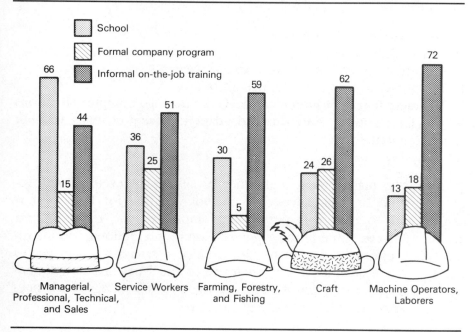

321

in Carnevale's analysis of census data—those who benefited from informal training improved their earning by 13 percent over their peers, while the productivity return for on-the-job training was 12.6 percent for those who were college-educated and 19 percent for those without college. Other studies also confirm the conclusion that learning on the job contributes significantly to work productivity.

PEAK PERFORMANCE

Such findings buffer our arguments in this book for high performance leadership. The landmark research of clinical psychologist and mathematician Charles Garfield (1986) of the University of California's Medical School in San Francisco provides further insight. In a recent work, *Peak Performers: The New Heroes of American Business,* he shares the results of his studies with 1500 prominent top performers. Garfield concludes that these high performers, whether in management, marketing, or the professions, excel because they *learned* a basic set of skills and thus leveraged their potential. The peak performers profile that emerged in his investigations indicated the presence of these six attributes:

1. A strong sense of mission
2. Well-defined goals
3. A capacity for self-observation and self-analysis
4. The ability to bring out the best in others
5. The mental agility to steer a critical path through complex situations
6. The foresight to anticipate and adapt to major changes without losing momentum

Obviously, management and other professional development programs would be well advised to include training for high performance and to use high performing employees as "trainers" and problem-solvers. Some of the suggested input, interactions, and instrumentation offered in our own volume helps the learning manager to cultivate these qualities in one's self and others. They are complimentary to a range of strategies that Wlodkowski (1985) suggests are necessary to enhance adult motivation to learn.

HR RELATED ISSUES

Among the driving forces changing the manager's role in human resource management and development, two are of significance to those aspiring to high performance leadership:

1. The alteration in our perception of the corporate human resources' function.

For the past several years, The Conference Board has conducted an annual meeting on this topic. In reporting on this event, *Business Week* (December 2, 1985, pp. 58-59) observed that managers who deal with the people issues (hiring, firing, promotion, pay, benefits, discipline, training, and union relations) are rising in power and influence. Human resources (HR), whether considered a staff or line function, is taking on the business-driven attributes of sales, marketing, and finance. The change in corporate philosophy is another reflection of the competitive business environment—acquisitions, mergers, spin-offs of divisions, entering new businesses or getting out of old ones. Strategic decisions are involved in these continuous organizational changes, and HR considerations are primary (e.g., matching skills with jobs, retaining key personnel and retraining them, coping with the human and cultural problems associated with introduction of a new technology or the closing of a plant). Those in management with HR insights and competencies are increasingly used by enlightened CEOs as advisers to keep the corporation on the competitive edge, especially in terms of productivity. As unions decline in power, those with personnel and training skills are valued to deal with broad labor and social issues involved in redeployment, offshore activities, intrapreneurialism, and many other organization innovations.

2. The involvement of line managers in HR issues, whether of personnel or training matters.

In the microcomputer, line managers have a new tool for taking on human resource management activities. Miner (1985) believes that practicing managers can be enabled to understand and take action on employee difficulties on the job, so as to turn around the performance situation. Furthermore, a decentralization is occurring relative to the HRD responsibilities.

The *Training & Development Journal* (January 1986, pp. 47-48) interviewed Paul Chaddock, vice president for Leehmere, Inc., on the trend to putting training into line management hands. This Dayton-Hudson subsidiary, like its parent company, is strongly committed to the customer and the merchandising function. Furthermore, their HR corporate philosophy is client-centered—the line manager has the charter to improve subordinate's competencies; training is to solve performance deficiencies, to help people acquire the skill necessary to perform their jobs optimally. If a training or HRD department exists, then its function is to provide managers with the tools and resources for adult learning. For example, at Lechmere, they demonstrate to managers the link between competence and results, the connection between lack of knowledge and lack of productivity. HR professional provide managers with counsel, feedback systems, and training program aid. HR expert power is diversified, managers learn to become trainers and call upon an HR support function or skill bank. When a new store is opened, a training team is composed with the store manager as team leader, and the HR specialist is only a consultant; the team assesses the learning needs of personnel and then deliver the training.

It is with such major HR developments in mind that this text has been revised and directed. In conclusion, I would like to direct reader attention to ten more HR issues worthy of their further study and consideration; the references and resource sections to follow may provide information on these trends.

3. The whole culture is in transition toward information processing, technology, and computers (Pagels, 1985).

Therefore, learning, whether in formal institutions of education or within organizational training settings, must focus on these subjects. Anthropologist Edward Hall (1987) reminds us that any culture is primarily a *system* for creating, sending, and storing information. Communication underlies everything, he notes, and I might add that the new communication technology is the means for learning advancement.

4. Information technology, wisely employed, provides leverage to greater productivity and performance pay-off (Strassman, 1985).

Corporate strategies should give priority to learning its mastery for valued-added results. Since this technology is constantly advancing, continuing education is a necessity.

5. The impact of automation and robotics on work is profound, causing a transformation in relationships and the operations of offices and plants (Harris, 1985).

In this changed work environment, the vital role of information resource manager is emerging (Ferreira and Harris, 1986), which again requires new learnings on the part of today's management. The spread of office automation, telecommunications, and work-at-home capabilities not only causes a reduction in office personnel, but changes the design and purpose of the office, as well as the role office managers.

6. Learning strategy may have to include pretraining for those workers who never learned how to read and study properly, or have forgotten such skills.

To benefit more fully from technical and other training, effective presentations may be insufficient; some personnel have to be prepared to learn how to acquire and apply the information being presented more efficiently. This may be especially important for managers whose backgrounds in science and technology are deficient.

7. To convince top management that proposed learning programs can bring a return on such investments, the cost of learning will have to be quantified and perceived as a capitalization of human assets, not merely as expenses to be written off.

Training programs can be so evaluated, productivity improvement is measurable, employee turn-over and lay-off losses can be reduced by employing human resource accounting methods (Flamholtz, 1985).

8. How an organization uses leadership development programs, whether internal or external, can affect the outcome of the learning (Van Velsor, 1984).

If there is to be a transfer from these programs to on-the-job per-formance, pre-program assessment and planning contribute to content relevancy. But learning applications in the work environment are en-hanced when:

- There are overall organizational and strategic goals for the learn-ing

- Key management attends and models behavioral change as a result of the learning experience
- Such programs are linked to promotions and new assignments
- Assessment results obtained in the learning process are fed back to participants in a confidential, supervised setting
- Discussions involve peer interaction on real-work issues
- Post-program support is evident through management debriefings, establishing of informal "alumni" groups, further career development is rewarded, and follow-up training is periodically made available

9. Managers and trainers are well advised to exercise HRD leadership in the creation of high performance teams (Harris, 1986b).

Promoting competent team management is in harmony with the new work culture, and is another means for effectively capitalizing on organizational human assets. The winning companies are even convincing unions that the team concept contributes to worker satisifaction, participation, and productivity. But such teams require planned development and new learnings.

10. The metaindustrial environment emphasizes work for enjoyment and satisfaction, rather than for punishment or fear.

Building upon the research of psychologist, B. F. Skinner (1986), behavior management provides on-the-job positive reinforcement of desirable behavior such as high performance. Management can do this in a systematic fashion, such as by the redesign of assembly-line jobs so the worker is more involved in the finished product, or offering sustained psychological or other rewards for productive behavior. Again new learnings are implied in this applied behavior methodology or modification.

11. Giving employees "ownership" in learning or an organization tends to improve their performance.

This can be accomplished figuratively or literally (Rubenstein, 1987). For example, some companies use top performing workers as instructors, tutors, or mentors with new trainees, while other corporations offer stock options to their personnel (95 percent of the 1500 plus firms listed on the New York Stock Exchange have such schemes). However, the latter is often supplemented by performance-related rewards.

12. HRD increasingly directs its attention to developing global managers for global business (Murray and Murray, 1986; Harris and Moran, 1987).

The globalization of business and markets requires managers and technical representatives who are cross-culturally skilled. Going international means training not only in foreign area studies and economics, but how to cope with cultural differences to produce synergy.

High performance leadership is also manifest in the promotion of synergy between and among various disciplines, industries, systems and nations (Moran and Harris, 1982). It is what Landau and Rosenberg (1986) have dubbed *The Positive Sum Strategy* in their volume on harnessing technology for economic growth. This strategy needs wider applications through learning managers who foster synergy in their organizations and communities.

In contrast to the above twelve human resource trends, consider two recent reports that confirm the validity of the author's insights in a perverse way. Massachusetts Institute of Technology inaugurated a faculty commission on Industrial Productivity. Their findings were that United States businesses are losing their competitive edge because of preoccupation with the bottom line at the expense of research and development, poor management, and a lack of foreign market development (*Insight,* March 14, 1988, p. 46). Topping the list for declining productivity was inadequate capital investment for maintaining technological leadership (witness the struggles of NASA to get sufficient funding for a space station).

In another, European study, Professor Peter Doyle of Warwick University discovered that few companies abroad give their personnel departments the same status as their finance departments. The survey of 356 big British companies found that 89 percent of them had a finance director on their board of directors, but only 32 percent had a personnel director there (*The Economist,* February 13, 1988, p. 61). A comparable investigation of American firms would likely reveal even less representation of human resource experts on such boards, despite the importance of human assets to organizational success. *The Economist* article entitled "The Power of People" described myriad ways compa-

327

nies are now trying to motivate employees' productivity. Among the strategies being utilized:

- Paying more attention to workers, such as by including them in media shows of new products and services and appealing to their needs for power, achievement, and affiliation
- Devising schemes for financial reward that link rewards to performance, such as by "gainsharing," in which operating units share in company savings for which they are responsible, or flexible compensation plans that allow employees so many dollars worth of benefits, which they can then spend on a menu of options from health to child care
- Training managers of nonprofit agencies and associations to operate their activities as if they were businesses.

Readers who act upon the messages in this book will discover for themselves the "pay-off" in higher performing personnel.

Appendix A

Directory of Human Resource Organizations and Publications

INTRODUCTION

Information and knowledge are the new currencies of the metaindustrial work culture. For executives and managers who wish to stay on the cutting edge of their fields, the following listings have been provided. For *High-Performance Leadership* readers who seek to capitalize more effectively on human assets, write or call these sources and request to be placed on their mailing lists, especially for catalogs and announcements. One inquiry form letter can be sent to all the resources of interest. Since it is impossible to record all the organizations and publishers related to executive and management development, this is a select and representative sampling of resources which the author found helpful in his consulting practice and which he hopes will prove useful to learning managers. We welcome reader feedback on recommended additions for the next edition. . . . Philip R. Harris, Author.

ASSOCIATIONS, CENTERS, AND PROFESSIONAL SOCIETIES

ACADEMY OF MANAGEMENT, Drawer KZ, Mississippi State, MS 39762. A professional society for professors of business with special divisions in organizational behavior, managerial consultation, international management, etc. In addition to a placement service and student division, the Academy publishes a newsletter and annual proceedings. Managers may wish to subscribe to the Academy's publications: *Executive, The Journal* and *The Review.*

ADULT EDUCATION ASSOCIATION, 810 18th St., Washington, DC 20006. Clearinghouse for information on all types of adult education. Conduct conferences and workshops, as well as issue publications.

AMERICAN ACADEMY OF POLITICAL AND SOCIAL SCIENCE, 3937 Chestnut Street, Philadelphia, PA 19104. Publishes *The Annals* for interdisciplinary discussions of today's vital issues, such as in the areas of politics, economics, international and urban affairs, public policy and social issues. Back issues are available on such themes as robotics, unionism, technology transfer, environment and quality of life.

AMERICAN ASSOCIATION FOR COUNSELING AND DEVELOPMENT, 5999 Stevenson Ave., Alexandria, VA 22304 (703-823-9800). A professional association for counselors with 13 divisions, such as employment and rehabilitation counseling. In addition to conferences, publish books (such as, on women issues, work/life counseling for older people, or assertiveness training, or directory of counseling services) and audio-visual aids (such as, videotapes on impacts of technology on future workplace, or films on career development).

AMERICAN COUNCIL ON EDUCATION PUBLICATIONS, c/o Macmillan, 866 Third Avenue, New York, NY 10022. Membership in ACE is for institutions of higher education and educational associations. However, some of its published research studies are useful in HRD, such as: *Accredited Institutions of Postsecondary Education; Guide to the Evaluation of Educational Experience in the Armed Services; The National Guide to Educational Credit for Training Programs.*

AMERICAN INSTITUTE OF ECONOMICS AND TECHNOLOGY, P.O. Box 396, Old Greenwich, CT 06870. Distribute unique audiocassette series on management development topics with outstanding leaders (e.g., authors Blanchard and Johnson "One Minute Manager," Tom Peters' "In Search of Excellence," Alec MacKenzie's "How to Delegate," and Robert Townsend's "Leadership in Business").

AMERICAN MANAGEMENT ASSOCIATIONS, 135 West 50th St., New York, NY 10020 (212/586-8100). Leading supplier of live and packaged management courses. Have Extension Institute with self-study programs—audio, video and computer disc. AMACOM, the publishing division of management books like the *Human Resource and Development Handbook* and periodicals, such as *Management Review* and *Intrapreneurial Excellence;* its Management Book Club which offers both their own AMA books and those of other publishers. Operates Management Centers around the world, and subsidiaries like The Presidents Association for CEOs and the International Management Association, etc. Conducts an annual HR Conference for managers and trainers.

AMERICAN PRODUCTIVITY CENTER, 123 North Post Oak Lane, Houston, TX 77024 (713/681-4020). Engages in research, training, reports and visual aids to improve productivity and the quality of work life. Services include employee involvement, productivity measurement, labor/management cooperation, as well as video/film series on such issues.

AMERICAN SOCIETY FOR ASSOCIATION EXECUTIVES, 1575 I St., N.W., Washington, DC (202/626-2723). Although a professional organization for directors of trade and professional associations, it offers HR aids for meeting planners like a directory, *Finding the Right Speaker,* as well as helpful audio/videocassettes.

AMERICAN SOCIETY FOR HEALTHCARE EDUCATION AND TRAINING, 840 N. Lake Shore Drive, Chicago, IL 50511 (312/260-6111). Conferences and publications in HRD for hospitals and health service institutions.

AMERICAN SOCIETY FOR PERSONNEL ADMINISTRATORS, 606 North Washington St., Alexandria, VA 22314. A professional organization for personnel specialists which conducts HR conferences and workshops, as well as publish a journal and reports.

AMERICAN SOCIETY FOR MACRO-ENGINEERING, c/o Polytechnic Institute, 333 Jay St., Brooklyn, NY 11201 (212/643-8755). For management of large scale projects, conducts conferences, publishes proceedings and international journal, *Technology in Society.*

AMERICAN SOCIETY FOR TRAINING AND DEVELOPMENT, 630 Duke St., Box 1443, Alexandria, VA 22313 (703/683-8100). Professional society for human resource specialists with numerous divisions (such as, organization development, sales, media, international), as well as local chapters. ASTD Press not only publishes ASTD reports (such as on trainer competencies or human capital, or volumes like *The Training and Development Handbook*), but through its Book Service makes available texts of other publishers on management and HRD subjects. Audio cassettes are available of prominent national conference speakers, as well as a periodical, *Training & Development Journal*. Distributes directories of members and HRD suppliers. Affiliated with the INTERNATIONAL FEDERATION OF TRAINING & DEVELOPMENT ORGANIZATIONS.

ASSOCIATION FOR EDUCATIONAL COMMUNICATION AND TECHNOLOGY, 1126 Sixteenth St., N.W., Washington, DC 20036 (202/833-4180). Instructional technology society that provides a magazine, *Instructional Innovator*; an annual *Human Resource Directory* of members; two quarterlies, *Educational Communication & Technology Journal* and *Journal of Instructional Development*, as well as special divisions for members, and an annual convention/exhibition.

ASSOCIATION OF HUMAN RESOURCES MANAGEMENT AND ORGANIZATIONAL BEHAVIOR, PO Box 64841, Virginia Beach, VA 23464. Professional group of university professors and practitioners who meet annually to present and discuss papers on HRM/OB themes. Proceedings are available for purchase.

ASSOCIATION FOR MEDIA-BASED CONTINUING EDUCATION OF ENGINEERS, 225 North Ave. N.W., Atlanta, GA 30313-9990 (404/894-3362). Concerned about production and distribution of audio-video learning programs for the professional development of engineering. Their color video-cassette packages include lecture notes and textbooks on such subjects as, *New Product Development*.

ASSOCIATION OF RESEARCH LIBRARIES/Office of Management Studies, 1527 New Hampshire Ave., N.W., Washington, DC 20036 (202/232-8656). Assists librarians on managerial and human resource dimensions of libraries. Provides consultation, self-studies, training, and research publications. Focus is upon improving management skills in academic libraries.

ASSOCIATION FOR SYSTEMS MANAGEMENT, 24587 Bagley Road, Cleveland, OH 44138 (216/243-6900). Professional society to improve business systems education. Conduct annual conference and sell cassettes of presentations, published proceedings. Also publish *Journal of Systems Management* and valuable HR books, like *Peopleware in Systems* and *Systems Film Catalog*. For those interested in living systems theory, SOCIETY FOR GENERAL SYSTEMS RESEARCH (P.O. Box 64025, Baltimore, MD 21264) publishes a journal, *Behavioral Science*.

BUREAU OF NATIONAL AFFAIRS, 1231 25th Street, N.W., Washington, DC 20037 (202/452-4200) [also an international office in London, telephone:

01-222-8831]. Conducts research, publishes reports and books, and produces films/videocassettes on subjects related to employee relations, human resource development, and issues of concern to management (e.g., new "Environment Reporter," information resource service on environmental protection and pollution control. Recommend free newsletter, *Bulletin on Training.*

CENTER FOR APPLIED HEALTH CARE MANAGEMENT, 27299 W. Grand Blvd., Detroit, MI 48202. Coordinates and distributes information about organizational member activity in health care services. For example, the Fairlane Health Services (313/271-6550) has an Organization Development Group that offers team management and consulting to health care institutions, including multimedia programs on OD, future studies, patient relations, performance.

CENTER FOR CREATIVE LEADERSHIP, 5000 Laurinda Drive, Greensboro, NC 27402-1660 (919/288-7210). (San Diego Branch—Suite 620, 4275 Executive Square, LaJolla, CA 92037 619/453-4474). Established by the Smith Richardson Foundation to improve the practice of management and develop leadership potential. Engages in research, training, and contract programs; publishes useful reports (such as, *The CEO: An Annotated Bibliography*) and a free newsletter, *Issues & Observations;* library and information search service on leadership.

CENTER FOR INTERACTIVE PROGRAMS, University of Wisconsin—Extension, 610 Langdon St., Madison, WI 53703. Resource on teleconferencing and electronic communications. CIP produces books, newsletter, software, and learning materials on the teleconferencing industry.

CENTER FOR INTERNATIONAL STUDIES, Brigham Young University, Box 61 FOB, Provo, UT 84602 (801/378-6528). Provides publications on international areas and cultures, including briefings on major countries of the world and special bulletins.

CENTER FOR MANAGEMENT RESEARCH, Opinion Research Corporation, 850 Boylston St., Chestnut Hill, MA 02167 (671-738-5020). An Arthur D. Little Company, this professional research firm conducts employee surveys and publishes reports of interest to executives and managers. For example, *Managing Human Resources, 1983 and Beyond* examined attitudes and trends among personnel in American industry.

CENTER FOR RESEARCH IN CAREER DEVELOPMENT, Columbia University, 815 Uris Hall, New York, NY 10027. University research that results in conferences and publications on career development. For example, these recent publications are available—*Human Resources Management: Issues for the 1980s; Career Unrest: A Source of Creativity.*

CONFERENCE BOARD, THE 845 Third Avenue, New York, NY 10022. Research and reports on topics of interest to management subscribers (e.g., economics, labor relations, and HRD). Conduct special seminars, including annually the Human Resource Outlook series.

COUNCIL ON THE CONTINUING EDUCATION UNIT, 13000 Old Columbia Pike, Columbia, MD 20904. Promotes research and certification of CEU credits for corporate or extension courses and training. Publishes reports, such as *Principles of Good Practice in Continuing Education.*

HUMAN RESOURCE PLANNING SOCIETY, P.O. Box 2553, New York, NY 10163 (617-837-0630). Professional HR planning group which conducts regional meetings.

INSTITUTE OF CONSTRUCTIVE CAPITALISM, University of Texas, 2815 San Gabriel, Austin, TX 78705-3594 (512-474-9298). Sponsored by the RGK Foundation, this is an innovative center for the study of democratic capitalism and free enterprise system, especially entrepreneurialism and technology venturing. Conducts invitational seminars and publishes proceedings (such as in 1985, on *Frontiers in Creative and Innovative Management*). Promotes two new publications *Journal of High Technology Marketing* and *Leading-edge Technologies.* IC2, also an affiliate, INSTITUTE FOR LARGE SCALE PROGRAMS engaged in research on macroengineering projects and macromanagement.

INTERNATIONAL SOCIETY FOR GENERAL SEMANTICS, P.O. BOX 2469, San Francisco, CA 94126 (415/543-1747). Professional society that explores how language shapes human society and behavior. Publishes a quarterly journal, ETC., research studies, and special monographs, such as the excellent *Communications: The Transfer of Meaning* by Don Fabun. Provides book and media services on language, words, and their meaning, such as audio cassettes on general semantics by Sanford Berman.

INSTRUCTIONAL SYSTEMS ASSOCIATION, 84 State St., Boston, MA 02109. For those in field of education in business and industry, provide annual meetings, reports on education industry data, and networking among professional training organizations.

INTERNATIONAL ASSOCIATION OF QUALITY CIRCLES, 801-B West Eighth St., Suite 301, Cincinnati, OH 45203 (513/381-1959). Professional society for those interested in quality circles, employee motivation, and participative management. Services include conferences and workshops, as well as training materials and audio-visual aids.

INTERNATIONAL CONSULTANTS FOUNDATION, 11612 Georgetowne Ct., Potomac, MD 20654 (301/983-2709). Worldwide network of consultants and training specialists who publish a directory of member qualifications, a newsletter, and proceedings of annual conferences (e.g., *Helping Across Cultures* and *Innovations in Global Consultation*). Request catalog, *The Source.*

INTERNATIONAL LABOUR OFFICE, Management Development Programme, 1211 Geneva 22, Switzerland (99 68 55) [ILO, Suite 330MA, 1750 New York Ave., N.W., Washington, DC 20006 (202/376-2315)]. Worldwide membership of states offering both labor and management services. Inquire about publications list which include such titles as, *Management Consulting, Practice of Entrepreneurship, Case Method in Management Development.*

NATIONAL AUDIO-VISUAL ASSOCIATION, 3150 Spring St., Fairfax, VA 22031 (703/869-7200). Provides special services for those using A-V media in training and communicating. These include annual convention, special institutes, equipment and membership directory, publications.

NATIONAL AUDIO VISUAL CENTER, Washington, DC 20409 (1-800/638-1300). As part of the National Archives Trust Board, offer film and videocassette sale and rentals on diverse business subjects (such as, market development, personnel management, communications, employee enrichment, women and retirement), as well as distributor of Foreign Language Institute's Language Instruction Series (language kits in variety of foreign languages produced by the U. S. State Department).

NATIONAL FOREMAN'S INSTITUTE, 24 Rope Ferry Road, Waterford, CT 06386 (1-800-243-0876). Publish *The Productivity Improvement Bulletin,* and monographs, such as *Quality Circles* and *The Executive Standard Desk Manual.*

NATIONAL INFORMATION CENTER FOR EDUCATIONAL MEDIA, University of Southern California, University Park, Los Angeles, CA 90007. Publish various indexes for slides, film, video and other A-V media, as well as for the special education of the handicapped.

NATIONAL SAFETY COUNCIL, PO Box 11933, Chicago, IL 60611 (1-800/621-7619). Offers training programs, courses, and materials in all areas of safety, including employees to managers. Learning aids of books and films or cassettes on industrial hygiene, occupational health, fire and job safety, including home courses.

NATIONAL SOCIETY FOR PERFORMANCE INSTRUCTION, 1126 16th St., N.W., Suite 315, Washington, DC 20036. For those interested in instructional technology and computer assisted learning, this professional group conducts an annual conference, as well as publishes a journal and member directory. Local chapters.

OD NETWORK, 1011 Park Ave., Plainfield, NJ 07060 (201/561-8677). Society for professionals in field of organization development. Conduct conferences, such as on wellness and ecology of work, and publish a newsletter, *OD Practitioner.*

SOCIETY FOR INTERCULTURAL EDUCATION, TRAINING, AND RESEARCH INTERNATIONAL, 1414 Twenty-second St., N.W., Washington, DC 20037 (202/862-1990). Global network of practitioners in the field of cross-cultural training who conduct annual conference and special workshops on intercultural interaction. Publish newsletter, journal, and special publications for trainers and consultants.

TECHNOLOGY TRANSFER SOCIETY, 611 North Capitol Ave., Indianapolis, IN 46204 (Regional office: 9841 Airport Blvd., Suite 800 AIAA, Los Angeles, CA 90045.) Professional association concerned about all forms of transfer of technology (e.g., defense to commercial), but especially overseas application, assessment, and forecasting of technology. Conducts annual international conference and special seminars on advanced technology; publishes a newsletter and journal; contracts for activities, such as establishment of The Productivity Improvement Council.

WORLD FUTURE SOCIETY, 4916 St. Elmo Ave., Bethesda, MD 20814-5089 (301/656-8274). Interdisciplinary organization of futurists with chapters throughout the world. Conduct convocations and workshops, publish proceedings and special reports, plus journal, *The Futurist* and *Futures Research Quarterly.* Have a book service of discounted volumes on future studies, such as *Work Now and in the Future.*

MANAGEMENT AIDS—DIRECTORIES, REPORTS, SERVICES

A1 MENTOR, Inc., 1000 Elwell Court, Suite 205, Palo Alto, CA 94303. Produce *Performance Mentor,* a computer-based expert system for goal setting and performance appraisal of personnel. Software disk with user's guide and reference manual.

ABBOTT, LANGER & ASSOCIATES, P.O. Box 275, Park Forest, IL 60466. Publish quarterly *Personnel News and Products.*

ABLEX PUBLISHING CORPORATION, 355 Chestnut St., Norwood, NJ 07648 (201/767-8450). International publishers of outstanding research in the field of communication and information sciences (e.g., *American Communication in a Global Society, Information Strategies: New Pathways to Management Productivity, Handbook of Organizational Communication,* and *Emerging Office Systems.*

ADYTUM, INC. P. O. Box 2629, San Francisco, CA 94126 (415/482-0325). Provides consultation and services in high technology business development and management, especially related to biotechnology, agricultural technology, and university technology transfer.

A. M. BEST COMPANY, Ambest Road, Oldwick, NJ 08858 (201/439-2200). Publish *Best's Safety Directory* on industrial safety, hygiene, and security resources.

AMERICAN COLLEGE TESTING PROGRAM, P.O. Box 168, Iowa City, IA 52243 (319/337-1053). Provides national testing program (PEP) in business and professional subjects which can be used as part of an external degree program. (In New York State, call 518/474-3703 and request brochures, *Regents External Degrees, How to Study Independently,* and *Directory of External Degree Programs.*)

BALLINGER PUBLISHING COMPANY, 54 Church St., Cambridge, MA 02138 (1-800/638-3030). Publish books on management strategy, business policy, international business, finance and economics. Titles include *Managing Corporate Culture, Frontiers of Creative and Innovative Management* and *Space Commerce.*

BEHAVIORAL SCIENCES NEWSLETTER, Whitney Road, Mahwah, NJ 07430 (201/891-5757). Bimonthly confidential report on HRD, motivation, productivity, absenteeism, retirement, safety, MBO, job enrichment and like topics regarding people at work.

BRITTANNICA TRAINING & DEVELOPMENT, 1488 South Lapeer Rd., Lake Orion, MI 48035. Educational corporation of encyclopedia fame who publish books and training aids, such as A. Richard De Luca's video on *Project Management,* and Rosabeth Kanter's video, *The Change Masters.*

BUSINESS INTERNATIONAL CORPORATION, One Dag Hammarskjold Plaza, New York, NY 10017 (212/750-6335). Publish weekly reports on doing business in various foreign countries, offer reference services and research on international business, provide political and economic forecasts, as well as special briefings.

CAHNERS EXPOSITION GROUP, 1350 East Touhy Ave., Des Plaines, IL 60018. (312/299-9311). Conduct worldwide exhibits and conferences, such as one on Office Information Systems.

CAREER DEVELOPMENT REVIEW, P.O. Box 376, New York, NY 10024. A quarterly journal for counselors and trainers in education, business, and government.

CAREERTRACK PUBLICATIONS, INC., 1800 38th St., Boulder, CO 80301. Books, audio/video cassettes, and seminars on career development.

COMMERCE CLEARING HOUSE, P.O. Box 66333, Airport Station, AMF O'Hare IL 60666. Biweekly newsletters on employment relations, EEO, personnel practices, and human resource management.

CONSULTANTS BOOKSTORE, Templeton Rd., Fitswilliam, NH 03447 (603/585-2200). Clearinghouse for current books on consulting and management, executive search and special directories. Publisher of *Consultant News.*

CONTINUING EDUCATION INTERNATIONAL, 412 S. Lyon St., Santa Ana, CA 92701 (714/667-7000). Subsidiary of Vedax Sciences Corporation, provide seminars, workshops and speakers for management development, as well as videotapes. Same address can also provide information on THE EXECUTIVE COMMITTEE, a network of small CEO groups.

DIDACTIC SYSTEMS, Inc., Box 457, Cranford, NJ 07016. Specializing in management and business games, the annual catalog also carries management books from all publishers.

THE DIEBOLD GROUP, 475 Park Avenue, New York, NY 70016 (212/684-4700). Consultants in management information systems to corporate clients. Conduct plenary conference and working sessions and publish summaries of proceedings along with specialized research reports, videotapes and books. Diebold research program also in Europe.

DOW JONES & COMPANY INC., Educational Services Bureau, 200 West Monroe St., Chicago, IL 60606 (312/648-7600). [Offices in Atlanta, GA., Princeton, NJ, and Palo Alto, CA, plus Dow-Jones—Irwin Publishers in Homewood, IL.] Corporate inservice and university programs centered around *The Wall Street Journal* and *Barron's* on American business. DJ-I has bookstore of volumes on management, finance, accounting, computers, etc., as well as business games.

EDUCATION RESEARCH, P.O. Box 4205, Warren, NJ 07060. Specializes in business and management games.

EMPLOYMENT MARKETPLACE, P.O. Box 31112, St. Louis, MO 63131. Publishes annual resource directory on personnel/human resources, recruitment, placement, search and employment, consulting aids.

ERICS/CAPS PUBLICATIONS, 2108 School of Education, University of Michigan, Ann Arbor, MI 48109. Information data base capable of Dialog computer searches from Educational Resources Information Center, plus a document reproduction service. Publications vary from *Outplacement Counseling* and *Career Development in Organizations* to *Broadening Career Options for Women* and *Counseling Women for Life Decisions.*

EXECUTIVE TELECOM SYSTEMS, INC., 6015 Guion Road, Indianapolis, IN 46254. Provide Human Resource Information Network for professionals, and quick computerized exchanges of data on HRD.

FERREIRA ASSOCIATES, 3376 Deerhaunt St., Yorktown Heights, NY 10598 (914/245-5662). Executive consultants on management information systems particularly with role transitions of EDP personnel.

FOLLETT PUBLISHING COMPANY, 1010 W. Washington Blvd., Chicago, IL 60607. Specialize in adult learning and group work books; offerings range from *Invitation to Lifelong Learning* to *Strategies for Adult Education— Practices in Western Europe.*

GALES RESEARCH COMPANY, Book Tower, Detroit, MI 48226 (1-88/521-0707). Publish variety of useful reference books and directories from multinational enterprises and consulting organizations, to encyclopedia of business information services and business organization/agencies. Have a series

339

on employee training, including *Training and Development Organizations Directory* and *Management Media Directory.*

GOODMEASURE, Inc., 330 Broadway, PO Box 3004, Cambridge, MA 02139. Provide innovative tools for enterprising managers from videotapes and books to management tool kits and talking authors.

G. P. Publishing, Inc., 10650 Hickory Ridge Road, Columbia, MD 21044 (1-800-638-3838). Request *Achieve* catalog of human resource, training, self-improvement and management books and videos. Central clearinghouse of many publishers, such as Nichols Publishing' books—*High-Risk Training* by G. Ward and *Leadership Training Through Gaming* by E. W. Christopher and L. F. Smith; or GP Courseware's *Performance Management,* a video training program.

HARRIS INTERNATIONAL, 2702 Costebelle Drive, LaJolla, CA 92037 (619/453-2271). Behavioral science management and organization development consulting. Customized programs in executive and management development on such topics as new work culture, high performance, management of change and transitions, organizational communications. Management books; seminars also by the author. Cross-cultural training and foreign deployment systems. Action learning and research, as well as training trainers, conference mangement and futures research.

HIGH-TECH MATERIALS ALERT, 158 Linwood Place, Fort Lee, NJ 07024 (201/944-6204). A monthly intelligence service from Technical Insights, Inc. on developments in advanced materials and new technologies. Also 8-10 page weekly reports relative to R&D on such subjects as *Industrial Robotics International, Biomass Digest,* and monthly *Genetic Technology News.*

HOPE REPORTS, 1600 Lyell Avenue, Rochester, NY 14606 (716/458-4250). Market research reports on A-V communications, television, theatrical entertainment, global media, U.S. training business.

HR REPORTER, 201 N. Robertson Blvd., Suite C2, Beverly Hills, CA 90211. Monthly newsletter for executives on human resource management, including dialogues with practitioners, cases, HRD profiles, and updates.

INTERCULTURAL PRESS, Inc., P.O. Box 768, Yarmouth, ME 04096. In addition to carrying intercultural publications of other sources, they publish their own books and monographs related to cross-cultural training, overseas country briefings, and international communications/negotiations.

INTERNATIONAL REFERENCE AND COORDINATION CENTRE FOR EDUCA-TIONAL FACILITIES, 17 Rue du Cendrier, 1201 Geneva, Switzerland. ICREF is an information center on general education and training worldwide. It is a meeting and educational exhibit place, as well as a learning and resource center with data bank and library. It offers consulting services on global hardware and software and exchange of HRD information.

INTERNATIONAL RESOURCE DEVELOPMENT INC., 30 High St., Norwalk, CT 06851 (1-800/243-5008). Reports, newsletters, and directories on various markets (such as, facsimile, simulator, artificial intelligence, factory automation), and subjects like electronic mail, executive directory or interactive video systems/services.

INSTITUTE FOR MANAGEMENT & AUTOMATION, Management International, PO Box 1510, FDR Station, New York, NY 10150. Reports include *Management and Career Perspectives for MIS Executives* and *Long-Range Strategic Planning for EDP.*

INTEGRATED COMPUTER SYSTEMS, 5800 Hannum Ave., PO Box 3614, Culver City, CA 90231 (1-800/421-8166). Seminars and course materials on microprocessors, computer system design, digital signal and image processing, networks, knowledge-based systems, software development and tools, technical manager skills.

JOHN NASIBITT TREND LETTER, PO Box 33309, Washington, DC 20033. Biweekly update on megatrends affecting our lives by best selling author and forecaster.

KNOWLEDGE INDUSTRY PUBLICATIONS, 701 Westchester Ave., White Plains, NY 10604 (1-800/431-1880). Among many useful publications, seek *The Teleconferencing Resource Directory* and *The Teleconferencing Handbook.*

LIBRARIES UNLIMITED, P.O. Box 263, Littleton, CO 80160. Reference books such as *Educational Media Yearbook* and *Online Reference and Information Retrieval.*

MANAGEMENT BOOKS INSTITUTE, PO Box 442, West Nyack, NY 10995. Membership includes discount purchase of latest, select books of interest to managers for personal and professional growth.

MANAGEMENT RESEARCH SYSTEMS/Talico Inc., 2320 South Third St., Ste. #75, Jacksonville Beach, FL 32250 (1-904/241-1721). Distributor for popular management data-gathering instruments and simulations for career development, leadership effectiveness employee survey, supervisory practice, training needs assessment, time management, safety audit, etc. Distributes Harris International instruments by this author that appear in *High-Performance Leadership*.

MBO, Inc., 157 Pontoosic Road, Westfield, MA 01086. Reports and publications on Odiorne's approach to Management by Objectives.

MARQUIS PUBLICATIONS, Dept HM, 200 East Ohio Street, Chicago, IL 60611 (1-800, 428-3898). Publishes a variety of reference works from *Who's Who in America* and *Who's Who in Frontier Science and Technology* to *Directory of Online Professionals* and *Marquis Profiles Database* for current information on individuals in high technology fields.

MASTERICAO PRESS, P.O. Box 7382, Ann Arbor, MI 48107 (1-800-443-0100, Ext. 230, except California, where it is 772-3545, Ext. 230). A central source of discount price books, multimedia programs, programmed instruction and courses on business, management, and HRD; includes most publishers, such as this author's AMACOM sequel, *New Worlds, New Ways, New Management*.

MCB University Press, 62 Toller Lane, Bradford, England BD8 9BY. Publisher of numerous British books (e.g., *Action Learning, How to Lead a Winning Team*) and journals (e.g., *Leadership and Organization Development, Journal of Managerial Psychology, Executive Development*).

MEAD DATA CENTRAL, 200 Park Ave., New York, NY 10166 (212/883-8560). [Offices in Atlanta, Chicago, Houston, Los Angeles, San Francisco, and Washington, D.C.] Provides NEXIS, a computer-assisted information service for searching world's most important media sources.

NATIONAL TECHNICAL INFORMATION SERVICES, U.S. Department of Commerce, Springfield, VA 22161. Provide information service, *Tech Notes*, with monthly reports on federally funded applied research from diverse government, industry, and academic sources. Packets of notes available in 10 categories from computers and engineering to manufacturing and physical/life sciences.

NATIONAL TRAINING AND COMPUTERS NETWORK, Sagamore Institute, Raquette Lake, NY 13436 (1-800/34-TRAIN). Publish *The Assist Journal* and free newsletter.

ORGANIZATIONAL TESTS, Ltd., PO Box Fredricton, N.B., Canada or International Publications, Ltd., Melbourne House, Parliament St., Hamilton 5-31, Bermuda. Management instruments for diagnosis of management and sales style, communication and change skills, culture shock and values inventories, organizational health, etc.

PERGAMON PRESS, Inc., Maxwell House, Fairview Park, Elmford, NY 10523; or Headington Hill Hass, Oxford QX3 OBW, England. Publish interesting management books, reports, and journals including *International Directory of Executive Education;* planning *Andragogy: An International Journal of Research and Studies* on adult learning activities.

PRINCETON UNIVERSITY PRESS, 3175 Princeton Pike, Lawrenceville, NJ 08648. Some books of interest to management, especially report on *Corporate Classrooms: The Learning Business.*

PRYOR RESOURCES, PO Box 1766, Clemson, SC 29633 (1-800-237-7967). Management consultant Fred Pryor publishes monthly newsletter, *The Pryor Report,* with practical ideas for managing people.

RAND CORPORATION, 1700 Main St., Santa Monica, CA 90406. Private think tank with major defense contracts. Reports include Business Intelligence Program and Study of Social Policy publications, such as *Handbook of Forecasting Techniques.*

RHINESMITH AND ASSOCIATES, INC. 443 Highbrook Avenue, Pelham Manor, NY 10803 (914/738-4415). Consultants in organization planning and development on domestic and international level, including relocation services.

SEMINAR INFORMATION SERVICE, Suite 3141, 175 Fifth Ave., New York, NY 10010 (212/229-5561). Publish workbook with guide to 3,000 business and technical seminars with listings by topic and sponsor, as well as upcoming programs.

SKEIBO, 44 Forster Ave., Mt. Vernon, NY 10552 (1-800/446-9111). Publish quarterly newsletter, *The Select Guide to Seminars,* which lists some discount offerings.

SOUNDVIEW EXECUTIVE BOOK SUMMARIES, 100 Heights Road, Darien, CT 06820. Subscription service of 4-6 page summaries for executives of latest books in business and management literature; usually selections of practical, "how to" nature.

SRI INTERNATIONAL, 333 Menlo Park, CA 94025 (415/326-6200). Formerly known as the Stanford Research Institute, this "think tank" provides a variety of consulting services and reports of a futuristic nature, ranging from education to forest product planning. They are knowledge specialists for industry.

STERLING INSTITUTE, 1010 Wisconsin Ave., N.W., Washington, DC 20007 (202/337-4000). Quality consulting and training service for general/sales/technical/human resource management, as well as acquisition/procurement/contract management. Have available instruments like *Management Practices Survey* and videocassette case studies, *Careers in Management* (see Harris International).

TELEOMETRICS INTERNATIONAL, 1755 Woodstead Ct., The Woodlands, TX 77380 (713/367-0060). Offer variety of learning instruments (seminars optional) on interpersonal relations and communications, motivation, management and leadership style, group/team/organization dynamics, plus A-V program on Managerial Achievement and Models for Management seminar.

UNIWORLD BUSINESS PUBLICATIONS, Inc., Suite 509, 50 E. 42nd St., New York, NY 10017 (1-800, 521-8110). Publish *Directory of American Firms Operating in Foreign Countries* and *Who's Who in Technology* among other resource volumes.

U.S. SMALL BUSINESS ADMINISTRATION, P.O. Box 19993, Washington, DC 20036. Publications, industrial innovation conferences, and local offices with counselors to assist entrepreneurs. Also provide grants to local consulting groups to assist small business with capital and consultants. (If the business is to operate in international market, contact U.S. Dept. of Commerce.)

WHARTON ECONOMETRICS FORECASTING ASSOCIATES, Inc., 4025 Chestnut St., Philadelphia, PA 19104. (University of Pennsylvania researchers who produce reports like, *The Wharton Quarterly Econometric Forecasting Model* and *The Wharton Annual and Industry Forecasting Model.*)

WORLDWATCH INSTITUTE, 1776 Massachusetts Ave., N.W., Washington, D.C. 20036. Publish variety of books, reports, and papers on technology, environment and resource management and the future (such as, annual reference volume, *State of the World.*)

HUMAN RESOURCE DEVELOPMENT ORGANIZATIONS AND PUBLISHERS

(Note: This partial listing is in addition to sources cited in the text or previously in this directory. Not included are the standard major publishers of management development texts, such as Random House, Harper & Row, D. C. Heath/Lexington, Holt-Rinehart-Winston, Prentice Hall, McGraw-Hill, Macmillan, etc., for which there is easy access; request information on their division catalogs of HRD, adult education, and management.)

ADDISON-WESLEY PUBLISHING COMPANY, One Jacobs Way, Reading, MA 01867 (617-944-3700). Major publisher of HRD/OD and management books, including *Breaking the Glass Ceiling* by A. M. Morrison, R. P. White, and E. Van Velsor—a research study of women who break through the barriers to the executive suite; as well as video systems such as *The Technical Manager.*

AT&T INFORMATION SYSTEMS, P.O. Box 8, Pine Mt., GA 31822-0008 (1-800/247-1212, Ext. 223). Through Institute for Communications and Information Management, offer variety of seminars in information resources, distribution or networking. Also request to be placed on the mailing list of AT&T Corporate Planning and Emerging Issues Group, Rm. 7211N2 N. Maple Avenue, Basking Ridge, NJ 07920—request annual study reports. Also request course information on management and training from AT&T Corporate Education Center, P.O. Box 1000, Hopewell, NJ 08525.

BRACE-PARK, THE HUMAN RESOURCE PRESS, P.O. Box 526, Lake Forest, IL 60045 (312/433-0434). Press specializing in HR publications, such as *Human Resource Planning, The Business of Human Resource Management, Strategic Human Resource Management,* and others.

CAREER COMMUNICATIONS, 1101 Whisnand, Bloomington, IN 47401. Complete learning system entitled, *Career Dimensions* of slides, audio cassettes, and lecture guide for 11 instructional modules, plus handbook, *Career Planning Today.*

COMPUTER TECHNOLOGY GROUP, Telemedia, Inc., 310 S. Michigan Ave., Chicago, IL 60604. (1-800, 323-UNIX). Offers public and on-site seminars in interactive, video-based training for individual or multiple audiences on various aspects of communication technology.

CONTROL DATA LEARNING CENTERS, P.O. Box O, Minneapolis, MN 55440 (1-800/328-1109, Ext. 65). A national network of learning centers offer data processing, computer and supervisory training courses for managers (PLATO, such as *Participative Management: Team Success* and wellness programs).

CRISP PUBLICATIONS, INC., 95 First St., Los Altos, CA 94022. Self-study books for management training, customer service and sales training, employee assistance programs, career guidance, and retirement/life planning.

DATAPRO RESEARCH CORPORATION, 1805 Underwood Blvd., Delran, NJ 08075 (1-800, 257-9406). Catalog available on seminars in data communications, microcomputers, and information systems, plus specialized reports on automation, software, microcomputers, etc.

EDUCATION DIMENSIONS TRAINING, Box 126, Stamford, CT 06904-0126 (1-800, 243-9020). Programs for HRD professionals and training managers in computers and high technology, such as computer graphics.

FREE PRESS, THE, 866 Third Ave., New York, NY 10022 (1-800, 223-1001.) A Macmillan division that publishes books on business, economics, strategy, MIS, finance, manufacturing, HRD, leadership and organization, management and executive development, marketing, and communication, etc.

GARRETT PARK PRESS, Garrett Park, MD 20896. Career development and job-finding publications, such as *The Professional and Trade Association Job Finder* which is a directory of employment resources.

GOWER PUBLISHING COMPANY, Gower House, Croft Rd., Aldershot, Hants GU11 3HR, England or Brookfield, VT, 05036. Variety of helpful books for HRD managers, such as *Action Learning in Practice, Behavior Technology, Improving Interpersonal Relations*. Also have management film catalog and distribute media.

GULF PUBLISHING COMPANY, PO Box 2608, Houston, TX 77007 (1-800, 231-6275). Publish 21 technical journals, plus books in HRD, international management, meeting management and adult education. Request list of the "Building Blocks of Human Potential Series." Videotapes available through subsidiary, International Training Company.

HARVARD BUSINESS SCHOOL PRESS, PO Box 1542, Hagerstown, MD 21741 (1-800-638-3030). HBS faculty and external experts are authors of these books for executive and managers, such as: *Competition in Global Industries* by M. Porter, *The Clash of Cultures—Managers and Professionals* by J. A. Raelin, *Managing in the Service Economy* by J. L. Heskett.

HONEYWELL INFORMATION SYSTEMS, 200 Smith St., MS486, Walthan, MA 02154. Programs in computer-based education and training, using CAN-8 instructional system. Also for course authoring, graphics, networking, info resource management, and BASIC.

HRD REVIEW, 105 Berkley Place, Glen Rock, NJ 07452 (201/445-2288). A monthly newsletter of professional opinion about HRD publications, learning systems, and media.

HUMAN RESOURCE COMMUNICATION GROUP, 2355 E. Stadium Blvd., Ann Arbor, MI 48104. Publish *The Directory of Human Resource Services & Products.*

HUMAN RESOURCES DEVELOPMENT PRESS, 22 Amherst Rd., Amherst, MA 01002. Specialized publications for HRD professionals, such as annual edition of *The Human Resource Information Systems Sourcebook, The Trainer's Resource* and *Performance Based Supervisory Development.*

HUMAN SYNERGETICS, 39819 Plymouth Rd., Plymouth, MI 48170 (313/459-1030). Publish management training materials and simulations (such as, for problem solving, project planning, plant closing, leadership styles, and team building.)

INSTITUTE FOR MANAGEMENT, IFM Bldg., Old Saybrook, CT 06475. Among its HRD publications and services, *How to Automate the Human Resource Function.*

INTERNATIONAL HUMAN RESOURCE MANAGEMENT, 137 Newbury St., Boston, MA 02116 (617/536-0202). HRD consulting and training service; publisher of such texts as *Training Resource Guide* for the petroleum industry, *Manpower Planning and Development* for Third World.

INTERNATIONAL UNIVERSITIES PRESS, 300 Raritan Center Parkway CN#94, Edison, NJ 08818. Publishing clearinghouse for books by university professors and researchers in business and social sciences (such titles as *The Irrational Executive, Human Relations in Modern Industry.*)

JOSSEY-BASS PUBLISHERS, 350 Sansome St., San Francisco, CA 94104 (415/433-1740). Inquire about their catalogues for management and behavioral science series, as well as books in continuing education.

JOHN WILEY & SONS, INC., P.O. Box 6793, Somerset, NJ 08875. Professional books offered by mail on free examination (such as *How to Be an Effective Trainer* by B. J. Smith and B. L. Delahays.)

347

LANSFORD PUBLISHING CO., 1088 Lincoln Ave, San Jose, CA 95155 (408/287-3105). Provide management training resources relative to instructional transparencies, slides, and videotapes.

LEARN INCORPORATED, Mt. Laurel Plaza, 113 Gaither Dr., Mount Laurel, NJ 08054. Communication skills training consultants and resource publisher (such as, *Meeting Management Corporate Grammar,* and *Working Together*).

LEARNING ALTERNATIVES, 186 East Paterson Ave., East Rutherford, NJ 07073 (1-800-323-1718). Audio cassette programs for personal and managerial development of popular authors, as well as recommended readings and musical programs.

LEXINGTON BOOKS, 125 Spring St., Lexington, MA 02173 (1-800-428-8071). A D.C. Heath subsidiary which publishes titles in areas of corporate strategy, management, international trade, finance.

LIFETIME LEARNING PUBLICATIONS, Inc. 10 Davis Dr., Belmont, CA 94002. Paperbacks on career development, such as *Every Women Works—A Manual for Women Reentering the Job Market or Changing Jobs, The Promotable Woman, Practical Management Skills for Engineers and Scientists, Managing Your Career Success.*

McGRAW-HILLS TRAINING SYSTEMS, P.O. Box 641, Del Mar, CA 92014-9988 (619/481-8184). Publish and distribute HRD books, learning systems and audio-visual aids on such varied topics as team and women management, worker motivation and pre-retirement, wellness subjects like computerphobia, managing stress and maintaining a healthy heart. Request to be placed on mailing list for free publication, *The Professional Trainer,* and for information on new supervision and management series.

MERRITT COMPANY PUBLICATIONS, P.O. Box 955, Santa Monica, CA 90406 (213/450-7234). Publish a *OSHA Reference Manual* with supplement, newsletter and management briefings.

MORELAND COMPANY, P.O. Box 4566, Pasadena, CA 91106. *Human Resources Index* is an annual compilation of information sources with quarterly updates.

ORYX PRESS, 2214 North Central, Phoenix, AZ 85004 (602-254-6156). Publish *Learning Packaged to Go: A Directory and Guide to Staff Development and Training Packages.* It facilitates use of ready-made, commercial media learning resources for HRD.

NADLER ASSOCIATES, Box 536 Berwyn Station, College Park, MD 20740 (301-935-5229). International consultants and services in professional human resource development, including presentations and publications.

NICHOLS PUBLISHING, PO Box 96, New York, NY 10024 (212-580-8079). In addition to publishing their own educational books, this source distributes European books of interest to multinational managers (such titles as *Education, Training, and the New Technologies; The Future of Management Education,* and *The Politics of Management.*)

NTL Institute, PO Box 9155 Rosslyn Station, Arlington, VA 22209 (703-527-1500). National Training Lab public and inhouse seminars for personal, professional, and management development. Also have Master's program in HRD in conjunction with American University, and sponsor conferences in conjunction with the OD Network, as well as training/consulting skills development. Publish *Journal of Applied Behavioral Science.*

ODT ASSOCIATES, PO Box 134, Amherst, MA 01004 (413-549-1293). Publish books, such as *How to Manage Your Boss* by B. Mezoff, and HRD "tip sheets" on practical topics, such as "How to Receive a Performance Appraisal" or "How to Manage a Sexist Boss."

PERSONNEL NEWS AND PRODUCTS, 548 First Street, Crete, IL 60417. A quarterly publication of Abbott, Langer & Associates. Digest summaries of recent HRD type articles, books, and other aids.

PITMAN PUBLISHING, 1020 Plain St., Marshfield, MA 02050 (617-837-1331). Now publishing management books with such titles as *The Executive Challenge: Managing Change and Ambiguity,* and *Readings in the Management of Innovation,* and *Power in Organizations.*

PRICE WATERHOUSE/HUMAN RESOURCE STRATEGIES GROUP, 600 B Street, Suite 1600, San Diego, CA 92101. Operates in many PW offices with assistance on HR strategies for compensation, practices, and executive search. Company also publishes a series of information guides to business abroad in various countries—contact headquarters, 1251 Avenue of the Americas, N.Y., NY.

RESEARCH SCIENCES, Inc. 5500 Interstate North Parkway, Suite 470, Atlanta, GA 30328 (404-953-3460). Publish *Human Resource Management National Directory* of HRM executives and companies.

ROUNDTABLE CONFERENCES FOR PROFESSIONAL WOMEN Four Linden Square, Wellsley, MA 02181 (617-235-5320). Series of Friday evening/Saturday sessions for women to share information and strategies relative to career development.

SAGE PUBLICATIONS, 2111 West Hillcrest Dr., Newbury Park, CA 91320. Publish professional journals and proceedings, as well as books on work and human resources, small group behavior, women policy studies, organizational and research studies (such as the annual *Technology Forecasts and Surveys* and *Intercultural Interactions*).

SCHRELLO ENTERPRISES, P.O. Box 1610, Long Beach, CA 90801 (213-437-2230). Training consultants, HRD direct market specialists, and publishers (*The Seminar Market, Marketing In-house Training Programs,* and *How to Market Training Programs, Seminars & Instructional Materials*).

SCOTT, FORESMAN AND CO., Professional Publishing Group, 1900 East Lake Ave., Glenview, IL 60025. (312/729-3000). This textbook publisher has begun an innovative series of management volumes (*Back in Working Order: How America Can Win the Productivity Battle*), as well as business applications series on computer software.

STRATEGIC MANAGEMENT GROUP, Inc., 3501 Market St., Philadelphia, PA 19104 (215-387-0120). Management consulting and executive development in finance and strategic planning, including case study, "The Strategic Management Game."

SONY CORPORATION OF AMERICA, Sony Drive, Park Ridge, NJ 07656. Produce Sony Video Responder System for interactive tape-based communication between speaker and audience.

TEN SPEED PRESS, PO Box 1723, Berkley, CA 94707. Among wide variety of popular publications, series of practical books on business, career development, and lifestyle.

TIMEPLACE, 460 Totten Road, Waltham, MA 02154. Personal computer courseware database, EdVENT and TRAINET.

TRAINING HOUSE, P.O. Box 3090, Princeton, NJ 08540 (609-452-1505). Live and packaged training programs on topics ranging from leadership to team building with methods from simulation games to slide/tape presentations.

TRANSFORMATIONS, INC., PO Box 6254, Athens, GA 30604 (404-548-3313). Focus is upon consulting and training to assist local government in managing the future, including in-house ADEPT program (Assessing, Developing Executive Productivity through Training).

U.S. GOVERNMENT PRINTING OFFICE, Washington, DC 20402. Inquire for the *Consumer Guide to Federal Publications* to learn about many free and inexpensive offerings by the Superintendent of Documents. For example, there is a whole section for business and management, adult education, consumers, labor/management relations, NASA, personnel management, health and safety. Book stores in 25 major cities. Subscription available for newsletter, *The Federal Trainer.*

UNIVERSITY ASSOCIATES, 8517 Production Avenue, San Diego, CA 92121 (619-578-5900). Major resource of training materials, games, and books for professional trainers and HRD specialists. Conduct annual HRD conference and have graduate programs in HR management.

UNIVERSITY TELEVISION, 1330 North Vine St., Hollywood, CA 90028. Teleconferencing network for speakers and authors to present management and university lectures/courses.

VAN NOSTRAND REINHOLD, 7625 Empire Dr., Florence, KY 41042. Publish both management and HRD volumes, such as *Costing Human Resources* and *HRIS Development* on human resource information systems.

VENICOMPASS, Inc. 155 W. Eighth St., Erie, PA 16501. Video training programs utilizing both video cassettes and personal computer disc.

VIDEOSTAR CONNECTIONS, Inc., 10850 Wilshire Blvd., Suite 600, Los Angeles, CA 90024. A satellite networking company that provides global broadcasting services for transmission of meetings, seminars, and conferences.

VIDEODISC/VIDEOTEX, Meckler Communications, 520 Riverside Ave., Westport, CT 06880 (1-800-243-4223). Magazine quarterly on video technologies, both hardware and software. Promotes annual conference.

WADSWORTH, Inc., 10 Davis Dr., Belmont, CA 94002 (415-595-2350). Among its many publications in accounting, business communication, computer science, and management, this company also produces interesting books in HRD/training (such titles as *Managing Human Relations, Career Development, In Training* and *Understanding Organizational Behavior*).

WALDENTAPES, P.O. Box 4142, Huntington Station, NY 11746. Audio cassettes on management and career development, such as *How to Manage People for Peak Performance.*

WORLDTEN—World Technology Executives Network, 1900 Avenue of the Stars, Suite 1185, Los Angeles, CA 90067 (213/282-0558). International network of decision-makers in technology companies. Affiliated with Southern California Technology Executives Network.

XEROX LEARNING SYSTEMS, P.O. Box 10211, Stamford, CT 06904. Advanced, self-administered learning systems and guides on such subject as *Negotiating Self-Taught* and new publication series, *Working Smart.*

MANAGERIAL JOURNALS, PERIODICALS, AND NEWSLETTERS

(Beside the many academic business journals and popular business magazines, the following may be especially useful for managers in transition.)

BERKELEY WELLNESS LETTER, University of California School of Public Health, P.O. Box 10922, Des Moines, IA 50340. Informative newsletter for those dedicated to a wellness lifestyle with timely health and fitness counsel.

BOTTOM LINE PERSONAL, Millburn, NJ 07041. Practical tips and information for personal management from financial to computers.

BULLOCK, DONALD H., Box 217, Simpsonville, MD 21150. Publisher of *Training Consultants Memo,* a monthly newsletter.

CONSULTATION, Human Sciences Press, 75 Fifth Avenue, New York, NY 10011. A professional journal for consultants.

THE ECONOMIST, PO Box 904, Farmingdale, NY 11737-9808 (1-800/628-0677). A quality weekly news magazine for global managers seeking a cosmopolitan viewpoint. Also publishes intelligence reports and traveler's guides on doing business in various countries.

EXECUTIVE EXCELLENCE, Suite 201, 226 West 2230 North, Provo, UT 84604. Sophisticated quarterly newsletter on personal development, managerial effectiveness, and organizational productivity.

EXECUTIVE HEALTH REPORT, PO Box 27287, San Diego, CA 92128.

HARVARD BUSINESS REVIEW, PO Box 3010, Woburn, MA 01888. A cutting-edge journal for managers that gives the viewpoints of both the academic and the practitioner. Also a reprint/book service.

HEALTH TIPS NEWSLETTER, C. I. Bete Co., 200 State Road, So. Deerfield, MA 01373. For those into the wellness life style.

HR REPORTER, Suite 1400, 1221, St. Louis, MO 63103. A newsletter on current trends and resources for HR professionals.

HUMAN RESOURCE MANAGEMENT JOURNAL. John Wiley & Sons, 605 Third Ave., New York, NY 10517-0228. Readable and practical HR periodical edited by Noel Tick of the University of Michigan, School of Business Administration.

INC., 38 Commercial Wharf, Boston, MA 02110. Popular magazine for managers of small companies. From the publisher of *High Technology*.

INFORMATION STRATEGY: THE EXECUTIVE'S JOURNAL, Auerbach, 6560 North Park Drive, Pennsauken, NJ 08109. Quarterly on information management for the non-MIS specialist.

INFOWORLD, 375 Cochituate Rd., Framingham, MA 01701. Popular weekly magazine for microcomputer users.

INTERNATIONAL LIVING, 2201 St. Paul St., Baltimore, MD 21218. Helpful 16-page newsletter for those who do business internationally.

JOURNAL OF BUSINESS STRATEGY, THE, Warren, Gorham & Lamont, Inc., 210 South St., Boston, MA 02111. Wide-ranging quarterly that examines issues of strategic planning and management.

MCB University Press, 62 Toller Lane, Bradford, West Yorkshire, England BD9 4JQ. Publish a range of European professional journals (such as, *Leadership and Organization Development, The Journal of Management Development, Journal of Human Resource Development, Journal of Managerial Psychology, Journal of European Industrial Training* and others) as well as monographs.

NATIONAL PRODUCTIVITY REVIEW, 33 West 60th St., New York, NY 10023 (212/489-5903). A quarterly review of Executive Enterprises, Inc, on productivity improvement, quality circles, work redesign and enrichment, robotics and CAM, systems controls, technology and the workplace.

NEW AGE JOURNAL, 342 Brighton, MA 02135. Sprightly monthly that acts as a forum for postindustrial thinkers and provides networking opportunities for Aquarians.

NEW MANAGEMENT, John Wiley & Sons, 605 Third Ave., New York, NY 10518-0012. "Classy" magazine for innovative managers produced by USC's Graduate School of Business Administration under Prof. James O'Toole as editor.

ON ACHIEVING EXCELLENCE, PO Box 2189, Berkeley, CA 94702 (1-800/327-9893). Monthly newsletter of Tom Peters. PATTERNS OF TOP PERFORMANCE package of cassettes, case histories, and special handouts.

ORGANIZATIONAL DYNAMICS, AMACOM, PO Box 1026, Saranac Lake, NY 12983. Among many periodicals published for managers and personnel administrators by the American Management Associations, this one is the best. Combination of scholarly and practical analysis of organizational behavior and development.

PERSONNEL JOURNAL, 866 W. 18th St., Costa Mesa, CA 92627. Popular, monthly periodical for those into personnel administration.

PERSONNEL PRACTICE IDEAS, Warren, Gorham & Lamont, 210 South St., Boston, MA 02111. Human resource newsletter with emphasis on changing employment legislation.

SLOAN MANAGEMENT REVIEW, Massachusetts Institute of Technology, Cambridge, MA 02139. A scholarly journal for innovative managers with articles largely by MIT professors, plus the SMR Forum of viewpoints of managers and other academics. Also a reprint service.

SUCCESSFUL MEETINGS, Bill Publications, 633 3rd Ave., NY 10017. For those involved in meeting planning and incentive travel, this popular monthly magazine and annual meeting site directory is free.

SMALL BUSINESS INNOVATION NEWS, P.O. Box 17730, Washington, DC 20041. Bimonthly newsletter to track trends in high tech, incentives, procurement, federal regulations, and opportunities, especially from the Washington perspective.

THE TARRYTOWN LETTER, Tarrytown House, East Sunnyside Lane, Tarrytown, NY 10591. Insights of the creative minority thinkers of The Tarrytown Group on "New Age" issues; also reports on their School for Entrepreneurs.

TRAINING, THE MAGAZINE OF HUMAN RESOURCE DEVELOPMENT, 50 South Ninth St., Minneapolis, MN 55402 (1-800/328-4239). Lively monthly journal, one of the many HRD projects of Lakeside Publications which include a newsletter, *Training Directors' Forum* and "Mesh Kit" of audio tapes, as well as major regional training conferences in the East and West.

TRAINING & DEVELOPMENT JOURNAL, ASTD, Box 1443, Alexandria, VA 22313. "The" journal for those who would be HRD professionals.

VENTURE, P.O. Box 10771. Des Moines, IA 50349. Popular monthly for venture capitalists and entrepreneurs that deals with business plans, franchises, patents, and other management concerns.

WARREN/WEINGARTEN, Inc., 38 Chauncy St., Boston, MA 02111 (617-542-0146). Publish three excellent, newspaper-like organs entitled *Training News, Data Training,* and *Information Center.* Also conduct national conferences for subscribers and practitioners in these fields.

MANAGEMENT DEVELOPMENT FILM AND VIDEO PRODUCERS AND DISTRIBUTORS

(Note: A-V aids offer variety of input in training and meetings. Films or video-cassettes can be purchased, leased, or rented. Catalogs from the following sources will provide complete details about their offerings. Major associations and corporations, such as Aetna and Chevron, also have Film Libraries that distribute their own productions, usually for rental or without charge. In addition to any listed above, this is a partial listing of sources. Also consult the annual April "Business Film Guide" in *Successful Meetings* magazine.)

AGENCY FOR INSTRUCTIONAL TECHNOLOGY, Box A, Bloomington, IN 47402.

AFL-CIO FILM DIVISION, Dept. of Education, 815 Sixteenth St., N.W., Washington, DC 20006.

AMA FILM/VIDEO, 85 Main St., Watertown, MA 02172. (1-800-225-3215).

AMERICAN MEDIA INCORPORATED, 5911 Meredith Dr., Des Moines, AT 50324.

BARR FILMS, P.O. Box 5667, Pasadena, CA 91107.

BNA COMMUNICATIONS Inc., 9439 Key West Ave., Rockville, MD 20850.

CALLY CURTIS COMPANY, 1111 North Las Palmas Ave., Hollywood, CA 90038.

CHURCHIL FILMS, 622 North Robertson Blvd., Los Angeles, CA 90069 (health & fitness films, including one on AIDS).

COMMUNICATIONS PARK VIDEO & FILM, P.O. Box 4000, Mount Kisco, NY 10549.

CONSORTIUM OF UNIVERSITY FILM CENTERS, c/o Audio-Visual Services, Kent University, Kent, OH 44242.

CONSUMERS UNION FILM LIBRARY, 470 Park Ave. S., New York, NY 10016.

COPELAND GRIGGS PRODUCTIONS, 411 15th Ave., San Francisco, CA 94118 (intercultural awareness/service films).

CORONET/MTI FILM & VIDEO, 108 Wilmot Road, Deerfield, IL 60015 (1-800-621-2131). (Request information on videocassette workshop on *Peak Performers* by Dr. Charles Garfield.

CRM FILMS, 2233 Faraday Ave., Carlsbad, CA 92008 (1-800-421-0833). Excellent series of management development films/videos.

DARTNELL INC., 4660 Ravenswood Ave., Chicago, IL 20850.

EDUCATIONAL RESOURCES INCORPORATED, 5534 Bush River Rd. Columbia, SC 29210 (1-800-845-8822).

ENCYCLOPEDIA BRITTANICA FILMS, 1488 South Lapeer Rd., Lake Orion, MI 48035 (1-800-554-6970).

FILMS INCORPORATE, 733 Green Bay Rd., Wilmeete, IL 60091.

FRED A. NILES COMMUNICATIONS CENTERS, Inc. 1058 W. Washington Blvd., Chicago, IL 60607.

GLASS, J.M., PO Box 9999, Spokane, WA 99209. Videotapes on "Sexual Harassment is Bad Business."

GULF PUBLISHING COMPANY, P.O. Box 2608, Houston, TX 77252 (1-800-231-6275).

MODERN TALKING PICTURE SERVICE, 5000 Park Street N., St. Petersburgh, FL 33709.

MTI TELEPROGRAMS INC., 3710 Commercial Ave., Northbrook, IL 60062.

NATIONAL AUDIOVISUAL CENTER, Archives and Records Services, General Services Administration, Marketing Branch YS, Washington, DC 20409.

NATIONAL CHAMBER OF COMMERCE FILMS, 1615 H Street, N.W., Washington, DC 20062.

NATIONAL EDUCATIONAL MEDIA, Inc., 21601 Devonshire St., Chatsworth, CA 91311 (1-800-245-6009).

OLYMPIC FILM SERVICE, 471 West 21st St., New York, NY 10011.

PYRAMID FILM & VIDEO, P.O. Box 1048, Santa Monica, CA 90406.

RAMIC PRODUCTIONS, 4910 Birch St., Newport Beach, CA 90404.

ROUNDTABLE FILMS, 113 N. San Vincente Blvd., Beverly Hills, CA 90211.

SALENGER EDUCATIONAL MEDIA, 2635 Twelfth St., Santa Monica, CA 90404.

SANDLER INSTITUTIONAL FILMS, Inc., 7449 Melrose Ave., Hollywood, CA 90046.

STEPHEN BOSUSTOW PRODUCTIONS, P.O. Box 2127, Santa Monica, CA 90406.

TELEMETRICS INTERNATIONAL, P.O. DRAWER 1850, Conroe, TX 77301.

TIME-LIFE VIDEO, P.O. Box 644, Paramus, NJ 07652.

UNIVERSITY MICROFILMS INTERNATIONAL, 300 North Zeeh Road, Ann Arbor, MI 48106. In addition to their university dissertations on HRD and management topics, inquire about their special services, such as Japanese Technical Information Service.

VANTAGE COMMUNICATIONS, Inc. Nyack, NY 10960.

VIDEO PUBLISHING HOUSE, 1011 East Touhy Ave., Suite 580, Des Plaines, IL 60028. (1-800-824-8889).

VIDEO LEARNING SYSTEMS, 354 West Lancaster Ave., Suite 105, Haverford, PA 19041.

WALT DISNEY EDUCATIONAL MEDIA, 500 South Buena Vista St., Burbank, CA 91521 (1-800-423-2555).

XICOM, Inc., Sterling Forest, Tuxedo, NY 10987.

ELECTRONIC NETWORKS

INTERNATIONAL BUSINESS ISSUES NETWORK, The Executive Board, Inc., 3819 El Camino Road, Carlsbad, CA 92008 (619/729-9447). A global network for executives to discuss business issues either by teleconferencing or computer.

THE META NETWORK, Metasystems Design Group, Inc., 2000 North 15th Street, Suite 103, Arlington, VA 22201 (703/243-6622). Computer network of professionals and managers seeking mind-to-mind connections on leadership and management futures, organizational transformation, education and technology, networking theory, and so on.

A CONCLUDING OBSERVATION—Learning managers utilize information networks to advance their own and their colleague's career development. In addition to commercial electronic networks to which one may subscribe, such as *The Source,* we can form personal and computer linkages with like-minded managers or trainers within our own company, industry, or region for exchange purposes on human resource development and management.

A final insight comes from A. Paul Protos, a Coopers & Lybrand partner in an interview on "Human Resources: Systems Are Key" (*The Consultant Forum,* 5:2, pp. 16-20). He believes that HR managers and personnel need to link both personally and electronically with the corporate management information specialists. Thus, human resource activities can integrate with other corporate information and services, particularly when there is a merger or acquisition. In this manner, the human resource function can become more cost effective and contribute to higher performance by the organization.

Appendix B

References and a Bibliography for Learning Managers

Abrams, G. "Spotting Secrets of Success in High Achievers," *Los Angeles Times,* September 18, 1984, pp. 1,6.

Adair, J. *Effective Teambuilding.* Hants, UK: Gower Publishing (Croft Road, Aldershot GU11 3HR), 1986.

Argyris, C. *Reasoning, Learning, and Action—Individual and Organizational.* San Francisco: Jossey-Bass, 1982

Argyris, C., Putnam, R., and Smith, D. M. *Action Science: Concepts, Methods, and Skills for Research and Intervention.* San Francisco: Jossey-Bass, 1985.

Armstrong, J. S. *Long-Range Forecasting.* New York: John Wiley & Sons, 1985.

Bard, R., Bell, C. Stephen, L., and Webster, L. *The Trainer's Professional Development Handbook.* San Francisco: Jossey-Bass, 1987.

Bass, B. *Leadership and Performance Beyond Expectations.* New York: The Free Press, 1985a.

Beckhard, R. and Harris, R. T. Organizational Transitions: Managing Complex Change. Reading, MA: Addison-Wesley, 1987.

Behling, O. and Rausch, C. F. "A Functional Perspective on Organizational Leadership," *Organizational Dynamics,* Spring 1985, 13:4, pp. 51-61.

Belcher, J. G. *Productivity Plus—How Today's Best-Run Companies Are Gaining the Competitive Edge.* Houston: Gulf, 1987.

Bellman, G. M. *The Quest for Staff Leadership.* Glenview, IL: Scott, Foresman, 1987.

Beer, S. *Diagnosing the System for Organizations.* New York: John Wiley & Sons, 1985.

Bennis, W., and Nanus, B. *Leaders: The Strategy of Taking Charge.* New York: Harper & Row, 1985.

Blake, R., Moulton, J., and Allen, R. *Spectacular Teamwork*. Somerset, N.J.: John Wiley & Sons, 1987.

Block, P. *The Empowered Manager—Positive Political Skills at Work*. San Francisco: Jossey-Bass, 1987.

Bomers, G. B., and Peterson, R. B. *Conflict Management and Industrial Relations*. Hingham, Mass.: Kluwer Academic Publishers, 1982.

Bradford, D. L., and Cohen, A. R. *Managing for Excellence: The Guide to Developing High Performance in Contemporary Organizations*. New York: John Wiley & Sons, 1984.

Brandt, S. C. *Entrepreneuring in Established Companies*. Homewood, Ill.: Dow-Jones-Irwin, 1986.

Brislin, R. W., and Cushner, K. *Intercultural Interactions: A Practical Guide*. Beverly Hills: Sage Publications, 1986.

Broder, J. M. "Business Adapting to a New Climate." *Los Angeles Times,* Nov. 24, 1985.

Buchholtz, S. (ed). *The Positive Managers*. New York: John Wiley & Sons, 1984.

Burch, J. G. *Entrepreneurship*. New York: John Wiley & Sons, 1986.

Burke, W. W. *Organization Development: A Normative View*. Reading, MA: Addison-Wesley, 1987.

Burns, J. M. *Leadership*. New York: Harper & Row, 1978.

Business Week. Gaining the Competitive Edge: A Conference for Human Resource Executives (Proceedings). New York: McGraw-Hill Publishing/Business Week, 1985.

Business & Legal Reports. *Beating the Drug & Alcohol Problem in the Workplace: Detection, Control & Treatment*. Madison, Conn.: Bureau of Law & Business, 1986.

Camp, R. R., Blanchard, P. N., and Huszezo, G. E. *Toward a More Organizationally Effective Training Strategy and Practice*. Englewood Cliffs, N.J.: Prentice Hall, 1986.

Carnevale, A. P. "The Learning Enterprise," *Training and Development Journal,* January 1986, 40:1, pp. 18-29.

Christie, B. (ed). *Human Factors of Information Technology in the Office*. New York: John Wiley & Sons, 1985.

Clark, M. B. *Leadership Education*. Greensboro, N.C.: Center for Creative Leadership, 1987.

Cook, J. R. *The Start-up Entrepreneur*. New York: Truman Talley/E.P. Dutton, 1985.

Conger, J. A. and Kanungo, R. N. *Charismatic Leadership: The Elusive Factor in Organizational Effectiveness*. San Francisco: Jossey-Bass, 1988.

Connor, J. P., and Carson, W. M. *Manpower Planning and Development: The Developing World*. Boston: IHRDC, 1982.

Connors, M. M., Harrison, A. A., and Atkins, F. R. (eds). *Living Aloft—Human Requirements for Extended Spaceflight.* Washington, D.C.: U.S. Government Printing Office, 1985.

Cox, C., and Beck, J. *Management Development: Advances in Practices and Theory.* New York: John Wiley & Sons, 1984.

Daloz, L. A. *Effective Teaching and Mentoring.* San Francisco: Jossey-Bass, 1986.

Dalton, G. W. *Novations: Strategies for Career Management.* Glenview, IL: Scott, Foresman, 1987.

Dartnell Staff. *How to Develop and Conduct Successful In-Company Training Programs.* Chicago: Dartnell Corporation, 1986.

Deming, W. E. *Out of the Crisis.* Cambridge, Mass.: Massachusetts Institute of Technology. (Accompanied by 13 videotapes on Deming's way to improve productivity.)

Drucker, P. E. *Innovation and Entrepreneurship.* New York: Harper & Row, 1985.

Dyer, L. *The Human Resource Planning Guide.* New York: Random House, 1986.

Dyer, W. G. *Team Building: Issues and Alternatives.* Reading, MA: Addison-Wesley, 1987.

Eitington, J. E. *The Winning Trainer.* Houston: Gulf, 1984.

Elgood, C. *Handbook of Management Games.* Brookfield, Vt.: Gower Publishing, 1984.

Famularo, J. J. (ed). *Handbook of Human Resources Administration.* New York: McGraw-Hill Book Company, 1985.

Ferguson, H. *Tomorrow's Global Executives.* Homewood, IL: Dow Jones-Irwin, 1988.

Ferreira, J., and Harris, P. R. "The Changing Roles of Information Resource Management Professionals," *Information Strategy: The Executives Journal,* Fall 1985, 2:1, pp. 18-22.

Fiedler, F. E. and Garcia, J. F. *New Approaches to Effective Leadership.* Somerset, N.J.: John Wiley & Sons, 1987.

Fisher, G. *Mindsets: The Role of Culture and Perception.* Yarmouth, MA: Intercultural Press, 1988.

Fitzenz, J. *How to Measure Human Resource Management.* New York: McGraw-Hill Book Company, 1985.

Flamholtz, E. G. *Human Resource Accounting.* San Francisco: Jossey-Bass, 1986.

Fombrun, C., Tichy, N. M., and Devanne, M. A. *Strategic Human Resources Management.* New York: John Wiley & Sons, 1984.

Forester, T. (ed). *The Microelectronics Revolution—The Complete Guide to the New Technology and its Impact on Society.* Cambridge, Mass.: MIT Press, 1985.

Foulkes, F. K. *Employee Benefits Handbooks*. Boston: Warren, Gorham & Lamont, Inc., 1985.

French, W. C., and Bell, C. H. *Organizational Development*. Englewood Cliffs, N.J.: Prentice-Hall, 1984.

Gabarro, J. J. *The Dynamics of Taking Charge*. Cambridge, Mass.: Harvard Business School Press, 1987.

Garfield, C. *Peak Performers: The New Heroes of American Business,* New York: William Morrow, 1986.

Gerstein, M. S. *The Technology Connection: Strategy and Change in the Information Age*. Reading, MA: Addison-Wesley, 1987.

Gibson, C. F., and Jackson, B. B., *The Information Imperative*. Lexington, Mass.: Lexington/D.C. Heath, 1987.

Gomez-Mejia, L. R. and Lawless, M. W. *Managing the High Technology Firm*. Boulder, CO: Center for High Technology Research, University of Colorado, 1988.

Greiner, L. E. and Schein, V. *Power and Organization Development*. Reading, MA: Addison-Wesley, 1988.

Grove, A. *High-Output Management*. New York: Random House, 1983.

Gryskiewicz, S. G., Shields, J. T., and Drath, W. H. (eds). *Selected Reading in Creativity*. Greensboro, N.C.: Center for Creative Leadership, 1983.

Gudykunst, W. B., Stewart, L. P., and Ting-Toomey, S. (eds). *Communication, Culture and Organizational Processes*. Newbury Park, CA: Sage Publishing, 1985.

Gutek, B. A. *Sex and the Workplace: The Impact of Sexual Behavior and Harassment on Women, Men, and Organizations*. San Francisco: Jossey-Bass, 1985.

Gutek, B. A., and Larwood, L. (eds). *Women Career Development*. Newbury Park: Sage Publications, 1986.

Hall, E. T., and Hall, M. R. *Hidden Differences: Doing Business with the Japanese*. Garden City, NJ: Doubleday, 1987.

Hall, R. H. *Dimensions of Work*. Newbury Park, CA: Sage Publications, 1985.

Hanna, D. P. *Designing Organizations for High Performance*. Reading, MA: Addison-Wesley, 1988.

Harris, P. R. *Planned Change in the Military Justice System—Professional Development Institutes* (Action Research Reports for the Office of Naval Research, No. 1,2,3; DOD Contract #N000-14-72-C-0165/P00001). LaJolla, Calif.: Management & Organization Development Inc., 1972/73.

Harris, P. R. *Effective Management of Change* (Unit One, Increasing Managerial Effectiveness with People Series). Pittsburgh: Westinghouse Learning Systems, 1976.

Harris, P. R. *New Worlds, New Ways, New Managements*. Ann Arbor, MI: Masterco Press/AMACOM, 1983.

362

Harris, P. R. *Increasing Leadership Effectiveness with People.* LaJolla, CA: Harris International/Management & Organizational Development Inc., 1983 (NOTE: This is the revised version of the First Edition, which appeared in 1973 under the title, *Organizational Dynamics*).

Harris, P. R. (ed). *Global Strategies for Human Resource Development.* Alexandria, VA: American Society for Training & Development, 1984.

Harris, P. R. *Management in Transition—Transforming Managerial Practices and Organizational Strategies for a New Work Culture.* San Francisco: Jossey-Bass, 1985.

Harris, P. R. "The Influence of Culture on Space Developments," *Behavioral Science—Journal of the Society for General Systems Research,* January 1986a, 31:1, pp. 12-28.

Harris, P. R. "Building a High Performance Teams," *Training and Development Journal,* April 1986b, 40:4, pp. 28-29.

Harris, P. R. "The New World of Creative Work," in R. L. Kuhn, ed., *Handbook for Creative and Innovative Managers.* New York: McGraw-Hill, 1987, pp. 555-566.

Harris, P. R., and Moran, R. T. *Managing Cultural Differences—Strategies for Global Management.* Houston, TX: Gulf Publishing, 1987.

Harvard Business Review. Executive Success: Making It in Management; Strategic Management. New York: John Wiley & Sons, 1983; 1985.

Hersey, P., and Blanchard, K. *Management of Organizational Behavior: Utilizing Human Resources,* 5th Edition. Englewood Cliffs, N.J.: Prentice Hall, 1988.

Hersey, P. *The Situational Leader.* San Diego: University Associates, 1988.

Huczynski, A. *Encyclopedia of Management Development Methods.* Brookfield, Vt.: Gower Publishing, 1984.

Hunt, J., Hoskins, D. Schresheim, C., and Stewart, R. (eds). *Leaders and Managers.* New York: Pergamon, 1984.

Iacocca, L., with M. Novak. *Iacocca: An Autobiography.* New York: Bantam Books, 1984.

Jandt, F., with Gillette, P. *Win-Win Negotiating.* New York: John Wiley & Sons, 1985.

Kakabadse, A. *The Politics of Management.* Brookfield, Vt.: Gower Publishing Co., 1984.

Kakabadse, A., Ludlow, R., and Vinnicombe, S. *Working in Organizations.* Hants, UK: Gower Publishing (Croft Road, Aldershot GU11 3HR), 1987.

Kidder, R. M. *An Agenda for the 21st Century.* Cambridge, MA: MIT Press, 1988.

Kilmann, R. H., Saxton, M. J., and Serpa, R. *Gaining Control of the Corporate Culture.* San Francisco: Jossey-Bass, 1985.

Kilmann, R. H., and Covin, T. J. *Corporate Transformation.* San Francisco, CA: Jossey-Bass, 1987.

Kirkpatrick, D. L. *How to Manage Change Effectively.* San Francisco: Jossey-Bass, 1985.

Kizer, W. M. *The Healthy Workplace: A Blueprint for Corporate Action.* Somerset, N.J.: John Wiley & Sons, 1987.

Keil, J. M. *The Creative Mystique.* New York: John Wiley & Sons, 1985.

Knapp, M. L., and Miller, G. R. (eds). *Handbook of Interpersonal Communication.* Beverly Hills: Sage Publications, 1985.

Knowles, M. S. *Andragogy in Action: Applying Modern Principles of Adult Learning.* San Francisco: Jossey-Bass, 1984.

Knox, A. B. *Helping Adults Learn.* San Francisco: Jossey-Bass, 1986.

Kozmetksky, G. *Transformational Management.* Cambridge, Mass.: Ballinger/ Harper & Row, 1985.

Kuhn, R. L. (ed). *Handbook for Creative and Innovative Managers,* New York: McGraw-Hill, 1987.

Landau, R., and Rosenberg, N. (eds). *The Positive Sum Strategy: Harnessing Technology for Economic Growth.* Washington, D.C.: National Academy Press, 1986.

Lawler, E. F., et al. *Doing Research That Is Useful for Theory and Practice.* San Francisco: Jossey-Bass, 1985.

Lawler, E. F. *High Involvement Management.* San Francisco: Jossey-Bass, 1986.

Likert, R. *New Patterns of Management.* New York: McGraw-Hill, 1961.

Lippitt, G. L., Langseth, P., and Mossop, J. *Implementing Organizational Change.* San Francisco: Jossey-Bass, 1985.

Loden, M. *Feminine Leadership.* New York: New York Times Books, 1985.

London, M. (ed). *Assessment Centres and Management Development.* Bradford, UK: MCB University Press, 1985.

London, M. *Change Agents: New Roles, Strategies for Human Resource Professionals.* San Francisco: Jossey-Bass, 1988.

London, M., and Mone, E. M. *Career Management and Survival in the Workplace.* San Francisco: Jossey-Bass, 1987.

Lund, R. T., and Hansen, J. A. *Keeping America at Work: Strategies for Employing New Technologies,* New York: John Wiley & Sons, 1986.

Lynch, D. *Your High-Performance Business Brain—An Operator's Manual.* Fort Collins, Col.: Brain Technologies Corp., 1986.

MacCrimmon, K. R., and Wehrung, D. A. *Taking Risks: The Management of Uncertainty.* New York: The Free Press, 1986.

McClelland, D. C. *Human Motivation.* Glenview, Ill.: Scott, Foresman, 1984.

McGregor, D. *Human Side of Enterprise—25th Anniversary Printing.* New York: McGraw-Hill, 1985.

McManus, M. L., and Hergert, M.L. *Surviving Merger and Acquisition.* Glenview, Ill.: Scott, Foresman, 1988.

McPhee, R. D., and Tompkins, P. K. (eds). *Organizational Communications: Traditional Themes and New Directions.* Beverly Hills: Sage Publishing, 1985.

Martel, L. *Master Change: The Key to Business Success.* New York: Simon & Schuster, 1986.

Mendell, J. S. Nonextrapolative Methods in Business Forecasting. Westport, CT: Quorum Books, 1985.

Merwin, J. *Effective Evaluation—Strategies and Techniques.* San Diego: University Associates, 1986.

Miller, D. B. *Managing Professionals in Research and Development.* San Francisco: Jossey-Bass, 1986.

Miller, J. G. *Living Systems.* New York: McGraw-Hill, 1978.

Miner, J. B. *People Problems: Executive Answer Book.* New York: Random House, 1985.

Moran, R. T., and Harris, P. R. *Managing Cultural Synergy.* Houston, TX: Gulf Publishing, 1982.

Morrison, A. M., White, R. P., and Van Velsor, E. *Breaking the Glass Ceiling—Can Women Reach the Top of America's Largest Corporations?* Reading, Mass.: Addison-Wesley, 1987.

Mosvick, R. K., and Nelson, R. B. *We've Got to Start Meeting Like This: A Guide to Successful Business Meeting Management.* Glenview, Ill.: Scott, Foresman, 1987.

Mumford, A. (ed). *Action Learning.* Bradford, UK: MCB University Press, 1987.

Mumford, A. (ed). *Handbook of Management Development.* Hant, UK: Gower Publishing (Croft Road, Aldershot GU11 3HR), 1986.

Murdick, R. G., and Cooper, D. R. *Business Research—Concepts and Guides.* Columbus, OH: Grid Publishing Inc., 1982.

Murray, F. T., and Murray, A. H. "Global Managers for Global Business," *Sloan Management Review,* Winter 1986, 27:2, pp. 75-80.

Nadler, L. (ed). *The Handbook of Human Resource Development.* New York: John Wiley & Sons, 1984.

Nadler, L., and Nadler, Z. *The Conference Book.* Houston, TX: Gulf Publishing Co., 1977.

Nadler, L., and Nadler, Z. *The Comprehensive Guide to Successful Conferences and Meetings.* San Francisco, CA: Jossey-Bass, 1987.

Nadler, L., and Wiggs, G. D. *Managing Human Resource Development.* San Francisco: Jossey-Bass, 1986.

Nash, M. *Making People Productive.* San Francisco: Jossey-Bass, 1965.

National Academy of Engineering. *Information Technologies and Social Transformation.* Washington, D.C.: The National Academy Press, 1985.

Nelson, R. B. *Decision Point.* New York: AMACOM, 1987.

Norman, R. *Service Management—Strategies and Leadership in the Service Businesses.* New York: John Wiley & Sons, 1984.

O'Donnell, M. P., and Ainswoth, T. H. *Health Promotion in the Workplace.* New York: John Wiley & Sons, 1984.

Opinion Research Corporation, *Employee Training in America.* Alexandria, Va.: American Society for Training and Development, 1986.

Osborn, A. *Applied Imagination.* New York: Charles Scribner's & Sons, 1963.

O'Toole, J. *Vanguard Management.* New York: Doubleday, 1985; paperback ed., New York: Berkley Publishing Group, 1987.

Ouchi, W. *Theory Z: How American Business Can Meet the Japanese Challenge.* Reading, Mass.: Addison-Wesley, 1981.

Pagel, H. R. (ed). *Computer Culture—The Scientific, Intellectual, and Social Impact of the Computer.* New York: New York Academy of Science, Vol. 426, 1985.

Passmore, W. A. *Using Sociotechnical Systems to Design Effective Organizations.* New York: John Wiley & Sons, 1985.

Pennings, J. M. *Organizational Strategies and Change.* San Francisco: Jossey-Bass, 1985.

Peters, T. *Leadership Alliance.* New York: Alfred Knopf, 1989.

Peters, T. *Thriving on Chaos: Handbook for a Management Revolution.* New York: Knopf, 1987.

Phillips, J. J. *Handbook of Training Evaluation and Measurement Methods.* Houston, TX: Gulf Publishing, 1983.

Phillips, J. J. *Improving Supervisory Effectiveness.* San Francisco: Jossey-Bass, 1985.

Rae, L. *How to Measure Training Effectiveness.* Hants, UK: Gower Publishing, 1986.

Rausch, E., with Frisch, M. H. *Win/Win Performance Management/Appraisal.* New York: John Wiley & Sons, 1986.

Reddy, W. B. and Jamison, K. *Team Building: Blueprints for Productivity.* San Diego, CA: University Associates, 1988.

Reich, R. B. *The Next American Frontier.* New York: New York Times Books, 1983.

Revens, R. W. *The Origins and Growth of Action Learning.* London: Chartwell-Bratt Publishers, 1982.

Robson, M. (ed). *Quality Circles in Action.* Brookfield, Vt.: Gower Publishing, 1984.

Rubinstein, S. (ed). *Participative Systems at Work.* New York: Human Sciences Press, 1987.

Saunders, G. *The Committed Organization—How to Develop Companies to Compete Successfully in the 1990s.* Brookfield, Vt.: Gower Publishing, 1984.

Sayles, R., and Wright, R. V. "The Use of Culture in Strategic Management," *Issues & Observations,* Nov. 1985, 5:4.

Schein, E. *Organizational Culture and Leadership.* San Francisco: Jossey-Bass, 1985.

Schein, E. *Process Consultation: Its Role in Organization Development.* Reading, MA: Addison Wesley, 1988.

Schein, E. *Process Consultation: Lessons for Managers and Consultants.* Reading, MA: Addison Wesley, 1987.

Sears, W. H. *Back in Working Order: How American Institutions Can Win the Productivity Battle.* Glenview, Ill.: Scott, Foresman, 1983.

Sears, V. *Staffing for Optimum Performance: How to Use the Training and Experential Method to Identify Superior Candidates.* New York: Executive Enterprises Inc., 1986.

Sears, V. *How to Attract, Recruit, Select and Retain High Performers.* Englewood Cliffs, N.J.: Prentice Hall, 1988.

Sears, W. H. *Service First! Winning the Competition for Consumer Dollars.* (In Press, 1989).

Shea, G. F. *Building Trust for Personal and Organizational Success.* New York: John Wiley & Sons, 1987b.

Shea, G. F. *Creative Negotiating.* New York: CBI/Van Nostrand Reinhold Co., 1983.

Shea, G. F. *Company Loyalty: Earning It and Keeping It.* New York: American Management Association, 1987a.

Shea, G. F. *Managing a Difficult or Hostile Audience.* Englewood Cliffs, NJ: Prentice Hall, 1984.

Shetty, Y. K., and Buehler, V. M. *Quality, Productivity, and Innovation.* New York: Elsevier Science Publishing, 1987.

Sinetar, M. *Ordinary People as Monks and Mystics—Lifestyles for Self-Discovery.* Mahwah, N.J.: Paulist Press, 1986.

Sinha, M. N., and Willborn, W. O. *The Management of Quality Assurance.* New York: John Wiley & Sons, 1985.

Skinner, B. F. *Upon Further Reflection.* New York: New York University Press, 1986.

Smilor, R. W., and Kuhn, R. L. (eds). *Managing Take-off in Fast-Growth Companies.* New York: Praeger, 1986.

Strassman, P. A. *Information Pay-off: The Transformation of Work in the Electronic Age.* New York: Free Press/Colliers Macmillan, 1985.

Sudit, E. F. *Productivity-Based Management.* Hingham, Mass.: Kluwer Academic Press, 1984.

Susjara, K. *A Manager's Guide to Industrial Robots.* Englewood Cliffs, N.J.: Prentice Hall, 1982,

Sweeney, N. R. *For Those Who Would be President: 16 Management Skills for the Top Job.* Glenview, Ill.: Scott, Foresman, 1986.

Tannenbaum, R., Margulies, N., and Massarik, F. *Human Systems Development—New Perspectives on People and Organizations.* San Francisco: Jossey-Bass, 1985.

Theobald, R. *The Rapids of Change: Social Entrepreneurship in Turbulent Times.* Indianapolis, Ind.: Knowledge Systems Inc., 1987.

Thomas, K. "Conflict and Conflict Management," in M. Dunneete (ed), *Handbook of Industrial and Organizational Psychology.* New York: Rand McNally, 1976, pp. 889-937.

Thurow, L. *The Management Challenge: Japanese View.* Cambridge, Mass.: MIT Press, 1985.

Tichy, N. M. *Managing Strategic Change—Technical, Political, and Cultural Dynamics.* New York: John Wiley & Sons, 1983.

Tichy, N. M., and DeVanna, M. A. *The Transformational Leader.* New York: John Wiley & Sons, 1986.

Toffer, B. L. *Tough Choices—Managers Talk Ethics.* New York: John Wiley & Sons, 1986.

Tjosvold, D. *Working Together to Get Things Done—Managing for Organizational Productivity.* Lexington, Mass.: Lexington/D.C. Heath, 1986.

Tubesing, N. L., and Tubesing, D. A. (eds). *Structured Exercise in Stress Management,* Vols. I & II; Structured Exercises in Wellness Promotion, Vols. I & II. Duluth, Minn.: Whole Person Press, 1983.

Tung, R. L. *The New Expatriates: Managing Human Resources Abroad.* Cambridge, Mass.: Ballenger/Harper & Row, 1987.

Tyson, S. and Kakabadse, A., eds., *Cases in Human Resource Management.* London: William Heinemann Ltd., 1987. [Plus a *Teacher's Case Guide* volume.]

Universal Training Systems, *How to Review and Evaluate Employee Performance.* Chicago: Dartnell Corporation, 1987.

Van Velsor, E. "Can Development Programs Make A Difference?" *Issues & Observations,* Nov. 1984, 4:4.

Walton, R. E. *Innovating to Compete.* San Francisco: Jossey-Bass, 1987.

Walton, R. E. *Managing Conflict: Interpersonal Dialogue and Third Party Roles.* Reading, MA: Addison Wesley, 1987.

Walton, R. E., and Lawrence, P. R. (eds). *Human Resource Management Trends & Challenges.* Boston: Harvard Business School Press, 1985.

Wheelright, S. C., and Makridakis, S. *Forecasting Methods for Management.* New York: John Wiley & Sons, 1985.

Whitefield, D. "Entrepreneurs Wanted." Los Angeles Times, Nov. 27, 1985.

Wlodkowski, R. J. *Enhancing Adult Motivation to Learn.* San Francisco: Jossey-Bass, 1985.

Yates, D. *Analysis of Selected Top Performers Success Experience.* San Diego: United States International University, 1979. (Unpublished doctoral dissertation available from University Microfilms International, 300 North Zeeb Road, Ann Arbor, MI. 48106, U.S.A.).

Yates, D. T. *The Politics of Management.* San Francisco: Jossey-Bass, 1985.

Index